Gambling on War

The First World War left a legacy of chaos that is still with us a century later. Why did European leaders resort to war and why did they not end it sooner? Roger L. Ransom sheds new light on this enduring puzzle by employing insights from prospect theory and notions of risk and uncertainty. He reveals how the interplay of confidence, fear, and a propensity to gamble encouraged aggressive behavior by leaders who pursued risky military strategies in hopes of winning the war. The result was a series of military disasters and a war of attrition which gradually exhausted the belligerents without producing any hope of ending the war. Ultimately, he shows that the outcome of the war rested as much on the ability of the Allied Powers to muster their superior economic resources to continue the fight, as it did on success on the battlefield.

Roger L. Ransom is Distinguished Professor of History and Economics, Emeritus at the University of California, Riverside. He is best known for his work with Richard Sutch on the American Civil War and his many publications include the books *One Kind of Freedom* (co-authored with Richard Sutch) (Cambridge, 2001), *Conflict and Compromise* (Cambridge, 1989), and *The Confederate States of America: What Might Have Been* (2005). He was the president of the Economic History Association in 2005, and was awarded a Guggenheim Fellowship, and the distinguished teaching award from the University of California, Riverside. He also won the Arthur Cole prize from the Economic History Association and the Clio Can award from the Cliometric Society.

Gambling on War

Confidence, Fear, and the Tragedy of the First World War

Roger L. Ransom

CAMBRIDGE
UNIVERSITY PRESS

CAMBRIDGE
UNIVERSITY PRESS

University Printing House, Cambridge CB2 8BS, United Kingdom

One Liberty Plaza, 20th Floor, New York, NY 10006, USA

477 Williamstown Road, Port Melbourne, VIC 3207, Australia

314–321, 3rd Floor, Plot 3, Splendor Forum, Jasola District Centre, New Delhi – 110025, India

79 Anson Road, #06-04/06, Singapore 079906

Cambridge University Press is part of the University of Cambridge.

It furthers the University's mission by disseminating knowledge in the pursuit of education, learning, and research at the highest international levels of excellence.

www.cambridge.org
Information on this title: www.cambridge.org/9781108485029
DOI: 10.1017/9781108600101

First published 2018

Printed in United Kingdom by TJ International Ltd. Padstow Cornwall

A catalogue record for this publication is available from the British Library.

Library of Congress Cataloging-in-Publication Data
Names: Ransom, Roger L., 1938– author.
Title: Gambling on war : confidence, fear, and the tragedy of the First World War / Roger L. Ransom, University of California, Riverside.
Other titles: Confidence, fear, and the tragedy of the First World War
Description: New York, NY : Cambridge University Press, [2018] |
Includes bibliographical references and index.
Identifiers: LCCN 2018003780 | ISBN 9781108485029 (hardback)
Subjects: LCSH: World War, 1914–1918. | World War, 1914–1918–Economic aspects.
Classification: LCC D521 .R25 2018 | DDC 940.3–dc23
LC record available at https://lccn.loc.gov/2018003780

ISBN 978-1-108-48502-9 Hardback
ISBN 978-1-108-45435-3 Paperback

To my family:
Connie
Charlotte and Bob
Leslie
Jared
Jack
and to my faithful kitty, Cleo

CONTENTS

FIGURES

MAPS

TABLES

PROLOGUE

In their book *Power and Plenty*, Ronald Findlay and Kevin O'Rourke identify three "great world-historical events" that touched off dramatic changes in the demographic, economic, and socio-political structure of societies throughout the world. The first of these was the response to the Black Death of the fourteenth century; the second was the discovery and incorporation of the New World into the Old World at the end of the fifteenth century; and the third was the industrial revolution at the beginning of the nineteenth century.[1] Each of these eras introduced new and profound changes in the institutional arrangements throughout the world. My experience teaching and researching world history has persuaded me that the Great War of 1914–18 and its aftermath should be added to Findlay and O'Rourke's list of major historical events that changed the world.[2] The puzzle of war and economics has attracted a large body of research in both the humanities and the social sciences. One of the things that makes the puzzle so difficult to piece together is the apparent "irrationality" behind decisions to wage war or engage in risky speculations that produce economic crises. Economists and political scientists are particularly wedded to the notion that human behavior involves some sort of rationality.

As someone who is a "cliometrician" with a research background in both economics and history, the idea that the course of history can be profoundly changed by significant events such as wars and panics appeals to me.[3] One of the more successful efforts to offer such an interpretation from a historian's perspective is Donald Kagan's book *The Origins of War*.[4] Kagan sought a methodology that could explain wars that took place in three very different places and eras of history: the Peloponnesian Wars of Ancient Greece, the First World War, and the Cuban Missile Crisis of the twentieth century. He starts by citing the Greek poet Archilochus, who argued that "The fox knows many tricks, the hedgehog only one; one big one." Social scientists, Kagan argues, "are the hedgehogs; they seek to explain a vast range of particular phenomena by the simplest possible generalization." Historians, he says, "should in the first instance, be foxes, using as many tricks as they can to explain as many particular things as accurately and convincingly as possible." Neither group, Kagan cautions, should "expect to find the one big trick that will explain everything," but they should be able to "draw upon the lesser generalizations and other understandings of the evidence that has been examined."

Kagan calls his approach a "narrative history," a term that appeals to me because it stresses the need to keep the timeline of events at the center of the analysis. For the economist, time and place are an essential part of the analysis. Theories – or to use the economists' term, economic models – involve assumptions that must be set in a particular time and place. Kagan is a narrative "fox" who turns to the "hedgehogs" for assistance as needed in his discussion of three very different wars. My approach, which I will call a *cliometric narrative*, is to be a "hedgehog" who turns to the historian "fox" for help identifying the major tipping points in our story that need to be examined in greater detail using the quantitative and theoretical tools of a cliometrician. This book offers a narrative that examines the First World War as a series of situations where political leaders and generals consistently decided to gamble that starting or continuing a war was preferable to looking for options that might produce a more peaceful solution. Our narrative begins with the formation of the German Empire in 1871 and follows the course of events through the First World War and efforts to construct a peace settlement in 1919 that would shape the world in the aftermath of that war.

Chapter 1 presents some historical background on the evolution of war since 1500 and develops some analytical concepts showing how the notion of what the British economist John Maynard Keynes termed "animal spirits" and more recent work in behavioral economics help to explain wars and their aftermath. Chapter 2 examines how Otto von Bismarck's successful use of war to create the German Empire in 1871 changed the balance of power in Europe and encouraged others to choose war over diplomacy in 1914. Chapter 3 discusses the war plans of the various powers in the years leading up to 1914, with particular attention to the plan devised by General Alfred von Schlieffen for Germany to attack France in the event of a two-front war with Russia and France. Chapter 4 examines how the failure of Schlieffen's plan produced a strategy of bloody attrition that led to a stalemate that lasted for three years. Battles such as Ypres, Verdun, the Somme, and Passchendaele produced horrendous casualties and brought about little or no change in the chances of victory for either side.

Chapter 5 argues that this was an economic war, one which would be decided not only on the battlefield, but by the ability of economies to meet the needs of mobilization for war. Mobilization produced dramatic changes in the allocation of resources in every country, and the imposition of economic blockades by both sides produced shortages of supplies. At the end of 1916 both sides were near exhaustion, yet neither side was willing to settle for a negotiated settlement to end the fighting. Chapter 6 carries the narrative through 1917, when the United States entered the war as a partner of the Entente Powers and the Russians found themselves in the midst of a revolution that would eventually overthrow the Tsar and take Russia out of the war.

Chapter 7 deals with the final efforts by both sides to break the stalemate and win the war with a final grand blow. At the beginning of 1918, the commander of the German High Command, Erich Ludendorff, launched one last offensive against the Allied forces on the Western Front. When that gamble failed, the Allies countered with a series of offensives that led to an armistice on November 11, 1918 that finally ended the fighting on the Western Front. Since Austria-Hungary, the Ottoman Empire, and Bulgaria had all reached ceasefire agreements earlier in the month, the ceasefire with the Germans completed the collapse of the Central Powers.

Chapter 8 deals with the chaos of victory and the efforts to restore the world to some form of "normalcy." Five years of fighting had not only resulted in 30 million military casualties; it also displaced millions of civilians and destroyed the institutional framework that had governed the global economic and political systems for more than a century. The leaders at the Paris Peace Conference in 1919 did their best to rebuild their shattered world, but their efforts could not cope with the enormity of social, political, and economic instabilities throughout the postwar world.

Unfortunately, the series of postwar catastrophes did not end in 1919. The First World War was touched off by decisions taken by leaders of all the major powers of Europe to gamble on war rather than seeking a peaceful solution for a crisis in the Balkans. Neither side was willing to end the fighting so long as they believed they still had a chance to win the war. Whether or not the decisions to go to war in 1914 were the consequence of "rational" decisions, the price the world paid for the gambles on war seems extraordinarily high for what was gained. The First World War turned out to be a conflict that nobody wanted, nobody understood, and even today nobody can forget.

This book presents a narrative tour that examines why the leaders of nations at war thought that gambling on the risky strategies that started and continued the war was a "rational" policy, and why the people in those countries were willing to put up with the enormous costs of a war that would eventually produce a solution whereby no one had "won" the war.

To maintain the flow of narrative, details of various events and points of interest, together with citations to additional materials of interest have been consigned to endnotes at the back of the book.

1 CONFIDENCE, FEAR, AND A PROPENSITY TO GAMBLE

> The objective nature of war makes it a matter of assessing probabilities ... No other human activity is so continuously or universally bound up with chance. And through the element of chance, guesswork and luck come to play a great part in war.
>
> In the whole range of human activities, war most closely resembles a game of cards.
>
> Carl von Clausewitz (1832)[1]

In his book *The Age of Extremes*, historian Eric Hobsbawm offers the following description of European society at the end of the nineteenth century:

> This civilization was capitalist in its economy; liberal in its legal and constitutional structure; bourgeois in the image of its characteristic hegemonic class; glorying in the advance of science, knowledge and education, material and moral progress; and profoundly convinced of the centrality of Europe, birthplace of the revolutions of the sciences, arts, politics and industry, whose economy had penetrated, and whose soldiers had conquered and subjugated most of the world; whose populations had grown until (including the vast and growing outflow of European emigrants and their descendants) they had risen to form a third of the human race; and whose major states constituted the system of world politics.[2]

The British economist John Maynard Keynes provides a detailed description of the comforts available to a middle-class Londoner on the eve of the First World War. "But most important of all," he concluded, the Londoner would have

> regarded this state of affairs as normal, certain, and permanent, except in the direction of further improvement, and any deviation from it as aberrant, scandalous, and avoidable. The projects and politics of militarism and imperialism, of racial and cultural rivalries, of monopolies, restrictions, and exclusion, which were to play the serpent to this paradise, were little more than the amusements of his daily newspaper, and appeared to exercise almost no influence at all on the ordinary course of social and economic life, the internationalization of which was nearly complete in practice.[3]

The possibility that somehow this world might collapse in a cataclysm of social, political, and economic confusion never entered their mind.

Seldom have so many people been so misguided by their optimism about the future. Two decades into the twentieth century, the world of European states and empires was in ruins, destroyed by the most destructive war the world had ever seen. In a conversation with President Woodrow Wilson at the Peace Conference at Versailles in 1919, French Premier Georges Clemenceau described the war that had just ended as a "series of catastrophes that resulted in victory."[4] Unfortunately, "victory" in the Great War did not end the series of catastrophes. It soon became apparent that the challenge of building a new world on the ruins of the old was a more daunting task than anyone imagined. When the last of the diplomats headed for home in January of 1920, the map of eastern Europe and the Middle East had been completely redrawn. The Hohenzollern, Habsburg, and Ottoman monarchies that had dominated central Europe for several centuries had been replaced with a panoply of newly created nation-states extending from the North Sea through central and eastern Europe and the Balkans to the northern coast of Africa. The Russian Empire was in the grip of a bitter civil war to determine who would fill the political vacuum left by the collapse of the Romanov Dynasty in 1917. The "Great War" was followed by three decades of additional calamities in the form of the worst economic collapse in modern times in the 1930s and another world war that finally ended in 1945.

The Gunpowder Revolution

In his book *Why Did Europe Conquer the World?*, historian Phillip Hoffman imagines a time machine that could take you anywhere in the world a thousand years ago. "As you consider the possibilities," he warns, "avoid Europe at all costs. Why reside there when it was poor, violent, politically chaotic, and by almost any yardstick, hopelessly backward?"[5] Yet by the beginning of the twentieth century, Europe ruled the world. What was the source of this remarkable change in the fortunes of Europeans? Hoffman points out that looking back from the world of the twenty-first century, it is easy to conclude that the industrial revolution, which allowed Europeans to build their economic and military capabilities far beyond those of other states around the world, was the primary force behind European supremacy. There is, however, a problem with this explanation. The industrial revolution was still in its infancy at the end of the eighteenth century, and by that time European powers already controlled more than 80 percent of the world. The most significant factor behind European success in developing military technology was their development of modern weapons and military organization; what historians refer to as the "gunpowder revolution." But that begs another unanswered question. Why was it the Europeans who embraced the revolution in weapons and military organization? The Chinese and other areas of Eurasia had been developing uses for gunpowder for centuries. Why were these empires, which in 1500 were economically as developed as Europe, unable or unwilling to copy the European example in arms development and stave off the European onslaught? Hoffman's answer to this puzzle is that European states put far more effort into the development of sophisticated military technology and tactics because they were constantly at war with one another. Between the late Middle Ages and the nineteenth century, European rulers were engaged in what he calls a "tournament" of wars that

> repeatedly pitted the continent's rulers and leaders against one another in warfare that affected the lives of people around the globe. The prize for the rulers engaged in this grim contest was financial gain, territorial expansion, defense of the faith, or the glory of victory ... In Europe, political conditions made it possible to mobilize gigantic sums for armies and navies, and

military conditions favored the gunpowder technology, which,
because it was new, had enormous potential for improvement
by the sort of learning by doing that was going on in Europe
before 1800.[6]

Hoffman's model of tournament warfare not only explains the fre-
quency of wars between the kingdoms and principalities of Europe in
the late medieval and early modern world; it also explains the energetic
efforts of rulers to advance the gunpowder revolution. He postulates
four conditions for the tournament model of warfare to explain the
steady advancement of gunpowder technology in Europe in the early
modern era. There must be constant warfare between European
princes; the prize for victory must be valuable enough to warrant the
costs; and governments must be willing – indeed, eager – to use the
gunpowder technology that emerges from their constant wars. Finally,
there must be no major obstacles that would restrict the adoption
of gunpowder technology. Hoffman argues that "all four conditions
required for advancing the gunpowder technology held in western
Europe throughout the late Middle Ages and the early modern period.
The result, so the model implies, should be uninterrupted productivity growth in western Europe's military sector. And that is just what
happened, at rates unheard of in preindustrial economies."[7]

All this worked well enough in the late Middle Ages, but things
were gradually changing in ways that would dramatically alter the
paradigm of war in Europe by the middle of the eighteenth century.
The lure of prizes, the promise of glory, and fighting to defend the
faith had been replaced by the perceived gains from colonial imperialism and the rising influence of nationalism among western European
nations. A further discouragement to the waging of "tournament
wars" with other states was the increasing possibility that rulers might
be overthrown or countries lose their independence in the event of a
defeat. The lower value of rewards and the increased risk from defeat
produced a situation where it was often preferable to negotiate a
peace rather than carry on an expensive and risky war. The Battle of
Waterloo in June of 1815, which ended Napoleon Bonaparte's effort
to gain the grand prize of an empire that would stretch from Paris to
Moscow, marked the beginning of a new era of global warfare.

Europeans in 1815 confidently observed their position on top
of the world like a sailor viewing a sea that was calm as far as the eye

could see. What they failed to appreciate was that beyond that calmness was the legacy of three centuries of incessant European conflicts that had made warfare an integral part of the global system of politics and economics. People accepted the fact that the gunpowder revolution had made the use of force to maintain their position of power in the world a necessary part of their world, and they endorsed the costs of military preparedness, as well as the use of military action in times of crisis. After the Congress of Vienna in 1815 European armies no longer spent as much of their time fighting neighbors. They now traveled all over the world in search of colonial conquests while European navies ruled the seven seas and controlled the global trading routes. Imperial rivalries prompted occasional political crises that might cause a call to arms, but there were few major conflicts between rival nations on European soil for more than a century. It was, unfortunately, the calm before the storm.

European Warfare, 1815–1914

To understand how a culture of war emerged in Europe it will be useful to look at the pattern of warfare in the century before the First World War. Figure 1.1 presents data on the number of wars and battle-related deaths from those conflicts involving European nations in the nineteenth century. The data is organized into three categories of wars. *Interstate wars* were conflicts between two or more states, at least one of which was a European state.[8] *Nationalist and civil wars* were a group of wars that dramatically changed the balance of power in Europe between 1848 and 1871. The most important wars in this group were the conflicts that created the Italian nation in 1867 and the formation of the German Empire and the French Third Republic after the Franco-Prussian War in 1871. This group also includes the American Civil War, which restructured the political and social arrangements of the American Union after 1865.[9] The third category of wars were *Imperial wars*, most of which constituted what the Correlates of War Project terms "extra-state" wars. These conflicts, which were the last vestiges of the constant warfare that had been characteristic of interstate European warfare of the late medieval and early modern period, involved at least one European state and a "non-state entity." Though most of them were relatively small wars, they accounted for just over 70 percent of all the wars in Figure 1.1.

The wars in Figure 1.1 are organized around three broad categories of wars. Interstate wars are wars between states with at least one of the combatants being a European country. Imperial wars are

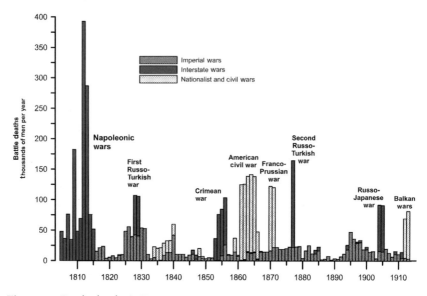

Figure 1.1 Battle deaths in European wars, 1805–1914

Sources: There are no reliable figures for battle-related deaths in the Napoleonic wars. Michael Clodfelter presents annual estimates for battle deaths from 1805 to 1815 for French troops and estimates of total battle deaths for the same period for Great Britain, Prussia, Austria, and Russia. His numbers suggest that a conservative estimate of deaths incurred by all the belligerents would be 13.1 million. This total is distributed over the entire fifteen-year period by applying the share of French losses for each year to the total deaths of all combatants. See Michael Clodfelter, *Warfare and Armed Conflicts: A Statistical Reference to Casualty and Other Figures, 1500–2000*, 2nd edn (Jefferson, NC: McFarland & Company, 2002), 191–3.

The data on the annual number of battle deaths from 1816 to 1914 are constructed from the Correlates of War Project (COW) data sets. The COW data sets give the total deaths for each war for each country. This figure is then converted to an annual average for each year that country participated in the war. The definition of a "war" in the Correlates of War data sets is that a conflict "must involve sustained combat involving armed forces resulting in a minimum of 1,000 battle-related fatalities in a minimum within a twelve month period." COW identifies three categories of war which served as a rough guide for the categories used in Figure 1.1: Inter-State Wars, which primarily take place between/among states; Intra-State Wars, which take place within a state; and Extra-State Wars which take place between/among a state(s) and a non-state entity.

conflicts or uprisings in territories that are controlled by a European colonial power or a war in which a European state acquired a new colonial territory. Nationalist and civil wars are situations where the conflict resulted in a significant institutional change in one or more of the combatants. The most significant wars in this category include the the wars for Italian unification, the Seven Weeks War between Prussia and Austria, the American Civil War, the Franco-Prussian War, and the conflicts between Romania, Greece, Bulgaria, and Serbia in 1912–13 that set the stage for the crisis that touched off the First World War. Wars that did not include European states and the United States of America are not included in the figure.

The first thing to note from the data displayed in Figure 1.1 is the relatively small number of interstate wars that Europeans fought among themselves. After Waterloo, in the nineteenth century there was no interstate war of any consequence involving major European states until the Crimean War of 1853–56, a conflict that began as a quarrel between the Ottoman Empire and Russia over the treatment of Christian minorities in the former. It expanded when Britain and France became involved because of their concern that a victory for the Russians might give them control of the Dardanelles. Historian Trevor Royle describes the war as a "punctuation mark that emerged almost halfway ... between Waterloo in 1815 ... and the fighting in Flanders in 1914. More than 600,000 men died on both sides during the war, only 20 percent of them from wounds on the battlefield."[10] The conflict is best remembered today for Florence Nightingale's pioneering efforts to advance the care and nursing of wounded British soldiers, and for the heroic – albeit tragically misguided – charge of the British "Light Brigade" at Balaklava that was memorialized in Alfred Lord Tennyson's poem.

The third quarter of the century was dominated by the nationalist and civil wars that dramatically changed the political structure of the North Atlantic community. While they paled in size compared with the Napoleonic wars, they stood out from the other wars of the period, and they ushered in a new struggle for a balance of power that would persist to 1914. There were only two other significant interstate wars between 1880 and 1914. One was the Russo-Turkish War of 1878, which was a continuation of the efforts by Russia to push the Ottoman Empire out of Europe. The Russian success prompted a meeting of the major powers in Berlin to discuss the problem of how to deal with the gradual abandonment of European territory by the Ottoman Empire. The other war was the Russo-Japanese War which broke out in 1904 when the Japanese attacked the Russian fleet at Port Arthur. Eventually 2.5 million men were called up for action by the two combatants and more than 150,000 of them died in battle. The most notable military event of that war was the destruction of the Russian Pacific Squadron of dreadnoughts by the Japanese Imperial Navy in the Straits of Tsushima in May 1905. This was the largest naval engagement since Nelson's victory at Trafalgar a century earlier, and the decisiveness of the Japanese triumph both impressed and surprised Western observers.

The Russo-Japanese War marked the emergence of Japan as a naval power to be reckoned with in the Far East, a development that was to have profound implications for the future economic and political balance of power in Asia. The war also had a significant impact on the political stability of the Russian Empire, where the humiliating defeats incurred by the Russian military forces at the hands of the Japanese contributed to a series of domestic uprisings against the Tsarist regime in early 1905. Largely lost in the discussion of that war was the extent to which economic factors played a major role in bringing about an end to the fighting. Although they were winning the battles, difficulties in financing the cost of the war effort had forced the Japanese to substantially scale back their military effort by early 1905. When Theodore Roosevelt offered to help negotiate a peace to end the war in March of that year, General Gentaro Kodama, the Japanese commander in Manchuria, made a special trip to Tokyo to urge his government to accept the offer and actively pursue a solution that would end the war while the Japanese still held the upper hand. The Russians were having their own problems with the war effort, and in the fall of 1905 both sides signed the Treaty of Portsmouth.

Table 1.1 presents data on battle deaths and the number of wars involving European nations and the United States between 1880 and 1914, organized by the categories of wars used for Figure 1.1 and the countries participating in the wars. The countries are listed by total number of casualties.

Perhaps the most surprising fact to emerge from this data is that the United States, which fought in only three interstate wars in the entire century, experienced more battle-related deaths than any other country. The American Civil War was the largest and deadliest war fought anywhere in the world between 1815 and 1914.[11] Europeans

Table 1.1 Battle deaths (in thousands) and number of European wars, 1816–1914

Country	Interstate wars		Imperial wars		National wars		All wars	
	Wars	Deaths	Wars	Deaths	Wars	Death	Wars	Deaths
United States	2	16.2	3	22.1	1	618.0	6	656.3
Ottoman Empire	7	355.4	17	158.4	–	–	24	513.8
Russia	5	341.7	11	88.4	–	–	16	430.1
Spain	4	3.7	11	283.1	–	125.0	15	411.8
France	4	105.5	25	110.9	4	168.2	33	384.6
Great Britain	1	22.0	48	325.5	1	2.5	50	350.0
Netherlands	–	–	8	269.6	–	–	8	269.6
Japan	2	85.4	3	30.9	–	–	5	116.3
Balkan states[a]	–	–	–		8	93.1	8	93.1
Germany[b]	–	–	2	21.6	4	65.1	6	86.7
Austria[c]	–	–	1	6.0	5	45.9	6	51.9
Portugal	–	–	5	37.2	–	–	5	37.2
Belgium	–	–	1	25.0	–	–	1	25.0
Italy	2	8.2	–	–	5	13.6	7	21.8
Total wars	27		135		28		190	
Total deaths		938.1		1,378.7		1,131.4		3,448.2

[a] Balkan states involved in the Balkan wars of 1912–13 were Serbia, Greece, Romania, and Bulgaria.
[b] Totals for Germany include Prussia, plus the North German Federation States of Hanover and Mecklenburg for the Seven Weeks War in 1868.
[c] Totals for Austria include South German Federation States of Saxony, Hesse, Bavaria, Wurttemberg, and Baden for the Seven Weeks War in 1868.
Source: Correlate of Wars data sets on wars. www.correlatesofwar.org/data-sets/COW-war

had little interest in the United States' struggle, which they regarded as nothing more than a fratricidal squabble between obstreperous Americans. The only major interstate war in recent memory in 1914 was the Russo-Japanese War, which Europeans also largely ignored, since it was several thousand miles east of London, Paris, or Berlin. Some of the old veterans in Germany and France might remind their countrymen of the Franco-Prussian War, but the memories of that war were pretty dim by the end of the century.

Imperial Wars

The years between Waterloo and the outbreak of the First World War are often referred to as the "Age of Imperialism." One of the "prizes" European nation-states valued from warfare after 1815 was the rewards associated with colonial territories. They were constantly fighting wars or putting down rebellions to expand and control their colonial empires. These military actions usually involved a relatively small European military force, often supported by naval power, that was pitted against peoples who were no match for European weaponry and military skill. But even small wars have their price. The total number of deaths from imperial wars was just under 1.4 million men – or about 10,000 men per war.

The conflicts that had the strongest hold on most people's attention in 1914 were the imperial wars that expanded empires. The race for territory was led by the British, who fought forty-eight imperial wars and the French who added twenty-five more in Africa, the Middle East, India, Southeast Asia, and China. The Netherlands, Belgium, and eventually the United States and Germany also pursued colonial interests that were scattered across the globe. The Russians fought two bloody wars with the Ottomans and suffered 430,000 deaths in their military efforts. Not all of the imperial wars waged by Europeans were successful. The Spanish and Portuguese fought sixteen imperial wars, most of them in an unsuccessful effort to hold on to their colonies in South America. All told, the price of empire was not cheap for the mother countries; the total number of deaths from the 135 imperial wars included in Table 1.1 was just under one and half million men.

What could Europeans in 1914 learn from these wars? The most obvious lesson was that waging war had become a costly business in terms of both lives and economic resources. To European eyes, nineteenth-century wars had been short and bloody, and they had been settled by agreements among the contesting parties, or with the help of third parties who negotiated a settlement. Crises came and went, and European governments remained confident that, for those willing to pay the costs, waging a war could be a useful, albeit expensive, policy option. The German victory over the French in 1871 produced a prolonged period of peace for the last three decades of the century, but beneath the seeming calm was a growing tension that could explode into violence.

The American Civil War

There was one major war outside Europe in this period that did not follow the pattern described above. The American Civil War provided some rather clear indications of what conflicts in the twentieth century might be like. Despite the horrendous cost of the war in terms of men and dollars, the two sides consistently rejected the idea of a settlement. They continued fighting until one side (the South) could no longer sustain the horrific cost. The American conflict also clearly demonstrated the growing significance of economic factors in determining the outcome of future conflicts. Addressing a group of Confederate veterans shortly after the war, Confederate General Jubal Early insisted that by the time the Army of Northern Virginia surrendered in the spring of 1865, the Southern forces "had been gradually worn down by the combined agencies of numbers, steam-power, railroads, mechanism, and all the resources of physical science … [Four years of fighting] had finally produced that exhaustion of our army and resources, and that accumulation of numbers on the other side, which wrought the final disaster."[12] Sadly for Early and his comrades, he was right; the military genius of Confederate General Robert E. Lee was not enough to overcome the economic might of the Union military establishment.

The human and economic consequences of the American Civil War also provide a rather prophetic look into the future of warfare. The ability of Abraham Lincoln's administration to orchestrate a partnership of private enterprise with government that was able to finance and consolidate the best-fed and best-equipped army the world had ever seen was a key to the Union victory. This was accomplished through considerable sacrifice; by the end of the war price levels in the United States had doubled and the national debt – which was almost non-existent at the outset of the war – had reached more than $2 billion.[13] An important part of the Union high command's "Anaconda Plan" was a naval blockade of Southern ports that by 1864 had managed to cut off importation of most consumer goods from abroad and interfered with the coastal trade of these ports, which contributed to the eventual collapse of the Confederate economy. All of these aspects of economic warfare reappeared in the Great War of 1914–18.[14]

Another element of the American Civil War that presaged twentieth-century warfare was the Union's commitment to a "total war" in the final year and a half of the conflict. William Tecumseh Sherman's famous "March to the Sea" from Atlanta to Savannah in the summer of 1864 and Phillip Sheridan's destruction of property in the Shenandoah Valley in the same year were conscious efforts to undermine the ability of the Confederate economy to supply troops in the field and to demoralize the rebel population.[15] In the east, Ulysses Grant introduced a commitment to a war of attrition in the summer of 1864 with his determination to fight a series of battles against the Confederates. Lee was forced to resort to digging a line of trenches that stretched from Richmond to Petersburg – a vivid precursor of the miles of trenches that would characterize the Western Front of the First World War.[16]

There were also lessons that could be learned from the economic effects of the war long after the fighting had stopped. A postwar fiscal policy of the federal government that stressed budget surpluses and debt retirement contributed to the longest deflation in American history, the consequences of which could be seen in a period of tumultuous politics. Finally, there were the costs associated with the benefits to widows of those who died in the war and the pensions for those who survived. At the end of the century, federal expenditures on pensions for a million Union veterans were the largest line item outside the war department in the federal budget.[17]

Warfare in the Twentieth Century

In the decades after the American Civil War, new weapons, faster means of transportation and communication, and the creation of huge standing armies and navies revolutionized the way wars were planned and fought on the battlefields and at sea. Behind the scenes of all of this military buildup was the increased importance of the industrial revolution and explosion of economic growth in determining the outcome of wars. Jubal Early's lament about the forces that "wrought the disaster" of Lee's defeat in 1865 would be repeated by those who lost in 1918 and again in 1945.

The scale of warfare in the period 1914–18 grew to a point far beyond anything people could ever have imagined at the turn of the century. "The count of casualties," writes Michael Clodfelter, "took a quantum leap in the Great War. Battle losses of World War I were totally unprecedented in human history. Even the greatest battles of the continental wars of the seventeenth and eighteenth centuries in Europe ... paled beside those of World War I."[18] Estimating deaths from war is an inexact science at best; we can only construct what might be called "orders of magnitude" for the number of men killed, wounded, or missing in action. Rough estimates of battle deaths for the major combatants suggest that for the First World War the total number of military deaths was 8.6 million. If we add the more than 700,000 battle deaths from the Russian Civil War, which began in 1917 and lasted until 1921, or the 250,000 men who died in eastern European conflicts between 1918 and 1920 as a result of wars following the collapse of the Austrian and Russian empires, the total number of military deaths in the Great War reaches close to 10 million men. This does not count the deaths of noncombatants associated with the movements of people as armies marched across Europe. Adding to the anguish associated with news of those who had died was a stream of wounded men returning from the endless battles. Clodfelter estimates the number of killed and wounded soldiers as 33 million – or the equivalent of a country the size of Italy in 1914.

The Second World War produced another quantum leap in casualties to a total of between 18 and 20 million men lost in battle, and 27.7 million men wounded, with approximately 9.4 million Allied soldiers and 8.3 million Axis soldiers.[19] Clodfelter argues that "when one adds up all the civilian victims of the Holocaust, of the Resistance in occupied Europe, of the terror bombings, of starvation, disease, and privation caused by the conflict, the toll of World War II, at the most conservative estimate, surpasses 30 million – with 40 million a more likely figure and some estimates going up to 55 million."[20] This implies that 70 million deaths is a reasonable estimate of the human toll from the Second World War, and it is not beyond reason to argue that as many as 100 million people died as a direct consequence of the two world wars.

The Aftermath of the Great War

Faced with the enormous demands of the war, military spending in all of the belligerent economies increased to a point where between a third and half of the gross domestic product (GDP) was devoted to supporting the war effort. This splurge of spending generated rapid increases in prices. Every country experienced at least a doubling of prices during the war, and for the defeated Central Powers, matters became much worse as the inflation of prices got completely out of hand. While Germany suffered the most extreme case of inflationary excesses, Austria, Poland, and Russia also experienced runaway inflation during and immediately after the war. The conscription of young men into the military required major adjustments in the labor force during the war, including the widespread recruitment of women into the labor force for the first time. When the war ended, demobilization of military personnel meant a sudden flow of male labor back into the labor market and displacement of many of the women who had worked in the war industries. The initial impact of these changes was widespread unemployment for several years after the end of the war. The final element of wartime disruption was the disintegration of international trade patterns under the pressures of blockades and sudden changes in demand. By 1925, some order had been restored to the international economy, but the interlude of relative "normalcy" was short-lived. In 1929, a series of banking crises, punctuated by the crash of the New York Stock Market in October, ushered in the worst depression in modern history. The combination of falling prices and a declining level of output together with unemployment created a hugely pessimistic economic outlook throughout the global economy. There had been economic downturns before, but there had never been anything comparable to the Great Depression.

The Puzzle of War

There is a growing body of research which suggests the Great Depression had its roots in the dislocations and disequilibria caused by the Great War, and that the strains from two decades of global economic insecurity played a significant role in exacerbating the problems that led to the Second World War.[21] This is not surprising; it is easy to find explanations suggesting that the causes of crises involving war and economic activity share some common features. In the introduction to his widely read book *Why Nations Go to War*, John Stoessinger notes that:

> Mortals made these decisions [to go to war]. They made them in fear and in trembling, but they made them nonetheless. In most cases, the decision makers were not evil people bent on destruction but were frightened and entrapped by self-delusion. They based their policies on fears, not facts, and were singularly devoid of empathy. Misperception, rather than conscious evil design, appears to have been the leading villain in the drama.[22]

Stoessinger accepts the assumption commonly made by students of war that the decision-makers are trying to act rationally. However, he points out that when the outcome of those decisions is based on inadequate information and fears, not facts, the results can be catastrophic. Stoessinger also claims that at the moment of crisis the decision-makers are under considerable pressure to act quickly on the basis of imperfect perceptions and instincts to make what proved to be erroneous decisions in terms of the eventual outcome. Military historians have long highlighted the irrational (and therefore unexplained) mistakes, miscalculations, and misperceptions that have led generals and politicians to so often choose war over diplomacy. Social scientists, on the other hand, have relied on notions of rationality, which insist that decision-makers operate in a fashion that will ensure rational outcomes even if individuals behave in irrational ways.

Animal Spirits

Writing about explanations for the Great Depression of the 1930s, John Maynard Keynes, the British economist who revolutionized economic thinking in the 1930s, claimed that "if orthodox economics is at fault, error is to be found not in the superstructure, which has been erected with great care for logical consistency, but in a lack of clearness and of generality in the premises."[23] He suggested that economic theorists needed to recognize that much more than mere "rationality" lay behind the decisions that households and businesses made every day.

> [A] large proportion of our positive activities," he wrote, "depend on spontaneous optimism rather than on mathematical expectation, whether moral or hedonistic or economic. Decisions to do something positive ... can only be taken as the result of animal spirits – of a spontaneous urge to action rather than inaction, and not as the outcome of a weighted average of quantitative benefits multiplied by quantitative probabilities.[24]

George Akerlof and Robert Shiller have taken Keynes' notion of animal spirits to "account for how [the economy] works when people act as *humans*, that is, possessed of all-too-human animal spirits."[25]

Keynes characterized his animal spirits as bursts of optimism that fueled the speculative excesses in financial markets. However, the same animal spirits that push people to be overly optimistic can be equally responsible for bursts of pessimism that fuel the panics that bring a crashing end to the boom of stock prices. With a touch of imagination, we can expand his notion of animal spirits to characterize the behavior behind the Great Depression and the decisions relating to the outbreak and prosecution of wars. The foundations for our analysis are three characteristics that are particularly susceptible to such "spontaneous urges" – of optimism and pessimism: *Confidence*, *Fear*, and a *Propensity to Gamble*.

Confidence

"The very term confidence," explain Akerlof and Shiller, "implies behavior that goes beyond a rational approach to decision making ... When people are confident they go out to buy; when they are unconfident they withdraw, and they sell. Economic history is full of such cycles of confidence and withdrawal."[26] On the face of it, diplomatic crises would seem to be very different phenomena from speculative financial bubbles. Yet the "road to war" follows a sequence of events that is remarkably similar to that of a speculative investment bubble. Carl von Clausewitz, a general who served in the Prussian army during the Napoleonic wars and later wrote a treatise titled *On War*, noted that war is simply an extension of state policy.[27] Policies demand choices. One can imagine a variety of "incidents" that create tensions between states that could gradually escalate into a diplomatic crisis. Most of the time there are options available that allow the parties to resolve the crisis without resorting to war. But suppose diplomatic measures do not reduce tensions and the situation continues to escalate. At each level of escalation, the number of options that might lessen the pressure on the confidence bubble dwindles – but war is invariably one of the options that does not get "taken off the table." Political leaders are gradually faced with a situation where they decide that force is the only policy that can actually resolve the dispute.

This brings us to the problem of *overconfidence*. Modern wars, like modern investment schemes, involve a great deal of planning. Planning requires a set of assumptions that provide the foundation for the plans that are being made. These assumptions are supposed to reflect conditions in the "real world." All too often, however, planners let their pursuit of victory cloud their choice of assumptions. Dominic

Johnson notes that positive illusions may not be the "all-encompassing explanation for war, but they … offer a compelling extra piece of the war puzzle."[28] Johnson makes the interesting point that the larger the scope of the problem, the more room there is for positive illusions to foment overconfidence. Johnson is hardly alone in his emphasis on overconfidence as a cause for going to war. It is a rather simple extension of his argument to say that the overconfidence of leaders is shared by the masses. Just as rumors of immense profits or unexpected changes in markets can reinforce the euphoria of a stock market boom, stories of military prowess can magnify the incessant beat of the "drums of war."

Both the military/diplomatic and the economic situations described above involve the evolution of a *confidence bubble* – a situation where *overconfidence* has produced a "bubble" that has been stretched to a point where the slightest dislocation may cause the bubble to "pop." The problem is that no one has found a way to gently "deflate" the bubble. This is when confidence begins to waver and fear becomes an ever-increasing element in the efforts to resolve the crisis.

Fear

Like the confidence multiplier, a *fear multiplier* can kick in if confidence is shaken by the course of events. As fears grow and confidence wanes, decisions become much more geared to the need for immediate solutions to defuse the imminent danger that a major war could break out at any moment. Less evident than the way fear triggers an attack is the subtle way that fear gradually pervades the decisions that lead up to the confidence bubble.

Military leaders are vulnerable to fear. They worry that their potential enemies will gain an edge by increasing their military strength, so they increase their armaments, thus touching off an "arms race" that increases the possibility of a preemptive war. Starting a war may gain victories in the short run; however, wars are rarely decided by the opening blow. Fear and falling confidence will play a major role in deciding the next move. Victories set the confidence multiplier spinning upwards; defeats puncture the confidence bubble, but offer little in the way of suggestions of where to go next. This interplay of fear and confidence brings us to the final element that influences decisions on war and economics: the propensity for humans to make risky gambles.

A Propensity to Gamble

The final element in our use of animal spirits to turn "rational" decisions into very "irrational" outcomes is the propensity people have to gamble. That propensity can increase dramatically in situations that involve high stakes and big losses. Decisions in times of crisis involve the ability to predict events that are subject to varying degrees of risk and uncertainty. The probabilities associated with market behavior in a world of uncertainty can be estimated using complex models that forecast future outcomes. But all of the "models" which predict the behavior of financial markets rely on some degree of "rational" decision-making, and for the most part they rely on behaviors in past crises. Since each crisis is different, people confronted with a new "confidence bubble" do not always know how to act "rationally" – particularly if they are afraid of disparate consequences. One of the effects of fear is to encourage people to take risks they might otherwise not consider.

All wars contain some element of chance and uncertainty. Simple choice theory suggests that political leaders would carefully look at the odds of winning or losing and select the option with the highest odds of winning. Economic theory suggests the same thing is true for investors. They should select those investments with the greatest chance of increasing their net wealth. However, making choices that involve risk is not that simple. In 1979, behavioral economists Daniel Kahneman and Amos Tversky developed a model they called "prospect theory" to analyze how people make decisions when facing risks.[29] Prospect theory argues that people will place less weight on assessing outcomes that are "merely probable" than they will on choosing outcomes that appear to be certain. This tendency, claim Kahneman and Tversky, "contributes to *risk aversion* in choices involving sure gains and to *risk seeking* in choices involving sure losses."[30] Prospect theory also postulates that people are much more concerned about losses than they are about acquiring gains. Jack Levy explains how these aspects of prospect theory explain the propensity to gamble when it comes to international war and diplomacy.

Given a tendency to place greater weight on avoiding losses relative to gains and a tendency to take risks involving possible losses, political leaders have a propensity to take more risks to maintain their international positions, reputations, and domestic political support against potential losses than they do to enhance their positions. It is reasonable to conclude that there are more leaders who are "likely to fight in order to avoid losses than to make gains. This reinforces the argument that wars are driven as much by fear as by the possibility of gains from victory – The same logic suggests that people will punish their leaders more for incurring losses than for the failure to make gains."[31]

Prospect theory is particularly useful for a narrative or historical approach to explaining wars because the calculations of risk for a specific situation are placed in the context of a reference point that "frames" the specific assumptions for each decision. Once the outcome of the decision is known, a new reference point must be established for subsequent decisions. The emphasis in prospect theory is on the importance of *changes* that are brought about by recent decisions, not the total level of activity. This allows us to view the outcomes of battles as marginal increments in the context of the larger war. The tendency for decision-makers to reframe their decisions based on what to do next in the face of changing situations produces a final way in which animal spirits influence their reactions to wars. We have seen how battles involve enormous costs, in terms of both human casualties and the resources to carry on the fight.[32]

The costs associated with these phenomena are what economists call "sunk costs." The logic of marginal economic analysis tells us to forget the past and concentrate on the added or *marginal* costs and benefits associated with what we anticipate might happen. Behavioral economists point out that there are many situations where animal spirits can trump logic when it comes to assessing how to deal with sunk costs. Daniel Kahneman notes that social incentives can

> shape our preferences and motivate our actions in a way that causes us to refuse to cut losses when doing so would admit failure, we are biased against actions that could lead to regret, and we draw an illusory but sharp distinction between omission and commission, not doing and doing, because the sense of responsibility is greater for one than for the other.[33]

In the case of wars, prospect theory suggests that the sunk costs in the form of casualties from wars persist in a way that creates a tendency for leaders to find ways to recover those costs, even if this choice involves higher risks rather than pulling back to "cut one's losses." As Levy and Thompson put it, "political leaders often continue to pursue costly interventions and wars, even in strategically unimportant areas, rather than risk the state's loss of power and prestige or their own loss of domestic support."[34] All of this is tied to what Robert Shiller calls "a basic human interest in gambling, seen in one form or another in all cultures, an interest that also expresses itself in speculative markets."[35]

Confidence, fear, and a propensity to gamble or take risks are instincts that always present themselves in the process of making decisions. Most of the time, these traits exert their influence within the boundaries of what we might call rational decision-making. In times of crisis, which usually involve a very short timeline to make decisions, the presence of animal spirits can "turbo-charge" these influences in a way that produces what might seem to be irrational behavior. Thus, confidence becomes overconfidence, fear becomes panic, and a propensity to gamble becomes recklessness. A major pitfall in the analysis of such situations is that there is not any systematic way to construct a quantitative variable that allows us to unequivocally determine how much of the action was due to animal spirits. For that, we must turn to the history "foxes."

Risk, Uncertainty, and Animal Spirits

Any decision for future action involves some level of risk and some degree of uncertainty. Both words deal with the prediction of future outcomes – whether losses or gains. There is, however, an important difference in the meaning of the two terms when used in decision theory. *Risk* refers to events where the various outcomes being considered are known and their effect on future events can be measured with some degree of accuracy. *Uncertainty* deals with situations where there is no way of ascertaining what is going to happen. Both are phenomena that will influence the fears and confidence with which a future action can be taken. Because the risk factor can be measured, generals and politicians develop plans which take account of "calculated risks" to boost their confidence as they go into battle. They cannot, however, make similar projections to deal with uncertainty, because they don't know what might happen. Risks can be estimated, but there is no way to accurately "calculate" the impact of uncertainty. A final word on risk and uncertainty is to note that the discussion of the role of risk and uncertainty rests on the ability of leaders to make accurate assessments of outcomes from their actions. When people are excited by animal spirits they are more likely to be overconfident, as a result of the way things are going. A higher level of uncertainty increases the margin of error in the estimates of what will happen.

Stories

This brings us back to the question of how individuals – and groups of individuals – formulate what they believe to be a "rational" calculus of decision-making. People base their decisions on *perceptions*, and those perceptions are shaped by the information available to them. Most people have a tendency see things as they *want them to be*, not as they *actually are.* Even when reliable information about the situation exists, people fall victim to systematic biases that exaggerate the gains and minimize the risks of some action. "A root cause of war," notes Stephen Van Evera, "lies in the opacity of the future and in the optimistic illusions that this opacity allows. These illusions lead states to a false confidence in victory, or Pyrrhic victories."[36] John Vasquez sums up the net effect of all these problems by noting that "as one examines the actual consequences of each action that is taken, one finds that it is anything but rational. Misperception, miscalculation, self-fulfilling prophesies, and errors often produce disasters that might have been avoided if actors had behaved differently."[37]

Every explanation of war or economic speculation must take into consideration the issue of inaccurate or insufficient information. Akerlof and Shiller add a further dimension to the problems surrounding information when they note that a substantial amount of information comes in the form of "stories" that convey information formally or informally among groups of people. Stories, they argue, give us "our sense of reality, of who we are and what we are doing," which is "intertwined with the story of our lives and of the lives of others. The aggregate of such stories is a national or international story, which itself plays an important role in the economy." Quantitative historians – both those who study economic history and those pursuing military history – shy away from a reliance on stories as a basis for modeling behavior. In part, this reflects the difficulty of assessing the accuracy of what a lawyer might call hearsay evidence; in part it reflects the difficulties in quantifying statements involving magnitudes that are stated as "large" or "small" without any numer-ical accuracy. Stories, in other words, cannot easily fit into quantitative models of behavior. Yet, everyone hears stories that are passed on by relatives or friends giving advice regarding questions of public policy. Whether or not the stories are accurate, people trust them because they trust the source. Word of mouth becomes an important way that infor-mation is disseminated throughout society.

Paradigms, Anomalies, and Tipping Points

Why was it so difficult for people to return to the prewar world of 1914 after the Great War ended? It should be apparent by now that we are not likely to come up with a simple answer to this question. The world of 1900 had numerous checks and balances that had evolved over the past century, and things had worked well enough so long as there were no major "displacements" that required significant alter-ations to the global status quo. The Great War changed all that. People were forced to deal with a whole new set of challenges. The hardest changes were those that called for a new way of looking at things.

In his study of scientific revolutions, Thomas Kuhn uses the concept of "paradigms" to explain the structure of scientific revolutions.[38] Kuhn identifies paradigms as accepted bodies of know-ledge that the scientific community took for granted in their research agenda.[39] He contends that, precisely because they "worked" most of the time, paradigms were not only accepted, they were resistant to major changes. In fact, most research projects were designed to test the validity of existing paradigms, not discover new paradigms. Only if someone found some "anomaly" – an event that could not be reconciled with the implications of the paradigm – would there be an incentive for scientists to launch a search for new paradigms. Since no paradigm could explain everything, there were always a few anomalies that could not be reconciled with the paradigm. Only anomalies significant enough to pose a serious "crisis" for the use-fulness of the paradigm would challenge the existing paradigm. As Kuhn put it:

> So long as the tools a paradigm supplies continue to prove cap-able of solving the problems it defines, science moves fastest and penetrates most deeply through confident employment of those tools. The reason is clear. As in manufacture so in

science – retooling is an extravagance to be reserved for the occasion that demands it. The significance of crises is the indication they provide that an occasion for retooling has arrived.[40]

Kuhn's logic of scientific revolutions has been applied to the social sciences using what John Kenneth Galbraith called the "conventional wisdom" governing the world of economics.[41] In the years following the Great War, people experienced hyperinflation, persistent unemployment, the collapse of security markets and the unexplained decline of money income, and the demise of governments that had existed for centuries. All of this constituted a massive group of anomalies, suggesting that the existing paradigms for wars and economic crises might no longer be an accurate reflection of the way that the world actually worked. As such, a new set of paradigms was needed to understand what was happening.

Unfortunately, it is seldom easy to change people's view of the world. John Maynard Keynes commented on the power that existing paradigms exert on people when he wrote in the closing paragraph of his *General Theory of Employment, Interest and Money* that:

> [T]he ideas of economists and political philosophers, both when they are right and when they are wrong, are more powerful than is commonly understood. Indeed the world is ruled by little else. Practical men, who believe themselves to be quite exempt from any intellectual influences, are usually the slaves of some defunct economist. Madmen in authority, who hear voices in the air, are distilling their frenzy from some academic scribbler of a few years back. I am sure that the power of vested interests is vastly exaggerated compared with the gradual encroachment of ideas.[42]

"Practical men" in western Europe and the United States at the turn of the twentieth century had an unrelenting belief that markets were stable, efficient institutions that promoted exchange and specialization throughout the world. They were not about to give up those beliefs simply because of some rather unfortunate anomalies in the form of inflation, unemployment, and falling income that seemed to linger when they should have disappeared. Eventually, stubbornness might give way to a grudging recognition that things *had* changed and that new ideas must therefore be developed to deal with the postwar world. But the process by which those new ideas took hold were usually neither simple nor quick. Ideas that challenge the conventional wisdom seldom triumph on their intellectual or ideological appeal alone. They are accepted in response to changes that proceed gradually over time, a process that is so gradual that it may barely be noticeable behind the screen of everyday events.

The resistance to changing paradigms involves more than just a resistance to new ideas. Cliometricians have spent considerable effort examining a phenomenon that they call "path dependence." Once people have taken the time to learn how to do something, it can be expensive to retrain them to a new system. A new machine or technique of production may promise to be more efficient; however, if companies have invested large sums of money on existing equipment and techniques for a specific task, they may be reluctant to incur the risks associated with the costs of adopting a new technology. Generals searching for ways to win a war are particularly susceptible to the problem of path dependence because the stakes for using a new idea can be very high, and there is seldom time to work out the kinks. It is worth noting that despite the enormous costs in the form of casualties, the conventional wisdom that success rested on the use of large units of infantry to "break through" enemy lines did not significantly change on the battlefield until the end of 1917.[43]

Once in a great while, something comes along that produces sudden changes that force people to quickly reassess their world. Such epochs of economic and social change have involved myriad much smaller historical turning points that historians call "tipping points." Tipping points are instances when people must respond to changes in the short run that could have a significant effect on some aspect of a military or economic crisis. This could involve events as disparate as the outcome of a battle, "regime changes" that alter political alignments, or disruptions in the economy that might affect the course of military or economic crises. These are the instances when the animal spirits of confidence, fear, and a propensity to gamble will most forcefully come into play. The outbreak of the First World War has posed major challenges to scholars trying to interpret the period after 1914. This is particularly true for those who seek "rational" explanations for the irrational environment created by two wars and a global depression. Why were the paradigms and institutional arrangements of 1900 unable to contain the forces of change unleashed by the crisis of 1914?

An Age of Catastrophes

Let us return for a moment to Eric Hobsbawm's description of a time when Europeans confidently ruled most of the inhabited areas of the world. That confidence was based on a set of paradigms about how the world "works." In 1900 the progress of the past century provided ample evidence for those inclined to believe they were sitting atop a world that belonged to them and promised a bright future. To be sure, the peace following the fall of Napoleon in 1815 had been interrupted by major military actions such as the Crimean War, the American Civil War, the Franco-Prussian War, and the Russo-Japanese War. And there was always the soft but constant drumbeat of imperial wars in the background. For the most part, the consequences of these military and economic events were contained and isolated from each other so that they did not create global crises.

Unfortunately, this approach tends to ignore the possibility that more than one thing can happen at the same time. Most paradigms or theories deal with some particular problem or set of problems that are of interest to us. To simplify matters the analysis assumes that everything else remains unchanged. Economists call this approach a "partial equilibrium" analysis that isolates the effects of the variables we are interested in. But what if the other variables that might affect our problem do not remain unchanged? In that case, we would need to expand our analysis to a general equilibrium theory that could account for the possibility that there is an interdependence between the variables we are looking at and the rest of the things that might affect our situation. A common example is the use of simple marginal "cost–benefit analysis," which compares the change in the level of costs and benefits to measure the net impact of some decision. The analysis looks at the effects on prices in a set of particular markets without considering the effects of other markets or variables that could affect the market under investigation. A "general equilibrium" approach is much more complicated, involving a set of simultaneous equations to account for the effects of other variables.

Too much of a good thing can sometimes lead to very bad things. By the end of the nineteenth century people living in Hobsbawm's European world of confidence had developed an over-confidence that made them blind to the reality that beneath the veneer of world peace and economic growth and progress was a world that was racked by intermittent economic turmoil and military conflict. The panics and wars that began with Archduke Ferdinand's assassination in June of 1914 may indeed have been anomalies; however, they were an integral part of a process of historical change that was reshaping the global political and economic environment in the years leading up to the crisis of 1914. Viewed through the lens of accepted paradigms they were interruptions that could not be easily explained at the time. "The decades from the outbreak of the First World War to the aftermath of the Second," Hobsbawm wrote, "was an Age of Catastrophe. For forty years, [Western civilization] stumbled from one calamity to another. There were times when even intelligent conservatives would not take bets on its survival."[44]

The Composite Index of National Capability (CINC) Score

Any study of warfare in the twentieth century must involve some attempt to assess and compare the ability of rival states or groups to wage war. The basic tenet of the narrative presented in this book is that the outcome of wars rested not only on the military prowess and skill of the various belligerent countries or empires, but also on their relative economic strength. A major challenge for quantitative historians is to find measures of the military capability of states involved in the various conflicts. One of the most ambitious efforts to meet this challenge is the research by the Correlates of War Project (COW) at the University of Michigan established by David Singer in 1962. Singer was a political scientist whose objective was to undertake "the systematic accumulation of scientific knowledge about war." Together with historian Melvin Small, the COW Project began to assemble "a more accurate data set on the incidence and extent of inter-state and extra-systemic war in the post-Napoleonic period."[45] The COW data sets have served as a major resource for scholars working on the causes and outcomes of war.[46] What makes these data sets particularly useful for our study is that they combine a huge body of data collected using the same definitions of six important variables for many areas of the world for a period of more than two hundred years.

One of the objectives of the COW Project was to construct a set of "scores" that could "provide an index that reflects the breadth and depth of the resources that a nation could bring to bear in instances of militarized disputes."[47] The Composite Index of National Capability (CINC) score combines the economic and military capabilities of a country in a way that will reflect "the ability of a nation to exercise and resist influence."[48] The CINC score is constructed from six variables representing the demographic, industrial, and military indicators as the most effective measures of a nation's material capabilities. The six variables included in the CINC score are:

1. Military personnel (thousands of men): defined as troops under the command of the national government, intended for use against foreign adversaries, and held ready for combat as of January 1 of the referent year.

2. Military expenditures (thousands of current dollars): defined as the total military budget for a given state for a given year.

3. Total population (thousands): defined as the number of people living in a given state.

4. Urban population (thousands): defined as the number of people living in a city of 100,000 or more people.

5. Primary energy consumption (thousands of coal-ton equivalents): computed using data about four broad categories of sources – coal, petroleum, electricity, and natural gas. The raw data for each commodity is converted into a common unit and then summed to produce the total energy consumption for a given state in a particular year.

6. Iron and steel production (thousands of tons): defined as all domestically produced pig iron before 1899 and steel after 1900.

For each of the six variables in the data set the share of each country's production can be computed as the ratio of that country's production divided by the global production to obtain the "country ratio." The composite CINC "score" for a country is the sum of all six country ratios divided by six. Multiplying the CINC ratio by 100 gives us what I call %CINC index, which provides a measure of the relative share of military and economic power of countries across territories and time.[49] However, it is important to emphasize that the aggregate %CINC score measures the overall capability of a state's military and economic power, not the actual ability to wage war at a point in time. Whether or not the country actually realizes that capability depends on the degree to which the resources measured by the CINC score can be mobilized into an effective system of economic and military organization to fight a war.[50]

Can an index constructed from six aggregate variables that are spread across dozens of states over a period of nearly two hundred years capture all – or even most – of the subtleties and capricious outcomes that decided a world war? Probably not. The data can, however, add support and provide interesting insights to our analytical narrative of how animal spirits such as confidence, fear, and the propensity to gamble affected the decisions that led to turning points in history.

Appendix 1 presents a set of tables containing the %CINC scores and values for the military, economic, and demographic component values for the major powers of the world between 1850 and 1939.

2 OTTO VON BISMARCK AND THE CHANGING PARADIGM OF WAR

The government of a state engaged in war must look in more directions than towards the scene of the struggle only. The task of the commanders of the army is to annihilate the hostile forces; the object of war is to conquer peace under conditions which are conformable to the policy pursued by the state.

Otto von Bismarck (1866)[1]

While there are many competing explanations for the "origins" of the First World War, there is general agreement on when the European states started on the "road to war." "More than anything else," writes historian Joachim Remak, "what set in motion the course of events that led to disaster in 1914 was the Franco-Prussian War of 1870–71, and the peace that followed it. For it was that which opened a new age in European history."[2] No one understood that war had become an extension of state policy better than Otto von Bismarck, who in slightly more than a decade transformed a Prussian state that had been a second-level power in Europe for more than two centuries into a nation-state that dominated central European politics by the end of the nineteenth century.

It All Started with Bismarck

In 1862, when King Wilhelm I appointed Otto von Bismarck as Minister-President of Prussia, the German states and principalities organized loosely into the German Federation, which had been created following the Congress of Vienna at the end of the Napoleonic wars. Although it had managed to survive the political turmoil that swept over Europe during the 1850s, the Federation struggled to deal with the rivalry between the Habsburg Empire and Prussia, each of which vied for leadership of the entire Federation.[3] Within weeks of his appointment as Minister-President of Prussia, Bismarck made it clear that he intended to pursue a policy to unify these states under Prussian leadership. In a speech to the Prussian Landmark that would come to personify Bismarck's career as the leader of a united Germany, he announced that unification would be achieved, "not by means of speeches and majority verdicts ... but by iron and blood."[4]

The Schleswig-Holstein Question

In November 1863, the death of King Ferdinand of Denmark offered Bismarck an opportunity to put his "iron and blood" approach to a test by reopening a longstanding dispute over who should govern the duchies of Schleswig and Holstein, which are located on an isthmus of land connecting Denmark to the German states of Hanover and Mecklenburg. Christian IX, now King of Denmark, proposed that his country should be allowed to annex Schleswig, but not Holstein. Disputes surrounding the "Schleswig-Holstein Question" had already spawned a war between Denmark and the German states in 1849–53 which ended with a treaty signed in London giving the governing rights for both states to Denmark. The issue was complicated by confusion over the line of inheritance for the Danish throne and by the fact that a large fraction of the population in Schleswig was essentially Danish in terms of customs and language, while most Holsteiners spoke German and were more closely allied with their southern neighbors as a member of the German Federation.

Bismarck strongly objected to the proposed annexation by the Danish king, and he made it clear that he was prepared to use force, if necessary, to ensure that neither Schleswig nor Holstein would be annexed to Denmark. Austria, which also wanted to keep both duchies in the German Federation, went along with Bismarck's objections, and when the Danes refused to back down from their intent to annex Schleswig, Prussia and Austria declared war on Denmark. Prussian forces quickly overran the Danish defenses, and by the end of July 1864 they had occupied all of Schleswig and crossed over into Denmark. Unable to check the Austro-German advance, the Danes accepted the outcome of a conference meeting in Vienna to resolve the dispute. Christian renounced his claims to both Schleswig and Holstein and agreed to an armistice. The Treaty of Vienna, signed on October 30, 1864, stipulated that Austria was to become the administrator of Holstein and Prussia was to become the administrator of Schleswig.[5] Bismarck's iron and blood approach had won its first military encounter with relative ease, and the victorious campaign cemented the close relationship of the three men who would forge the war policy of the Prussian government over the next decade. Bismarck was Minister-President and foreign minister; Albrecht von Roon, who had overseen a well-functioning military organization, was Minister of War; and Helmuth von Moltke had proved to be a skillful commander in the Danish war. Bismarck could now turn his attention to the larger problem of dealing with Austria's rivalry with Prussia and the German Federation.

The Zollverein

Long before he became prime minister in 1868, the economic foundation of Bismarck's plan to unify Germany had been laid by the creation of a customs union known as the Zollverein. As early as 1828 several German states had experimented with the idea of forming customs unions to cut down the barriers on trade among the various states. In 1834 Prussia took the lead by joining with a group of nine other German states to sign agreements to form the Zollverein.[6] Prussia was by far the biggest state, with a population of 13.6 million; the populations of the remaining states in 1836 totaled just under 10.5 million. The Habsburg Empire was not included in the Zollverein, partly because it pursued a protectionist trade policy and partly because of its rivalry with Prussia. By 1865, when the Zollverein treaties were up for renewal, the number of member states had increased to eighteen, with four more states expressing strong interest. Bismarck had persuaded all the states in the Zollverein to accept Prussian control of their economic policies as the price of renewal. Even for states that were not particularly happy with Prussia's economic dominance, the economic gains offered by membership in the Zollverein were substantial and Prussia's presence in the union gave the group a military strength that protected them against rival powers. Austria-Hungary responded by trying to set up a rival customs union around the southern German states – most notably Bavaria, Wurttemberg, Hesse-Darmstadt, and Nassau. In May of 1865 the Zollverein was renewed for another twelve years under conditions set by Bismarck. The new arrangements left Prussia effectively in charge of interregional trade among the German states. Austria-Hungary remained outside the Zollverein.

The renewal of the Zollverein customs union was an important part of Bismarck's campaign to unify the German states; indeed, it was probably more important than the military success against Denmark. Economic integration can be a powerful unifying force – a factor that Bismarck and his allies used to their advantage throughout the rivalry of the 1860s in gaining support for a unified German economy and a political state that would include all the German Federation – and still exclude Austria-Hungary. The Zollverein had already produced an economic expansion that benefited all the German states through the period 1840–67.[7] By early 1866 the struggle between the two rivals for dominance among the German states had reached a point where both sides were preparing for a war that Bismarck felt was inevitable. "Because of the policy of Vienna," he explained, "Germany is clearly too small for us both. In the not too distant future we shall have to fight for our existence against Austria and … it is not within our power to avoid that, since the course of events in Germany has no other solution."[8]

Bismarck realized that a war with Austria-Hungary involved some serious risks, but they were risks he was prepared to take in pursuit of unification of the German states. Most of the German states were likely to side with the Austrians in a war; however, the performance of the Prussian army in the Danish war convinced Bismarck that, so long as the other major powers did not take sides in the struggle with Austria, Moltke could take care of the Austrian military threat as well as any forces the Federation could muster.[9] His confidence was boosted by the fact that the Austrians were already engaged in a military conflict with Italy that was tying up a sizeable fraction of their troops. To cover the possibility that other powers might intervene, he managed to make a short-term alliance with Italy to join the war with Austria, and he made use of earlier ties to France and Russia to ensure that if there were a conflict between Austria and Prussia, those powers would remain on the sidelines. With everything in place, starting a war against the southern German Federation and Austria seemed worth the risk.

The Seven Weeks War

The war began with a setback for the Prussians at the hands of Hanoverian troops at the Battle of Langensalza in northern Saxony. However, the use of railroads to rush Prussian reinforcements to the scene quickly reversed that outcome and Hanover was subsequently occupied by Prussian troops. Thereafter Federation troops, who were neither well trained nor well led, did not pose a serious threat to the Prussian plans. In addition to demonstrating the mobility of the Prussian forces, this early fighting demonstrated one of the huge tactical advantages the Prussians enjoyed because of the superior fire-power that their breech-loading "needle guns" gave their infantry. Not only did the needle gun allow a much faster rate of fire; it also allowed the Prussians to load while lying prone on the ground. The Austrians had no answer to this new weaponry. The decisive battle of the war was on the Bavarian plains near the town of Sadowa on July 3, 1866. Moltke had gathered three Prussian armies totaling 220,000 men and attacked an Austrian army of roughly the same size. The Battle of Königgrätz was a stunning victory for the Prussians.[10]

Already pressed by the demands of their war with Italy, the Austrians decided to reach a quick settlement with the Prussians. An armistice was signed on July 26, 1866 and Bismarck had once again won his military gamble. The stakes were higher this time, and the spoils of victory were greater. In fact, the challenge now was to keep things focused on why Prussia went to war in the first place. Victories such as Königgrätz tended to stoke the ambitions of generals and politicians alike – not to mention the passions of the populace back home. Bismarck discovered to his dismay that his king was not going to be satisfied with the Austrian offer of letting Prussia have its way with the German Federation without any accompanying territorial concessions. Only the intervention of the crown prince – normally not one of Bismarck's supporters – saved the day for the prime minister by convincing the king that Prussia should not press for any territorial concession from the Austrians.

Moltke's overwhelming victory at Königgrätz should not obscure the fact that the Prussians had taken a significant risk on the outcome of that battle. Geoffrey Wawro considers a counterfactual scenario predicting that if Austria had won the battle,

> the Prussians could have expected no mercy. Barring French or Russian intervention, they might have been reduced to something like the Tilsit frontiers of 1807 ... Vienna would have stunted Prussia's economic growth by a debilitating schedule of reparation payments, the amputation of industrial provinces like Silesia, Lusatia, and the Ruhr, and by the forcible attachment of the underdeveloped Austrian Empire to the Prusso-German *Zollverein*.[11]

Like all counterfactual scenarios, this is just one of many possibilities. A rout of the Prussians by Austrian forces would be as unlikely an outcome as was the overwhelming Prussian victory. The point remains that even a lesser victory by Austria could have stymied Bismarck's goal of forcing Austria out of the German Federation.

Bismarck's struggle to persuade his monarch to resist making territorial demands from Austria points to one of the most likely pitfalls in policy that rests on military success. There is always a threat that the animal spirits spurred on by victories of war will cause elements in the government to abandon the initial policy objectives that lay behind the decision to go to war. Thanks to the crown prince's help, Bismarck had been able to maintain Prussia's commitment to a long-term policy of German unification led by the Prussian monarchy. For Bismarck, who became the Chancellor of Germany, cutting Austria out of the German Federation without exacting additional territories from the Habsburg Empire was a sufficient reward for the Prussian army's success at Königgrätz, and it was important to Bismarck's goal of German unification that Austria not become an implacable foe. Bismarck's restraint bore fruit. Within two years the German Chancellor had orchestrated the reorganization of a north German union that would clearly be dominated by Prussia, an action that was the first concrete step toward the creation of a unified German state.

Austria-Hungary and several states which now formed a South German Federation were excluded from the Northern Federation. Bismarck did not make a serious effort to include these states in his expanding empire because he feared that the French, and possibly other European powers as well, might interfere with his negotiations with Austria-Hungary at the end of the Seven Weeks War. The French

Emperor Louis Napoleon had made it clear that he would not accept Prussian domination of the southern German states and Bismarck was not yet ready for a war with France, so he did not directly pursue the inclusion of these states in the North German Federation. In fact, as it turned out, he did not need to do anything. The states in the South German Federation could clearly see the writing on the wall, and within a year they had all signed secret military treaties that tied them to Prussia in the event of another war with either Austria-Hungary or France.

The final step in Bismarck's plan for a German Empire was the rivalry between Prussia and France. Once again the dynastic intrigues of Europe assisted the German Chancellor. In September 1868 Queen Isabella of Spain abdicated her throne, touching off a search for a new monarch. Bismarck publicly championed the candidacy of a Hohenzollern related to King Wilhelm of Prussia, an action that he knew was sure to incense Louis Napoleon. In the furor that followed, Bismarck further aggravated the situation by publishing a carefully edited telegram that made it seem that the French ambassador had insulted the Prussian monarch in a private meeting. In his memoirs – which are notorious for displaying his own actions in a favorable light – Bismarck says little of the editing, but he makes it clear that his purpose in making the king's message public was to stir up the passions for war both at home and in France. Bismarck's purpose in publishing what became known as the "Ems Telegram" was clear enough. He hoped to provoke a crisis that would lead to war with France, and he wanted Louis Napoleon to be the one to initiate the conflict. He was helped along in this effort by the fact that the French emperor was as convinced as Bismarck that a conflict between Prussia and France was inevitable. Louis Napoleon took the bait and on July 19, 1870 France declared war against Prussia.[12]

It was a disastrous decision on the part of the French. The Prussian army, under the skillful leadership of Moltke, had gained a series of victories culminating in the defeat of the French army and the capture of Louis Napoleon at Sedan in September 1870. Although some French insurgents in Paris continued to resist, French troops were able to subdue the rebels by January of 1871 and the Third Republic became the successor to the Second Empire. Once again Bismarck was faced with the problem of bringing a war to an end while keeping the turbo-charged animal spirits from inducing his king to ask for too much amid the euphoria of victory. Bismarck was anxious to end the hostilities before other powers had time to think up reasons to intervene. The major sticking point to reaching an agreement on a treaty was strong pressure from the Prussian generals and many politicians to annex the French provinces of Alsace and Lorraine. Bismarck reluctantly went along with the pressure of popular opinion in demanding annexation at the peace talks, and the two countries eventually signed the Treaty of Frankfurt ending hostilities on February 26, 1871.[13] Alsace and Lorraine were both annexed to the newly formed German Empire, and France agreed to pay a substantial indemnity to Germany. The animal spirits subsided, but the lingering legacy of the German annexation of French territory remained a smoldering ember that would resurface years later.

To everyone's surprise, the French paid off their indemnity in just two years. As Dennis Showalter points out, "Much of the indemnity eventually went into public circulation, through war-loan repayment, railway and military building programs, and pensions to veterans and families."[14] Not only were the French defeated, by 1872 it was apparent that the other powers of Europe would not oppose the annexation of the South German Federation into the German Empire. The Prussian victory put the states of the South German Federation in a position where they no longer saw any reason to postpone their annexation into the German Empire. They had supported Prussia in the recent war, and it was apparent that neither Austria nor France was likely to protect their long-term interests. Bismarck's use of military force was an example of "policy wars" that began with a clear policy objective attached to success, together with a reasonable chance of victory. His successes were a result of his willingness to gamble on war combined with an ability to recognize opportunities that presented themselves with odds that made the risks involved in a war acceptable. With the crowning of Emperor Wilhelm I, Bismarck realized his dream of a unified German state under the guidance of Prussia. He was promptly elevated to Chancellor of the Empire – a post he would hold for the next eighteen years. Map 2.1 shows the components that led to the formation of the German Empire in 1871.

The Congress of Berlin

At this point Bismarck's policies changed from an aggressive effort to establish Prussia – now known as the German Empire – as a

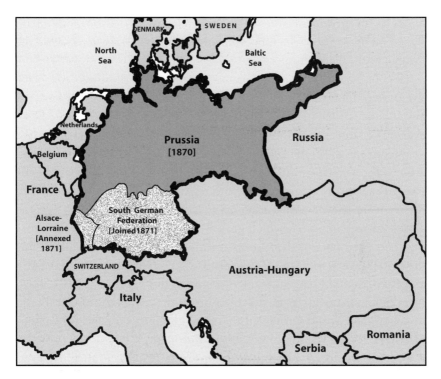

Map 2.1 The formation of the German Empire, 1870–1

major power in the world of European politics. He assured everyone Germany had reached the bounds of its ambitions and was therefore "satiated" and contemplated no further territorial ambitions. What this meant in practice was that Bismarck followed a foreign policy that put much less emphasis on threats of war, and much more on the construction of an intricate network of treaties and alliances that would protect the interests of the young German Empire against European rivals – particularly France or Russia.

Bismarck was basically a conservative monarchist. In his view, it was the "international revolutionary and social struggles" that had threatened monarchies in Europe in the 1850s. To protect those monarchies Bismarck worked to create an alliance of three emperors – Kaiser Wilhelm I of Germany, Tsar Alexander II of Russia, and Emperor Franz Joseph of the Habsburg Empire. He wasted no time in putting this new approach into action. In September 1872 Bismarck arranged a meeting of the three emperors in Berlin, and followed the success of this meeting by having Kaiser Wilhelm visit St. Petersburg and Vienna in October. His hopes for an agreement were realized when Germany, Russia, and Austria signed an agreement which became known as the *Dreikaiserbund* – the League of the Three Emperors.

In broad terms, the League sought to tie the three conservative monarchies into an alliance with one another that would forestall any alliances that might include France or Britain. There was, however, an obvious problem with this arrangement which severely limited its effectiveness. While Austria-Hungary and Russia both professed an affinity for a partnership with Germany, they had a serious antipathy toward each other – particularly with regard to the Balkans. Thus, when Russia went to war with Turkey 1877 and forced the Turks to sign the Treaty of San Stefano – which gave Russia sizeable territories in areas that had been part of the Ottoman Empire – the Austrians, as well as the British, were very upset. Concerned that a conflict between Austria and Russia would tear his fragile League of the Three Emperors apart, Bismarck managed to persuade the European powers to come to Berlin to negotiate a broad settlement that could maintain a peaceful balance of power among the major powers of Europe.[15]

Representatives from Russia, Great Britain, France, Austria-Hungary, Italy, Germany, and the Ottoman Empire all assembled in Berlin on June 13, 1878.[16] The main item on the agenda of the Congress was to sort out the boundaries of the Balkan states created by the defeat of the Ottoman Empire in its recent war with Russia. The European powers all agreed that it was time to end Ottoman rule over Christian populations in the Balkans, but the Austrians and British were not happy with the terms set forth in the Treaty of San Stefano. At issue was how the area taken from the Ottomans was to be ruled and the question of who should control the Dardanelles which was an important trade route between the Mediterranean and the Black Sea. To ensure that there would be no surprises at the Congress, a variety of secret meetings between representatives from Britain, Russia, and Austria-Hungary worked out agreements that all three were willing to accept regarding the division of the Balkans into several principalities along ethnic lines. Bismarck, who was kept informed about all this, was able to preside over the proceedings with a firm hand as the delegates worked out the details of the final agreement. When they had finished their deliberations, the Congress had established a new set of borders for Bulgaria, Romania, Serbia, and Montenegro that everyone was willing to accept, and agreed that control of the Dardanelles would remain in the hands of the Turks, with guarantees of passage for ships of all countries.

Bismarck was sufficiently pleased with the results of his Congress that in his closing remarks, he noted that it had, "within the limits of what was possible, done Europe the great service of keeping and maintaining the peace."[17] However, while the Treaty of Berlin managed to maintain the peace, it also revealed the limits to diplomacy as a means of solving the issues raised by the sudden emergence of Italy and the German Empire as new forces in European politics, and the vacuum of power created by the gradual demise of Ottoman influence in the Balkans after their defeat in the war with Russia. For Bismarck, the most serious problem was that the continuing rivalry between Austria-Hungary and Russia over the situation in the Balkans was forcing him to choose which of his two partners he should support in the tug of war for influence there. The Russians – who clearly believed they had come out on the short end of the arrangements reached at the Congress of Berlin – were furious with him because they felt that the German Chancellor had consistently supported Austrian interests at the expense of Russian interests in the boundary disputes between Serbia, Bulgaria, and Romania.

The tensions between Russia and Austria-Hungary reached a point where Bismarck decided to secretly negotiate a separate agreement with the Habsburg Empire known as the Dual Alliance, which committed both countries to come to the other's aid in the event of an attack by Russia. Bismarck did eventually manage to smooth Russia's ruffled feathers enough to reinstate the Three Emperors' League in June of 1881; however, by that time it was clear that *Dreikaiserbund* did not have a promising future. In May of 1882 Bismarck therefore negotiated a new agreement – the Triple Alliance – that bound Germany, Austria-Hungary, and Italy to assist one another in case of an attack by another power. In a final effort to protect the German Empire from an attack by Russia, Bismarck negotiated a secret "Reinsurance Treaty" between Germany and Russia in June of 1887, which stipulated that each party must remain neutral in case of a war with another power, except in the case of an aggressive war by Germany against France or Russia against Austria.

Germany was not the only country seeking treaties and secret agreements to protect itself against various threats of attack by another power. The French were actively courting the Russians, and the British remained involved in the arrangements in the Middle East because they needed a route to India. The problem with all these machinations was that, while they provided some protection against attacks by one power against another, the ease with which treaties and secret agreements could be changed meant that they did not instill any lasting confidence that the protection offered by a treaty would be enforced. A change in government or the outcome of some international dispute could cause a chain of adjustments in existing treaties that would create a whole new set of problems.

The risks associated with relying on diplomatic agreements for security explain why war was always one of the policy alternatives still on the table in times of crisis. David Singer observes that, "There are quite a few roads to interstate war, and all of them have fairly frequent exit ramps. On the other hand, some of these exits are not clearly marked, and even when they are, the protagonists fail to see them."[18] Bismarck, of course, was not looking for exits; he was looking for opportunities to use military force to further his objective of building a unified Germany.

So long as Wilhelm I was the German Kaiser, Bismarck's relationship with his monarch allowed him to exercise a firm grip on German foreign policy. He could therefore orchestrate actions that would maintain peace among the great powers. But in June of 1888 Wilhelm I died, and Bismarck did not have the same close relationship with the new ruler of Germany. Wilhelm II had dreams of expanding the German Empire into an even greater power, an ambition that went against Bismarck's approach of consolidating the gains that had been reached with the wars of unification. On March 18, 1890, the Chancellor was summarily dismissed by the new Kaiser, bringing an abrupt end to the Bismarckian era of war and diplomacy.

Bismarck's policy of "iron and blood" had elevated Germany into the most powerful country in central Europe. Bismarck's wars, claims historian Brian Bond, "were near-perfect examples of Clausewitz's celebrated axiom that war is an instrument of policy ... [I]t was mainly due to Bismarck's statecraft that these wars were politically controlled and yielded lasting political gains to the victor."[19] Bismarck understood that to use wars as state policy it was important to control the animal spirits raised by success on the battlefield. His success also points out the dangers of using war to further state policy. He was able to restrain his Kaiser from pushing Austria too far after the victory at Königgrätz. However, even his diplomatic skills could not persuade the Kaiser that Germany should resist the urge to demand that the French relinquish control of Alsace-Lorraine to the newly formed German Empire.

Racing to Armageddon

"In an age of diplomatic confrontations when governments repeatedly contemplated war," writes historian David Herrmann, "the military strength of the European powers was a subject of increasingly vital interest to the public as well as to policy makers in Germany, Austria-Hungary, France, Russia, Great Britain, and Italy."[20] What Herrmann termed "the arming of Europe" became a race to further advance the gunpowder revolution. Each year more men were conscripted into the armies of every major power. Within a decade of Prussia's victory over France in 1871 the armies of the five major powers totaled about 2.5 million men; by 1913 that number had risen to 3.7 million men – an increase of more than 50 percent.[21]

This rise in the size of armed forces on the part of all the European powers was the product of conscious decisions on the part of each country to maintain the status quo of military preparedness. The pace of the "arms race" was constrained by the availability of manpower, and that in turn was dictated by the growth in European populations.[22] By 1880 all of the countries except Great Britain had regulations in place for the conscription of young males into the army, and all of them followed roughly the same procedures. Much has been made of the extent to which the British relied on the Royal Navy to protect their "island fortress" and on volunteers for their army, which was primarily concerned with keeping peace in the Empire. Herrmann estimates that the size of their available forces to fight on the continent in 1914 was 192,000, which is well below the number of troops available to their continental counterparts. However, this estimate does not consider Britain's ability to maintain the largest navy in the world, and to muster additional armed forces from its colonial possessions and from the Commonwealth in the case of a major war. Table A1.1 of Appendix 1 shows that Great Britain had the highest potential for waging war of all the continental powers. This meant that population growth by itself could account for much of the increase in the number of men serving in the army, a conjecture that is supported by the fact that the fraction of the population serving in the armed forces remained relatively stable in all five countries, Austria-Hungary, France, Germany, Great Britian, and Russia. In each calendar year generals and politicians could count on "harvesting" a new crop of recruits. They did not need to wait to see if their friends or adversaries had increased the size of their armies; they simply assumed – correctly as it turned out – that everyone would move in lock-step with the growth in the population of young men. The result was the formation of a "bubble" of military personnel that grew larger each year. By the summer of 1914, 3.3 million men were organized to leap into action.

Maintaining and arming huge armies required an enormous expenditure of resources. Figure 2.1 presents estimates of the total military expenditures by all five major powers from 1880 to 1913. In 1880 the military expenses of all five powers totaled £114 million each year; by 1913 annual expenses tripled to £346 million, an annual increase of 3.2 percent each year. Over the final five years there was a particularly rapid burst of spending that averaged 8 percent each year.

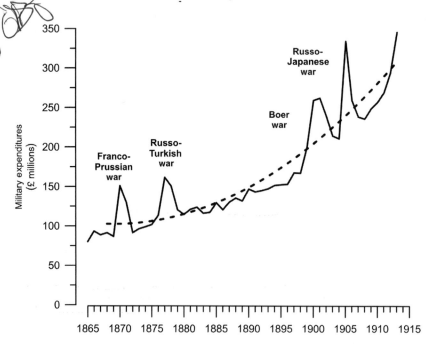

Figure 2.1 Military expenditures of the five major powers (Austria-Hungary, France, Germany, Great Britain, and Russia), 1865–1913

Sources: Data from the Correlates of War data set. "Military expenditures" are the total military budget for a given state for a given year in current dollars.

At least two major factors caused this acceleration of military spending. The first was the Russian defeat in their war against Japan. By 1906 that war had essentially bankrupted the Russian treasury and destroyed a major part of the Russian navy at the Battle of Tsushima. The immediate effect of the war was an outburst of rioting and unrest in 1905–6 that forced Tsar Nicholas II to make some concessions to the protesters by approving the formation of a Duma while promising further constitutional reforms, most of which were never made. While scholars agree that unrest triggered by the defeat of 1905 planted the seeds for the Revolution of 1917, historian John Grenville points out that "from the low point of his reign in 1905 to the outbreak of war nine years later, the Tsar managed better than many would have foretold at the outset."[23] Nicholas and his prime minister, Pyotr Stolypin, effectively suppressed the rebellion, revitalized and reformed the Russian army, and initiated an ambitious naval program through large increases in military spending.[24] The Russians added an additional 300,000 men in uniform by 1913. This was seen by the Germans and the Austrians as a major threat to the status quo, and they responded by increasing the size of their armies by 200,000 men. The French, who had the highest fraction of eligible men serving in their military, added just over 100,000 more recruits. In the space of seven years, the total number of men in the armed services of the continental powers rose by more than 20 percent.

The Naval Arms Race

Maintaining massive armies was not the only area of military spending that accelerated growth of military preparedness at the beginning of the twentieth century. According to his wife "Vicky" (who was Queen Victoria's daughter), Wilhelm's "one idea is to have a Navy which shall be larger and stronger than the Royal Navy."[25] To accomplish that task, Wilhelm elevated Rear Admiral Alfred von Tirpitz to the position of State Secretary for the Navy in June of 1897. Tirpitz developed a strategy – which he called "risk theory" – whereby the German fleet only needed to be strong enough to inflict serious losses on the Royal Navy in any major naval engagement. His reasoning was that because the resources of the British fleet were thinly stretched across the globe protecting the vastness of the British Empire, the British Admiralty could not risk an engagement with the German High Seas Fleet that might produce serious losses. The Germans would therefore be free to roam the high seas without having to actually engage the British navy in a full blown naval battle involving the capital ships of both navies.[26]

One problem with Tirpitz's theory was that it assumed that the British would ignore his announced intention of building more capital ships. In fact, the British did not stand still; they reacted to the German increase in capital ships by increasing the size of the Royal Navy. In November 1904, John Arbuthnot Fisher was appointed First Lord of the Admiralty of the Royal Navy. "Jacky" Fisher was one of those military figures whose place in history rests not on victories won at sea, but on victories in budget battles that were won within the halls of the Admiralty and in the House of Commons. In September 1884, while still a captain in the Royal Navy, Fisher had coauthored an article to the *Pall Mall Gazette* which claimed that "the truth about the navy is that our naval supremacy has ceased to exist." Coming from the pen of a British officer this was sheer heresy. Naval supremacy had been the cornerstone of Britain's military strategy since Nelson's victory at Trafalgar almost a century earlier. The article caused a major uproar in the press, prompting Parliament to increase the funds given to the navy.[27]

Fisher would spend the rest of his career championing the need for a larger and more modern Royal Navy. When he became First Lord of the Admiralty, he promptly retired more than forty old vessels and launched a campaign to replace them with a completely new class of warships. The crowning success of this program was the launching of a warship that combined speed (18–21 knots per hour), firepower (ten 12-inch guns), and size (18,000-ton displacement) in a single warship. *Dreadnought* was completed in February of 1906, and with the launch of a single ship a large fraction of the world's battleship fleets were instantly obsolete.[28]

The repercussions of *Dreadnought*'s highly publicized success were both immediate and far-reaching. Other countries – most notably the United States and Japan – had been experimenting with ships that combined speed and heavy armament, but no one had put ships embodying all of Fisher's ideas to sea in 1906. Between 1907 and 1913 Britain and Germany engaged in a frantic competition to gain the upper hand in naval supremacy of the North Sea. When, in 1908, the Reichstag approved a new naval building program for Germany, Fisher urged his government to expand the British naval construction program. Parliament wanted to add only four new ships to the budget; the Admiralty insisted it needed six. Winston Churchill described the outcome of the ensuing debate: "In the end a curious and characteristic solution was reached. The Admiralty had demanded six ships: the economists offered four and we finally compromised on eight."[29] The result of this rivalry involving both naval and army expenditures among the powers can be seen in Figure 2.1, where the military expenditures move sharply upwards in the four years just before the outbreak of war.[30] The Germans were not able to keep pace with the expansion of the British naval program, but they did expand their fleet of dreadnought-class battleships, and they made a considerable fanfare over their intent to eventually gain mastery in the North Sea, an objective that did not sit well with the British Admiralty – or the British public.

The data on manpower and military expenditures can easily be interpreted as evidence that the five major powers of Europe were engaged in arms races. However, the implications of this growth in military preparedness are less clear. David Stevenson points out that "the sporting metaphor was in currency before 1914 and is a convenient shorthand, but misleading. The contestants in an arms race may know neither the location of the finishing tape (the timing of the outbreak of war) nor even if there is a tape at all."[31] The absence of a finish line is what feeds the arms race despite a growing fear that the costs may be too much for the budget to bear. Rivals do not want to fall behind, because they do not know when something might end the race and they would face the prospect of a war they might not win. Not surprisingly, the military spending for the five major powers were bunched rather closely together, so that no one power would have a huge advantage in a war with any of the other four powers.[32] Confidence that a strategy of increasing arms brings security is therefore susceptible to erosion and replaced with a rising fear that something must be done to end the arms race. Writing in 1926, Sir Edward Grey, the British foreign minister in 1914, observed that "the enormous growth of armaments in Europe, the sense of insecurity and fear caused by them – it was this that made war inevitable."[33] Grey understood that, by the summer of 1914, the five powers were dealing with an armaments bubble that had gradually grown to a point where the option of whether or not to use all that military power to avoid losing a war overshadowed all the other options. There was a fragile equilibrium that could be broken by a very small event that would set off the beginnings of a major war. As the stockpile of arms grew larger, the fears about when – or how – this race to Armageddon would end also grew larger. Since no one knew the answer, military commanders of every country had to consider the possibility that falling behind in an arms race would lead to disaster. If the cost of keeping up or staying ahead in the race gets too high, the option of starting a preemptive war might be put on the table even if the odds of victory are not all that favorable. This is a situation where animal spirits are likely to become energized.

Bismarck knew how fragile the peace was. "Europe today is a powder keg and the leaders are like men smoking in an arsenal," he observed at one point during the Congress of Berlin, "A single spark will set off an explosion that will consume us all … I cannot tell you when that explosion will occur, but I can tell you where … Some damned foolish thing in the Balkans will set it off."[34]

3 SCHLIEFFEN'S GAMBLE

The essential element of the entire operation is a strong right wing,
the formation of which will help to win the battles and allow
the relentless pursuit of the enemy and bring defeat to him again
and again.
> If you march into France, see to it that the man on the
utmost right brushes the Channel coast with his sleeve.
> Alfred von Schlieffen (1906)[1]

By the summer of 1914 the nations of Europe had become
entangled in a patchwork of treaties, alliances, and secret agreements
designed to maintain a precarious equilibrium that would prevent a
major war. The Triple Alliance consisted of Germany, Austria, and
Italy; the Triple Entente had been formed by a set of agreements
between France, Britain, and Russia finalized in 1906. Each of these
alliances was bound together by additional agreements – some of
them secret arrangements – that protected a country in one group
from being attacked by a country from the other group. An unin-
tended result of these agreements was that they created a situation
where any military action between major powers could result in a
conflict among all the powers.[2] Diplomacy managed to maintain a
delicate balance of peace over the two decades before 1914. Beneath
the veneer of peace, however, the possibility of a general war was
growing ever so much closer. The political and military leaders of the
major powers all professed to have a strong commitment to avoiding
a "European war," but they took the precaution of devoting a great

deal of time and effort to planning how to deal with just such a war. Those plans were always on the negotiating table at times of crisis, and once they were put into motion they greatly reduced the chance of a negotiated settlement.

Planning for War

The challenge of planning for a really big war was complicated by the fact that the last conflict big enough to involve all the powers of Europe had been the Napoleonic wars a century earlier. The scale of operations, the number of men, and the technology of new weapons, forms of communications, and speed of transportation had changed the face of war. No one was really prepared for what might happen in a European war, but that did not prevent them planning for one.

Planning for war in the early twentieth century entailed much more than simply conscripting men every year for military training or adding weapons for them to fight with or ships to the fleets. Every country conducted regular maneuvers each year to train and equip their armed forces and try out the latest plans and weapons in preparation for hostilities. David Herrmann describes these "war games":

> Tens of thousands of troops formed two sides to fight a simulated battle lasting several days over many hundred square kilometers. The generals and staffs commanding each force underwent the rare experience of handling very large bodies of troops in the field. The high command could experiment with new equipment, regulations, and tactics. The cost was colossal, the atmosphere festive, and the spectacle an attraction for heads of state, foreign dignitaries, the press, and the local population, all of whom turned out in force to watch the action.[3]

No one pursued this practice with greater scale and seriousness than the Germans. They organized annual war games that were designed to tweak and perfect the latest ideas of the generals. The results of these exercises were not only to prepare the soldiers for a war; they also had an effect in boosting confidence among the population at large that their leaders were prepared for the next war. There was a subtle risk to all this military activity. Herrmann points out that a decision to increase the number of men in arms by one country "created the impression of aggressive intent toward others." Moreover, all this activity "demanded the engagement of popular chauvinism, a sense of national emergency, and the risk of domestic reaction against the new sacrifices, all of which made war ... a more acceptable option in the event of a crisis."[4]

German military and civilian leaders faced the prospect of a two-front war involving Russia and France. In the years following their victory over the French in 1871, General Helmuth von Moltke and the German General Staff planned for the contingency that involved a simultaneous attack by France from the west and Russia from the east. Moltke's approach was to split the German army into two roughly equal groups and hope that interior lines of transportation would work to the advantage of the Germans. When he stepped down as head of the German General Staff in February 1891, Moltke was replaced by Alfred von Schlieffen. Throughout his tenure as commander-in-chief, Schlieffen devoted his energies to solving the problem of how to defeat Russia and France in a two-front war. The results of his thinking have become etched into virtually every historical account of the period as the "Schlieffen Plan."

Schlieffen's Plan

Schlieffen insisted that the Germans should not split their forces equally between two fronts; they should concentrate most of their forces for an attack against one of their enemies before turning to deal with the other. His overriding contribution to the development of German military planning was to persuade his colleagues that the best chance Germany had for winning the next war would be to invade France with overwhelming force immediately upon declaring war, while fighting a holding action against Russia in the east. Schlieffen never actually developed a full-scale "plan" of action for the German army in the event of a war with France or Russia. His ideas were outlined in a pair of memoranda that he wrote in January/February of 1906, just before he stepped down as the head of the General Staff. The memos outlined a deceptively simple idea for how to annihilate the French while holding the Russians at bay in the east.

What Schlieffen proposed was a broad sweep of German troops through Belgium and Holland to a position well west of Paris (see Map 3.1). The entire operation in the west would work like a

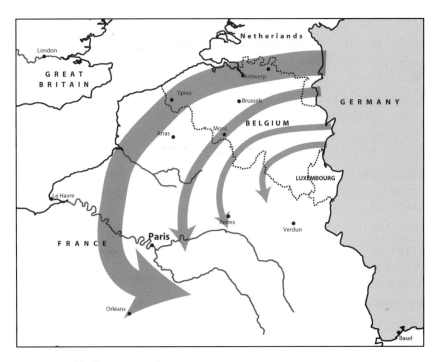

Map 3.1 Schlieffen's 1906 plan

giant door swinging across Belgium, Holland, and northern France. Schlieffen recognized that massing so many troops on the right wing of the western army involved a considerable gamble. "If the right wing is to be made very strong," he conceded, "this can only occur at the expense of the left, on to which will probably fall the task of fighting against a superior force." He went so far as to point out that, if necessary, those forces might even have to withdraw in the face of a French advance. While there would be an obvious risk to such a withdrawal, Schlieffen saw this possibility as a "revolving door" that would work to the Germans' favor because the advancing left wing of the French army would eventually be cut off by the center of the German army marching through France.[5]

There remained the question of how to deal with the Russians in the east. Writing at the end of 1905, Schlieffen was disposed not to take the eastern threat too seriously. Noting the poor performance of Russian troops in their recent war with Japan, he wrote that the defeat of the Russians by the Japanese "represents not only a great weakening of the Russian strength in Europe in terms of numbers and value, but also a great weakening of the army's organization." He also tended to minimize the impact of any British interference with German armies as they marched through Belgium. "If the English await a favorable moment for their intended landing," he speculated, "they will hardly find this before the first battle. If this falls to the Germans, the English will give up their hopeless enterprise." The British, after all, had only about 150,000 men to commit to the battle – hardly enough to blunt the German advance of a million and a half men.[6]

What worried Schlieffen far more than the number of Russian or British soldiers was the small size of the German army. His proposal was, he recognized, "an enterprise for which we are too weak." When he wrote his 1906 memos, the German army had around 600,000 regular army troops, and could perhaps mobilize an additional force of roughly the same size. Throughout his tenure as chief of staff, Schlieffen argued that Germany needed to increase the size of its standing army to at least 800,000. Although his efforts to increase the size of the army through more liberal appropriations were not very successful, Schlieffen was confident that eventually the politicians would come to their senses and authorize funds for more troops. Therefore, in his invasion plans for Holland and Belgium he simply "created" an additional eight corps for the right wing that never materialized – but they remained on the books as troops that would be available for the invasion. It is perhaps ironic that amid all the tinkering with the details of Schlieffen's plan after his retirement in 1906, increasing the size of the German army – the one significant step that he thought would increase the plan's chances of success – was not enacted by the Landtag until 1912. By that time, it was too little, too late.

Schlieffen died in 1913 without knowing whether the plans spawned by his idea of concentrating strength in the west would actually work in the event of a war. Upon his retirement, responsibility for the success of the German war machine fell on to the shoulders of Helmuth von Moltke – the nephew of the legendary general who had served with Bismarck in the wars against Austria and France. By 1914 the younger Moltke had reorganized the command structure of the German army, creating a supreme army command called the *Oberste Heeresleitung* (OHL). He had also made some significant changes to Schlieffen's original memorandum. One of the most important of these changes was to reject the idea of going through both Holland and Belgium. "I cannot agree," Moltke wrote in 1911, that "Dutch neutrality as well as Belgian neutrality needs to be violated." Not only did he think that "a hostile Netherlands at our rear could have disastrous consequences for the advance of the German army to the west," he also insisted that Holland's neutrality could provide "the windpipe through which we can breathe."[7] Schlieffen had been willing to risk violating Holland's neutrality in order to gain the space needed for the swing west of Paris that was an essential part of his plan. Moltke's caution reveals a very different perspective on the situation in 1914. Fear, not confidence, was becoming the dominant factor in his decisions about the two-front war. The immediate effect of these early concerns about Holland was the significant altering of the path of the German right wing to the south, a modification that had a profound impact on the outcome of the first great battle of the war. Moltke was also afraid that the left wing of the German army was too small and that the French would be able to advance into Germany and cut across the rear of the center of the German forces as they invaded northern France. This, in fact, was precisely what Schlieffen hoped for. He envisioned a "revolving door" where the French forces in the south would move eastward through Alsace-Lorraine into Germany and be trapped there as the great "wheel" of the right wing of the German army enveloped the French army around Paris and would then be free to deal with any remaining French troops.

It was a grand scheme that has triggered an extensive debate over who was responsible for the "plan" that led to the invasion of France through Belgium in 1914. Years after the war, some historians still dispute whether there ever was a "Schlieffen Plan." Terence Zuber insists that too many details remained to be filled in from the outline in Schlieffen's 1906 memorandum to call him the architect of the plans implemented in 1914.[8] The vigor with which these writers carry on the debate masks a deeper issue. After the war, Schlieffen became something of a scapegoat for masterminding a plan that did not work. His defenders argued that Schlieffen should not be blamed for the way things turned out, since he was no longer in command, and he would probably not have approved of some of the changes made after his retirement. Yet it is clear that Schlieffen's 1906 thoughts left a permanent imprint on German preparations for the war that erupted in 1914. His assumption that the only way to deal with a two-front war was a massive preemptive strike against France remained the foundation of German military preparedness throughout the various crises leading up to the outbreak of war in 1914. One reason for this was the simple fact that, as Richard Hamilton and Holger Herwig point out, "Schlieffen's critics lacked a viable alternative. Put bluntly, to concede that the vaunted Prussian General Staff could no longer conduct short wars of annihilation was to admit that war had ceased to be a viable option by the start of the twentieth century."[9]

The adoption of Schlieffen's principle of "France First" did more than define the parameters of German military strategy. It also severely limited the options of Germany's civilian leaders by explicitly choosing France as the initial target of any general war, and it violated Belgian and Dutch neutrality, actions that were almost certain to bring Britain into the conflict as part of the coalition arrayed against Germany. Everyone knew that there were enormous risks to this possibility. Yet it is clear from what transpired in the summer of 1914 that the Kaiser, his ministers, and his generals all felt that implementing an attack in the west was the only action that promised any hope of a favorable resolution to the situation of a two-front war that faced Germany in 1914. Annika Mombauer sums up the debate by saying, "Whatever we want to call the German deployment plan, the fact remains that Germany attacked France via Belgium (and Luxembourg) in 1914, thus implementing a deployment plan which had been updated and adopted annually by Moltke."[10]

Joffre's Plan XVII

While the Germans drafted and redrafted their plans to deal with a two-front war, everyone else was drafting their own plans to deploy in the event of a war. All of these plans shared one common feature with the Schlieffen Plan: they were driven by a conviction that the only way to wage wars was to attack. "During the decades before the First World War," writes Stephen Van Evera, "a phenomenon which may be called a 'cult of the offensive' swept through Europe. Militaries glorified the offensive and adopted offensive military doctrines, while civilian elites and publics assumed that the offense had the advantage in warfare, and that offensive solutions to security problems were the most effective."[11] Nowhere was this doctrine practiced more fervently than in France. General Joseph Joffre, who became the commander-in-chief of the French armies in 1911, decided that the existing plan for a possible war – imaginatively called Plan XVI – needed a heavy infusion of *élan*. Rather than just modifying existing plans, Joffre began to work on a brand-new scheme that became Plan XVII.

Joffre had an easier task than either Schlieffen or Moltke because, unlike the Germans, he only had to worry about fighting on one front. However, his task was made more difficult in that he had to factor in the willingness of his two allies – Russia and Great Britain – to coordinate with the French plans. Russia did not require a lot of attention; from the French perspective, all they had to do was launch an attack that would draw some of the German troops away from the "western front." Britain, on the other hand, was reluctant to commit to a firm plan. Indeed, it was not at all clear that the British would supply any ground troops to repel a German attack on France. Joffre knew that he must depend on French armies, not the British, to hold off the initial German attack. However, the French were eager for the British to join the war because of their naval power and their considerable economic prowess. So the main problem for Joffre was making sure the British would intervene. Once they committed troops to the battle, Joffre was confident they would not be willing to withdraw them. S. R. Williamson relates a conversation between British General Henry Wilson and French General Ferdinand Foch: "'What would you say was the smallest British military force that would be of any practical assistance to you in the event of a contest such as we have been considering?' Wilson asked. 'One single private soldier,' responded Foch, 'and we would take good care that he was killed.'"[12]

Confident that the British would eventually come to France's aid, the important element in any French plan for Joffre was the need to *attack*. "Any other conception," he claimed, "ought to be rejected as contrary to the very nature of war." Ferdinand Foch, the man who would eventually command the Allied armies in 1918, agreed with this sentiment. He described the offensive spirit of French military doctrine as "a single formula for success, a single combat doctrine, namely, the decisive power of offensive action undertaken with the resolute determination to march on the enemy, reach and destroy him."[13] The question Joffre wrestled with in 1912 was not whether to launch an attack against the invading forces; it was where to launch the attack. He did not have a clear answer to this question, so he organized his forces into five armies and deployed them as shown in Map 3.2, which includes the original plan for Schlieffen's invasion. Firm in his belief that the main German attack would come in the south, three French

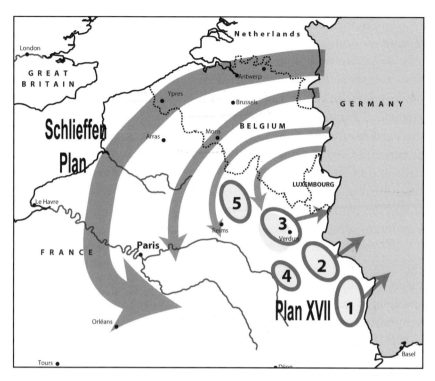

Map 3.2 Joffre's Plan XVII and Schlieffen's 1906 plan

armies were placed along the frontier with Alsace, stretching from a point north of Verdun and extending south to the region around Epinal. These units would form spearheads for an invasion of Germany as soon as the war began. A fourth army was stationed as a reserve to be used as needed to support the attack in Alsace, and a fifth army would be stationed along the Belgian frontier in the north to deal with what Joffre was certain would be a smaller German force. In all of this Joffre was deliberately vague about the details of his plan, insisting that any plan must be flexible. David Stevenson notes that, "As regards the strategic offensive, Plan XVII was a concentration plan, but did not prescribe the course of operations beyond that point. Joffre's guiding principle was to commit his reserves at once, in order to keep the initiative, to adhere to the convention with Russia, and to protect France from invasion."[14]

Joffre turned out to be wrong about the German plans. He badly misread the number of troops the Germans would commit to the invasion through Belgium, and he thought that even if the Germans attacked in the north, they would not have enough troops to carry out that attack and still meet the threat of the Russians in the east. He also assumed that reserves would not be used by the Germans in the front lines. Consequently, his estimate of German strength was 800,000 men, while in fact the Germans had almost 1.5 million men for the attack on Belgium.[15] Plan XVII proposed to do exactly what Schlieffen wanted the French armies to do. If Schlieffen's plan worked as he hoped it would, the German armies would sweep in a wide arc to the west of Paris and be in a position to attack the three French armies in Alsace from the rear. Joffre was not completely blind to this possibility, which is why he placed the Fourth French Army in a position to assist the Fifth Army along the Belgian frontier if needed.

Joffre's caution was rewarded. Moltke became sufficiently concerned with the possibility that a French invasion through Alsace might actually be successful that he increased the number of men in the left wing of the German army at the expense of troops whom Schlieffen wanted to include in the march through Belgium. The circular flow of armies through Belgium, west of Paris, and then east again as part of Schlieffen's "revolving door" is evident in Map 3.2, as is Joffre's placement of French armies to put them in a position to attack the German flank as it advanced into France. Things did not go exactly as planned for either side. But, as is often the case in military operations, mistakes and confusions on one side can be offset by mistakes and confusions on the other side.

War, as Clausewitz reminds us, is a game of chance.

The Other Plans

While the German and French generals spent most of their time planning for war against each other, the planners from the rest of Europe pursued their own rivalries. The outcome of another war between Germany and France was never a principal concern for either the Austrians or the Russians, both of whom were far more worried about protecting their own competing interests in the Balkans and Middle East. While the Franco-German rivalry had simmered for four decades without erupting into a new war, a series of wars had swept through the Balkan states. At the core of these conflicts was the declining influence of the Ottoman Empire, the intense rivalries between the Balkan states, and the growing presence of Russia in the Middle East. Looking back from the twenty-first century, Russia in the last quarter of the nineteenth century appears to be an economic and military disaster waiting to happen. However, contemporaries saw a Russian state that was by far the largest nation in Europe and one that was aggressively extending its authority to the east and south. As Niall Ferguson observed: "Between the well-known defeats of the Crimea and Tsushima, Russian generals won countless obscure victories in Central Asia and the Far East. By 1914 the Russian Empire covered 8.6 million square miles and extended from the Carpathians to the borders of China."[16]

In addition to the expansion of its territory, Russia was experiencing a significant growth of its economy and population. By 1913, Russia was second only to the United States in global wheat production, and although the industrial sector was small, it was rapidly expanding. As Paul Kennedy notes, "it seems that Russia in the decades prior to 1914 was simultaneously powerful *and* weak – depending on which end of the telescope one peered down."[17] Looking through one end of the telescope one could see that Russia was still an overwhelmingly rural society, with only 5 percent of the population living in cities, and a transportation infrastructure that was primitive. Looking the other way, its sheer size made the Russian Empire an economic and military force to be reckoned with. The %CINC measures of military capability in Table A1.1 of Appendix 1 confirm the impression that the military threat from Russia should not be taken too lightly. Based largely on its huge population, the Russian Empire's %CINC score in 1914 was essentially the same as Germany's.

The Austrians and the Russians both had plans to deal with each other in the event of another war in the Balkans. However, in the event of a war involving France and Germany these plans were secondary to their commitment to aid their ally. The British tried to avoid making any commitments that were tied to specific actions, preferring to join less formal alliances where it was understood that there was a mutual sharing of interests between countries. The most promising rewards for this sort of diplomacy seemed to be agreements with the French and the Russians, both of whom shared colonial aspirations with the British in the Middle and Far East, and both of whom worried about the aims of the Germans and the Austrians in that part of the globe. As a result, the Triple Entente was not really an alliance; indeed, as a British diplomat in the foreign office pointed out to his colleagues in a memo written in 1913, "an entente is nothing more than a frame of mind, a view of general policy which is shared by the governments of two countries. But which may be or may become so vague as to lose all content."[18] In addition to being vague, some of the details contained in the "agreements" reached at the meetings between British and French officials regarding British military support for the French in the event of a war with Germany were kept secret from members of the British cabinet and from members in Parliament. The only "plan" the British actually had openly considered was that an "Expeditionary Force" *might* be sent to France if the Germans attacked.

Viewed in isolation, none of these individual plans suggest that the assassination of Archduke Franz Ferdinand would lead to a general European war. Annika Mombauer convincingly argues that "there is no interpretation, no 'factual' account of the events that led to war, that could not be criticized or rejected by historians who favour a different explanation of the origins of the war – after all, this is precisely why this debate has occupied historians for nearly a century."[19] Each party had confidence in the success of its plans and each of them feared the consequences of *not* going to war. Seldom in the course of history has so much depended on a set of decisions by such a small number of men. In Berlin, London, St. Petersburg, Paris, and Vienna, the leaders of the Western world acted more out of fear than from reason; they were following plans that were based on their "animal spirits."

Two Shots Heard around the World

On June 28, 1914, Gavrilo Princip, a young Serbian nationalist, fired two shots into the automobile carrying the Archduke Franz Ferdinand of Austria and his wife, Sophie, during a visit by the royal couple to the Bosnian city of Sarajevo. Both Franz and Sophie suffered fatal wounds from the two shots. The news of their deaths sent shockwaves throughout the world and touched off a month of frantic diplomatic activity. Monarchs and their ministers exchanged notes with one another, called for conferences and meetings to discuss the situation, and checked with their generals to explore military options if diplomacy failed and war broke out between Austria-Hungary and Serbia. The possibility of such a conflict made the leaders of Europe uncomfortable, but this was not the first time there had been a diplomatic and military crisis in the Balkans. Why did this crisis spur anything more than another war in the region?

One reason was that none of those earlier wars had involved direct military intervention by any of the major European powers fighting against each other. This time was different. By 1914 Serbia had emerged from the wars against the Ottoman Empire and other Balkan states as a major rival to the Austrians in the region. There was a strong movement in the country toward creating a "Greater Serbia" that would include additional territory to the west. The Russians, who had their own interests in the Balkans, strongly supported the Serbs in their rivalry with Austria-Hungary. Despite the fact that officials in both Belgrade and Vienna were well aware of the dangers associated with a visit by the heir to the Habsburg throne, yet everyone concerned – including the Archduke himself – chose to ignore the need for extra precautions for the visiting dignitaries. The result was a comedy of errors that led to the shooting of the Archduke. On the way to the Governor's Palace a bomb was thrown at the Archduke's car, but it missed its target and exploded behind the convoy of cars, so the Archduke and his party proceeded to their destination. The route was changed, but no one told the drivers. While this oversight was being corrected, the cars made a wrong turn and came to a halt about five feet from a surprised Gavrilo Princip, who then fired his two shots at the royal couple

The assassination of the Archduke and his wife by a Serbian infuriated the Austrians, and it offered them an excuse to take some sort of strong action against the Serbs. Count Franz Conrad von Hötzendorf, the Chief of the General Staff of the Austrian army, had been strongly in favor of a war against Serbia for several years. He now pressed his case upon increasingly receptive ears in Vienna. Eager to "punish" the Serbs for Franz Ferdinand's death, the Austrians knew all too well that if they acted precipitously in dealing with the Serbs, there almost surely would be a confrontation with Russia that could be disastrous. So they sought assurance that their German ally would stand behind them in the event that the Russians became bellicose. The Kaiser hastened to assure Emperor Franz Joseph that Germany would indeed support an Austrian attack on Serbia regardless of the consequences. On July 26 Theobald von Bethmann-Hollweg, the German chancellor, sent a message that amounted to a "blank check" for the Austrians to take action against the Serbs. "The Emperor

Franz Joseph," Bethmann-Hollweg wrote, "may rest assured that His Majesty will faithfully stand by Austria-Hungary, as is required by the obligations of his alliance and of his ancient friendship."[20]

Buoyed by such strong support from a powerful ally, the Austrians brought things to a head by issuing an ultimatum on July 23 insisting that the Serbian government accept responsibility for the assassination; that the Serbs restrict all publication of "propaganda" against Austria-Hungary; and that the Serbian government initiate an investigation – which must include representatives of the Austrian government – into the operation of the persons who were allegedly behind the assassination. When this ultimatum was rejected by the Serbs on July 25 – as the Austrians hoped it would be – Austria-Hungary severed diplomatic relations with Serbia and began to mobilize its armies. On July 28 the Austrians declared war against the Serbs. Meanwhile Tsar Nicholas II secretly ordered a partial mobilization of Russian forces in the hope that it would not aggravate the Germans. Two days later Austrian warships bombarded the Serbian capital of Belgrade. The question now was whether the Austrian action against Serbia would trigger a strong military response from Russia and the other European powers.

There had been two "Balkan wars" between 1911 and 1913, and neither of them produced global conflict. The Austrian declaration of war against Serbia was the first step toward a third, and potentially much larger, war in the Balkans. All the European powers – including Austria-Hungary and Russia – had stayed on the sidelines of those earlier conflicts. This time the Austrians were already involved in the fight, and Russia was making it clear that the Tsar and his generals were considering entering the war on the side of the Serbs. All eyes now turned to the Kaiser and the Tsar. It was Wilhelm's assurance of support for any action Austria-Hungary might take against the Serbs that had bolstered the tone of its ultimatum against Serbia and ultimately led to the Austrian declaration of war. Could he now convince Nicholas to keep Russia out of the war?

The Willy–Nicky Telegrams

Wilhelm began by asking the Austrians to stop at Belgrade and he asked the Russians to hold off any overt military action long enough to consider what could be done to prevent an Austro-Russian war. What followed was an exchange of messages between the Kaiser and the Tsar that are known as the "Willy–Nicky Telegrams."[21] The telegrams illustrate the role of both fear and confidence in the decisions to go to war. Both rulers professed a deep fear of the consequences of a "European war." Yet the cold reality was that for some time both of them had been preparing for just such a war. On July 29 they exchanged a series of messages that crossed in the night. Nicholas appealed for Wilhelm's assistance by claiming that:

> An ignoble war has been declared to a weak country. The indignation in Russia shared fully by me is enormous. I foresee that very soon I shall be overwhelmed by the pressure forced upon me and be forced to take extreme measures which will lead to war. To try and avoid such a calamity as a European war I beg you in the name of our old friendship to do what you can to stop your allies from going too far.[22]

Wilhelm's note to Nicholas was conciliatory – but he remained firmly committed to Austria's declaration of war against Serbia: "It is with the gravest concern that I hear of the impression which the action of Austria against Serbia is creating in your country," he assured the Tsar,

> and I fully understand how difficult it is for you and your Government to face the drift of your public opinion.
>
> Therefore, with regard to the hearty and tender friendship which binds us both from long ago with firm ties, I am exerting my utmost influence to induce the Austrians to deal straightly to arrive to a satisfactory understanding with you. I confidently hope that you will help me in my efforts to smooth over difficulties that may still arise.
>
> Your very sincere and devoted friend and cousin,
> Willy[23]

When he received Nicholas' telegram on the night of the 29th the Kaiser was less than pleased with the Tsar's description of the crisis. But he offered his help as an intermediary to avert a war between Austria-Hungary and Russia. He noted that he could not consider Austria's action against Serbia an "ignoble" war, and he went on to suggest that:

> It would be quite possible for Russia to remain a spectator of the Austro-Serbian conflict without involving Europe in the most

horrible war she ever witnessed. I think a direct understanding between your Government and Vienna possible and desirable, and as I already telegraphed to you, my Government is continuing its exercises to promote it.

Of course military measures on the part of Russia would be looked upon by Austria as a calamity we both wish to avoid and jeopardize my position as mediator which I readily accepted on your appeal to my friendship and my help.

Willy[24]

Nicholas responded by reminding his cousin that he had taken steps for a mobilization "on account of Austria's preparations." He went on to say that he valued Wilhelm's efforts at mediation, and that he needed Wilhelm's "strong pressure on Austria to come to an understanding with us."[25]

On July 31 the tone of the exchanges became less cordial. Wilhelm again telegraphed the Tsar, saying that he was deeply troubled by the fact that he had "news of serious preparations for war on my Eastern frontier," an action that he felt made his mediation "almost illusory." He reminded Nicholas that "the peace of Europe may still be maintained by you if Russia will agree to stop the milit. [sic] measures which must threaten Germany and Austro-Hungary."[26] Nicholas sought to defuse the situation by assuring the Kaiser that "as long as the negotiations with Austria on Serbia's account are taking place my troops shall not make any probably provocative action. I give you my solemn word for this."[27]

The Willy–Nicky Telegrams illustrate the problems of relying on diplomacy to avert war in a world where preparations for war are already well under way. Both the Kaiser and the Tsar had the authority to lessen the pressure of the crisis by pulling back their demands. However, once the two leaders reached the point of mobilizing their armies, their ability to avoid going to war decreased. Facing a potential enemy who was mobilizing his troops, neither monarch was willing to override the concerns of his military advisors and be the one who backed away from preparing for war. The fear that the other side might gain an edge through mobilization of their forces was stronger than the confidence that negotiations might prevent a war. On August 1 Germany declared war on Russia.

The next country to be drawn into the struggle was France, which had a firm commitment under the terms of the Triple Entente to come to the assistance of the Russians in the event of an attack by either the Germans or Austria-Hungary. News of the German declaration of war against Russia prompted French President Raymond Poincaré to sign an order mobilizing the French army on August 1. In Berlin, the Kaiser and his generals met to discuss their options. The French mobilization meant that the Germans now faced the prospect of fighting both the French and the Russians in a two-front war. The Schlieffen Plan had been developed for just such an occasion, However, Schlieffen assumed the next war would begin with an invasion of France, not Russia, and the Germans were caught off guard by the need to react to the change in venue. They had already declared war on Russia; now they had to quickly decide whether or not that meant they should immediately expand what was rapidly becoming a European war by implementing Schlieffen's plan to invade Belgium and France. The French were already mobilizing, and time was not on Germany's side. If they were to launch the Schlieffen Plan they needed to act quickly. A key element in that plan was the invasion of Belgium. On August 2 the German foreign office sent an ultimatum to the government of Belgium demanding free passage of German troops through their country to counter an alleged attack organized by the French. The message was written in a way that gave little option to the Belgians, and not surprisingly, they quickly refused.[28] In a tense meeting on the evening of August 3 of the Kaiser and his generals, Germany declared war against France and orders were sent to put the Schlieffen Plan into motion.

Great Britain Enters the European War

There was still one major power in this tangle of agreements that was not yet fully committed to joining the war. In London, the British cabinet was badly split over the question of British intervention in a war centered in central and eastern Europe. Foreign minister Edward Grey firmly believed the British could not simply stay on the sidelines if Germany and France went to war. "If Germany dominated the Continent," Grey told his colleagues, "it would be disagreeable to us as well as to others, for we would be isolated." Grey's position was supported by the Prime Minister, Herbert Asquith, and he also had the support of the First Lord of the Admiralty, Winston Churchill. Acting on his own authority, Churchill had already mobilized the British fleet by sending it to war stations on July 26. Yet a majority of the cabinet

were still opposed to sending British troops to fight in France. On
August 1, twelve of eighteen cabinet members had declared themselves
opposed to war; that was followed by a nineteen to four vote against
intervention in a Liberal MP caucus later in the same afternoon.

There was, however, another possibility that might persuade the
British to intervene. In 1839 the British had signed a treaty agreeing to
protect Belgian neutrality. On August 2 they sent a stern warning to the
Germans that Britain would honor this commitment. When Germany
ignored the British note and proceeded with an invasion of Belgium, the
British cabinet declared war on Germany late in the evening of August 4.

The story of the last three agonizing days of peace has been
told and retold many times. There was no single declaration of war.
What transpired was a web of agreements that touched off wars
between individual countries that merged into a single world war.
Figure 3.1 offers a schematic diagram that traces the way in which the
major powers of Europe were drawn into the war between Austria-
Hungary and Serbia in the summer of 1914. On the right-hand side of
the figure are the states aligned with the Triple Alliance – the Habsburg
Empire, the German Empire, and Italy; on the left are the states aligned
with the Triple Entente – the Russian Empire, France, and Great
Britain. A glance at the schematic quickly reveals the significance of
Wilhelm's "Blank Check" that bolstered Austria's decision to declare

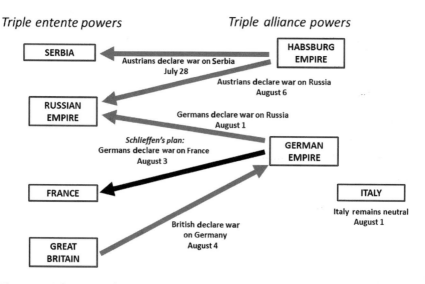

Figure 3.1 The crisis of 1914

war on Serbia. When Wilhelm's effort to restrain Russia's mobilization failed, he was eventually put in a position of declaring war on Russia or abandoning his impetuous ally, Austria-Hungary. On August 1, Germany went to war with Russia.[29] The Kaiser then faced the reality that the war with Russia also necessitated implementation of the Schlieffen Plan and the invasion of France. That, in turn, involved the invasion of Belgium, which brought Britain into the war. What all this meant, in the words of historian Martin Gilbert, is that "by midnight of August 4th, five European empires were at war: Austria-Hungary against Serbia and Russia; Russia against Austria-Hungary and Germany; Germany against Russia, France, Belgium and Britain; France against Germany and Britain against Germany."[30] This was the war that no one really wanted, yet no one was willing or able to prevent.

Why did Germany accept the gamble of supporting Austria-Hungary even though this would almost surely produce a war with both Russia and France? One line of reasoning suggests that the answer lies with the fact that the German High Command firmly believed that sooner or later a war against both France and Russia was inevitable. They had invested considerable effort into developing the Schlieffen Plan to win such a two-front war and the dispute between Austria-Hungary and Russia provided them with a window of opportunity to put their plan into action. Germany's greatest fears were the continuing buildup of Russian military power and the alliance between France, Russia, and Great Britain after the Russo-Japanese War. They also feared that anything less than strong support for Austria-Hungary would jeopardize their relationship with the only other major power that was likely to be an ally in the event of a war against France and Russia. Finally, there was the need to act quickly. Every hour of delay threatened to lower the odds of success for the plan. Having to make the decision quickly allowed animal spirits to elevate the confidence of both the Austrians and the Germans. The Schlieffen Plan depended on speed of deployment and every day of indecision lowered the odds of its success.

The Kaiser elected to roll the dice.

Stopped at the Marne

Responsibility for the success of the German war machine now rested on the shoulders of Helmuth von Moltke. By 1914 Schlieffen's 1906 memos had grown into a set of plans detailing everything down to the schedule of trains that would bring troops to the railheads from which the invasion would be launched. Unfortunately for the Germans, Moltke was not well suited to lead the German army into battle with Schlieffen's plan. Though he had accepted the basic foundation of the plan, he had real doubts that the Germans could pull off the victory that Schlieffen had predicted. Moltke was sixty-six years old, with a heart problem that was exacerbated by the anxieties of command. His most serious shortcoming, however, was that he was simply not a gambler, and the Schlieffen Plan entailed a huge gamble that Germany could win the war with one crushing attack that would destroy the French armies in time for the Kaiser's troops to turn and defeat the Russians. The cancer of fear was already firmly rooted in Moltke's mind before any German troops set foot in Belgium. Schlieffen had discounted the Russians because of the fiasco of the war with Japan in 1905. Yet one of the things that plagued Moltke through the first months of the Great War was a nagging fear of a disaster in the east. He was constantly worrying whether or not he should reinforce the Eastern Front with troops from France. Telegrams from the eastern commanders screaming for reinforcements did little to calm his already jangled nerves.

Despite their commander-in-chief's misgivings, things started out well for the Germans. Their troops moved forward into Belgium on August 4. Through the first two weeks of the campaign the German armies continued to move through Belgium and into northern France. But it gradually became apparent that the armies could not keep up the rapid pace called for in the plan. After nearly a month of intensive fighting and marching, the armies of Generals Alexander von Kluck and Otto von Bulow on the German right wing were nearing exhaustion. Kluck's First Army – which by Schlieffen's calculations should have been west of Paris by this time – was in fact still well to the east of Paris and its commander was requesting permission to move even further east. Moltke granted that permission, but he elected to not reinforce either Kluck or Bulow with additional forces. Map 3.3 shows the paths the invading armies actually took in 1914 compared with the idea that Schlieffen put forward in 1906. The confidence in the underlying strategy for the grand advance west of Paris was being rapidly undermined by the confusion and uncertainty created by tactical decisions made on the spur of the moment.

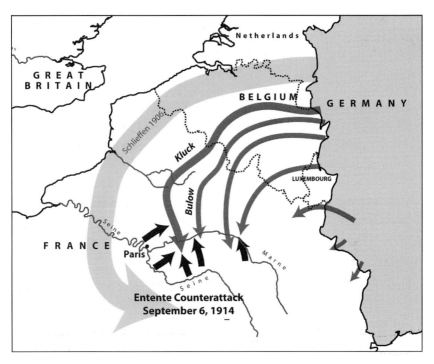

Map 3.3 The German invasion of France, September 1914

By the beginning of September the two armies on the German right wing had become separated from one another and from the center of the German advance. The alterations in the routes taken by Kluck and Bulow presented the French and British forces with an opportunity to attack the right flank of the German First Army and drive a wedge between Kluck and Bulow. Finally realizing the precarious position of his right wing, Moltke ordered the German advance to stop and regroup on September 4.

While the Germans struggled to reorganize their forces, the Entente armies counterattacked. French troops under General Michel-Joseph Maunoury launched an attack against Kluck's exposed flank on September 5. The next day the British Expeditionary Force (BEF) under Sir John French struck at the gap between the German First and Second Armies, and French forces under Ferdinand Foch attacked Bulow's advancing troops. In all, eighty Entente divisions attacked roughly the same number of German troops. Exhausted by their efforts of the previous month, the German troops were forced back. As they did so, the spirits that had been so high when they crossed into Belgium and France wilted in the summer heat. Among those who felt the most pressure was their commander-in-chief. In a letter written to his wife on September 8, Moltke revealed the depths of the fear that had been plaguing him since the onset of the campaign:

> It is going badly. The battles to the east of Paris will go against us. One of our armies must withdraw [Bullow's?], the others will have to follow. The opening of the war, so hopefully begun, will turn into the opposite ... The campaign is not lost, no more than it was until now for the French, but French spirit, which was on the point of being extinguished, will now flare up tremendously and I am afraid that our nation in its headlong careening towards victory will scarcely be able to bear this misfortune.[31]

By September 13 the Germans had pulled back to the Marne River, where they regrouped and managed to stop the Allied offensives.

The First Battle of the Marne was a major setback for the Germans. They had, as Corelli Barnett observed, stumbled within thirty miles of victory. In the end, Schlieffen's gamble to win the war in one bold stroke came up short, partly because of a growing fear of disaster. On the other side, Entente troops felt a surge of optimism because they had stopped the German advance.

The Race to the Sea

While the Germans were moving through Belgium, the French had launched their Plan XVII with a push into Alsace and Lorraine. In a series of actions that became known as the "Battles of the Frontiers," the Germans threw back the invading French armies with heavy losses on both sides. Despite its shortcomings, Plan XVII actually had a silver lining for the French. By pushing the French units back into France, the German successes actually put the French in a better position to reinforce their beleaguered armies around Paris in September. The French effort in the south also induced Moltke to send reinforcements to that area of the battle. Williamson argues that "the French Plan XVII fitted into the original Schlieffen Plan like a glove, but by placing powerful armies in Lorraine and driving the French back on their own fortress barriers, Moltke effectively nullified his chances of victory."[32]

With the southern flank stabilized for the moment, the two adversaries turned their attention back to the north and started what

became a "race to the sea." The last major ac
on November 24 near the Belgian city of Ypres,
managed to blunt an effort by the Germans to r
ports." By the end of November, a line of hastily constructed
stretched from the English Channel to the Swiss border. Map 3.4 shows
the situation on the Western Front at the beginning of 1915. Neither
side won the race to the sea. As each side paused for the Christmas
break, the generals were confronted with a new form of warfare for
which they were not at all prepared.

When all was said and done, the Schlieffen Plan turned out
to be one of the biggest gambles in military history. What made that
gamble "rational" in the eyes of German planners was the conviction
that the only way that Germany could survive a war with both Russia
and France was to deal with each separately – an idea that was initially put forward by the elder Moltke. The wild card in all of this was
Germany's ally, Austria, whose quarrel with Russia forced Germany
to declare war on both Russia and France and invade Belgium – an
action that drew the British into the war. What made them take this
risk was the overconfidence that animal spirits had injected into the

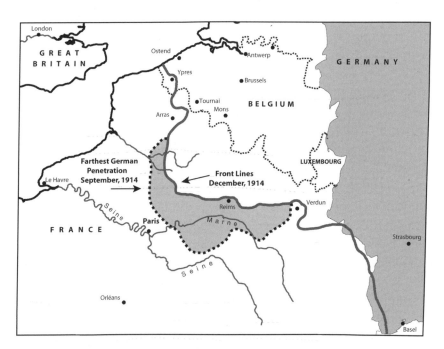

Map 3.4 The Western Front, December 1914

...ations made in the course of the battle. After an initial surge of ...ccess, the Germans saw their confidence gradually turn into a fear that induced them to be cautious, and the Entente commanders had their confidence boosted by their success on the Marne.

All of which eventually produced a stalemate on the Western Front for the next three years.

The Eastern Front

If the situation in the west was less than what the Germans had hoped for by the end of 1914, the situation in the east was somewhat of a mixed bag. Austrian war plans envisioned two major objectives. They were determined to invade Serbia and occupy Belgrade; and they were committed to launch an offensive action against Russia to support their German ally. General Franz Graf Conrad von Hötzendorf, the Austrian commander-in-chief, devised a complicated mobilization scheme to meet these objectives. The Austrian army was divided into three groups. The largest force was stationed along the border in Galicia for an offensive against the Russians. A second group was stationed on the frontier between Austria and Serbia, ostensibly to keep the Serbs from attacking Austria, and the third group was held in reserve and would have the lowest priority for timing in a general mobilization.

The German and Habsburg chiefs of staff had worked together since 1909 in the hope that there would be a clear understanding of what each side must do in the event of a war with Russia. One might think, therefore, that the highest priority for the Austrians would be mobilizing troops for the attack against the Russians. However, Conrad had a passionate hatred for the Serbs, and he was determined to concentrate as many men as possible for an invasion of Serbia, an operation that he was confident would not take very long to successfully complete. When Moltke got wind of this idea he was furious and insisted that Conrad should concentrate his troops against Russia and ignore Serbia for the time being. Conrad reassured Moltke that the invasion of Russia would proceed as planned, but he remained focused on punishing Serbia. The invasion of Serbia that commenced on August 12 turned into a complete fiasco for the Austrians. The Serbian army had capable generals and a large complement of veterans who had served in the recent Balkan wars. Three unsuccessful Austrian offensives into Serbia produced 250,000 casualties without signifi-cantly changing the territory occupied by either side. The Austrians finally managed to occupy Belgrade in early December; however, two weeks later the Serbs liberated their capital and pushed the Austrians back across the Danube.

Tannenberg and the Masurian Lakes

All of this was little more than a sideshow for the main event on the Eastern Front, which would be played out along the borders that Germany and Austria-Hungary shared with Russia. One of the many assumptions behind Schlieffen's strategy was that it would take the Russians at least ten or twelve weeks to mobilize their forces for an attack on East Prussia. The first sign of trouble in the east for the German High Command was the appearance of two Russian armies advancing into East Prussia a week and a half after the war began. The Russian plan was to trap the outnumbered German army between a Russian army advancing from the east, and a second army converging from the south. The Russian armies totaled about 450,000 men, compared with roughly 200,000 Germans. However, as Michael Clodfelter notes, the Russian army was "lacking in everything except for raw numbers and the raw courage of those numbers. Few soldiers in the world could endure better the strains and sacrifices demanded by war, both on and off the battlefield."[33] The idea of a pincer movement that would encircle the German forces was sound enough, but the execution by the Russians fell far short of expectations. On August 17, a series of attacks by Russian forces were repulsed with heavy losses, causing the Russian general Paul Rennenkampf to pull back several miles. Though German troops had succeeded in checking the Russian advance, General Maximillian Prittwitz, the German commander in the east, realized that he was greatly outnumbered, and he frantically called Moltke in Berlin demanding reserves and permission to pull back behind the Vistula River – a retreat that would effectively abandon East Prussia to the Russians.

Moltke was alarmed at the suggestion that the Germans should abandon East Prussia, and voiced a larger concern that the entire Eastern Front might collapse altogether in the face of the Russian advance. His confidence in Prittwitz, was totally shattered, and in an effort to stabilize the situation, he hurriedly contacted Paul von Hindenburg, a 66-year-old veteran who had fought in the Franco-Prussian War and served on Alfred von Schlieffen's staff before retiring in 1911, to ask if he would assume command in the east. Hindenburg's reply was short and to the point: "I am ready!" Keegan relates the story that, while Hindenburg may have been ready for the assignment, he did not have a gray field uniform as issued by the imperial army in 1914; he had to wear the blue uniform of the nineteenth-century German army as he headed east to take charge of his new command.[34] Moltke had already decided upon Erich Ludendorff, a younger general who had just distinguished himself in the march through Belgium, as the person to be Hindenburg's chief of staff.

Hindenburg and Ludendorff did not know one another. They met for the first time on the train carrying them east to their new assignment in Prussia. However, as John Keegan points out, "their qualities, natural authority in Hindenburg, ruthless intellect in Ludendorff, complemented each other's perfectly and were to make them one of the most effective military partnerships in history." Years later Hindenburg would observe that their collaboration turned out to be "a happy marriage."[35]

By the time the new commanders arrived at the Eighth Army headquarters on the evening of August 25, things had settled down somewhat. The two Russian armies – which had initially hoped to catch the Germans in a pincer movement and overpower them with superior numbers – were still too far apart to effectively work with one another. Rennenkampf seemed content to stay put, and Luddendorf and Hindenburg quickly realized that this provided the Germans with a chance to concentrate all of their forces against Alexander Samsonov's troops and postpone any serious encounter with Rennenkampf's forces. On August 26 they seized the opportunity and inflicted a crushing defeat on Samsonov at the Battle of Tannenberg. The Germans then quickly moved south and attacked Rennenkampf's army at the Battle of the Masurian Lakes on September 8 forcing the Russians to withdraw to the east. These stunning successes removed – at least for the time being – any serious threat to East Prussia on the part of the Russians. More significantly, it catapulted Hindenburg and Ludendorff into the limelight as Germany's most successful generals.

The victories at Tannenberg and the Masurian Lakes raised the morale and confidence of the Germans, but the victories did little to change what was still a rather dire strategic situation for the

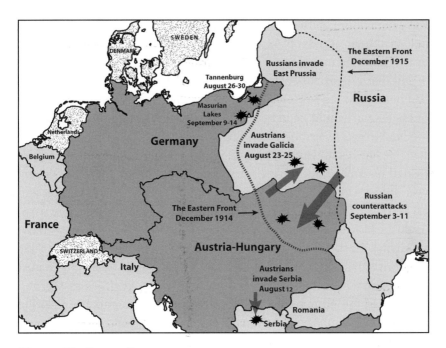

Map 3.5 The Eastern Front, 1914–15

Central Powers in the east. While the Germans had succeeded in blunting the advances of the Russians armies into East Prussia, much larger campaigns were being waged to the south between the Russians and the Austrians, and those conflicts did not go so well for the Central Powers. Unlike the situation in the west, where the two sides settled into a network of parallel trenches that stretched from the English Channel to the Swiss border, the Eastern Front became a war where armies moved rapidly over a wide area. Map 3.5 provides a quick view of the activities along the eastern borders of Germany and Austria-Hungary over the last four months of 1914, and the changes in the position of the front lines by the beginning of 1915.

The Galicia Campaigns

The Austrian commander, Conrad von Hötzendorf, planned to attack Russia along the northern border of Galicia before the Russians could mobilize. He anticipated having three armies, each with about 300,000 men. They would push into Polish Russia southeast of Warsaw, which would threaten Russian supply lines and hopefully lessen the

Russian pressure on the Germans fighting in East Prussia. The Austrians launched their attack on August 23, only to discover that the Russians by this time had managed to gather 1.2 million men under the command of Nikolai Ivanov for their own offensive plans. Like Conrad, Ivanov had been planning to attack the enemy as soon as possible. The strength of his assault would be aimed at the fortified Austrian positions at the fortified towns of Lemberg and Premysl.

The result was that two huge and very poorly organized armies rushed at each other paying very little attention to what the enemy was doing. On the north end of the battlefield the Austrians initially carried the day as their troops pushed the Russian armies back in some disarray. However, these Austrian victories were offset by events to the south, where the Russian attackers overwhelmed the Austrian forces. The rout of Habsburg forces in the south was so complete that by August 30 the Russian forces had to halt their advance in order to regroup because of the poor roads and confusion from the pursuit of fleeing Austrian soldiers. The Austrians eventually were forced to withdraw westward to the base of the Carpathian Mountains, abandoning their fortifications at Lemberg and Premysl. By the middle of September, the Russians controlled almost all of Galicia. Norman Stone reports that "both armies were exhausted. The Austro-Hungarians had suffered casualties of nearly fifty per cent – 400,000, of which the Russians took 100,000, with 300 guns; the Russians had lost 250,000 men, 40,000 as prisoners, with 100 guns."[36]

The disastrous defeat of the Austrian army alarmed the Germans, who feared that the Russians might be able to press their advantage and invade Silesia. Taking advantage of the German railroad transportation, Hindenburg and Ludendorff rushed four army corps south to Cracow in order to stabilize the northern end of the Austrian army. They were then able to launch a German counterattack against the Russians on September 28 that eventually reached the outskirts of Warsaw. Russian manpower stymied the Germans, who ultimately withdrew to their original position just east of Cracow. The situation had been stabilized, but as Ludendorff remarked to the German commander-in-chief Erich von Falkenhayn, in January 1915, "Austria's emergency is our great incalculable."[37]

It was clear to both generals that the Germans, who could not afford to let the Eastern Front simply collapse, would have to transfer men there to support the Austrians. With the Kaiser's approval, a decision was made to launch a major offensive against the Russians, and on May 2, 1915 a combined Austro-German attack was launched against the Russian forces occupying Galicia. The results exceeded even the most optimistic expectations. By the end of September, the Austrian and German troops had recaptured Galicia and occupied virtually all of Russian Poland (see Map 3.5). The Russian army had been eliminated as an offensive threat to either Germany or Austria, and the Russian economy had been dealt a devastating blow from the loss of territory that accompanied what became known as the "great retreat."[38]

At the end of 1915 the ambitious objectives envisioned by Schlieffen had not been reached. On the other hand, the Central Powers now controlled all of Belgium, a significant portion of northern France, and much of Russian Poland. Things could have been worse.

Stalemate

The battles that took place in the early months of the First World War set the tone for the rest of the war. Battles were no longer settled in a matter of days; they went on for weeks or even months. Nor did battles produce decisive outcomes. Five months of furious fighting had produced nothing more than a stalemate. The *élan* that was the cornerstone of confidence underlying all the prewar military plans was eroded by the horrendously high casualties encountered by both sides. More than seven million men were killed, wounded, or taken prisoner in the five months from August through December of 1914 – a total that accounts for more than 20 percent of all the casualties suffered by all the combatants in fifty-four months of fighting. The French and the Germans lost a million men each; the original British Expeditionary Force was virtually annihilated; and the Austrians and the Russians lost two million men each fighting for Galicia.[39] The enormous casualty lists documented the extent to which the firepower of modern armies had revolutionized warfare. While the machine gun attracts much of the attention for increasing the casualty rates, it was artillery shells that accounted for 60 percent of all wounds suffered by infantry units in the war.[40]

High casualties were bothersome, but in 1914 there were still plenty of young men who could be conscripted into new armies that could be trained and sent off to the front to launch suicidal offensive attacks on fortified positions. Conscripting more men could fill the depleted ranks of the armies, but what were the soldiers going to fight with? Everyone had prepared for war by stockpiling what they hoped would be sufficient arms, ammunition, and other supplies necessary to implement their plans – and presumably win the war. No one had anticipated prolonged and expensive stalemate. Nor had anyone realized how enormous the appetite of an army of several million men could be in an actual war. The first months of fighting quickly exhausted inventories of supplies on all sides. Historian Gerd Hardach provides an example that illustrates the magnitude of the supply problem: "Daily output of the 'seventy-five' shell, the [French] field artillery's standard projectile, amounted to 14,000 units at a time when a single battery was expending as much as 1,000 rounds in a day. In September the French Commanders in the field were calling for supplies of 700,000 shells a week." To emphasize how great the increase in the rate at which armies used ammunition seemed to people at the time, Hardach notes that the German artillery expended more ammunition during the Battle of the Marne than in the entire war of 1870–1.[41] What became known as the "munitions crisis" was experienced to greater or lesser degrees by every army, and there were literally hundreds of lesser supply crises that had to be dealt with as the armies settled down to a war of attrition.

In the summer and fall of 1914 the Germans had almost succeeded in defeating the French. Perhaps the most prescient verdict on the success of the Schlieffen Plan at the time was put forward by General Erich von Falkenhayn, the man who replaced Helmuth von Moltke as commander-in-chief of the German army. In a conversation with Chancellor Theobald von Bethmann-Hollweg, Falkenhayn suggested that Germany should immediately seek a negotiated settlement with the Entente Powers to end the war. "If Russia, France, and England hold together," Falkenhayn insisted, "we cannot defeat them in such a way as to achieve acceptable peace terms. We are more likely to be slowly exhausted." He went on to suggest that the Germans agree to a peace without any territorial annexations.[42] Bethmann-Hollweg agreed with Falkenhayn, but the Kaiser and his other advisors, driven by animal spirits and overconfidence combined with a propensity to gamble, elected to fight on.

Looking back after one hundred years, it is clear that Falkenhayn's suggestion was unerringly correct: Germany would never be in a better position to negotiate and any settlement would surely have been better than the one finally reached in November of 1918. Whether or not they would have been in a position to capitalize on that advantage is a counterfactual exercise with a multitude of answers, and all of them involve some rather imaginative "what ifs." To cut a deal with the French and British the Germans would almost surely have to give back the areas they occupied in northern France, and they would have to work out some way of negotiating an arrangement for Belgium to be a buffer state between Germany and France that would be acceptable to the British. In the east the prospects for negotiation were perhaps more optimistic. The Germans were not impressed with the performance of their Austrian allies – in private the German military described the alliance as being "tied to a corpse"– and Tsar Nicolas and Kaiser Wilhelm might have been willing to work out an arrangement after the fiasco for both countries in Galicia.[43]

But none of these imaginary counterfactuals worked out, and the pursuit of victory prevailed over common sense.

Was Schlieffen's Gamble a Good Bet?

On the face of it, Schlieffen's 1906 memorandum was a risky proposal. He proposed that Germany should concentrate its forces against one opponent at a time, and he felt that France offered the best opportunity for a quick German victory. He therefore recommended that between two-thirds and three-quarters of the German army be prepared to sweep through Belgium and Holland and on into France in a broad arc that would carry them west of Paris so that they would be in a position to annihilate the French army in a single battle as it had in 1871 (see Map 3.1). The proposal depended on speed of movement and successful coordination of a huge mass of troops, most of whom had no experience under combat conditions. It constituted a violation of both Belgium's and Holland's sovereignty, which would almost surely bring the British into the fray. We have already examined the plan in some detail as it existed in 1914, and we have seen how it eventually ended with the First Battle of the Marne and a stalemate on the Western Front.

How improbable were the chances of success for Schlieffen's plan? The metrics in Figure 3.2 present the %CINC scores for 1914.

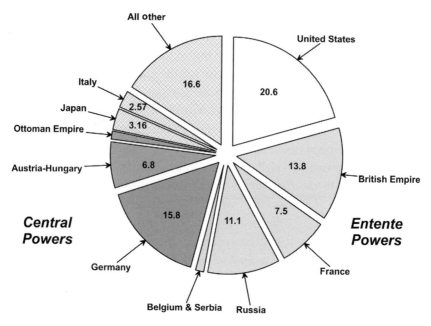

Figure 3.2 Global %CINC scores in 1914
Source: Table A1.1, 1914.

They underscore the importance of a quick and overwhelming victory against the French if the plan was to succeed. The Combined Military Capability [%CINC] scores of the three Entente Powers in 1914 was 32.5 while that of Germany and its Austrian ally totaled only 22.6. Given the uncertainty of what the United States – with a %CINC of 20.6 – might do, Falkenhayn's estimate that the longer the war, the lower the odds of a German victory seems correct. Schlieffen recognized the urgency of a quick victory, and that is why he was willing to violate the neutrality of both Holland and Belgium in order to create an invasion route that would quickly take his armies deep into northern France. His confidence in a piecemeal approach of tackling the French first and then confronting the Russians in the east was based not on the total weight of forces arrayed against Germany, but on the fact that Germany would be fighting them one at a time. This judgment is not contradicted by the metrics presented in Figure 3.2, which shows the global %CINC scores for 1914. Germany held a substantial edge in %CINC scores against the French (15.8 to 7.5), while being close to that of Russia (15.8 to 11.1). Schlieffen's dismissal of the importance of British intervention might be considered somewhat overconfident in the context of a long war; however, he was correct in assuming that in a short war the British would have only about 160,000 troops available for duty on the continent, and that would not be enough to turn the odds against the 1.5 million German troops invading France.

Grand schemes for total victory that fall short of their goal tend to get worse reviews than those which end in victory. We saw that things started out well enough for the Germans. The invading forces swept through Belgium and reached the French border two weeks later. They eventually almost reached Paris. However, at this point the exhausted troops had to pull back to the Marne, and this ended any hope of the quick and total victory Schlieffen envisioned in 1906. However, the invasion was hardly a total failure. By the end of 1914 German troops occupied almost all of Belgium and a significant portion of northern France. Looking past the immediate success, it is worth noting that they held most of that territory throughout the rest of the war. Moreover, Schlieffen's assessment of the situation in the east was not far off the mark. The stunning victories over the invading Russian troops at the battles of Tannenberg and the Masurian Lakes orchestrated by Generals Hindenburg and Ludendorff served to keep the Russians out of East Prussia and buy the time that Schlieffen had hoped for in the east. By the end of the year the Galician front had been stabilized. As late as the spring of 1918 the Germans were militarily still in the fight. The failure of the final offensives orchestrated by Erich Ludendorff was partly a product of overconfidence, but the real problem was not so much poor military strategy as it was that the German war effort in 1918 was running on empty after four years of debilitating fighting. Schlieffen's plan had given Germany a chance to win the war – or at least negotiate an outcome favorable to Germany – but neither Schlieffen nor any of the other generals realized the effort that would be required to carry their forces to victory.

Gambling on war involves taking chances, and the larger the military plans the greater the uncertainty and risks associated with the outcome. The decision to go ahead with Schlieffen's plan in 1914 was taken in the context of a German view that time was not in their favor. The window of opportunity to defeat both Russia and France was there and it was not clear when it would be there again. Animal spirits pushed German confidence to an overconfidence where invading France seemed worth the risk.

History suggests that the Germans should have taken Falkenhayn's advice to end the war in December 1914.

4 A WAR OF ATTRITION

In Flanders fields the poppies blow
Between the crosses, row on row,
That mark our place; and in the sky
The larks, still bravely singing, fly
Scarce heard amid the guns below.

We are the Dead.
Short days ago
We lived, felt dawn, saw sunset glow,
Loved and were loved, and now we lie
In Flanders fields

Take up our quarrel with the foe:
To you from failing hands we throw
The torch; be yours to hold it high.
If ye break faith with us who die
We shall not sleep, though poppies grow
In Flanders fields.
                John McCrae (1915)[1]

After four months of fighting, a war that began with optimistic projections of early victories had settled into a very bloody stalemate. The overconfidence of August had been replaced with a pervasive pessimism and fear that this was not going to be a short war ending with a decisive victory for either side. The French and the British had narrowly managed to avert disaster by turning back the German invasion just outside Paris. As the two armies took a deep breath at the end of 1914 the Germans still controlled all of Belgium and a significant part of northern France. In the east the Russians had been stopped in East Prussia, but the Austrian forces need help from the Germans to keep them out of Galicia. Despite the failure of the various plans, the military situation in December 1914 remained very uncertain and neither side was anxious to accept Erich von Falkenhayn's idea of returning to the *status quo antebellum* in northern Europe. Leaders on both sides still held out hope that the stalemate could eventually be broken and they could claim a victory. More than five million men had been killed or wounded in four months of fighting, and the result was a stalemate. That statistic alone should have extinguished any enthusiasm for continuing the war. Yet, far from discouraging more fighting, the casualty lists acted as a rallying cry to take the torch and hold it high to carry on the fight. To not do so would "break the faith" with those who already lay beneath the poppies in Flanders fields. John McCrae's poem was a classic example of how wartime casualties can form a collective memory of sunk costs that become a burden of the war that must somehow be "repaid" by carrying on the fight.

There had been one remarkable incident when soldiers did stop fighting in 1914. Beginning on Christmas Eve and on into the following day, there was a spirit of fraternization on both sides that became known as the "Christmas truce." "That Christmas Day," reports historian Martin Gilbert, "fraternization between the Germans and their enemies took place almost everywhere in the British No-Man's Land, and at places in the French and Belgian lines. It was almost always initiated by German troops, through either messages or song."[2] The full extent of such behavior remains unclear; however, it was common enough to be noticed by Sir John French, who issued orders to "prevent any recurrence of such conduct, and called the local commanders to strict account, which resulted in a good deal of trouble."[3] The Christmas truce of 1914 was not repeated in subsequent years.

The War Expands

The new year brought little prospect of an end to the stalemate on the Western Front, but it did bring the possibility that more countries could be enticed to join the fighting. "None of the original belligerents in 1914," argues Hew Strachan, "went to war in pursuance of so-called war aims. Most of the war's later entrants did. They exercised choice, and they sold their services to the highest bidder."[4] The choices were difficult. Experience showed that the potential gains were never guaranteed even if your side won, and winding up on the losing side could be very costly. Between the outbreak of the war in August of 1914 and the end of 1916, six more countries entered the war.[5]

Turkey Joins the Central Powers

First to jump in was the Ottoman Empire, which had been involved in a series of wars with Russia and the Balkan states – Greece, Serbia, Romania, and Bulgaria – dating back to the last quarter of the nineteenth century. Those conflicts left the Turks with only a small portion of European territory that had once comprised most of the Balkan states. A faction of "Young Turk" leaders in Istanbul had hopes of regaining at least some of the territories lost in the Balkan wars, and Germany had carefully played upon this sentiment to develop close military and economic ties to the Turkish government. On August 2, 1914 the Turks and the Germans agreed to a secret alliance that committed the Ottoman Empire to join the Central Powers in the war that had just broken out between Russia and Germany. Because of a lack of unanimity among the Turkish leaders when the treaty was drawn up, there were delays implementing this agreement and it was not until the end of October that the Turks formally entered the war on the side of the Central Powers with a naval bombardment of some towns along the Russian coast of the Black Sea.

The entry of Turkey on the side of the Germans posed several threats to the Entente, the most serious of which was the possible closure of the Dardanelles and Bosporus Straits, which were crucial transportation links between Russia and the Mediterranean Sea. The Turks were also in a position to threaten the Suez Canal, which was a vital link between Great Britain and India. On the other hand, the decision of the Turks to side with the Germans also offered the British and French an opportunity to further dismantle what remained of the Ottoman Empire. As Edward Grey, the British Secretary of State for Foreign Affairs, noted in a memo dated August 15, 1914: "if Turkey sided with Germany and Austria, and they were defeated, of course we could not answer for what might be taken from Turkey in Asia Minor."[6]

With all this in mind, Britain and France declared war against the Ottoman Empire on November 5, 1914. Neither side was prepared for extensive military action in the Middle East. In January of 1915 a force of Ottoman troops crossed the Sinai Peninsula and reached the Suez Canal; however, their attempt to cross the canal was easily repulsed by the British forces in Egypt. Though unsuccessful, the attack on Suez served notice to the British that the Ottoman entry into the war was a very real threat to their interests in the Middle East and could pose problems with the supply routes to India. The Russians, who were fighting the Turks in the Caucasus region on the northern border of Turkey, urged Lord Kitchener, the British Secretary of State for War, and Winston Churchill, the First Lord of the Admiralty, to support Russian efforts by launching an amphibious attack to occupy the Gallipoli Peninsula. Kitchener and Churchill succeeded in persuading Herbert Asquith, the British Prime Minister, to support the formation of a Mediterranean Expeditionary Force (MEP) that would operate out of Egypt against Ottoman forces in Palestine. Reinforcements were brought in from India and Australia/New Zealand, and the French contributed a complement of men who would eventually bring the strength of the MEP to more than 70,000 troops.

The Gallipoli Campaign

Hoping that a victory in the Middle East could change the course of the war, First Lord of the Admiralty Winston Churchill was confident that his Royal Navy, backed up by troops from the MEP, could drive Turkey from the war by a joint sea and land operation against the Ottoman Empire. His enthusiasm produced one of the most celebrated military gambles to emerge from the war: an expedition organized by the French and British in April 1915 with a plan to open the Dardanelles through a joint naval and army attack. The plan was to send a fleet of sixteen British and French battleships to clear the Dardanelles of mines and disable the Turkish shore artillery batteries guarding the southern opening of the straits. On March 18, the naval squadron attacked the main defenses at the southern mouth of the Dardanelles. The battle quickly turned into a major disaster for the Entente ships. Three of the battleships struck mines and subsequently sank, and three more were seriously damaged by mines and fire from shore batteries. Appalled at the losses they had suffered, Sir John de Robeck, the British admiral commanding the squadron, ordered his fleet to withdraw, and insisted that his fleet could not clear the Turkish minefields in the Dardanelles.[7] A subsequent naval attack by the Russian Black Sea Fleet ten days later against Turkish forts defending the Bosporus Straits to the north of Istanbul was also driven off by Turkish batteries assisted by the German battle cruiser *Goeben*.

Despite the inability of the combined naval attacks to clear the Dardanelles and Bosporus of Turkish defenses, Churchill and Lord Kitchener were resolved to persevere with their plan to attack the Turkish capital from the south with an amphibious assault by the MEP on the southern tip of the Gallipoli Peninsula (see Map 4.1). Unfortunately, the organization of the MEP in Egypt had required more than a month of preparation, and by the time the expedition left for Gallipoli in mid-April, any element of surprise had dissipated. Under the guidance of Liman von Sanders, the German advisor to the Ottoman Empire troops, the Turks had constructed formidable defenses along the coast of the peninsula where the British intended to land their troops.

On April 25, 1915, Entente forces landed troops at five beachheads on the Gallipoli Peninsula. Things did not go well for the attacking forces. Though they were able to get their troops ashore at

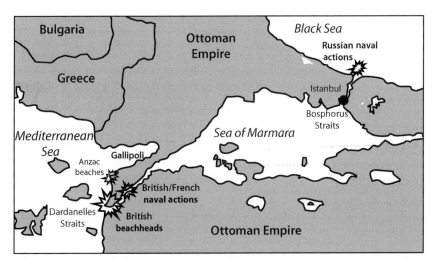

Map 4.1 The Gallipoli campaign, 1915

or near the appointed places, the troops of the MEP could not exploit their early advantage and they soon found themselves pinned to the narrow beachheads where they had landed. Kemal Ataturk, the Turkish commander, proved to be extraordinarily adept at managing his forces to keep the enemy bottled up close to the sea. The French troops were landed on the northern side of the peninsula, and the Australian and New Zealand forces – popularly referred to as ANZACs – managed to gain a foothold further north at Suvla Bay. None of these efforts was able to break through the Turkish lines and the fighting eventually evolved into a stalemate not unlike the fighting on the Western Front. Frustrated by the drain on their resources, and seeing no appreciable promise of success, the expedition was eventually abandoned in early January 1916. Ironically, one of the few things that went right for the Entente troops at Gallipoli was the evacuation of the troops. The Turks were not even aware they had abandoned their positions until several hours after the last troops had left. The fighting on Gallipoli took the usual toll of casualties on both sides. The 400,000 British Empire and French troops who eventually saw action there suffered 250,000 casualties, including 46,000 battle deaths. The Turks fielded 500,000 men, half of whom became casualties, including 65,000 killed or missing in action.[8]

The failure of the Gallipoli gamble meant that British and French interests in the Middle East remained at risk of attack from the Ottoman Turks. The British transferred the troops evacuated from Gallipoli to Egypt and reorganized them into a new army group, renamed the Egyptian Expeditionary Force (EEF). Their hope was that the EEF would be able to move north along the coast toward Jerusalem and Damascus. However, Turkish forces were able to form an effective line of defense between the towns of Gaza on the Mediterranean coast and Beersheba on the edge of the desert. Two British offensives in 1916 failed to break the Turkish line, and in March of 1917 Alfred Murray, the British commander of the EEF, was replaced by Edmund Allenby. Allenby had come up through the ranks as a cavalry officer of some note, and when offered command of the EEF he welcomed the opportunity to escape the trench warfare in France in favor of the more open spaces of the Arabian desert, which offered one of the few chances where cavalry might still play a significant role. Allenby's appointment would bode well for the future, but he would have to wait until events on the Western Front had played out before he would have the necessary resources to make any serious advance toward Jerusalem.

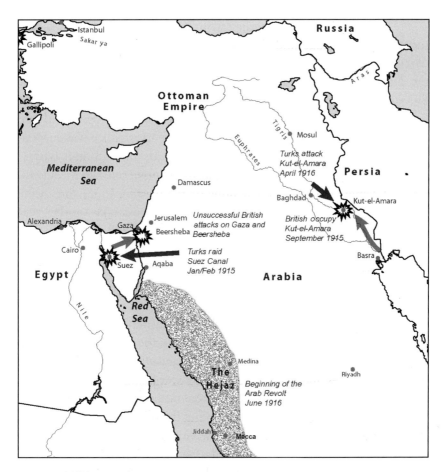

Map 4.2 Palestine and Mesopotamia, 1916/17

Elsewhere in the Middle East, the British sought to further weaken the Ottoman Empire by occupying the Tigris and Euphrates river basin in Mesopotamia (see Map 4.2). British and Indian troops had occupied Basra in November 1914, and began a steady advance that eventually reached Ctesiphon, a town within twenty miles of Baghdad. At this point, the Turks launched a counterattack that forced the British to retreat and fall back to the town of Kut-el-Amara, where General Charles Townshend and 11,000 troops were surrounded and eventually forced to surrender. The dispiriting defeat at Kut-el-Amara, which came close on the heels of the equally discouraging setback in Gallipoli, spurred a parliamentary investigation and reorganization of the British troops in Mesopotamia.

New leadership and two divisions of reinforcements increased the strength of the British contingent in Mesopotamia and by December of 1916, General Stanley Maude was ready to begin a new push up the Tigris toward Baghdad. By the end of 1916 the situation for the Entente Powers in the Middle East had stabilized, but after the military setbacks at Gallipoli and Kut-el-Amara there was little to cheer about. As David Fromkin notes, the Turks' wartime performance was surprisingly successful. "Engaged in a three-front war, the Ottoman Empire defeated Britain and France in the west in 1915–16, crushed the advancing armies of British India in the east at the same time, and in the north held off the Russian invasion forces."[9] It would take another year of hard fighting before British troops finally reached Jerusalem and were prepared to advance on to Damascus.

The Arab Revolt

The Entente forces were not the only group in the Middle East fighting the Ottoman Turks. For years before the war, Arabs living in the Ottoman Empire chaffed under the weight of Turkish rule. The war offered the Arabs an opportunity to break free of the Ottoman Empire. In the spring of 1916 the resentment flared into open rebellion in Hejaz, an area of western Arabia that runs along the eastern shore of the Red Sea and includes the Holy City of Mecca and the port city of Jiddah (see Map 4.2). On June 10 Sharif Hussein ibn Ali, the King of Hejaz, proclaimed a rebellion against the Ottoman Empire. What eventually became known as the "Arab Revolt" had actually started five days earlier when two of Hussein's sons led an unsuccessful attack against the Ottoman garrison at Medina. Hussein's effort at Mecca succeeded in gaining control of the city; however, it soon became apparent that his forces were not strong enough to withstand the efforts of Ottoman troops sent south to control the rebellion. Hussein therefore sought help from the British, who had actively encouraged him to take up arms against the Turks. The roots of Hussein's decision to seek British help involved considerable intrigue on both sides. David Fromkin argues that Hussein would have preferred to stay with the Ottoman leaders until he discovered that the Young Turks in Istanbul planned to replace him. When troop movements indicated that they were implementing their plans to overthrow him, Hussein decided to turn to the British.[10] The British responded by having the Royal Navy rush to the scene with a flotilla that included HMS *Ben-My-Chree* – a ship carrying aircraft – to the scene. With the help of the carrier's seaplanes the British forced the Turks to retreat and by the end of July, Jiddah and two other ports on the east coast of the Red Sea were in Arab hands and protected by the Royal Navy. Control of the Hejaz coastline was critical to the British because it provided them with ports that were closer to the battles in Palestine.

Hussein had grandly promised that his revolt would draw thousands of Muslims to support the fight against the Ottomans, but those dreams never materialized. Consequently, the Arab rebels were confined to limited raids on Turkish posts and a continuation of the guerilla tactics against the Turkish railway. These attacks served a useful purpose by tying down Ottoman troops sent to protect their rail and communication routes in the Hejaz, but they did not offer substantive support to Edmund Allenby, who wanted the EEF to strike north along the Mediterranean coast. By May of 1917, the British Arab Office in Cairo was ready to write off the effort to support Hussein's revolt as a failed – and rather expensive – experiment. A memo summarizing the situation stated "That the Hejaz Bedouins were simply *guerillas*, and not of good quality at that, had been amply demonstrated, even in the early sieges; and it was never in doubt that they would not attack nor withstand Turkish regulars." The best that could be hoped for in the future from Hussein's Arab movement, the memo argued, was that it would "just hold its own in place." Nevertheless, Britain had spent £11 million on the Arab Revolt and the military advisors insisted that they should continue to support Hussein's effort in order to preserve Britain's standing among the Arabs.[11]

At this point a new face appeared on the scene who would dramatically change the course of the desert war. T. E. Lawrence was a junior British officer included in a group of military advisors sent to Hejaz to encourage Hussein to take some organized action against the Turks. He was hardly an imposing figure. At age twenty-eight. he was short, looked younger than his age, and had no military record of accomplishment. However, Lawrence had managed to accumulate a strong background in Arabic language and culture, and he quickly gained the confidence of Hussein's son, Faisal. Lawrence managed to persuade Faisal that an attack against Aqaba, which was the last major Red Sea port still held by the Turks, was feasible. With the support of the Royal Navy, an Arab force of about five thousand men attacked

Aqaba on July 2 and forced the small Turkish garrison to surrender. The capture of Aqaba was a relatively minor event in terms of military significance; however, Lawrence's heroics during the battle and the defeat of a Turkish garrison proved to be a huge confidence-builder for Faisal and his men. Lawrence and Faisal were to provide valuable support to the British forces under Allenby as they moved northward toward Damascus later in the year.

The Sykes–Picot Agreement

The military setbacks for Entente forces in Gallipoli, Palestine, and Mesopotamia did not stop the British and French governments from making plans for the eventual division of the Ottoman Empire in the Middle East after the war. Throughout the second half of the nineteenth century the British had propped up the crumbling Ottoman Empire as a buffer against the southern expansion of Russia. The rivalry between Britain, France, and Russia over the Middle East had led to the Crimean War in 1854–6, and the two western powers had quietly backed the Turks in their conflict with Russia in 1878. The collapse of the Gallipoli campaign caused the British and French to rethink their positions on the Ottomans, and by the end of 1915 the British foreign office decided that their operations out of Cairo needed to be reorganized. The man who emerged as the prime mover in this effort was Sir Mark Sykes, a protégé of Lord Kitchener, who had a strong background in Arabic languages and history. Sykes had just returned from an extensive tour of India and the Middle East, and he proposed that all the diplomatic affairs for the Middle East should be handled through a single office. The Arab Bureau was established in Cairo and became the focus for diplomatic action in the region. As evidence of the disorganization of the British handling of diplomatic affairs in the region, Sykes pointed out that there were eighteen agencies that had to be consulted before a decision could be reached on any major issue.[12] Though Kitchener was nominally the head of the Bureau, it was Sykes who served as his voice there.

There were now four major groups vying for control of the Ottoman territories on the Arabian Peninsula: Britain, France, Russia, and the Arabs in the region who hoped to break free from Ottoman control. The British were in the difficult position of simultaneously trying to maintain complex – and sometimes conflicting – commitments to all the other three groups. They sought to assist the Arabs in their fight against the Turks and the Germans, while dealing with their rivalry with the French and Russians over the territorial control of the region by each country. Sykes was given the task of negotiating an understanding with the French over territorial control of the region. He met with his French counterpart, Georges François Picot, on almost a daily basis at the French embassy in London during December 1915 in an effort to hammer out the details of an agreement that would spell out which areas each country would "control" or have a "controlling interest in" after the war. The two men eventually drafted a document that became known as the Sykes–Picot Agreement. All that remained was to bring the Russians into the circle of their agreement, so Sykes and Picot traveled to Petrograd, where they worked with the Russian foreign minister, Sergei Sazonov, to get Russia to agree to the draft of their proposal. By the end of March 1916, all three governments had agreed to accept the areas of "control" and "influence" depicted in Map 4.3. Partly because each government interpreted the rather vague

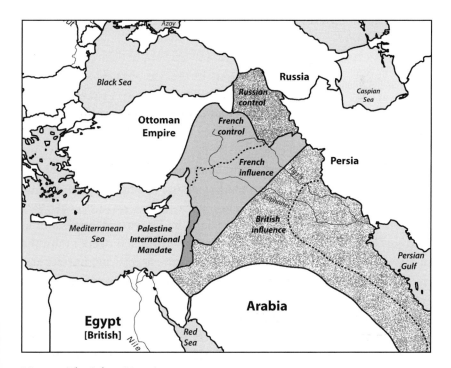

Map 4.3 The Sykes–Picot Agreement, 1916

terms of the agreement as they saw fit, everyone was happy with what they thought they would get from the arrangement. The French were given unfettered control over Syria in the north; the Russians were now free to push southward; while the British were given free range in Gaza and Mesopotamia. All three powers agreed that Palestine and the city of Jerusalem would be set aside as an area that would be "internationally" controlled.

These arrangements were carried out with utmost secrecy, which was essential because they involved several provisions that contradicted promises that the British had already made to the Arab population to secure their support for the war against the Ottoman Empire on the western side of the Arabian Peninsula. And, of course, the agreement depended on military success by the Entente in the Middle East – which was far from certain in the spring of 1915. The Sykes–Picot Agreement remained quietly filed away until its contents were unexpectedly made public by the Russian Bolshevik government in November 1918 – much to the dismay of the British and French governments. Despite all that happened between 1916 and end of the war, the arrangements worked out by Mark Sykes and François Picot formed the foundation for the reshaping of the Middle East in 1919.

Italy Joins the Entente Powers

The most significant European country still deciding whether to join the war in 1915 was Italy. When war broke out in the summer of 1914, Italy was allied with Germany and Austria by the terms of the Triple Alliance. That treaty committed each of the signees to support the other two in the event of an attack by another great power. However, the Italians balked at entering the fight in 1914 because they claimed that the Austrians and Germans had been the aggressors in starting the war. Their reluctance actually went much deeper than the terms written into the Triple Alliance. Since the unification of Italy and the formation of an Italian state in 1867, there had been contentious relations between the Italians and the Habsburgs over disputed territory between the two countries. The Italians had watched with alarm as the Habsburg Empire gradually acquired the territories abandoned by the Ottoman Empire along the eastern Adriatic coast, including the city of Trieste. These were areas that included a substantial Italian population who would welcome an annexation by Italy, and the terms of the Triple Alliance stipulated that if Austria expanded its boundaries to include additional territories once controlled by the Ottoman Empire, Italy would receive some form of territorial compensation. Most Italians felt this would include the region around Trieste. When Austria refused to consider ceding any territory to Italy, the Italians had announced they were no longer bound by the terms of the Triple Alliance and would remain neutral in the war being waged by Austria and Germany against the Entente. This announcement touched off vigorous efforts by all the belligerents to gain their favor as an ally. From the outset of the bidding it was clear that what Italy expected was promises of territorial expansion. This put the Central Powers at a distinct disadvantage. Germany was willing to make such concessions in return for Italian assistance in the war; however, their Austrian ally balked at giving up any territory to the Italians. The British and the French, on the other hand, had no such compunctions; they assured the Italians that they would not only gain territorial rights to Trieste, but they could also have the region of Trentino, which jutted down into north-central Italy. These promises of territorial gains of areas belonging to the Habsburg Empire in the event of an Entente victory were enough to persuade the Italians to join the Entente in the war against the Central Powers on May 23, 1915.[13]

Declaring war against the Central Powers was relatively simple. Fighting a war in the mountainous region that divides Italy and Austria was a far more difficult task. Like most countries entering the Great War, the Italians were hardly ready for what lay ahead. Their army was ill equipped in terms of ammunition and artillery, and because the main military planning before the war had been directed toward France, not Austria, they were not at all prepared for fighting in the mountainous regions of northeastern Italy. The first Italian military effort was an offensive launched against the Austrians in June 1915 along the Isonzo River in the region that divides northeastern Italy and Austria. Over the course of the next three years the Austrians and the Italians would fight eleven "battles" along the Isonzo, in a stalemate that lasted into late 1917. There was also fighting in the Tyrolean Alps of Trentino, where the Austrians launched an unsuccessful attack. These attacks were all very bloody, and neither side was able to gain a significant advantage. It was, as Michael Clodfelter noted, "the Western Front transferred to a snowy and mountainous setting. Probably only the Somme, Verdun, and Ypres saw more bloodshed along their

crater-pocked lines than did the Isonzo."[14] Over a million battle casualties had been suffered by the two armies along the Isonzo and in
Trentino by the end of 1917. Since they tended to be on the attack
most of the time, the Italians bore the brunt of these losses by a ratio
of about 2:1.[15] Because the lines remained static from 1915 through
most of 1917, the Italian front has received relatively little attention
in general histories of the war. Yet the struggles along the Italian–
Austrian borders represented a significant drain on the resources and
manpower of both countries, and the possibility of a breakthrough by
either side in this theater of the war could create a major crisis for the
other side. The Austrians managed to hold off the Italian offensives,
but only by diverting troops and resources that could have provided
much needed support in the struggles of the Central Powers with
Russia to the north.

The Neutral's Dilemma: To Fight or Not to Fight?

While the major powers struggled to bloody stalemates,
everyone else was confronted with the problem of how they should react
to a war that was getting larger each month. Most of the other countries
in northern Europe had little direct interest in the conflict. However,
that does not mean they were indifferent as to the outcome of the war,
nor did it guarantee that they might not be drawn into the battles by the
fighting around their borders. The European countries which bordered
Germany and France – Holland, Denmark, Norway, and Sweden – all
chose to maintain an uneasy neutrality. They each had considerable economic ties to countries on both sides of the conflict, and they hoped to
avoid being directly involved with the war. Their success in maintaining
their neutrality depended on their ability to avoid offending either side.

The most successful of these neutral countries was Holland. In
addition to having strong ties to both Britain and Germany, Holland
was geographically situated between the two warring countries. The
Germans saw an obvious advantage to having the Netherlands as a trade
entrepot which could help offset the effects of a British naval blockade.
Schlieffen had proposed that the invasion of France go through Belgium
and Holland. When Helmuth von Moltke took over Schlieffen's position, he changed that part of the master plan because he recognized
the importance of a neutral Holland as a source of imports for the
Germans in the event of a war. The British also favored Dutch neutrality,

a view that was expressed by an internal memo of the Admiralty early in the war: "It is best that [Holland] should remain a neutral, favorably disposed to us. In any case, every effort should be made to prevent her from joining the enemy, even though trade concessions in some degree unfavorable to us should be necessary to obtain that end."[16] Both sides could implement policies that might seriously interdict Dutch shipping. By carefully managing the trade restrictions imposed by each of the belligerent countries, the Dutch were able to continue trade with both sides of the conflict until late in the war. During the first two years, exports of food to Germany from Holland rose dramatically and provided a significant source of food for the beleaguered German civilians. Moltke's decision not to invade Holland weakened Schlieffen's plan by making it more difficult for the right wing of the invading army to get west of Paris. Yet events showed that his decision may have been well-founded. Historian Marc Frey notes that Dutch exports to Germany more than doubled between 1914 and 1916, and Dutch foodstuffs "amounted to 50 percent of all German food imports." Frey cites a comment by German Chancellor Bethmann-Hollweg in August 1916 that Germany would have collapsed without food imports from neutral countries.[17] After the entry of the United States into the war in early 1917, the exports to Germany fell sharply due to an embargo against Dutch shipping. Holland was the most important of the European neutral states, and its success provided a model for the Scandinavian countries to stay out of the war.

A Bloody Stalemate

What was noticeably absent at the end of 1914 was any change in the underlying military strategy for winning this war. Determined that the Germans must regain the initiative they had lost at the Marne, Erich von Falkenhayn, the new commander-in-chief of the German army, decided to launch a major attack in April 1915 against the British forces at Ypres, a Belgian city at the northern end of the Entente lines. The most notable feature of the Second Battle of Ypres was the use of poison gas by the Germans for the first time on the Western Front. The Germans had used poison gas shells against the Russians on the Eastern Front in January 1915; however, the frigid temperatures prevented the gas from vaporizing. In July of 1915 the Germans also introduced the use of flamethrowers. By the end of the year the British had begun to employ poison gas in their offensive operations.[18] Despite the element of surprise the Germans were unable to exploit the gap in the British lines created by the first gas attack. Impressed by the fact that they had incurred heavy losses with little gain in territory, Falkenhayn abandoned plans for additional offensive actions in 1915. The Germans contented themselves with reinforcing their positions by constructing fortified lines and bunkers with as many as three lines of trenches.

The initiative along the Western Front thus went over to the French and the British. Entente commanders spent the rest of the year launching a series of futile assaults on German positions in the area between Ypres and Arras and further south between Reims and Verdun, hoping to find some point at which they could break through the enemy lines. Names such as Artois, Neuve Chapelle, Aubers Ridge, Champagne, and Loos do not spring quickly to mind in a list of First World War battles. Yet they were all sites of one or more efforts by British or French troops to break through the German trenches in 1915. Map 4.4 identifies the areas of fighting on the Western Front through

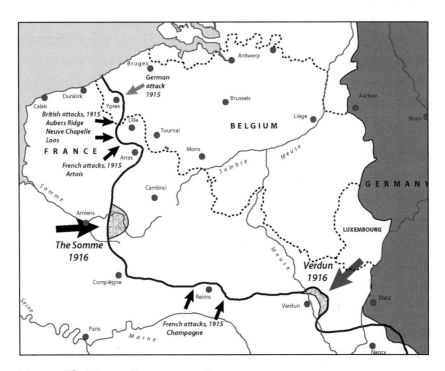

Map 4.4 The Western Front, 1915–16

1915. These were battles of incredible size, intensity, and bloodshed, pursued with a notable lack of strategic imagination. There are no definitive figures for the total number of casualties on the Western Front in 1915; estimates of the French losses range between 1.3 and 1.6 million men, whereas British losses totaled more than 250,000 men, and German losses ranged between 650,000 and 875,000 men.[19]

Far from easing, the intensity of fighting actually increased in 1916. In early December of 1915 the Entente leaders met at Chantilly to discuss how they could implement a common strategy to defeat the Central Powers. Representatives from Britain, France, Russia, and Italy eventually worked out a memorandum stating that the four Allies should coordinate their efforts in simultaneous attacks that would maximize the impact of their efforts on the outnumbered Germans and Austrians. In the west, there would be a Franco-British attack against the Germans along the Somme River in the center of the Western Front. This would be coordinated with a Russian attack against the Austrians in the east. Meanwhile, the Italians would renew their attacks against Austria in the south. Ideally, all these campaigns would be simultaneously launched in the spring of 1916. As the New Year dawned it soon became apparent that this timeline was far too optimistic. The French armies were exhausted by the heavy losses suffered in the first fifteen months of the war and the British needed time to recruit and train new armies to meet the demands of a new offensive. The Russians had suffered a series of humiliating defeats at the hands of the Germans toward the end of 1915 and were hardly ready to take the offensive in the east before early summer. The coordinated offensives were scheduled to begin at the end of June 1916.[20]

Verdun

While the Entente leaders were making plans for the coming year, the Germans were devising their own strategies. Erich von Falkenhayn, the new head of the OHL, had become convinced that a strategy based on throwing masses of infantry against fortified positions in the hope that they could "break through" the enemy lines was misguided. In a memo written to the Kaiser just before Christmas of 1915 he proposed that the Germans should create a situation where massive artillery bombardments could inflict heavy casualties on the enemy without incurring comparable losses among their own troops, and where the enemy would be put in a position where their troops would have to attack the German infantry. Falkenhayn's plan was diabolically simple. "Within our reach behind the French sector of the Western front," he noted:

> there are objectives for the retention of which the French General Staff would be compelled to throw in every man they have. If they do so the forces of France will bleed to death – as there can be no question of a voluntary withdrawal – whether we reach our goal or not. If they do not do so, and we reach our objectives, the moral effect on France will be enormous. For an operation limited to a narrow front, Germany will not be compelled to spend herself so completely.[21]

Falkenhayn was convinced he had found the perfect place to implement this new strategy: the city of Verdun. At first glance, this would seem to be a strange choice. The city was one of the most heavily fortified positions on the Western Front, with armed forts connected by intricate tunnels, supply centers, and infantry shelters. That did not deter Falkenhayn; his plan was not to occupy the city, but to attack the surrounding forts with artillery. Because it was situated in a salient that jutted out of the French lines, their positions would be vulnerable to artillery fire from two sides. Moreover, because the strength of the Verdun defenses was so formidable, the French would hardly expect a German attack in that sector, so the initial attack would have the advantage of surprise. Finally, and most importantly to Falkenhayn's objective of inflicting heavy casualties on the French, his conviction was that Verdun was a city that the French would defend to the last man.

On February 21 after an intensive nine-hour artillery bombardment, the German infantry attacked the ring of French forts defending the city. Over the course of the next week German troops pushed back the French lines and captured Fort Douaumont – one of the largest of the forts that surrounded the town. However, as the German troops advanced, French resistance stiffened and the Germans came under artillery fire from French batteries. At this point, Falkenhayn had to decide whether to press on with new attacks or pull back. He chose the latter course of action, but he did not commit all his reserves to the effort. What Falkenhayn had not counted on was that the French had found a commander who was willing to defend Verdun by punishing the German forces as heavily as they punished the French. On the same day that Fort Douaumont fell, Henri Philippe Pétain was given command of the French troops in the Verdun sector of the front lines. Pétain was one of the few French generals who was not blindly wedded to the notion of *offensive á outrance* – the philosophy that the only way to win battles was to vigorously attack the enemy regardless of the casualties to the attackers. Rather than simply throwing his troops against the advancing Germans (who were waiting for him to do exactly that), Pétain ordered his commanders to tenaciously hold their ground and counterattack only to regain any additional ground that was lost to the enemy. He would not condone any other new offensive actions.

Pétain's emphasis on a defense strategy involved strengthening the forts that remained in French hands, organizing an efficient system of supply for his troops, and instituting a system of troop rotation that took units out of action on a regular basis to ensure that fresh troops were always available when needed.[22] Pétain's most remarkable achievement was the organization of supply routes to the troops at the front line. There was a single narrow-gauge train track and an accompanying road that stretched fifty miles from the supply depot at Bar-le-Doc to Verdun. By imposing strict rules for traffic, organizing supply points for unloading trains and trucks along the way when things got jammed up, and assigning units to maintain the condition of the road, his men were able to deliver troops, horses, and supplies in a steady flow to the front lines. What later became known as the *Sacré Voie* was the supply lifeline for French troops.[23]

By the end of April, the battle had degenerated into a very bloody stalemate, a situation that did not sit well with either the French army command or the political leaders in Paris. The fall of Fort Douaumont to the Germans had been announced with great fanfare in the German press in February, and with equal consternation in the French press. President Raymond Poincaré was particularly unhappy that the fort was still in German hands after two months of heavy fighting, and he pressured Joffre to do something to remedy the situation. Poincaré and Joffre both visited the front in the middle of April and decided that Pétain should be replaced with Robert Nivelle, one of Pétain's corps commanders. Nivelle had exhibited an aggressive attitude while under Pétain's restraint, and he assured his superiors that the time had come for the French troops to regain the offensive. The change in command was made effective on May 1. Pétain was not pleased with the decision, which involved "promoting" him to become commander of the Center Army Group while Nivelle was made commander of the Second Army at Verdun. This meant that Pétain was still involved with the decisions regarding Verdun, but he was no longer managing the day-to-day operations.

A stalemate was not what Falkenhayn and the OHL had envisioned either. After only a few weeks of fighting, Falkenhayn's plan to "bleed the enemy to death" was turning into a struggle where both armies were bleeding to death. Estimates of the French and German losses from the beginning of the battle to the end of August show that the Germans consistently suffered only slightly fewer causalities than the French each month.[24] The magnitude of the German casualties, together with the threat posed by Entente offensives on the Somme and in Russia as the summer wore on, caused the Kaiser and his advisors to become disenchanted with reports that they were winning the battle of attrition. The price was simply too high. On August 31 Falkenhayn was replaced as head of the OHL by the team of Paul von Hindenburg and Erich Ludendorff. One of Hindenburg's first actions was to cancel German offensive actions at Verdun. That did not end the fighting there, but it marked the end of Falkenhayn's idea of winning the war through a single battle of attrition. Estimates of the casualties in the battle for Verdun vary widely; Michael Clodfelter notes that "it is possible that as many as nearly 1 million soldiers of France and Germany were casualties of Verdun."[25] More than any other battle, Verdun came to symbolize the senseless carnage of the First World War.

The Somme

Northwest of Verdun, the British and French sectors of the front lines met at the Somme River (see Map 4.4). While the Germans were preparing a trap for the French at Verdun early in 1916, Sir Douglas Haig, the newly appointed commander of the British Expeditionary Force, was planning an Anglo-French offensive that would provide a "breakthrough" that would win the war for the Entente Powers. Like the Germans, Haig counted on artillery to pave the way for victory. His plan of attack was to have artillery bombard the German lines for a week prior to an attack by the infantry. The preparations for this attack involved placement of more than 1,500 British guns along the British lines and 2.5 million shells for the initial bombardment. It also required the construction of an extensive network of roads, supply depots, and hospitals to support the attacking troops. The troops themselves were, for the most part, units recruited to replace the depleted ranks of the BEF that had fought through the battles of the previous year. Partly because of the lack of experienced troops, the tactics for the infantry were relatively simple. British historian John Keegan describes the instructions for the infantry assault:

> What this meant, in terms of soldiers on the ground, was that two battalions each of a thousand men, forming the leading wave of the brigade, would leave their front trenches, using scaling-ladders to climb the parapet, extend their soldiers in four lines, a company to each, the men two or three yards apart, the lines about fifty to a hundred yards behind each other, and advance to the German wire. This they would expect to find flat, or at least widely gapped, and, passing through, they would then jump down into the German trenches, shoot, bomb or bayonet any who opposed them, and take possession. Later the reserve waves would pass through and advance to capture the German second position by similar methods.
>
> The maneuver was to be done slowly and deliberately, for the men were to be laden with about sixty pounds of equipment, their re-supply with food and ammunition during the battle being one of the things the staff could not guarantee. In the circumstances, it did indeed seem that success would depend upon what the artillery could do for the infantry, both before the advance and once it was under way.[26]

At the appointed time on July 1, the first troops went "over the top" and advanced across no-man's-land toward the German trenches. Unfortunately for the British infantrymen, the artillery assault had not accomplished its expected task. Alerted to the attack by the extensive bombardment, the Germans were prepared for the assault. The shells had ploughed up the no-man's-land between the trenches, and what the advancing troops encountered was a tangle of barbed wire and shell craters impeding their progress. The Germans had pulled back their troops from the fury of the shells falling on their forward trenches, and as the British troops advanced they quickly returned to their positions and laid down a devastating fire into the slow-moving line of men. The result was that more than 19,000 British troops were killed and another 35,000 were wounded on the first day of action. Urged on by the French, who were struggling to hold Verdun, Haig continued to press attacks against the German lines until the middle of November. By that time the British casualty lists had reached close to half a million men, and the Germans had lost about half that number. The British attacks had advanced their lines about seven miles beyond the initial point of attack. But the German lines held and Haig did not achieve his objective of a breakthrough. The attack on the Somme, he later claimed, had relieved the German pressure on both the French at Verdun and the Russians in the east, and he had conducted a "well thought out process whereby the German army was to be worn out in 'one continuous battle' over the next two years."[27] Most historians have rejected Haig's self-assessment of his management of the battle, pointing out that the Germans were able to divert troops to other theaters of war, and questioning whether Haig's notion of a "continuous battle" was in fact what wore the Germans out two years later.[28] The British War Cabinet was singularly unimpressed by the battle's outcome, but they lacked the will to make any changes in the British chain of command. When Haig offered to resign in October, they did not even discuss his offer. "This was the moment," according to Robin Prior and Trevor Wilson, "when civilian leadership indicated in the most dramatic way that it had lost the nerve to assert their authority over Haig and Robertson."[29] Haig would not only survive the debacle of the Somme; he would remain in command of British troops in France for the rest of the war.

Verdun and the Somme are widely recognized as the two quintessential battles of the Western Front, and the military strategy employed by both sides has been examined in excruciating detail. The inescapable conclusion is that few battles in military history have accomplished so little for such a huge effort expended and casualties suffered by all sides. Nor is it clear that anyone could claim they "won" either battle. Michael Clodfelter notes that the "Germans had held their ground [at the Somme] and thus can be said to have won a tactical decision, but the cost was so astronomical for all engaged that the word 'victory' must forever be inappropriate for the Somme."[30] The recapture of Fort Douaumont by French forces in early December was celebrated as a great victory by the French public, but the cost of that victory was enormous, not only in terms of the casualties suffered during the fight for Verdun, but in the effect it would have on the French army's effectiveness in subsequent battles. "The French Army," writes Alistair Horne, "was not the same; never again would it be able to repeat the stubborn heroism it had shown at Verdun."[31]

The Brusilov Offensives

The final element of the grand scheme of attack adopted at the Entente Chantilly Conference was that Russian forces would attack the German and Austrian forces along the Eastern Front in early June of 1916. At a meeting in April, Stavka – the High Command of the Russian Imperial Army – met to discuss how they could meet this commitment.[32] The situation facing the Russians did not offer any obvious course of action, and after the enormous losses suffered in the first year of the war, confidence was very low as the generals discussed their options. Unlike the Western Front, where the trenches had not moved more than a few miles in either direction for more than a year, the battle lines of the Eastern Front had shifted dramatically over a huge area. By the end of 1915, the Germans and Austrians had reoccupied the territory they had earlier lost in Galicia and pushed the Russian forces eastward out of Russian Poland, so that the front now stretched from the city of Riga on the Baltic Sea south through the eastern edge of Russian Poland to the Romanian border (see Map 4.5). The Russian

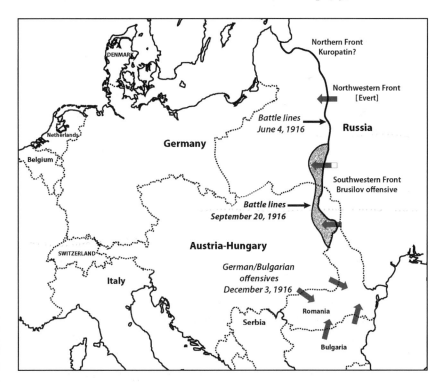

Map 4.5 The war in the east, 1916

commanders were particularly cool toward the idea of undertaking a major offensive action against the enemy. Their tactics of trying to establish "breakthroughs" in enemy lines using prolonged artillery bombardments and massed infantry units at the point of attack had proved singularly unsuccessful. The artillery attacks revealed the area that would be attacked, and that allowed the enemy to gather their forces to repulse the attacks. Moreover, artillery barrages turned "no-man's-land" into a morass of craters that reduced the mobility of the attacking infantry and prevented the artillery pieces from moving forward to provide continued support for the troops as they advanced. Finally, the need to make extensive preparations for large attacks in a concentrated area meant any element of surprise was out of the question.

Nevertheless, Mikhail Alekseyev, Chief of the General Staff, insisted that they must do something to help the French, who were pressing the Russians to take some immediate action that would lessen the pressure of the German assault on Verdun. Alekseyev pointed out that despite the setbacks of the previous campaigns, the Russians had managed to increase the size of their army by more than a million men, and they now held a significant numerical advantage over the combined Austrian and German forces. He suggested that they could undertake an offensive against the German troops in the northern sector of their front by the end of May. Generals Evert and Kuropatin, who commanded the armies in those sectors, demurred, insisting that their troops would not be ready for at least another two months. Urged on by their chief, the two commanders finally agreed to work on plans for such an offensive in the fall of 1916. At this point General Aleksei Brusilov, the commander of the Southwestern Front, spoke up and volunteered to launch a June offensive against the Austrians in the south. Such an action, he pointed out, would support the attacks of Evert and Kuropatin by forcing the Germans to move troops south to meet the threat. The immediate reaction to Brusilov's suggestion was stunned silence, but when he formally proposed it to Alekseyev two days later, the commanding general conditionally approved it with the clear understanding that Brusilov could expect no reinforcements. While most of the Russian generals doubted its chances of success, no one strongly opposed the proposal of a southern attack, which had the advantage that it would meet the Russian commitment to the French and British for an eastern offensive that would commence in early

June. The consensus was that Brusilov's attack would not amount to much, but there was no harm letting him go ahead with it so long as he did not need any additional resources. Brusilov himself was brimming with self-confidence. He assured Alekseyev that he already had sufficient troops and supplies at his disposal and he expected no reinforcements. As a measure of the lack of enthusiasm for Brusilov's proposal, Timothy Dowling reports that after the meeting a senior general asked Brusilov, "What made you expose yourself to such a danger? Had I been in your place I would have done anything in my power to avoid taking the offensive."[33]

In a war where it was rare to find a competent general, much less a brilliant one, Stavka had inadvertently selected one of the few truly outstanding field commanders in the Russian army to undertake a major offensive action that could materially change the situation on the Eastern Front. Brusilov was a cavalry officer who had served with considerable success during the Russian invasion of Galicia that had punished the Austrian forces in 1915. He had developed an approach to offensive operations that employed an artillery attack across a broad enough front that the enemy would not know where he intended to eventually concentrate the Russian infantry attack. Just a few hours prior to launching the infantry attack, a concentrated "lightning" artillery barrage at the point of attack would disrupt enemy positions and provide an opening for the infantry to pass through. An important key to his plans was to make sure that the artillery barrages were accurate – a skill that the Russians had exhibited in previous battles.

On June 4 Brusilov's forces attacked the Austrian forces near the city of Lusk on the northern end of his sector (see Map 4.5). The attack took the Austrians completely by surprise and the Russians managed to quickly open a 20-mile gap in the enemy lines. As planned, Brusilov's forces pressed their advantage and the Austrian forces fell back in disarray. An attack at the southern end of the front produced similar results. Within a few days the Habsburg army was on the verge of total collapse along the entire 150-mile front, and the Russians had advanced as far as 50 miles at some points. One of the more telling statistics of the battle was that more than 250,000 Habsburg troops surrendered in the face of the Russian advance. In desperation, the Austrian commander, Conrad von Hötzendorf, turned to the Germans for assistance, declaring that "the decision in the world war" hung in the balance. Falkenhayn, whose forces were already taxed to the limit fighting the French at Verdun and dealing with the British attack on the Somme, was appalled at the Austrian collapse, but he realized that the Germans could not afford to leave the Austrians to their fate. Troops and artillery from the Western Front were quickly put on trains and moved east in an effort to shore up his failing ally's resistance to the Russian attacks. German reinforcements were also dispatched from the northern sector of the Eastern Front, a situation made possible by the failure of Brusilov's colleagues to support his successes by vigorously attacking the Germans in the northern sector of the front.

By this time Alekseyev had become a believer in Brusilov's tactics and he supported efforts to sustain the Russian advances. However, the continued movement of German troops to the east and the replacement of Austrian officers with German commanders gradually turned the tide of battle back in favor of the Central Powers. Unfortunately, the other Russian commanders did not share Brusilov's audacity, and the cost of his success in terms of troops, horses, and supplies proved to be more than the Russian economy could sustain. A final drive by Brusilov's forces to capture the fortress at Lemberg resulted in a return to the tactics of mass attacks that had produced horrendous casualties earlier in the war. The German lines held, and on September 21 the Tsar asked Alekseyev to stop "our hopeless attacks." The Brusilov offensives had come to an end.

Shortly before Brusilov launched his offensive, Sergei Sazonov, the Russian foreign minister, had confidently predicted that "we have won the war, although the fighting will continue for several more years."[34] While Sazonov's confidence in a Russian triumph was not borne out by subsequent events, Brusilov's suggestion of a diversionary attack to support the Russian attacks to the north did produce the only significant victory for the Entente Powers in 1916. The Russians captured 15,000 square miles of territory, took 400,000 prisoners, and inflicted total casualties of more than 750,000 men on the Austrians and Germans. "The offensive," writes Michael Clodfelter,

> had forced the Austrians to halt their attacks against Italy, had weakened the German drive against Verdun by forcing Germany to transfer 18 divisions from the Western Front, and had come close to knocking Austria out of the war. The Habsburg Empire was nearly finished as a major military power and would become increasingly more dependent upon Germany's martial might.[35]

Brusilov's offensive marked the last major offensive action initiated against the Central Powers by Russian armies under the Tsarist regime.

The Romanian Fiasco

The Balkans had been the scene of almost continual conflict since the outbreak of the first Balkan War in the fall of 1912. Bulgaria had elected to join the Central Powers in September 1915 in the hope of regaining territories it had lost in the earlier wars. Its addition to the Central Powers guaranteed that there was a clear transportation route connecting the Austrians, Germans, and the Ottoman Empire. An unexpected consequence of the success of the Russian attack on Austria in the summer of 1916 was the entry of Romania into the war on the side of the Entente. Encouraged by the apparent collapse of the Austrians and the prospect of territorial gains promised by the French and the British, the Romanians signed a political and military alliance with the Entente Powers in Bucharest, and on August 27 they declared war against Austria. On paper, the addition of a half million Romanian troops encouraged the French and British generals to think that this could tip the balance of power on the Eastern Front in favor of the Entente.

In fact, Romania's entry into the war had exactly the opposite effect. The Romanians were ill-trained and totally unprepared to wage war. Norman Stone cites the comments of British observers who "felt that the operations of the Romanian army would make a public-school field-day look like the execution of the Schlieffen Plan; while the comments of Russians who had to fight side-by-side with the Romanians were often unprintable."[36] Although Britain and France had been eager to have Romania join the war, they could not offer any significant support to the Romanian war effort. Nor could the Russians, who were struggling to maintain their offensives against the Central Powers, and were not pleased by the prospect of sending troops to support a Romanian war against Austria. Even if they were willing to send aid, deficiencies in the transportation system would limit their ability to move large numbers of troops to support the Romanians. They eventually agreed to send a significant number of Russian troops to fight in the south when Bulgaria entered the war on the side of the

Central Powers; however, it took so long to organize and move the troops that they arrived too late to assist the Romanians.

The Germans were also taken by surprise by the Romanian decision to enter the war, but they quickly turned it to their advantage. Unlike the western powers, the Germans were in a position to quickly respond to the Romanian threat. Hindenburg and Ludendorff had been lobbying for some time that OHL should pay more attention to the east. Within a few weeks of Romania's declaration of war Ludendorff managed to assemble an army of 200,000 German and Bulgarian troops and move them by trains to Transylvania, where they were able to repulse the advance of Romanian troops. Erich von Falkenhayn was placed in command of the German and Austrian troops on the Romanian front, and by late November his forces were able to launch two major invasions into Romania: one from the south led by the German general August von Mackensen, and the other by Falkenhayn himself. Mackensen entered Bucharest on December 6 (see Map 4.5).

Though it did not produce any dramatic changes in the military capabilities of the two sides, the 1917 Romanian campaign was the beginning of a tipping point that would change the course of the war. The immediate effect was to give the Germans what Holger Herwig describes as the spoils of conquest: "more than two million tons of grain, 300,000 head of cattle, pigs, and goats, and 200,000 tons of timber."[37] While these supplies were welcomed by the occupying troops, a more significant result of the victorious campaign was its effect on the morale and confidence of the men at OHL. Coming on the failure of the Verdun campaign and the high cost of defending the Somme, the success in the east boosted the stature of the newly arrived team of Hindenburg and Ludendorff. As 1916 drew to a close, Ludendorff envisioned a grand strategy of German offensives in the east that could ultimately defeat Russia and set the stage for a final showdown in the west to win the war.[38]

The United States "Peace without Victory"

Watching all this from the sidelines was the most important neutral power, the United States of America. The Americans posed an interesting dilemma for both sides in the war. On the one hand, they were hardly prepared to engage in a major war several thousand miles from their shore. They had a formidable navy, but the armed forces of the United States totaled fewer than 180,000 men at the end of 1916, a total that would hardly make a difference on the Western Front. Even if they decided to enter the conflict and quickly mobilize their resources, it would take at least a year before American troops would be ready to fight. On the other hand, no one could ignore the fact that, whatever their level of preparedness, the United States was potentially the most powerful military force in the world.[39] Even if they did not actively enter the fray, the size of the American economy would play an important role in sustaining the war effort in Europe. Both the Central Powers and the Entente were acutely aware of this, and they therefore were careful not to push the United States into a position where it might enter the war on the other side.

President Woodrow Wilson had been narrowly reelected to a second term in November 1916, on a platform of keeping the United States out of the European war.[40] His hope was that the war had reached a point where the military stalemate in Europe had pushed both sides of the conflict to a point where they might be willing to accept a brokered peace. In an unusual personal appearance before the United States Senate on January 22, 1917, Wilson argued

> there must be a peace without victory ... Victory would mean peace forced upon the loser, a victor's terms imposed upon the vanquished. It would be accepted in humiliation, under duress, at an intolerable sacrifice, and would leave a sting, a resentment, a bitter memory upon which terms of peace would rest, not permanently, but only as upon quicksand. Only a peace between equals can last.[41]

Wilson's rhetoric was noble, but in Europe it fell on deaf ears. Given the huge expenditure of resources and lives already spent in seeking victory, none of the belligerents was likely to agree to forgo the possible fruits of that objective. Cynics could point out that Wilson's seemingly neutral objective of "no victory" would conveniently leave the United States alone at the top of the global power structure to dictate the terms of the peace that would govern the postwar world. Several weeks before his speech to the Senate Wilson had sent notes to the belligerents asking for a peace conference. "The Central Powers," he told Congress, were

> united in a reply which states merely that they were ready to meet their antagonists in conference to discuss terms of peace.

> The Entente powers have replied much more definitely and have stated, in general terms, indeed, but with sufficient definiteness to imply details, the arrangements, guarantees, and acts of reparation which they deem to be the indispensable conditions of a satisfactory settlement.[42]

Such enthusiasm in the response of the Entente Powers is understandable. The end of 1916 found them in the unenviable position of expending all of their available resources in a vain attempt to break the German lines. While they had every incentive to attend a conference to get Wilson's support for a negotiated peace, they had not spelled out what the terms of a satisfactory settlement would be. The lack of enthusiasm on the part of the Central Powers is equally understandable. Militarily, 1916 had ended rather well for the Germans, and the confidence of their new commanders-in-chief was rising. The Western Front had held firm. The Russians were in disarray along the Eastern Front, and facing increased political unrest at home. Hindenburg and Ludendorff had already developed a plan for an offensive in 1917 that would hopefully force Russia out of the war. Moreover, it was evident that if the United States was going to be drawn into the war, it would almost surely be on the side of the Entente Powers, and there was not a lot that the Germans could do about that. In his speech to the Senate Wilson made it clear that the United States would regard interruptions of trade as unacceptable. "The paths of the sea," he declared, "must alike in law and in fact be free by either side as unacceptable [sic]. The freedom of the seas is the sine qua non of peace, equality, and cooperation." Wilson had backed up his determination to keep sealanes open with a proposal for a program of naval expansion.[43]

The Statistics of Death

When the leaders of the Entente Powers gathered at Chantilly just before Christmas in 1915, they sketched out plans for three bold offensives that would strain the Central Powers to their breaking point. Yet, by the time Christmas of 1916 arrived there had been very little change in what John Keegan aptly terms "the face of battle." All along the Western Front there had been much fighting, and a great deal of digging, particularly on the German side. "The statistics of death," notes Martin Gilbert, were "being calculated by both sides, reaching unprecedented levels":

> In five months, more than twenty-three million shells were fired by the two contending armies at Verdun, on average more than a hundred shells a minute. Verdun itself remained in French hands, but the death toll there was 650,000 men. When added to that of the Somme, this made a five-month death toll of 960,459 men: almost a million. It was an average of more than 6,600 men killed every day, more than 277 every minute, nearly five men every second.
>
> On the Western Front, after all the savagery of the Somme and Verdun, 12.7 German divisions faced 106 French, 56 British, six Belgian and one Russian division: 169 divisions in all. The British Expeditionary Force, which in August 1914 had consisted of 160,000 men, was 1,591,745 strong by the end of 1916.
>
> The statistics of the confrontation reflected the intention, and the determination, of all the opposing armies to continue to fight.[44]

In the east the battles had covered more ground, but the end result was the same: a bloody stalemate that had shaken, but not yet broken, the will to continue the fight.

Yet amid all this slaughter and futility there were signs that things were changing. The strategic thinking of generals had not yet caught up with the changing technology of weapons and the ability to produce armaments far beyond the wildest dreams of military minds engaged in the arms races only a few decades earlier. But the generals on both sides were only gradually learning to appreciate how the power of new weapons was changing the battlefield. Artillery barrages for both offensive and defensive maneuvers became the key to any successful operation. One of the ironies of the fighting at Verdun was that Falkenhayn's idea of using artillery in the early stages of the battle to "bleed" the French army was later adopted by French artillery to do the same to the Germans in their counterattacks. The French artillery barrages against Fort Douaumont in December were so effective that the German troops abandoned the fort before advancing French troops arrived. The French also experimented with "creeping" artillery barrages that landed in no-man's-land just ahead of the advancing infantry.

Airplanes became a significant part of the battlefield as "eyes" for the artillery, and the Somme saw the first tactical use of tanks by the British. Pétain's efforts in operating the supply lines along the *Sacré Voie* at Verdun are celebrated as key to the French victory with their round-the-clock delivery of men, food, and munitions. Underlying that accomplishment was the ability of the home front to produce those supplies and transport them to the front. In early 1915 all the belligerents had faced serious shortages of shells and equipment for their military operations. A year later, the battlefields at Verdun and the Somme were littered with the debris from millions of artillery shells produced by the military-industrial plants in Germany, France, and Britain.

What had the high commands learned from all this? For the Entente the answer would appear to be "Not much." The French and the British generals were confidently planning for a resumption of offensive operations on the Western Front in 1917. They did so with the same approach that had failed over the first two years of the war and would produce new disasters that would further erode the confidence of both the people on the home front and the troops fighting in the trenches in 1917. The Germans were also making plans for 1917. The team of Hindenburg and Ludendorff had arrived from the Eastern Front to replace Erich von Falkenhayn as the head of OHL with a new approach to the conduct of the war. Schlieffen's vision of a quick defeat of France had not materialized, and Falkenhayn's scheme of bleeding the French to death had failed to end the stalemate on the Western Front. On the other hand, the stalemate could be interpreted as a German success in blunting the British and French offensives that had all been successfully turned back. Hindenburg and Ludendorff were confident that their success in the east offered an opportunity to win the war without a breakthrough in the west. In 1917 they proposed that the Germans should concentrate their efforts on the Eastern Front, where the Russian army appeared exhausted from the effort of the Brusilov offensives, and the Tsar's government was teetering on the verge of anarchy. Now was the time for a concerted effort on the part of the Central Powers to press the war in the east. If their effort to defeat the Russians worked, then the full weight of the German forces could be unleashed against the Entente armies on the Western Front.

While civilians talked of ending the war, the military chiefs on both sides saw 1917 as a chance to make one more try to end the stalemate. Robert Nivelle, the new French commander at Verdun, confidently assured his superiors that the tactics that had finally forced the Germans to ultimately abandon Fort Douaumont would produce even more spectacular results along the trenches northwest of Verdun, on a line known as the Chemin des Dames Ridge. Further north Douglas Haig, undaunted by the disaster of the Somme, was preparing a new set of offensive plans that would culminate in a final effort to pierce the German lines at Ypres. For the Germans, it was becoming increasingly evident that time was not on their side. If the United States decided to enter the war, the Central Powers would have to accomplish their aims before the Americans were able to mobilize their troops and get them to Europe. And while the military situation seemed to momentarily favor the Germans, the economic situation in Austria-Hungary and Germany was reaching a crisis level that threatened to undermine the ability of the Central Powers to carry on the war for another year.

Both sides hoped that 1917 would produce a tipping point in the war. Clausewitz would have warned them that you should be careful what you wish for.

5 ECONOMIES AT WAR

I can say without hesitation that, as circumstances are now, we
can force Britain to her knees within five months by means of
unrestricted U-boat Warfare.
                Admiral Henning von Holtzendorff (1916)

The war that had erupted in the summer of 1914 resembled a
massive earthquake that shook the economic and political foundations
of all the European countries, and the aftershocks quickly spread to
every part of the globe. We do not have anything like a Richter scale that
can measure the amplitude of such a quake, but data for Great Britain,
Germany, France, Austria-Hungary, Russia, and the United States allow
us to construct a set of statistical "economic snapshots" that provide a
rough indication of the economic displacements produced by the war.
These shocks not only affected the immediate welfare of the people in
each country in 1914, they set the stage for the enormous changes that
would follow. Nowhere was this more evident than in the economies
of the belligerent countries. The needs of the military suddenly became
the primary force driving economic decisions by governments. Warfare
could no longer be left to the generals and their military strategy and
tactics. Barbara Tuchman relates an incident early in the war when an
official presented Helmuth von Moltke with a memorandum dealing
with the need for an "economic general staff" to deal with problems
of supply. "Don't bother me with economics," snapped Moltke, "I am
busy conducting a war."[1] Several weeks later, the pressures of command
forced Moltke to resign as commander-in-chief of the German army.

His successors soon discovered that winning a war like this required an economic strategy as well as a bold military strategy.

The Shock of War

Despite all the planning and military preparation, none of the countries was prepared for the demands that the war would place on their economies in the first months of fighting. One of the first challenges was the impact that a sudden call up of reservists in the first months of the war had on the supply of labor – and the realization that many of the men might not return. Then came the realization that this was only the beginning of the military's demands for men. Table 5.1 shows the number of men available for military action on January 1, 1914 and the number who had been called up by the beginning of 1915. Putting all the various military plans into action in September of 1914 had involved sending 5 million men off to war. By the beginning of 1915 the total number of men serving in the armed forces of the belligerent powers had grown to more than 21 million – an increase of four and a half times in less than a year!

This massive transfer of men into the army created an immediate shortage of men in the labor force, and the shortage increased as time went on. Women stepped into some of the vacant jobs, but

Table 5.1 Military personnel of combatants, 1914–15 (thousands of men)

	January 1914	January 1915	Ratio of 1915/14
British Empire	532	4,350	8.18
France	789	4,997	6.33
Russia	1,321	5,500	4.16
Belgium	113	156	1.38
Total Entente Powers	2,755	15,003	5.45
Germany	862	3,813	4.42
Austria[a]	839	839	1.00
Ottoman Empire	249	790	3.17
Total Central Powers	1,950	5,442	2.79
Total	4,705	20,445	4.35

Note: [a] The estimates of military personnel for Austria-Hungary do not show the annual changes between 1914 and the end of the war.

Sources: COW Project data set; Component series for Military Personnel, version 4.0.

they could not immediately make up for the loss of labor – especially skilled labor. The impact of the labor shortage was not limited to industry. In a world where agriculture was still highly labor intensive and women already constituted a significant share of the farm labor force, the absence of men placed serious constraints on the production of agricultural output. The shortage of manpower in agriculture was compounded in the more developed economies by shortages of imported fertilizer. All of this created a crisis in the supply of food. Few people were starving. But a lot of people were hungry.

Historian Avner Offer presents an "agrarian interpretation" of the war which argues that:

> The First World War is often depicted as a great industrial war, fought by industrial methods. In fact, given a strong industrial capability on both sides, primary commodities were more decisive: food, industrial raw materials and that most primary of all commodities, people. Germany did not run out of rifles or shells. It suffered badly from shortages of food. Likewise the Allies: their agrarian resources decided the war. So not only a war of steel and gold, but a war of bread and potatoes.[2]

Another issue that every country had to deal with was the impact of the war on the international system of trade that linked the economies of the belligerents and of neutral countries. For some it was a matter of losing critical supplies of raw materials for their industrial systems; for others it was a matter of losing export markets for the goods churned out by their factories and farms. For almost everyone it was the challenge of replacing imported food supplies needed to feed their soldiers and their civilian populations. Unfortunately, it is extremely difficult to obtain reliable data on foreign trade during the war. The statistic that is most often used to measure trade is the total value of exports and imports. However, the high rates of inflation and price controls in all the countries make it difficult to infer the volume of trade from these series. There are, however, enough data for specific commodities to accept Findlay and O'Rourke's statement that "it is safe to conclude that the volume of trade fell sharply during the conflict, if by an unknown amount ... However, such aggregate effects mask a large range of individual country experience."[3]

Government Spending and the Inflation Tax

One of the most immediate challenges facing every economy was how to pay for the sudden shifts in demands created by the war. Public expenditures soared as governments scrambled to find revenues to pay troops and purchase supplies. The needs of the military created a level of government spending so large that the existing paradigms dealing with public finance no longer governed their fiscal policies. It soon became apparent that raising taxes to pay for the war was not a politically feasible solution to meet the enormous shortfall of revenues caused by the needs of the military. The problem was not only that taxes were unpopular; it was also that no one knew how much the war would cost. As the costs continued to rise, governments were forced to continually increase the tax rates to pay for the war. None of the major powers managed to cover more than a third of their expenditure deficits through tax revenues. One alternative was to simply print money that could be put in circulation to pay for purchases; another was to borrow the needed funds through the sale of bonds. Governments did both in abundance. Table 5.2 presents some summary data for government spending in Britain, France, Russia, Germany, and the Habsburg Empire from 1913 to the end of the fighting in 1918.

Deficit financing offered a solution to the immediate needs for cash to carry on the war; however, borrowing funds created other challenges for the treasuries. Printing money increased spending by producers, consumers, and government agencies and drove up prices throughout the economy in an inflationary spiral. Selling bonds had a more complex effect which involved persuading people to reduce their consumption expenditures by investing in government bonds, an action that would increase their savings without creating upward pressure on commodity prices. In this regard, the higher rates of inflation experienced by the Russian and Habsburg economies during the war reflected their inability to finance the deficit through bond sales rather than printing money. The "inflation tax" was their only option.

All of the belligerent countries experienced rates of inflation far above anything that had been seen in recent years. Simply put, price inflation was a hidden tax that meant that everyone – including the government – had to pay more each time they purchased the same "bundle of goods." Politically the inflation tax was a convenient fiscal tool for the wartime governments because it allowed the government

Table 5.2 Government outlays, deficits, and the money stock, five major powers, 1914–18

Country	1913	1914	1918	Total 1914–18
United Kingdom [million £]				
Government outlays	200	561	2,579	9,741
Deficit	34	334	1,690	6,860
Deficit as % outlays	–	60	66	70
Money stock index [1913=100]	100	108	190	
France [million francs]				
Government outlays	5,067	10,065	41,897	136,320
Deficit	34	5,516	34,276	108,819
Deficit as % outlays	0	55	82	80
Money stock index [1913=100]	100	404	172	
Russia [million rubles]				
Government outlays	3,383	4,858	40,706	105,975
Deficit	34	1,960	31,126	80,994
Deficit as % outlays	1	40	76	76
Money stock index [1914=100]	–	100	1,061	
Germany [million marks]				
Government outlays	–	2,532	13,147	38,863
Deficit	–	1,413	11,676	32,389
Deficit as % outlays	–	56	89	83
Money stock index [1913=100]	100	141	604	
Habsburg Empire [million crowns]				
Government outlays	3,469		22,169	–
Deficit	338	11,050	17,975	98,483
Deficit as % outlays	10	–	81	–
Money stock index [1914=100]	–	100	532	

Sources: *Money stock*: Stephen Broadberry and Mark Harrison, eds., *The Economics of World War I* (Cambridge University Press, 2005), Tables 2.16, 6.11, 7.4; Gatrell, *Russia's First World War: A Social and Economic History* (Harlow: Pearson, 2005), Table 7.2. *Government outlays and deficit*: Broadberry and Harrison, *The Economics of World War I*, Tables 2.14, 6.8, 7.7, 8.7.

to avoid having to maintain a cumbersome bureaucracy to collect the tax. As an economic policy it involved a risk that amounted to grabbing a tiger by the tail and hoping things would not get out of hand. Unfortunately, things did get out of hand. Consumers were not prepared for such a sudden shift to a world of rapidly rising prices after a long period of price stability stretching back to the middle of the nineteenth century.

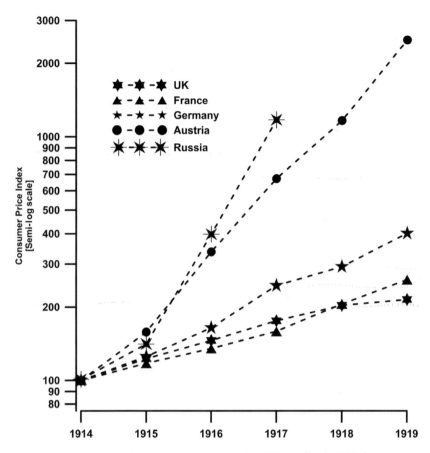

Figure 5.1 Consumer price indices in five major powers, 1914–21 (1914 = 100)
Sources: United Kingdom, France, Germany, Austria: Brian R. Mitchell, *European Historical Statistics, 1750–1993*. 4th edn (New York: Stockton Press, 1998), 866; Russia: Peter Gatrell, "Poor Russia, Poor Show: Mobilizing a Backward Economy," in Broadberry and Harrison, *The Economics of World War I*, 235–75, 270.

     Figure 5.1 traces the behavior of consumer prices in Great Britain, Germany, France, Austria, and Russia through the war years.[4] Table 5.3 presents annual rates of inflation in these countries and the USA over the same period. There are only six observations in the table that are not double-digit annual rates of inflation, and two of those are for the USA before it entered the war. By the end of 1917 inflation rates in Russia and Austria had reached a point where prices were more than doubling every year. In some countries a bundle of goods in 1918 could cost ten times what it had been four years earlier. For the Austrians and the Russians, the rate of inflation provides a vivid measure of the loss of confidence and economic collapse of governments which were

Table 5.3 Annual rates of inflation, 1914–19/20

	Great Britain	France	Germany	Austria	Russia	United States
1914/15	23	18	25	58	1	1
1915/16	19	15	31	113	40	8
1916/17	20	17	49	100	182	17
1917/18	16	30	20	73	147	18
1918/19	6	26	37	114	–	15
1919/20	16	16	146	16	–	16

Sources: European states: Mitchell, *European Historical Statistics*, 858–9. United States: Richard Sutch and Susan Carter, eds., *Historical Statistics of the United States: Earliest Times to the Present*, Millennial Edition, 5 vols. (Cambridge University Press, 2006), vol. III, Series Cc-1, p. 158.

unable to continue the war. The Germans managed to keep the inflationary pressures from exploding until the end of the war; however, with the collapse of the Kaiser's government in 1918, prices took off on a trajectory that mirrored the earlier path of hyperinflation in the defunct Habsburg and Romanov economies.

How much of this increase was due to the war? Measuring the impact of wartime spending is difficult because there are so many ways in which the military effort affected the activities of the government. Historian Gerd Hardach presents estimates of the inflationary impact of prices during the war by constructing counterfactual estimates of what "normal" peacetime government expenditures would have been and comparing those estimates with the actual wartime spending. The biggest problem in constructing such counterfactual estimates of war costs is defining which expenditures are "war related." Hardach finessed this problem by defining war expenditures as "the difference between total public expenditures and a notional 'peacetime' budget corresponding to public expenditure during the last year of peace." This method, he notes, "has the beauty of simplicity and recommends itself to anyone who ... wishes to establish comparisons and place a figure on the sum total of the world's wartime expenditure."[5] His estimates show that, without the expenses of a war, Britain, France, and Russia would have spent just over $20 billion. With the war, government outlays rose to just over $115 billion. Germany and Austria would have spent almost $9 billion if there had not been a war; with the war they spent about $70 billion. In other words, of the $185 billion that Hardach estimates were government outlays in these countries from

1914 to 1919, something on the order of $155 billion – or more than 80 percent of the total – can be attributed to the war. This is consistent with the numbers in Table 5.2. Even though these figures are little more than educated guesses, they provide us with an order of magnitude of the expansion and nature of government activity during the war that strongly supports the contention that the economic relationship between the private and public sector was dramatically altered in all the countries involved with the war. This change was an anomaly so large that it was no longer possible to use the existing paradigms of government spending to define what was "normal" after the war.[6]

Snapshots of Economies at War

No one had given a great deal of thought to the disruption that would be created by a prolonged conflict among all the powers in Europe. How government responded to the challenges outlined above would have a major influence on the outcome of the war. To illustrate the variety of responses from each country we have constructed "economic snapshots" that present various economic indices to measure the economic impact of the war on each of the major powers. The disruption created by the war makes it difficult to construct estimates of variables that are consistent across economies using definitions that were meant to reflect "normal times." The economic snapshots include indices that measure: gross domestic product (or national income); agricultural output – and where possible, food output; industrial output (or the fraction of GDP that reflects industrial production); the number of workers in the private sector labor force; and measures of imports and exports.

Germany

Figure 5.2 presents our economic snapshot for Germany. What is immediately striking is the enormous economic shock from the outbreak of war in 1914. By the end of 1915 gross domestic product had fallen to 80 percent of its 1913 level and the indices measuring industrial output and crop output suffered even larger declines. Germany's exports plummeted to a quarter of their prewar level, and imports declined by 40 percent. None of the variables shows any appreciable recovery over the course of the war. The picture presented in Figure 5.2

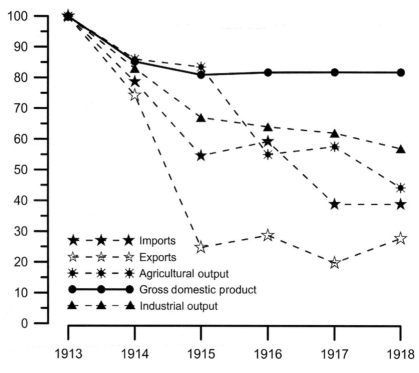

Figure 5.2 Economic indicators, Germany, 1913–18 (1913 = 100)

Source: Albrecht Ritschl, "The Pity of Peace: Germany's Economy at War, 1914–1918 and Beyond," in Broadberry and Harrison, *The Economics of World War I*, 71–6, Tables 2.2, 2.7, 2.14.

strongly reinforces Erich von Falkenhayn's pessimism at the end of 1914 regarding Germany's economic position during the war. Germany was a major player in the international marketplace. Its trade with the three Entente powers alone accounted for 31 percent of all exports and 27 percent of all imports over the period 1910–13. Northern Europe and the United States accounted for an additional 24 percent, and the Habsburg Empire for 10 percent of the total volume of trade.[7] The loss of some of these imports could be made up in the short term by redirecting import goods through Holland, Denmark, or Sweden; however, the closing of other international markets, whose volume of trade with Germany had plummeted to a quarter of the 1913 level by 1915, had more serious long-term effects. Without markets for their exports, the Germans had no way to pay for imports. Hardach points out that without the earnings from exports, "it appears that Germany had largely exhausted her credit facilities abroad." A significant portion of the German economy had simply disappeared with the coming of the war.

The second shock from the war was the withdrawal of labor that went into the armed forces. In 1913 the COW estimate for the number of military personnel in Germany was 860,000 men. By 1918 the Germans had ten times that number of men in their military.[8] While there is little reliable data on the civilian labor force for Germany during the war, it is clear that the mobilization of men into the army had a strong negative effect on the labor supply and this was a shortage that persisted throughout the war. Albrecht Ritschl presents data for the single years 1913 and 1918 showing that the number of males employed in German industry fell from 7.4 million to 5.8 million, a decline of 26 percent that was only partially offset by an increase in female employment from 1.6 million to 2.3 million.[9] The industrial labor force also suffered a significant shift of resources away from civilian industry – where employment fell by 40 percent over the course of the war – toward war-related production, where employment rose by 44 percent. These figures reveal an important element in the management of the German war economy. Priorities for producing goods and services strongly favored war materiel, not consumer goods. An indication of how severe the labor shortage had become by 1916 is that the Germans "contracted" to import foreign workers from occupied territories to work in both industry and agriculture. The experiment had only limited success; most of the workers were repatriated by mid-1917. Ritschl presents estimates for industrial employment for 1913 and 1918 showing that the Germans also employed large numbers of prisoners of war and workers both in Germany and in occupied countries.[10]

By 1918 the index of German industrial production had fallen to 57 percent of the 1913 level of employment, while the index of agricultural output had fallen to 44 percent of the prewar level. Both of these indices suggest that the declines in output were significantly greater than the shortfall in labor supply. Ritschl argues that for the German economy as a whole, "productivity per person employed seems to have fallen between 20 and 30 percent."[11] A look at the indices of industrial output and employment reveals that by shifting labor and other resources to war industries, the Germans managed to maintain their military forces in the field, but they did so at the expense of the provision of consumption goods for the rest of the population back home. Data on industrial output shows that war-related industries actually increased after 1915 to a level 10 percent above the 1913 level, while civilian industrial output continued to decline to a low of 41 percent of the 1913 level by the end of the war.

All of these numbers point to significant shortcomings in the efforts by German industry to meet the demands of the civilian population during the war. Perhaps the strongest indictment of Germany's inability to support the war effort was the collapse of the agricultural sector. Part of the problem was that Germany was heavily dependent on imports for a significant share of its food products. Avner Offer claims that 19 percent of the calories consumed by Germans came from abroad.[12] The shortage of food was exacerbated by the extent to which Germans had a strong preference to eat meat and animal products, which are an expensive way to get calories. These difficulties could have been diminished if German agriculture had been able to increase domestic agricultural output. That, unfortunately, was not the case. Although German industry ranked among the most advanced and efficient economies throughout the world in 1914, German agriculture relied on backward technology that was very labor intensive and depended on a heavy dose of imported nitrate fertilizers. These are unfortunate characteristics at a time when labor is suddenly in short supply and the supply of fertilizer is through imports that have been curtailed by the Entente blockade of German shipping.[13] By the winter of 1916, when bad weather severely diminished crop output throughout Europe, Germans were struggling to find enough food to eat, and they were forced to eat foods they once ignored. The result was not widespread starvation, but the food problem produced a growing opposition to the war on the home front.

Germany's difficulties in the international marketplace for food underscored a larger economic problem facing the Central Powers. Even if there had been no blockade by the Entente Powers, Germany and Austria-Hungary lacked access to the resources provided by "empires" that were available to Britain and France. As Jay Winter and Antoine Prost point out, "In going to war against the British Empire, Germany lost the war on its very first day. Germany fought the war to gain an empire, but she needed an empire to win the war."[14]

The Habsburg Empire

If the economic situation facing the German Empire seemed bleak, the situation of the Habsburg Empire was far worse.

Austria-Hungary might have started this war, but it was in no condition to finish it. The Empire's inability to deal with the military challenge has already been documented in our account of the 1915 Galicia campaign in Chapter 4. Figure 5.3 presents our economic snapshot for the Habsburg Empire. Simply put, the economy suffered a debilitating blow at the outset of the war from which it never recovered. Things proceeded to go from bad to worse. The decline in the civilian labor force was particularly pronounced. The number of males in the labor force fell to just over 50 percent of the 1913 level by the end of 1917. One statistic that is not directly evident in the snapshot was the declining war effort on the part of the central government. While the Germans and all the Entente Powers devoted an increasing share of their GDP to war

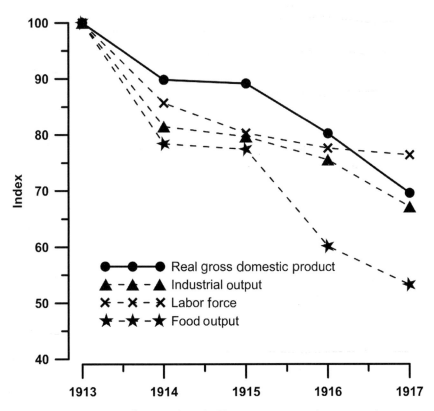

Figure 5.3 Economic indicators, Austria-Hungary, 1913–17 (1913 = 100)
Source: Max-Stephan Schulze, "Austria-Hungary's Economy in World War I," in Broadberry and Harrison, *The Economics of World War I*, 77–111, Tables 3.6, 3.10, 3.11.

expenditures that reached a peak of 59 percent in 1917, the fraction of government spending devoted to the war in Austria peaked at 30 percent in 1914/15 and had declined to 17 percent over the course of the war. Historian Max-Stephan Schulze, bluntly summarized the situation:

> To the extent that Austria-Hungary did fight this war on the cheap, that was not an outcome of choice, but of necessity in light of inadequate resources. Finally, the persistent and widespread food scarcity and resultant physical exhaustion of both the civilian population and the armed forces was a key factor in bringing about the collapse of the Habsburg Empire.[15]

While the economic effort of the Habsburg Empire would appear to have been an exercise in futility, one should not forget that the Austrian military effort, while it failed to live up to the expectations of its German ally, was nonetheless a considerable effort in terms of the number of men fighting and the level of casualties suffered in battles. In the first four months of fighting Russia, Serbia, and Italy, the Austrians suffered more than 1 million deaths, 1.8 million men wounded, and more than 1.5 million soldiers taken prisoner. The Germans may have felt at times that they were "shackled to a corpse," but the corpse played an important part in sustaining the war effort on the Eastern Front.

France

The French economy suffered the greatest initial shock from the war among the Entente states because of the loss of territory in northern France that was occupied by the Germans after the First Battle of the Marne. "The invasion affected all dimensions of the economy," writes historian Pierre-Cyrille Hautcoeur, "the production and supply of various goods, government resources, capital availability for investment, [and] transportation networks ... In the short run, the economic effect on the war effort was high, since the ten *departements* (out of a total of 87) that were occupied stopped producing for (and paying taxes to) France."[16] Gerd Hardach reinforces this view with estimates that the occupied territory accounted for 10 percent of the antebellum French population and 14 percent of the industrial workers in France. It also contained 64 percent of French pig iron production, 58 percent of steel production, and 40 percent of the coal mined before the war.[17]

Figure 5.4 presents our economic snapshot for the French economy. The effects of losing the territory in the north to the invasion are clearly evident, along with the loss of labor from mobilization and a sharp fall in exports. Real GDP and the production indices for industry and agriculture both drop sharply for 1913/14, and they do not show any marked recovery in the next two years. The French economy never recovered from the initial shock.

There is, however, one very important difference between the situation of the French and the Central Power economies. While the loss of export markets crippled the German effort to finance imports, the French were able to almost double their imports by 1917. They could do this because Britain and the United States were both willing to finance a French trade deficit that soared from 1.5 billion francs in 1913 to more than 20 billion francs in 1917. Imports from Great Britain and the United States increased from just under a quarter of all imports to a peak of 60 percent by 1918. What made this financing possible was government arrangements that allowed the Banque de France to abandon the rules of the gold standard and manage the exchange rate of the franc. In April 1915, the British and French governments signed an agreement guaranteeing the "financial solidarity" of the two governments to support a loan of £60 million. This became the basis for both governments to borrow funds to spend in the American market. The French trade deficit rose from an index of 100 in 1913 to a level of 532 in 1917.[18] Imports of foodstuffs alleviated to some extent the loss of food production that resulted from a pronounced decline in French crop production; imports of food were particularly helpful in dealing with the 1917 crop disaster. By this time France was importing more than 600,000 tons of food a month, including 275,000 tons of wheat. These imports were not sufficient to eliminate shortages; food prices rose and rationing for bread was instituted in 1917–18.[19] The French did not, however, experience a decline in food supplies anywhere near as severe as the situation in Germany or Austria-Hungary.

The supply of civilian labor was drastically reduced by the need for soldiers. From a level of just under 800,000 men in the fall of 1914 French armed forces had grown to 5 million men by the end of the year, a number that would remain fairly constant throughout the war (see Table 5.1). For a country that already had the highest fraction of its population in the armed services at the outbreak of the war, the conscription of an additional 4.2 million men was a sizeable

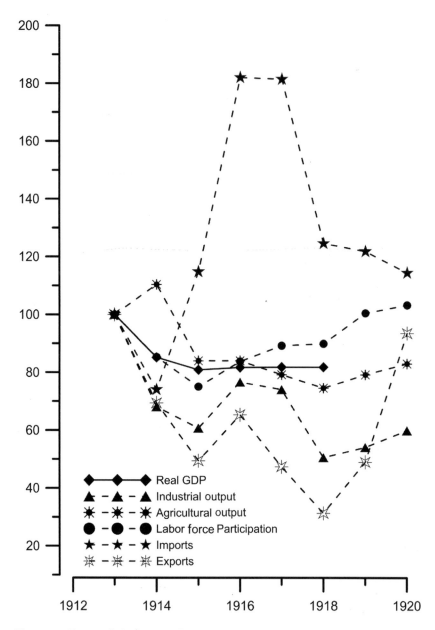

Figure 5.4 Economic indicators, France, 1914–20 (1913 = 100)

Source: Pierre-Cyrille Hautcoeur, "Was the Great War a Watershed? The Economics of World War I in France," in Broadberry and Harrison, *The Economics of World War I*, 169–205, Tables 6.1, 6.15.

jolt to the labor market. With the additional impact of labor lost from the German occupation of northern France, the private labor force by the end of 1915 had been reduced by one-fourth. The largest part of this decline in available labor occurred in non-defense-related private industry – employment in the consumption goods and construction trades – where employment fell by 40 percent or more by the end of 1915. The one sector that showed a significant rise in the private sector and output was "investment goods" – which included munitions. In itself, this was a notable achievement – an indication that the private sector was responding to the needs of the military effort.

All three of the economic snapshots presented thus far have portrayed countries under such extreme stress that they were never able to regain even a semblance of their prewar economic position. For Germany and Austria-Hungary, it is a statistical map of their eventual defeat in the war. For the French, the assistance of their allies allowed them to weather the storm, but just barely. All three of these economies had been driven toward the edge of collapse by the middle of 1917. The economic struggles on the home front were mirrored by the military efforts in the trenches. The French military effort virtually collapsed during the army mutinies of mid-1917, and they were never able to recover their *élan*. Both the Austrian and German armies had reached the limits of their endurance by the middle of 1918. Economics had become a controlling factor in the ability of these countries to wage war.

Great Britain

Our economic snapshot of the British economy during the war (Figure 5.5) presents a very different picture. The initial shock of the war on the British economy was nowhere near as drastic as it was for the continental powers. Real GDP rose slightly during the first two years of the war, and then evened out for the next three years at a level about 13 percent above that of 1913. The only variable that shows a large decline at the outset of fighting is the index for exports, which fell by 20 percent by the end of 1914 and an additional 10 percent in 1915. A significant portion of this decline reflects Britain's lost trade with Germany, which had accounted for about 14 percent of all British exports before the war.[20] By 1916 the level of exports was very nearly back to its 1913 level. However, imports tell a very different story.

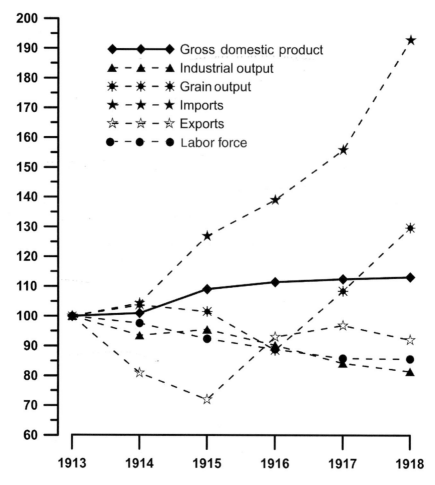

Figure 5.5 Economic indicators, United Kingdom, 1913–18 (1913 = 100)
Source: Broadberry and Harrison, *The Economics of World War I*. Stephen Broadberry, Stephen and Peter Howlett, "The United Kingdom During World War I: Business as Usual?" in Broadberry and Harrison, *The Economics of World War I*, 206–34, Tables 7.1, 7.2; Mitchell, *European Historical Statistics*, 311.

The British quickly turned to the global marketplace to supply their war effort. The annual level of imports nearly doubled over the course of the war. By far the largest increase was in imports from the United States. The increased volume of wartime trade – much of it carried on British vessels – produced a large inflow of income from shipping and insurance. These so-called "invisible" items on the external accounts covered roughly half the growing merchandise trade deficit. The British, like the French, were able to pay for a major part of their import needs through the financial largesse of the American capital markets, where they financed 75 percent of the £1.4 million they borrowed in foreign loans. However, unlike the French, the British were able to offset some of the burden from this debt by lending £1.7 million to their Allies.[21]

The British also managed to escape the initial shock from men leaving the labor force to enter the army. Their contribution to the war in 1914 was limited to the existing "expeditionary force" of 160,000 men. That situation did not last for long. By the end of 1915 the army had increased to 4.4 million men, thanks to Lord Kitchener's efforts in recruiting "New Armies" to fight in France (see Table 5.1). Women also helped fill the gap in the domestic labor force as female employment rose from 3.3 to 4.9 million, many of whom were employed in the armaments industries. Consequently, the private labor force was back to its prewar level by 1918. However, the aggregate figures mask a serious shortage of skilled labor, a problem that was more severe in Britain than other industrial countries, and the British also appear to have suffered from a greater number of hours lost through strikes by workers.

An area where the British fared significantly better than most of the other European war economies was the provision of foodstuffs for the civilian population. British agriculture was able to increase crop production at home by devoting more land to cereals. The result was that the output of cereal crops in 1918 was 23 percent above the 1913 level. This increase in home production greatly lessened the effects of a significant decline in food imports, particularly after 1916. There were no bread riots, although as Gerd Hardach notes, "the public was becoming increasingly discontented over rising prices."[22]

The British success in meeting the shock of war reflects the advantages of being one of the most developed economies of the day and having the financial center of a vast empire located in London. Even so, the costs of the war to the British were high. Their success was not so much that they kept the costs of waging war down as that they were able to use their financial markets to defer the costs until after the war.

Russia

Our economic snapshot of the British economy showed the advantages of wealth in withstanding the initial shock of war. At the other end of the spectrum was the Russian Empire, whose economy had experienced a considerable spurt of growth in the two decades before the outbreak of war, but still lagged far behind the other European powers and the United States in terms of most measures of economic performance. By 1914 the industrial sector had made impressive gains, and agricultural output had expanded to the point where Russia had become the major exporter of grains to Germany, Austria-Hungary, and eastern Europe.[23] This allowed the Tsar to reequip his military forces after the fiasco of the war with Japan, and improve the transportation network in the western part of his empire. In fact, of all the major European powers, the Russians were in the best position to absorb the shock of the outbreak of a major war in 1914. They had a large stockpile of munitions; they had a huge pool of men to recruit for their armies; and they did not face an immediate crisis of food.

In terms of immediate effects of the war our economic snapshot for the Russian economy, which is presented in Figure 5.6, provides some support for the impression that the Russian economy came through the initial impact of fighting rather well. Aggregate national income fell by only about 5 percent during the final months of 1914, and remained at that level through 1916.[24] There was a marked increase in the index of industrial production which reflects a strong response to demands from the military. Moreover, in sharp contrast to the experience of acute labor shortages in the other belligerent economies, the index measuring the number of people in the industrial labor force actually rose substantially in 1914/15. This appears to be the result of a migration of underemployed labor from farms to industry thanks to the expansion of military production. Perhaps the most surprising result shown in the snapshot is a sharp rise in agricultural income, which Peter Gatrell attributes to the possibility that rural consumption actually increased markedly until 1916 – a phenomenon that he attributes to the ability of peasants to sell food to the army. "Peasant incomes," he notes, "may have enjoyed a nominal increase of around 85 percent in their disposable income as against 1913."[25]

What this means is that during the first year of the war, Russia was actually experiencing a minor economic boom created by the needs of a war; something that none of the other belligerent countries experienced. This situation changed dramatically in 1916 as the German armies overran Galicia and Russian Poland. In addition to the loss of territory and economic activity, the German invasion created a huge flow of refugees fleeing east to escape the German occupation. By the end of 1916 the Russian economy faced some very difficult

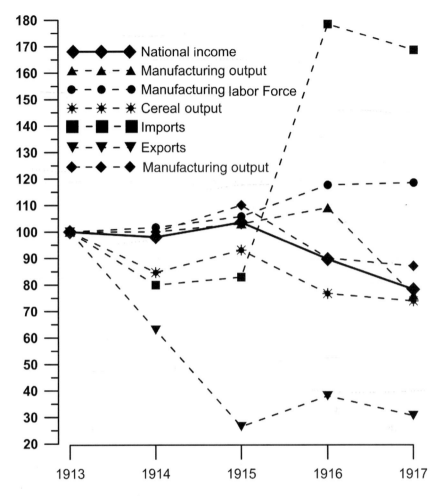

Figure 5.6 Economic indicators, Russia, 1914–17 (1913 = 100)
Source: Gatrell, "Poor Russia, Poor Show," Tables 8.3, 8.4, 8.5, 8.13, 8.16, 8.18.

problems which had been hidden by the sheer size of the Russian Empire and the cushion of food production that they had in 1914. While the huge manpower needs of the military did not create serious problems for the industrial sector in 1914/15, the continued drain of manpower into the army eventually led to labor shortages similar to those that characterized the other belligerents. Hardach estimates that military mobilization, which took 15 percent of able-bodied men in 1914, had risen to 36 percent per year by 1916. The impact of this loss of labor was masked by the rural unemployment on the eve of the war, but by 1916 the calls of the military began to particularly affect supply of labor on the large estates, which relied on hired labor more did than the family farms.[26] Gatrell places the overall number of military personnel through April of 1917 at 18.4 million, which represented 50.7 percent of males 18 to 60 years old in rural areas, and 24 percent of urban males that age.[27] The labor market was thrown further into disequilibrium by the huge flow of refugees and displaced persons that continued to grow every year.

An even larger problem was created by inefficiencies in the transportation and distribution system. Because of the prewar food surplus that was no longer exported, there was always more than enough food being produced each year to feed everyone. The problem was that the food was not reaching the towns, partly because the transportation system was so inefficient, but also because of the increasing reluctance of peasants to offer their crops for sale. As Hardach notes, "the peasants could obtain only a few industrial products at exorbitant prices and of indifferent quality at that, a better alternative seemed to be to consume more and more of their own produce."[28] William McNeill presents estimates showing that in 1917 only 15 percent of the crop harvest was brought to market, as compared with 25 percent of the 1913 harvest.[29] By the end of 1916 the Russian Empire was reaching the limit of its ability to mobilize sufficient economic and military resources in a manner that would allow it to carry on the war. This failure was not due to an absence of resources; it reflected the inability of institutional arrangements to organize those resources into a viable social and economic system. Gatrell points out that "growing economic prosperity before the war did not translate into social stability and political harmony. Longstanding peasant and working-class grievances remained acute, and divisions between the state and educated society would bedevil attempts to forge national unity in wartime."[30]

The United States

Our final economic snapshot is Figure 5.7, which shows the economic situation of the United States. The Americans did not enter the war as a belligerent until April 1917, and their troops did not engage German forces on the Western Front in any significant numbers until May of 1918. As a neutral country that was in a position to provide supplies and capital to the belligerents, the initial effect of the war was largely positive, and the American economy was large enough to absorb

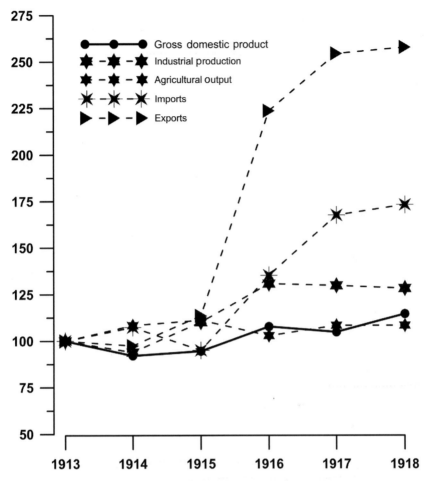

Figure 5.7 Economic indicators, the United States, 1913–18 (1913 = 100)

Source: Broadberry and Harrison, *The Economics of World War I*; Sutch and Carter, *Historical Statistics of the United States*, vol. IV, 652, Series Dd495; vol. V, 501, Series Ee362.

the economic effects of fighting in Europe throughout the war. Between 1913 and 1918 there was only a modest increase in industrial or agricultural production that produced an increase in GDP that economic historians have characterized as a "low growth economy."[31] There was, of course, an immediate demand for men to join the military forces once the Americans joined the war. With no need for a standing army, the United States had not bothered to construct the industrial facilities to produce armaments that were typical of the European countries in the years of the arms race before the outbreak of war. As Hugh Rockoff notes in his summary of the American war effort, "Our Allies produced most of the artillery used by American forces in France. Less than a quarter of the aircraft used by American pilots at the front were of American manufacture."[32]

The absence of American forces from the battlefield does not mean that the United States played no role in the war before 1917. The economic presence of the world's largest economy exerted a significant factor that both sides of the conflict had to consider from the beginning of the war. While President Wilson showed no enthusiasm for getting the United States involved in the bloody fighting on the Western Front, he was determined to protect a principle of "freedom of the seas" that would enable neutral countries to carry on worldwide commerce. While the American public may have been reluctant to participate in the fighting, they had no qualms about trading with the Europeans and lending them huge sums of money to pay for supplies of all sorts. Not surprisingly, the two variables in Figure 5.7 that show a significant change in terms of level of economic activity for the United States are imports and exports, which record dramatic increases. So long as someone was willing to pay, there was a steady flow of supplies across the Atlantic to Europe. This produced a situation where the economic activities of a "neutral" United States greatly favored Entente Powers, which had access to American ports and could obtain credit from capital markets to pay for the flow of exports. Though some American goods reached Germany through Holland, by 1917 this flow of goods had been greatly reduced. Adam Tooze presents figures showing that by 1916 the rest of the world was supplying 67 percent of the grain and 94 percent of the oil needs of Britain using credit extended from the United States.[33] The tensions between the American efforts to maintain freedom of the seas and German efforts to cut off the flow of goods to the Entente Powers played a central role in the eventual decision by the Americans to enter the war on the side of the Entente Powers.

Mobilizing for War

By the end of 1916 leaders were coming to the realization that this war was not following the usual paradigms of a quick, albeit bloody, war. Battles did not produce "victories" that led to the end of the war and the economic preparations for a longer war were proving to be woefully inadequate. Our economic snapshots of the economies of the six major powers reveal just how unprepared these economies were for a prolonged conflict. The scramble to mobilize men and resources produced an immediate expansion in the economic role of government. Figure 5.8 documents the speed and size of this increase in government spending for Germany, France, and Britain. In all three countries, government spending had accounted for less than 10 percent of national income in 1913. By the end of 1915 that fraction had risen to one third of national income in Great Britain and more than 45 percent in France and Germany.

This shift to a more controlled economy illustrates the different situations that existed in each country. The need to transfer such a large fraction of output to military objectives is a measure of the strain the war effort placed on production of goods and services for domestic consumption. All measures of economic activity in the German economy had declined dramatically by 1917. The steady increase in the government's share of national income meant that there was a steady decrease in goods and services for home consumption. If Germans on the home front were suffering from the demands of the war, their Austrian allies were experiencing a far worse situation. The less developed economy of the Habsburg Empire lacked the market organization required to direct production to meet the needs of both military and private consumption. After a vigorous response to mobilization at the outset of the war, the Austrians found it difficult to maintain their effort as the fighting wore on and economic production at home steadily collapsed. The British had a more modern agriculture that could feed their troops and still provide for food consumption in the private sector, while German troops could only be supplied at the expense of less food and fewer consumer goods for the home front.

A variety of arrangements were employed to accomplish this transformation in each country. The "war economies" in Britain, Germany, and France all relied on private production, but market-based decisions were complemented with government controls based on the needs of the war. The industrial economies left most of the production decisions in key areas such as raw materials and armaments in the hands of relatively small groups of people; however, the presence of well-developed markets was a key element in the economic mobilization. William McNeill argues that the belligerents actually did a reasonable

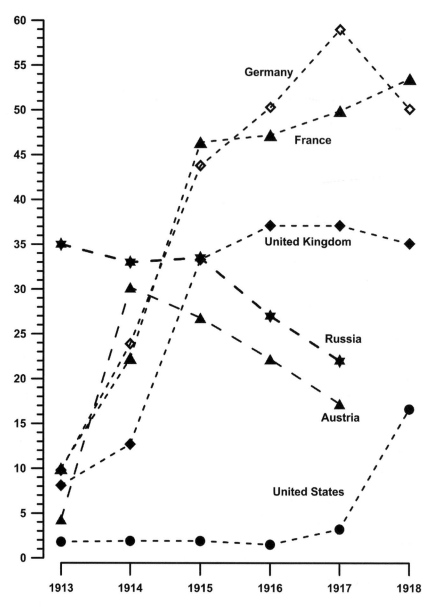

Figure 5.8 Government spending as a percentage of national income, six major powers, 1913–18

Source: Broadberry and Harrison, *The Economics of World War I*, 15, Table 1.5.

job under the circumstances. "Such a judgment," he concedes "would have seemed absurd" to contemporary observers during and right after the war – most of whom thought that the efforts to coordinate wartime production was haphazard at best. However, he argues that "in view of the global propagation of managed economies in the second half of the twentieth century, this is likely to seem the major historical significance of World War I in time to come."[34]

The War at Sea

All the industrial countries took advantage of the gains from specialization that came with the emergence of a global economy. The most important avenues of international trade were the oceans and waterways of the world. Strategists in all countries recognized that control of trade routes could provide a means of "starving" their opponents into submission. Establishment of a naval blockade against the enemy became a primary objective for the two largest navies in the world in 1914.

The idea of closing enemy ports with a naval blockade was hardly new in 1914. The British had instituted a naval blockade against France during the Napoleonic wars, and Napoleon had retaliated with the imposition of a "Continental System" of embargoes that closed European ports to British trade. The United States blockaded Confederate ports during the American Civil War as part of the "Anaconda Plan" to isolate the rebels from all external commerce. These experiences revealed the power of blockades, but they also revealed the difficulties posed by interfering with the rights of non-belligerent "neutral" countries whose trade was disrupted by the closing of international ports. Attempts to limit the trade of countries not involved with the conflict created major issues between neutrals and the blockading power. British efforts to block American trade with France was a major factor leading to the war of 1812 between Britain and the United States, and the Union blockade of the Confederacy in the American Civil War produced several diplomatic crises involving the British and the Union government.[35] Maintaining an effective naval blockade was not an easy assignment. It required not only the military ability to restrict entry or exit by ships from enemy ports; it also required diplomatic dexterity in dealing with the problems posed by "collateral damage" to neutrals who objected to the interference with trade.

The German High Command assumed that the British would establish a "close blockade" that would require ships to be stationed near the major German ports on the North Sea. However, the British quickly realized that the only way German ships could reach the Atlantic was either through the narrow opening of the English Channel or through the northern exit between Scotland and Norway. They therefore elected to set up a "distant" blockade by stationing ships to block the western end of the English Channel, and had their largest naval base at Scapa Flow in the Orkney Islands. From there they could intercept any German warships that might venture into the North Sea and they could effectively patrol the North Sea for contraband goods heading to Germany. This strategy not only provided an effective way of denying access to German harbors; it also meant that Admiral Tirpitz's "risk theory" was effectively checked. With the British fleet concentrated at Scapa Flow, there was no opportunity for the German High Seas Fleet to muster a sufficient advantage to harass blockading British squadrons or engage only a portion of the British fleet.

Blocking access to the Atlantic Ocean closed down the use of German merchant ships in the North Sea; however, the neutral countries on Germany's northern borders – Holland, Norway, Denmark, and Sweden – were still free to trade with Germany. Lance Davis and Stanley Engerman point out that,

> for Germany's Scandinavian neighbors, it appears that the blockade tightened, but only gradually. In all three countries, the 1918 exports to Germany still exceeded the prewar average. In the case of the Netherlands, the blockade appears to have been somewhat more effective; but a part of the reduction can almost certainly be attributed to the general breakdown of international trade.[36]

Jutland: The Battle of the Dreadnoughts

It gradually become apparent to the German Admiralty that the British "distant" blockade, while not perfect, was having a perceptible impact on the availability of important products that were needed both for the war effort and to feed the German population. The British saw no reason for the Royal Navy to present the High Seas Fleet with an opportunity to engage in the pitched battle that Tirpitz sought. The Germans therefore decided to take the initiative by challenging the British fleet in the hope of opening up access to the Atlantic through the North Sea. After several minor engagements in 1915 and early 1916 which were inconclusive, the High Seas Fleet put to sea in force on May 31, 1916, sailing north along the coast of Denmark under the command of Admirals Reinhard Scheer and Franz von Hipper. The intent was to lure portions of the British fleet into an action that would allow the Germans to engage the enemy piecemeal, without provoking a general engagement.

The German admirals got more than they bargained for. Alerted by the interception of German codes, the British Grand Fleet quickly reacted to the German sortie by dispatching three squadrons of ships to engage the High Seas Fleet. The two fleets collided off the coast of Denmark at Jutland, which resulted in the first – and only – great sea battle between the "capital ships" that were the pride of navies around the world. A total of 250 ships were involved in the Battle of Jutland: 151 in the British fleet and 99 in the German fleet. The Germans claimed victory because their ships performed very well and sank or damaged more capital ships than their foes; the British were content to point out that the Germans were eventually forced into a hurried withdrawal to escape a potentially disastrous duel with the heavier guns of the British battleships.[37] Though they lost more capital ships, hindsight suggests that it was the British – who had more ships to begin with – who clearly emerged the victors from this encounter. Shortly after the British battle cruisers got back to Scapa Flow, Admiral Jellicoe reported that his ships were ready to return to action on four hours' notice. The German outlook was less optimistic. In early July Admiral Scheer sent a report to the Kaiser that "the High Seas Fleet will be ready in the middle of August for further strikes against the enemy." Those strikes never came. Jutland effectively put an end to "risk theory." Germany, as John Keegan points out, "had built a navy for battle. In the only engagement fought by its united strength it had undergone an experience its leaders did not choose to repeat."[38]

Unrestricted U-boats

While the High Seas Fleet remained safely anchored at Wilhelmshaven for the remainder of the war, the German High Command turned their attention to the problem of how to set up their own blockade around the British Isles. There was no way for them to set up an effective "distant" blockade that would cut off commerce to Britain, and the presence of the Royal Navy ruled out any hope of a "close" blockade. One possibility was the use of commerce raiders – fast lightly armed cruisers that could sink or capture merchant ships – which had been a part of warfare at sea for years, and experience had shown that raiders could indeed disrupt trade. However, the Germans lacked logistical bases away from home that could keep their marauding cruisers supplied at sea, and if the raiders put into port they were vulnerable to attack or being bottled up by a blockading squadron of enemy cruisers. Commerce raiders could harass merchant ships trying to trade with the British, but their activities would not amount to an effective "blockade."

There was, however, a new and relatively untried naval weapon that navies had been experimenting with in the years leading up to the war: the submarine. By 1914 every navy had a small complement of submarines. They were still in an early stage of development, and no one had yet developed a plan of how to use them. A series of incidents shortly after the start of the war called attention to the possibilities opened by the development of this new weapon. Early in September 1914, a German U-boat sank the British cruiser *Pathfinder* in the North Sea with a loss of 259 lives. Two weeks later, a U-boat sank three more British warships off the coast of Holland with a loss of 1,459 lives. Both actions involved surprise attacks on the part of the U-boats, and the ease with which the warships were sunk startled civilian and military leaders in both countries. Otto Weddigen, the commander of the initial U-boat encounter, sank another British cruiser a month later and became an instant hero in Germany. He was awarded the Iron Cross for his efforts.[39] The potential threat that U-boat attacks posed to surface vessels of all kinds was now clear to everyone. In December 1914, Alfred von Tirpitz was asked by a newspaper reporter whether Germany would use U-boats to blockade Britain. "If pressed to the utmost, why not?," replied Tirpitz. "England wants to starve us into submission; we can play the same game, blockade England and destroy each and every ship that tries to run the blockade."[40]

Despite his enthusiastic response to the reporter's question, Tirpitz was initially rather cool to the idea of immediately setting up a U-boat blockade. The submarine was still an untested weapon, and Tirpitz believed that Germany did not have enough U-boats ready for action. However, other officers of the German navy were more enthusiastic. They insisted that the U-boats offered the only realistic way for the Germans to interfere with British trade. The success of U-boat commanders during the last four months of 1914, when German submarines sank a total of 252,000 gross tons of British merchant shipping with an average of only four submarines at sea each day, offered enough promise to eventually persuade Tirpitz and the Kaiser that an expanded campaign might cripple the British economy.[41] On February 4, 1915, the German government issued a declaration that "the waters around Great Britain and Ireland, including the English Channel, are hereby proclaimed a war region. Every enemy merchant vessel found in this region will be destroyed, without it always being possible to warn the crews or passengers of the dangers threatening." The notice went on to state that "Neutral ships will also be exposed to danger in the war zone, as … it is impossible to avoid attacks being made on neutral ships in mistake for those of the enemy."[42]

Figure 5.9 presents estimates of the tonnage of merchant vessels sunk by U-boats from August 1914 through November 1918. After a sharp rise in the number of ships sunk during the first half of

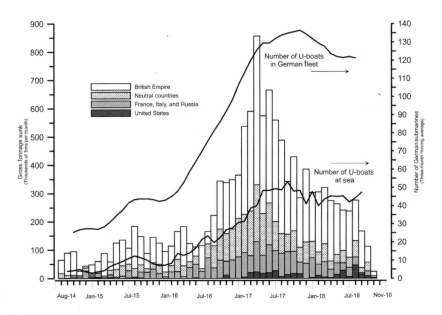

Figure 5.9 Gross tonnage of ships sunk by German U-boats, 1914–18

Source: Lance E. Davis and Stanley L. Engerman, *Naval Blockades in Peace and War* (Cambridge University Press, 2006), 182–3, 5.12.

1915, the tonnage lost each month remained about the same for the rest of the year. Admiral Tirpitz's pessimism that the use of submarines might be premature proved to be well-founded. Germany had twenty-seven U-boats available for action in February 1915; however, only four were likely to be at sea on any given day. Despite a steady growth in size of the U-boat fleet, the German navy was never able to consistently keep more than 30 percent of its boats at sea. Most observers agree with Gerd Hardach's observation that the unrestricted U-boat policy in 1915 was a "resounding failure ... [T]he expectations that Britain's economy would be grievously damaged proved illusory."[43] That said, the effort did provide valuable experience that would play an important role in planning for subsequent U-boat operations as the fleet grew to an appreciable size.

Encouraged by the success of the U-boat activity in 1915, "unrestricted" submarine warfare became a major element in the German plans for war. There were, however, some major drawbacks to the use of underwater craft to intercept international trade. By 1914 an international code of behavior had been worked out to govern the search and seizure of ships and their cargo by blockading ships during times of war. One of these rules of behavior was that the attacking vessel should give warning and make provision to allow the crew and passengers of the vessel under attack to escape before sinking their vessel. While this was a reasonable expectation for surface vessels, it was not always a practical approach for submarines, which tended to rely on surprise for their attacks to be successful. A U-boat's most fearsome weapon was a torpedo fired from a submerged vessel that destroyed its target without warning. This required that targeted ships be attacked without warning, and often without having been carefully identified as belonging to a neutral or a belligerent nation. Such attacks brought forth bitter complaints by neutral countries that their ships were being illegally attacked and sunk. President Woodrow Wilson replied to the German announcement of the blockade in 1915 with a statement that his government would be "constrained to hold the Imperial German Government to a strict accountability for such acts."

In May 1915, as the British passenger liner *Lusitania* prepared to set sail from New York, the German embassy posted warnings to prospective passengers that "travelers sailing in the war zone on the ships of Great Britain or her allies do so at their own risk." When the ship was torpedoed by a German submarine and sank off the coast of Ireland with a loss of 1,198 passengers – 123 of whom were Americans – the United States raised a strong protest. The possibility that sinking American ships might bring the United States into the war on the side of the Entente was too great a risk for the gains from sinking a few ships, and the Germans decided to rethink their U-boat practices. The High Command reduced the size of the "war zone" around Great Britain following the *Lusitania* disaster and four months later they rescinded the policy of unrestricted U-boat attacks.

The decision to end the unrestricted submarine attacks in 1915 did not end the debate among the German military and diplomatic corps over the effectiveness of U-boats as a weapon of economic warfare. In 1915 the German navy did not have the capability to seriously cripple the British economy with a U-boat blockade. However, by early 1917 the U-boat fleet had grown to more than a hundred boats and the tonnage sunk by them had grown from 100,000 tons a month to more than 600,000 tons per month (see Figure 5.9). The German naval staff confidently predicted their U-boats could "force Britain to her knees within five months."[44] On January 9, 1917 the Kaiser agreed with both his military and civilian advisors that Germany should resume unrestricted warfare around the British Isles. The result was a marked increase in the number of ships sunk, and when Germany refused to heed American protests over the U-boat attacks, the United States entered the war as a partner of the Entente Powers. The Germans were willing to gamble that the U-boat offensive could end the war before the Americans could mobilize their men and resources to rescue the Allied cause. Once again, they had allowed their overconfidence to dominate their assessment of the situation.

Blockades as an Economic Weapon

There is no question that the German U-boat effort had a perceptible effect on the enemy war effort. During the initial stages of the campaign in 1917 the U-boat commanders more than met their quota of 600,000 tons of shipping sunk each month. At that rate, one of every four vessels leaving the British Isles was being sunk by U-boats. "There were many in England," writes Gerd Hardach, "who voiced the opinion that the war would be lost within a matter of months failing the early discovery of an effective counter-measure."[45] Therein lay one of the fatal flaws in the German plan; they did not anticipate the countermeasures that could be introduced to reduce the losses from U-boat attacks. Arming merchant ships was one way to discourage submarines from surfacing for an attack that would allow the victim's crew to abandon ship. Grouping merchant ships into convoys that could be protected by warships proved to be an even more effective way of protecting them. The British Admiralty had resisted the use of convoys on the grounds that it limited the speed of the convoy to that of the slowest ships, and they claimed that the convoys would provide easier targets for submarines than ships scattered over a wide area. However, it was just as easy for an entire convoy to slip through the U-boat blockade as it was for a single ship to do so, and each time this happened, forty ships escaped instead of one. The final flaw in the German plan was that they badly underestimated the ability of the British and Americans to build new ships to replace the ships lost at sea.

The result of these changes can be seen in Figure 5.9, which shows that the tonnage lost per month in the last year of the war fell far short of the German projections, and in the data snapshots of the British and French economies showing that the level of imports into both countries rose steadily from 1916 to the end of the war. There were other subtler factors that also worked against the effective-ness of the blockade: for example, the substitutability of inputs and outputs in a market economy allowed both producers and consumers in the blockaded economy to adjust for the loss of imported goods and materials. Moreover, the assumption that the British depended on imports for an adequate supply of food proved to be far too sim-plistic. When the supply of foodstuffs from abroad was reduced, British farmers increased production of food crops. All of this meant that the German U-boat campaign could cause British civilians to tighten their belts, but despite the fears at the time, it never seriously threatened to destroy the British economy.

The British "distant" blockade was, by most accounts, far more effective than the German U-boat campaign. There is abundant evidence that cutting off imports led to a noticeable decline in the cal-oric intake of the German civilian population during the war.[46] How much of that decline was due to the blockade is less clear, because many of its effects were indirect – such as the cutting off of nitrate fertilizer inputs for agriculture. Davis and Engerman conclude that "It appears that the blockade directly accounted for about a quarter of the decline in German food production; the other three quarters of the fall can be traced to the decline in domestic production."[47] However, statistical measures do not capture the full impact of the blockade. The British did not lift the restrictions on German trade until the peace treaty at Versailles was signed by Germany in June of 1919. Germans considered this to be a continuation of an act of war after the signing of the ceasefire on the Western Front. Albert Ritschl argues that the German reaction to the continuing blockade was an important element in the planning for a future war with the British. "Whether real or imagined," he claims, "German planners interpreted the war as an inherently economic problem, and designed the aims for a war of revenge accordingly. Starting in 1915, public and internal debates on Germany's war goals began to shift away from the classical ambitions of German overseas imperialism and towards building up a continental empire in Eastern Europe."[48]

Total War and Total Mobilization

The arrival of a new team of generals at the head of OHL in 1917 marked a dramatic change in German strategy. Hindenburg and Ludendorff brought with them a view that Germany's hopes for winning the war rested on victory over the Russians in the east, rather than on further attempts to break through the French and British lines on the Western Front. They also believed that the need to wage a "total war" required "total mobilization" of the economy to meet the demands of war. One of their first orders of business, therefore, was to implement a series of changes in the way that the government organized the war effort by implementing what became known as the "Hindenburg Program" of reforms.

The Hindenburg Economic Program

The first step in the Hindenburg Program was to move the responsibility for controlling production of war materiel from the civilian war ministry to the military planners at the OHL. This had the effect of changing the way in which goals were set for production of military supplies in the hope of increasing the supply of weapons and gunpowder for the army. During the first years of the war, the war ministry had set production goals in terms that could be realized by the producers. The new system set goals based on what the military needed. In the words of one observer, the program demanded not "as much as is attainable, but rather definite increases of production by a definite time and at any price."[49] The result, by most accounts, was not a success. According to historian Gerald Feldman, the new program

> represented the triumph, not of imagination, but of fantasy. In his pursuit of an ill-conceived total mobilization for the attainment of irrational goals, Ludendorff undermined the strength of the army, promoted economic instability, created administrative chaos, and set loose an orgy of interest politics. His program represented the victory of heavy industry and the general staff over the War Ministry, and its chief architects were self-seeking industrialists and a ruthless military intriguer.[50]

In addition to shifting control of production of war materiel to the military, the new regime persuaded the Reichstag to pass the Auxiliary Service Law, which sought to reorganize the mobilization of labor by insisting that all males between seventeen and sixty not already serving in the military must work for the war effort. The law also stipulated that skilled workers could no longer be drafted and that specialists already in the army could be released to work in the war industries. As with the attempts to directly control the production of armaments, the efforts to "rationalize" the use of labor met with limited success. A shortage of labor was one of the major challenges facing Germany throughout the war, and the tug of war between the needs of the army and the need for skilled labor in the civilian sector did not have any simple resolution. The exemption of skilled labor pleased the industrialists, but the transfer of soldiers from the front had a perceptible effect on troop strength. Feldman presents estimates showing that by the middle of 1917 the number of exemptions had reached nearly two million men. He argues that the result was a decline in battalion strength from 750 to 713 on the Western Front and from 800 to 780 in the east.[51]

All the belligerents faced problems similar to those in Germany. The British and French instituted conscription and established bureaucratic control over production of war materiel, and all the countries relied on patriotic campaigns to support the war effort. They encountered difficulties in meeting goals that were unreasonable.

However, as we saw in the economic snapshots, the Entente countries were able to offset many of their shortcomings and mistakes by relying on international trade to provide the needed supplies. This was not an option that the Germans could make much use of because of the British blockade and their limited access to international trade routes.

While most writers argue that the Entente countries had more effective mobilization programs, the Germans did manage to make impressive increases in military supplies during the last two years of the war. The Hindenburg Program may not have been as "irrational" as its critics suggest. Subordinating everything to the immediate needs of the army was a gamble that Hindenburg and Ludendorff were willing to take to win the war. William McNeill insists that "victory did come very near in 1918 despite American intervention. Had the Germans won, Hindenburg and Ludendorff and their associates would have seemed paragons and heroes."[52]

6 WAR AND REVOLUTION

The [Russian] government considers it the greatest of crimes
against humanity to continue this war over the issue of
how to divide among the strong and rich nations the weak
nationalities they have conquered, and solemnly announces
its determination immediately to sign terms of peace to stop
this war on the terms indicated, which are equally just for all
nationalities without exception.

Vladimir Lenin (November 8, 1917)[1]

As the war entered its third year both sides once again gathered
their commanders to consider what the New Year would entail. The
war of attrition that both sides had been vigorously waging for two
and a half years produced horrendous casualties, but it had not created
an obvious advantage for either side. As they surveyed their options for
1917, everyone was searching for a tipping point that would break the
stalemate and offer an opportunity to win the war.

Hindenburg and Ludendorff

The appointment of Paul von Hindenburg and Erich Ludendorff
to head the OHL produced a new approach to the way the Germans
viewed their grand strategy. While they recognized that the Central
Powers would have to defeat the British and the French to eventually
win the war, Hindenburg and Ludendorff insisted that the next step in

achieving that goal lay in the east, not in the west. Accordingly, they proposed that the OHL develop a defensive strategy for the Western Front in 1917 and concentrate their offensive efforts on defeating the faltering Russian army in the eastern theater.

The Siegfried–Hindenburg Line

To facilitate the new strategy, the Germans began construction in the fall of 1916 on new fortifications along the Western Front consisting of a hundred miles of concrete bunkers, barbed wire, communication trenches, and artillery placements located fifteen to twenty miles behind the Somme battlefield (see Map 6.1). As soon as the Siegfried Line (which the French and British referred to as the Hindenburg Line) was finished, German troops began withdrawing behind the new fortifications. Operation Albrecht was completed without incident by

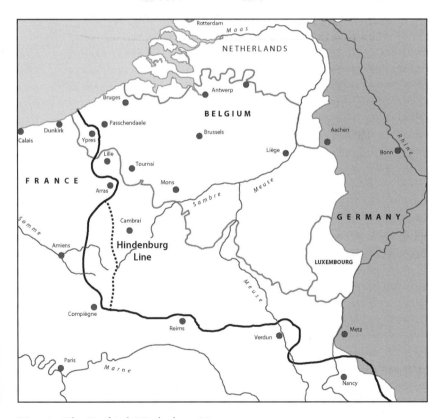

Map 6.1 The Siegfried–Hindenburg Line

the middle of March 1917. Ludendorff ordered that all territory that was abandoned as a result of the withdrawal was to be laid waste. The enemy, he claimed, must "find a totally barren land, in which their maneuverability was to be critically impaired."[2]

The German strategy caught the Entente leaders off guard. The British and the French generals hailed the "retreat" behind the Siegfried–Hindenburg Line as evidence that their own strategy of attrition was working and cited the withdrawal of troops as a sign that the German defenses had been weakened by the losses suffered at Verdun and the Battle of the Somme. Douglas Haig was so convinced of this that he wanted to resume the aborted offensive in 1917. In fact, the new German fortifications had greatly strengthened the German defenses along the Western Front by replacing the trenches first dug in the early years of the war with permanent defensive emplacements and by shortening the length of the Western Front by about thirty miles. Operation Albrecht allowed the Germans to release the equivalent of thirteen divisions to the Eastern Front for offensive operations against the Russians with little or no concern that there would be a breakthrough on the Western Front. Their confidence was well-founded; the Siegfried–Hindenburg Line would not be broken by Allied forces until October of 1918.

Still, the fact remained that no one had really "won" the battles of the past year. "The campaign of 1916," recalled Prince Maximillian of Baden in his memoirs written after the war, "ended in bitter disillusionment all round. We and our enemies had shed our best blood in streams, and neither we nor they had come one step nearer to victory. The word 'deadlock' was on every lip."[3] However, the prince's postwar recollection of the battles on the Western Front overlooks the extent to which the military deadlock was not entirely to Germany's disadvantage. At the end of 1916 German and Austrian forces controlled an area of northern and central Europe that stretched from northern France and Belgium to Russian Poland and Galicia and south to the Balkan states of Serbia, Albania, and Romania, while the Ottoman Empire had managed to keep the British bottled up in Palestine and Mesopotamia.[4]

Ludendorff's 1917 Plan

For the Germans, there were two ways of looking at this situation. A vocal bloc of deputies in the Reichstag and civilian branches of the government felt that the occupied territories gave Germany a strong negotiating position at the beginning of 1917. They urged the Kaiser to respond to President Wilson's call for a conference to discuss ending the war. Chancellor Bethmann-Hollweg personally favored pursing diplomacy because he was convinced that seeking to break the military deadlock by launching new offensives along the existing lines was not likely to succeed, and pursuing a more aggressive submarine warfare would almost surely bring the United States into the war. However, Bethmann-Hollweg was caught between a rock and a hard place. Though he personally favored diplomacy, he recognized that the chances of a diplomatic settlement that would be acceptable to the Kaiser and the OHL were slight, and he therefore vacillated between private assurances that he had serious doubts about the efficacy of unrestricted U-boat attacks, and public statements that he would support such a policy as "a military necessity" if that was what the generals wanted. The Chancellor was also unsure where the Kaiser – who had a tendency to vacillate when asked to choose between competing policy proposals – stood on this issue.

The generals at the OHL took a very different approach to their options. Hindenburg and Ludendorff firmly believed that 1917 offered Germany a window of opportunity to win the war, but they realized that this window might not stay open for very long. The key to their plan was to win a quick and decisive victory in the east. If the Central Powers could defeat the Russians, they could then use all of their resources to break the stalemate in the west. So while Bethmann-Hollweg and the German foreign office toyed with responses to Wilson's call for a peace without victory, the OHL was hard at work developing a grand military strategy to win the war.

By the end of 1916 Ludendorff was ready to present his ideas to the Kaiser. His goals were every bit as ambitious as those for the Schlieffen Plan that launched the war in 1914. The basic premise of Schlieffen's 1906 memo had been that the Germans should concentrate their forces on the west and defeat the enemy piecemeal. Schlieffen had argued that an initial attack in force against the French could be successful, and that a quick victory would release troops that could then be sent east to deal with the Russians. It is worth recalling at this point that the 1914 German invasion of France had very nearly succeeded. German troops got to within forty miles of Paris, and the Russians were stopped and eventually driven out of East Prussia by the end of 1915.

Ludendorff proposed to apply Schlieffen's divide-and-conquer logic to the situation facing the Germans at the end of 1916. As they surveyed the situation, the men at the OHL concluded that the Western Front was secure for the time being, and the collapse of the Brusilov offensives had left the Russian army disorganized and vulnerable to attack. A successful campaign against the Russians in 1917 would place Germany in a position to launch a final offensive against the British and French that could decide the outcome of the war. This was Schlieffen's approach turned 180 degrees toward the east. The initial German offensives in 1917 would be against the Russians and then they would turn around and deal with Britain and France. Moreover, the eastward focus of Ludendorff's plan involved much more than releasing troops for an offensive on the Western Front. It would also allow Germany to control large areas of western and southern Russia that included the food-producing regions of Belorussia and Ukraine.

Like Schlieffen's 1906 proposal, Ludendorff's proposal for enlarging the war in early 1917 entailed risks for the Germans. It involved putting all their military and economic resources into one huge final gamble where everything hinged not only on the favorable outcome of a series of battles, but also on timing. The defeat of French and British forces would have to be completed before the anticipated entry of the United States into the war could turn the military advantage back in favor of the expanded "Allied Powers." If one part of the plan got bogged down, the entire scheme could unravel.

None of these risks fazed Ludendorff in the spring of 1917. He remained supremely confident that the Russian forces were so demoralized that they could be defeated by the end of the year. He was counting on the proven efficiency of the German army to organize railway networks to meet the logistical challenge of moving troops back and forth between the two fronts, and he believed that the newly strengthened Siegfried–Hindenburg Line was secure enough that the Germans could safely shift men and resources to the Eastern Front. Finally, the men at the OHL were confident that new infantry tactics developed by German troops using attack units called stormtroopers during the 1916 campaign at Verdun would be able to break through the enemy trenches and create a war of movement that would ensure German successes in 1917 and 1918.

Déjà Vu: Unrestricted U-boats

There was, however, one huge uncertainty that was beyond Ludendorff's control. Ludendorff believed that defeating Britain was the biggest challenge to German success. In a secret memorandum on unrestricted U-boat warfare circulated within the OHL at the end of August 1916, Admiral Henning von Holtzendorff, Chief of the Imperial Navy, had pointed out that:

> Italy and France are already so severely weakened in their economic foundations that they are kept in the fight only through England's energy and resources. If we succeed to break England's backbone, the war will immediately be decided in our favour. England's backbone is the merchant tonnage, which delivers essential imports for their survival and for the military industry of the British islands and which ensures the [kingdom's] ability to pay for its imports from abroad.[5]

Everyone agreed with the admiral's observation that something had to be done to cut the flow of supplies to Britain from around the world if a German offensive against the British was going to drive them out of the war. The answer, Holtzendorff claimed, was to return to a policy of unrestricted U-boat blockade activity around the British Isles. The Imperial Navy had experimented with unrestricted U-boat warfare in 1915 and the results had been promising. However, at that point Germany possessed too few U-boats to operate an effective blockade. The admirals assured Ludendorff that things had changed. The submarine fleet was expected to reach more than 150 ships by the beginning of 1917, and Holtzendorff insisted that this would allow the navy to interdict the flow of food and supplies to the British Isles and "starve" the British economy. He estimated that his U-boats could sink 600,000 tons of merchant shipping a month.

Reinstating a policy of unrestricted submarine warfare required approval from the Kaiser. On January 9, 1917, a group of military and civilian leaders including the Kaiser, Generals Hindenburg and Ludendorff, Chief of the Imperial Navy Holtzendorff, and Chancellor Bethmann-Hollweg gathered in German-occupied Russia at the castle of Pless. The only item on the agenda was the August 1916 memorandum written by Holtzendorff proposing that "our clearly defined strategic objective is to force a decision in our favour through the destruction of enemy sea transport capacity." The admiral called for an immediate resumption of unrestricted submarine warfare.

> The exceptionally poor world harvest of grain, including feed grain, this year, provides us with a unique opportunity which nobody could responsibly reject. Both North America and Canada will probably cease their grain exports to England in February. Under such favourable circumstances an energetic blow conducted with all force against English merchant tonnage will promise a certain success.[6]

Holtzendorff knew that the Kaiser had resisted previous suggestions by the navy to reinstate unrestricted U-boat activity, partly because of President Wilson's clear warning that German infringements on the freedom of the seas would bring the United States into the war on the side of the Entente. That, Holtzendorff insisted, was a risk Germany must take. "A Campaign of unrestricted submarine warfare," he insisted,

> launched in time to produce a peace before the harvest of the summer 1917 – i.e. 1 August – has to accept the risk of American belligerence, because we have no other option. In spite of the diplomatic rupture with America, the unrestricted submarine warfare is nevertheless the right means to conclude this war victoriously. It is also the only means to this end.[7]

Before the meeting at Pless, the Kaiser had made it clear to the OHL that he was now leaning toward approval of a more aggressive submarine operation if it could win the war. Hindenburg and Ludendorff had both eagerly endorsed the idea. Wilhelm listened to the arguments for and against resumption of unrestricted submarine warfare and announced that he was prepared to approve the policy suggested in Holtzendorff's memorandum. It would take effect on February 1. The approval of unrestricted submarine warfare at Pless marked the end of Admiral Tirpitz's efforts to catch up with Great Britain in the number of capital ships. The admirals agreed to abandon two dreadnoughts and five battle cruisers currently under construction to facilitate the building of more submarines.[8]

Meetings like the gathering at Pless are meant to be "confidence builders." The danger of such gatherings is that the process of building confidence can lead to *over*confidence. In this case, the rhetoric of

Admiral Holtzendorff carried the day even though the argument was seriously flawed. The German admiral and his staff had underestimated both the ability of the Americans to mobilize their resources quickly and the ability of the British to withstand the shock of increased shipping losses from U-boats sinking their merchant ships. They also failed to consider the impact that America's entry into the war would have in boosting the confidence of Entente leaders, who now believed that it would be worthwhile for them to continue a vigorous fight in the short run while the Americans marshalled their resources for war. The final miscalculation was the assumption that the German fleet of U-boats – which in January 1917 numbered 103 – would be sufficient to sink enough shipping to create crippling shortages in the British economy.[9]

The decisions made at the Pless meeting committed Germany to a gamble that was based more on a deep-seated fear of defeat than a careful assessment of the odds that the outcome of a submarine offensive would be favorable. Ratcheting up the level of warfare with a U-boat offensive was not the only option the German leadership had in January 1917; it was a choice by the military commanders that eventually produced a "confidence bubble" that promoted their larger scheme to win the war. The decision received considerable support from a public anxious to see their government doing something to impose upon the British some semblance of the shortages they were suffering because of the British blockade of Germany, but the risks remained high. Once again, the Germans were looking at a situation where the odds of success were at best problematic, perhaps not even as good as those they had faced in 1914. A factor that contributed to the willingness of the OHL to accept these risks of the Ludendorff–Hindenburg plan was the ever-present hope that if the new commanders were right – and they had compiled a very impressive track record against the Russians in the east – it was possible that Germany might still be able to break the stalemate and win the war. The decision to go "all in" one more time was a calculated choice that produced another "tipping point" in the war.

The Zimmermann Telegram

In the midst of all this planning for military operations in the spring of 1917, Alfred Zimmermann, who had recently been appointed German State Secretary for Foreign Affairs, proposed a scheme that would entice Mexico to enter into an alliance with Germany and invade the United States in the event that the Americans entered the war on the side of the Entente. The Mexicans had been engaged in hostile activity along the American border for several years, and Zimmermann felt that Germany could offer them support for an invasion of the southwestern United States. Zimmermann's scheme was the latest in a string of efforts by the Germans to use Mexico's difficulties with the United States to their advantage. Had the scheme remained filed away in the German foreign office in Berlin, it would have been just one more idea. Zimmermann, however, decided to take the initiative and try to find out if the Mexicans would be interested in his scheme.

On January 17, 1917, he sent a coded telegram to Count Johann von Bernstorff, the German ambassador in Washington, DC, explaining his plan. Addressed "Most secret. For your Excellency's personal information and to be handed on to the Imperial Minister in Mexico by a safe route," the contents of the telegram informed Bernstorff that:

> We intend to begin unrestricted submarine warfare on the first of February. We shall endeavor in spite of this to keep the United States Neutral. In the event of this not succeeding, we make Mexico a proposal of alliance on the following basis: make war together, make peace together, generous financial support, and an understanding on our part that Mexico is to reconquer the lost territory in Texas, New Mexico, and Arizona. The settlement in detail is left to you.
>
> You will inform the President [of Mexico] of the above most secretly as soon as the outbreak of war with the United States is certain and add the suggestion that he should, on his own initiative invite Japan to immediate adherence and at the same time mediate between Japan and ourselves.
>
> Please call the President's attention to the fact that the unrestricted employment of our submarines now offers the prospect of compelling England to make peace within a few months.
>
> Acknowledge receipt.
> ZIMMERMANN[10]

Unfortunately for Zimmermann, the telegraph lines that the Germans used to send their "top secret" messages to their ambassador in the United States were not very secure. British naval vessels had succeeded in cutting the transatlantic cables on the bottom of the English Channel that connected Germany with the international cable system in August of 1914. This forced the Germans to send their military orders and other government messages outside Germany by transatlantic cables that were controlled by British or American companies. The Germans had set up an arrangement whereby the United States authorized the German government to send ciphered messages via telegraph to the US State Department, which then gave them to Bernstorff without reading their contents. Zimmermann used this route for his message, but to make sure it got through he sent copies using two other networks that were even less secure. All three routes were monitored by either the British or the Americans.

Within hours of its dispatch, British and American officials had copies of Zimmermann's telegram to Bernstorff. Although neither group took the time to completely decipher the contents of the message, they sensed that this was a message important enough to be placed in their files. When the Germans advised the American government on February 2 that they intended to resume unrestricted submarine activity around the British Isles, both the Americans and the British officials decoded the earlier message from Zimmermann to Bernstorff, and realized that it clearly revealed that the Germans were already committed to resuming unrestricted submarine warfare by the end of 1916.[11]

News of Zimmermann's scheme to involve Mexico and possibly Japan – which at this point was fighting on the side of the Entente Powers – as allies in a war against the United States quickly made headlines in the American press. On the morning of March 1 the *New York Times* announced that:[12]

GERMANY SEEKS ALLIANCE AGAINST U.S.
ASKS JAPAN AND MEXICO TO JOIN HER;
FULL TEXT OF HER PROPOSAL MADE PUBLIC

The public reaction on both sides of the Atlantic was a sense of incredulity over the revelation of a scheme – many reports referred to it as a "plot" – to form an alliance between Mexico and Germany, coupled with evidence that Germany had been secretly contemplating a return to unrestricted submarine warfare since the beginning of 1917. Advocates of America's entry into the war against the Central Powers felt that this should be enough to push President Wilson into taking action against Germany. Opponents of the war responded by challenging the authenticity of the telegram, insisting that it was a forgery planted by the British to excite public support for a declaration of war against Germany. However, when Zimmermann was asked by a Hearst reporter in Berlin whether he would deny the story, he replied "I cannot deny it. It is true."

The Zimmermann Telegram is widely regarded as one of the great diplomatic gaffes of the war. The hubbub over the alleged plot to ensnare the United States into a war with Mexico was one of those "stories" in the press that significantly moved US public opinion toward acceptance of the view that Germany was the villain in the European war and that the United States should enter the war on the side of the Entente. As Adam Tooze observes, "however hallucinogenic these associations may have appeared, the bizarre German scheme to seize the military initiative in the western hemisphere was the logical extension of Berlin's *idée fixe* that America was already committed to the Entente and that a declaration of war was under any circumstances inevitable."[13] Despite the furor, President Wilson remained committed to his belief that the only sensible way for America to deal with the conflict was to negotiate a "peace without victory," and he therefore stopped short of asking Congress to declare war over the incident. He did, however, break off diplomatic relations with Germany, and Bernstorff was recalled to Berlin.

On February 2, the day after the Germans resumed unrestricted submarine warfare, Wilson sent a strong note warning them that

> If it is still the purpose of the Imperial German Government to prosecute relentless and indiscriminate warfare against vessels of commerce by the use of submarines without regard to what the Government of the United States must consider the sacred and indisputable rules of international law and the universally recognized dictates of humanity, the Government of the United States is at last forced to the conclusion that there is but one course it can pursue.

The Germans were not swayed by the stern tone of Wilson's note. They replied with a note asserting their country's own right to "meet the illegal measures of her enemies" preventing ships from trading with England or France. Any ship that entered the coastal area of England or the English Channel zone "will be sunk."[14]

The German response did not lead immediately to America's entry into the war, but their commitment to U-boat warfare could not be easily dismissed. Zimmermann's note clearly demonstrated that Germany had been planning a new course of action since the beginning of the year. There no longer seemed any room for doubt that the United States would join the Entente as an ally if the German submarines began to sink American ships. It was, after all, anger over the submarine attacks that was the prime mover in swaying the American public toward a decision to go to war. Zimmermann had simply made that decision much easier with his ill-conceived "story" of German intentions that was widely believed by Americans who were anxious to get the United States to enter the war.

The War Goes On

The likelihood that the United States might enter the war if the Germans resumed unrestricted U-boat attacks was good news for the British and French leaders who were licking their wounds after the staggering losses at Verdun and the Somme in 1916 and their struggle to pay for their imports from America. It now appeared that the "Yanks" had finally decided to fight. The bad news was that American troops would not appear on the Western Front any time soon. One might reasonably think that after two and a half years of fighting on the Western Front had produced nothing but casualties, grief, shortages of food, and an intense frustration stemming from a long string of military failures, the Allied commanders would be content at this point to wait for the Americans to enter the war before they committed fresh troops to the front. But that was not how the Entente generals viewed the situation. They remained confident that their strategy of "attrition" on the Western Front was working, and they feared – with some justification – that lessening the offensive pressure on the Western Front would allow the Germans to force Russia – and possibly Italy – out of the war.

Mutiny on the Western Front

Still firmly committed to the idea that huge offensives were the key to victory in the west, Douglas Haig and Robert Nivelle were determined to launch new offensives on the Western Front. The generals' confidence was not shared by the political leaders in either country. Herbert Asquith, who had headed the coalition government in Britain since the beginning of the war, resigned in early December 1916. After several unsuccessful attempts to form a new government, he was finally replaced by David Lloyd George, who was committed to vigorously pursuing the war and pressing the Central Powers with offensive actions in 1917. However, Lloyd George, who had been highly critical of Douglas Haig's Somme offensive, was not inclined to support Haig's assertion that the war of attrition was succeeding. Unfortunately, the new prime minister lacked any military expertise himself, and he was unable to come up with a suitable candidate to replace Haig. Nor did he have a plan to put forward that might challenge Haig's view that his war of attrition was working. This meant that the British military remained committed to Haig's strategy of large offensive operations on the Western Front as the war entered its third year.

While the British were reviewing Haig's proposals for 1917, French political leaders were feeling pressure to replace Joseph Joffre as commander–in-chief of the French army. Still committed to the idea that offense was the key to victory, President Raymond Poincaré appointed Robert Nivelle, the general who had directed the assaults that finally drove the Germans out of Verdun, to replace Joffre. Nivelle enthusiastically outlined a plan for new offensives in the spring of 1917 based on the tactics that he had successfully employed at Verdun. Though Poincaré was skeptical, he approved Nivelle's plans, and even Lloyd George was sufficiently persuaded by the French general's optimistic enthusiasm that he agreed to have the British forces support the "Nivelle offensives" with a British offensive at Ypres. In effect, this meant that the Anglo-British forces on the Western Front would continue the strategy of persistent attacks in an attempt to gradually wear down the German forces.

In spite of the fact that the fighting around Verdun had decimated the ranks and seriously eroded the morale of the French army in 1916, Nivelle was convinced that the new tactics of "creeping artillery barrages" in front of advancing troops that had proved very successful in the final assaults to recapture Fort Douaumont in October 1916 would work in a much larger offensive operation against German trenches south of the Somme. He was quickly proved wrong. The Germans – aided by intelligence that provided ample warning of the impending attack, and with their troops firmly entrenched in a favorable position along a ridge known as the Chemin des Dames – repulsed the French attacks with heavy casualties. When Nivelle, who had assured his superiors that he would call off the attacks if there were no perceptible gains from the initial assault, continued the offensive into the first week of May with more heavy casualties, President Poincaré relieved him of his command and brought Henri Philippe Pétain back as his replacement.[15]

The Chemin des Dames disaster proved to be too much for many of the French troops to bear and morale collapsed to the point where men refused to move into the trenches, disobeyed orders to attack the enemy, and exhibited a general decline in discipline. By the beginning of April what became known as the "French Mutinies" had become widespread in many units of the French armies.[16] The angry complaints of the soldiers were aimed primarily at the casualties suffered in senseless attacks against heavily fortified enemy positions; however, the complaints also included demands for better treatment of soldiers at the front, and better care for the families of those killed or wounded.

Upon taking charge, Pétain quickly instituted courts-martial to deal with the more serious offenders, resulting in a number of executions and the immediate reassignment of some of the more obstreperous offenders to colonial posts in Africa.[17] He then turned his attention to ways in which he could restore order by responding to the complaints of the troops. His approach, which tended to rely more on the carrot than the stick, managed to calm the mutinous storm. However, the longer-term impact of the huge losses at Verdun and the Nivelle offensives remained, and the effect on morale was not limited to the men at the front.

The horrendous casualties suffered by the French army during the first two and a half years of the war and the crisis of morale in 1917 crippled its ability to vigorously support major offensive operations. Figure 6.1 shows the French casualties from the beginning of 1916 to the end of the war. Except for a sharp spike in April and May of 1917, when Nivelle launched his ill-fated attacks, Pétain's policy of limiting attacks that were not directly related to a defensive objective of holding positions lowered the casualty rate to less than a quarter of earlier periods.[18] The *poilus* did not refuse to fight; they just refused to continue to launch what they regarded as futile attacks on enemy positions

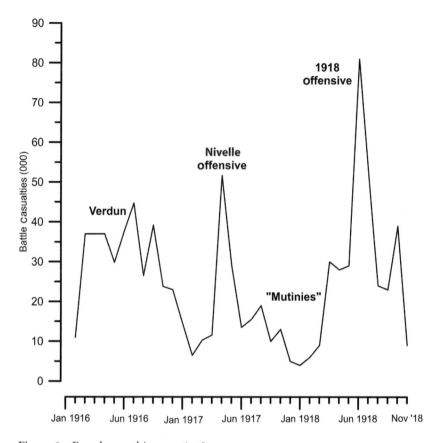

Figure 6.1 French casualties, 1916–18

Source: David Stevenson, "French Srategy on the Western Front," in Roger Chickering and Stig Forster, eds., *Great War, Total War: Combat and Mobilization on the Western Front, 1914–1918* (Cambridge University Press, 2000), 325–6.

en masse. Historian Eric Brose suggests that "what seized France was 'defencism', not defeatism."[19] One of the more remarkable aspects of the morale crisis was the ability of the French military authorities to keep information about the extent of the "mutinies" from reaching the French public. Pétain's success in restoring order at the front, together with some heavy-handed censorship, kept information on what was happening at the front from adding fuel to the growing opposition to the war at home. Incredibly, the Germans also remained largely unaware of the mutinous behavior. Although they became aware of breakdowns of discipline among the French units in May, official reports of the problems did not reach the OHL until late June, by which time it was too late for the Germans to plan any extensive responses.

Passchendaele

While the French struggled to keep their army in the field, Douglas Haig was eager to launch a new British offensive against the Germans in the fall of 1917. Haig, who always thought in terms of large-scale operations, offered two possibilities to the British Council of War. The first option was to continue attacking along the Somme battlefield in cooperation with the French. When Pétain showed little enthusiasm for such a scheme, Haig turned to a dream he had harbored since early in the war: a breakout from the salient in the British lines at Ypres at the northern end of the Entente lines. Haig was a classic example of a general who suffered from a strong tendency towards overconfidence. He firmly believed that his overall strategy of attrition was working, and that it was the Germans, not the British, who were near the breaking point. Moreover, he pointed out, a decisive break-through at Ypres could lead to the capture of the Channel ports of Ostend and Zebrugge, which were serving as German submarine bases.

While the possibility of destroying submarine bases caught the ear of the beleaguered prime minister and his staff who were trying to deal with the devastating losses of merchant ships off the coast of England, past experiences with battles in the Ypres area did not suggest that getting to the coast was a very realistic expectation. Lloyd George had grown weary of Haig's grand schemes for battles that invariably produced long casualty lists with little to show for the effort. Nonetheless, Britain's allies were all in the throes of major difficulties and it was clear that the burden of carrying on the war until the Americans arrived was going to fall on the British. Haig and Pétain met in July and the French general made it clear that after the disastrous losses from the Nivelle offensives and subsequent discipline problems facing the French army, they were in no condition to undertake any new attacks against the Germans. The situation in Russia was even more chaotic and there was not much that the British could do to stem further German advances into western Russia.

Lloyd George shared Haig's belief that the British must do something to prop up the Entente war effort. However, the prime minister no longer had any faith in Haig's judgment with regard to offensive operations. He proposed an alternative scheme whereby the British could send reinforcements to the Italian front, which also seemed to be shaky at this point. The notes of Colonel Maurice Hankey, the

Secretary of the War Cabinet, summarized Lloyd George's presentation of his case to the British War Cabinet in his notes on the meeting. The prime minister, claimed Hankey, wanted "to mass heavy guns on the Italian frontier, making use of Italian manpower, and dealing a blow which will compel Austria in her exhausted state to make peace."[20] Lloyd George's proposal was that the British should provide a large contribution of weapons and some additional manpower to the Italian forces, which would allow them to launch an offensive that could push Austria to the brink of collapse and force Germany to respond by sending troops from the Western Front to reinforce the Austrians. This scheme had the added advantage (to his way of thinking) that such an operation would not be under Haig's command – a point that was not lost on Haig and the members of the War Cabinet.

The two men were working from very different paradigms on how to proceed with the war, and their proposals reflected their very different backgrounds. Haig was a career soldier with a distinguished military background who still believed that the existing paradigm involving massive attacks against enemy positions would eventually produce victory. In his eyes the Somme had not been a failure; it had pushed the Germans to the limits of their resources and another offensive could tip the war in favor of the British. Moreover, like most military men, Haig refused to concern himself with public opinion. Lloyd George, on the other hand, was a politician with absolutely no military background, and he was very conscious of what the voters thought of his conduct of the war. His political instincts told him that the war of attrition was not working the way Haig claimed. "We have won great victories," he told the War Cabinet as they debated the options. "When I look at the casualty lists I sometimes wish it had not been necessary to win so many."[21] The prime minister's approach to the problem was to search for a weak spot away from the Western Front that could be exploited against the Austrians while holding the Germans at bay in France. A major attack against the German lines at Ypres did not meet these criteria. As Maurice Hankey noted in his journal, the prime minister felt that Haig's proposal had

> no decent chance of success. Russian & French cooperation are too insufficient; our superiority in men & guns too slight; the extent of the advance required in order to secure tangible results (Ostend & Zeebrugge) too great in his opinion to

justify the great losses which must be involved, losses which he thinks will jeopardize our chance next year, & cause great depression.[22]

Nonetheless, in the end, Haig's argument carried the day. Historians have debated at length why, given the deep reservations he had to Haig's proposed attack, Lloyd George gave in so easily. Two considerations seem to have determined his decision. First was his reluctance to simply overrule his military advisors. Second was the possibility – however remote it might seem – that Haig's attack might actually succeed in reaching the submarine bases along the Belgian coast – an outcome that could relieve some of the pressure on the supply lines from the United States and the empire. During the first six months of 1917 German U-boat attacks were sinking more than 600,000 tons of shipping each month, with a peak of just over 850,000 tons in June. This was enough to cause Lloyd George and the War Cabinet serious concern about the ability of the British economy to keep up their war effort. So the prime minister reluctantly agreed to let Haig proceed with his plans.[23]

It turned out to be a most unfortunate decision on the part of the prime minister. The Third Battle of Ypres – or as it is more often termed, the Battle of Passchendaele – opened on July 17 with an artillery barrage that lasted for more than two weeks and totally obliterated the German front lines, but left the second and third lines of defenses largely intact and left no doubt as to where the ensuing attack would take place. The statistics of the opening artillery salvoes of the battle show how far the armies had come from the days in 1914 when a "shell shortage" curtailed the availability of artillery to support the advancing infantry. British guns threw an estimated 3.5 million rounds on the German positions on Messines Ridge, a position that overlooked the British lines and had to be captured. As an added touch, they exploded a million pounds of high explosives in nineteen tunnels dug under the German position, creating a blast large enough that it could be felt in London.[24] The British troops moved forward over the "moonscape" left by the artillery barrage, but by August 2 the advance had been slowed to a crawl by German counterattacks. At this point it began to rain. Through the month of August there were only three days without rain; the total rainfall was more than double the usual average, and the battlefield turned into a quagmire of mud and water that adversely impeded all aspects of military activity. As Michael Clodfelter observes,

"It was hopeless, but some lemming-like impulse continued to drive the British army into the abyss of Passchendaele."[25] The push continued until a Canadian force finally reached the village of Passchendaele on November 6, which constituted a gain of just over five miles after four months of heavy fighting. At this point Haig mercifully called an end to one of the costliest battles of the war, with the closest British troops still thirty-five miles from the submarine bases at Ostend. Amphibious landings that were planned on the Belgian coast as the British advanced were never launched and Haig came under intense criticism for his handling of the battle, particularly for his stubbornness in continuing the fight when it was clear that the German resistance and the weather were crippling the efforts of his army to carry on the advance. None of his objectives had been realized, and if one measures his success by the expectations of his own paradigm of a war of attrition, the British had come up on the short end of the statistics. Passchendaele ranks with the Somme as another example of pointless killing. Nearly 70,000 British soldiers were killed in the muddy battlefield around Ypres, with little to show for their sacrifice.

The Russian Revolution

For the Russians, the military and political situation at the end of 1916 was even more precarious than that facing the French or British. Their army was larger than any other and the vastness of the Russian Empire offered ample resources to carry on the fight if they could be mobilized. However, the infrastructure of the Russian economy was on the verge of collapse and the political system had become dysfunctional. Food and fuel shortages in the cities had reached crisis proportions; at one point authorities in Moscow judged that there was less than two days of food available. The disruptions of the war meant that peasants tended to hoard their food and resist the growing labor demands of the army. Peter Gatrell comments that "In normal circumstances peasants entered the market to buy and sell food, in order to obtain cash needed to pay taxes and to buy consumer goods, but these arrangements were quite delicate and liable to be disrupted by changes in terms of trade between town and country." The war seriously disrupted the relations between rural areas and the cities. Refugees fleeing the advancing armies of the Central Powers created additional problems for an economy already stretched to the limit by the needs of war and civilian demands. In Turkestan and surrounding areas of Central Asia protests against the imperial government reached the point where they exploded into open revolt in the summer of 1916.[26]

The February Revolution

By the spring of 1917 the seeds of revolt had spread to the urban areas of Russia. On March 8, 1917, a large crowd of female garment workers gathered outside the Winter Palace in Petrograd to complain about shortages of food and to protest against continuing the war. By the following day the crowds of protesters had grown to several hundred thousand. This, Martin Gilbert notes, "was not just another antiwar protest, it was a challenge to the authority of the Tsar. For three days there were riots in the streets of the Russian capital."[27] On the morning of March 11, the Tsar, who at this point was with his army commanders at Mogilev, issued orders that troops be sent to restore order in Petrograd "the next day" and he ordered that the Duma, which was in session in Petrograd at this time, must be immediately dissolved. Far from restoring order, the Tsar's intervention fanned the flames of resistance in the capital. Troops loyal to the Tsar found themselves outnumbered by soldiers who had joined the protesters and armed clashes between the two groups resulted in more than a thousand deaths.[28]

The Duma refused to disband and remained in session trying to find a way to defuse the crisis. Mikhail Rodzianko, the chairman of the Duma and a man who had close personal ties to the royal family, responded to the Tsar's proclamations with a terse telegram to him:

> Position serious. Anarchy in the capital. Government paralyzed. Arrangements for transport, supply and fuel in complete disorder. General discontent is increasing. Disorderly firing in the streets. Part of the troops are firing on one another. Essential to entrust some individual who possesses the confidence of the country with the formation of a new government. There must be no delay. Any procrastination fatal. I pray to God that in this hour responsibility fall not on the wearer of the crown![29]

Rodzianko sent copies of his telegram to General Alekseyev, the chief of staff of the Stavka, and to each of the generals commanding army groups. The result was a flurry of telegrams to the Tsar from his generals advising him that the only way to restore order would be for him to abdicate and recognize the Provisional Government in Petrograd. The commanders made it clear that the army would not be able to support the monarchy any longer. Nicholas was on his way back to Petrograd on the morning of March 13 when his train was diverted to Pskov because the tracks ahead were in the hands of "unfriendly troops." Unwilling to cede any additional authority to the Duma, the Tsar agreed to abdicate his throne in favor of his brother, the Grand Duke Michael. However, Michael was not interested in becoming Tsar. He agreed to accept the honor long enough to issue a proclamation transferring power to the Provisional Government in Petrograd and he then followed his brother into retirement. Thus the longest reigning monarchy in Europe – a dynasty which could trace its ancestry back to the ascension of Mikhail I in 1603 – came to an abrupt and unexpected end on March 15, 1917.

The Provisional Government and the Petrograd Soviet

The protesters in Petrograd had hoped to get rid of Nicholas, but they had not intended to completely disband the monarchy. The sudden abdication of both Nicholas and his brother caught everyone by surprise, and it left the Russian Empire without a head of state to run the government. As if this were not enough to undermine any confidence they might have in the government, the politicians were now faced with the challenges of reconstructing a new Russian government from scratch, while simultaneously dealing with the imminent threat of invasion from the armies of Germany and Austria-Hungary perched along their western borders.

To meet the first challenge, the Duma formed a "Provisional Government" that took over the day-to-day responsibilities of running the government bureaucracy in Petrograd, a task formerly handled by the Tsar's Imperial Council of Ministers. As one government official observed, their efforts turned out to be surprisingly successful.

> Individuals and organizations expressed their loyalty to the new power. The Stavka [Army Headquarters] as a whole, followed by the entire commanding staff, recognized the Provisional Government. The Tsarist Ministers and some of the assistant Ministers were imprisoned, but all the other officials remained

at their posts. Ministries, offices, banks, in fact the entire political mechanism of Russia never ceased working.[30]

At the head of the new government was Prime Minister Georgy Lvov, a veteran politician who was a leading figure in the Cadet Party, a group that was viewed as the conservative wing of the Russian liberals who had dominated the Duma following the reforms enacted after the war with Japan in 1905. His immediate task was to organize elections for a Russian Constituent Assembly that would form the basis for a permanent government, a job that was complicated by the fact that the Provisional Government had no official electoral mandate to govern the country.

Adding to the political uncertainties of the moment, the Provisional Government was immediately confronted by a rival political group in Petrograd that claimed to also have the authority to govern. Following the disturbances of 1905, "Councils of Workers' Soviets" had sprung up in cities throughout Russia.[31] With the abdication of the Tsar, these soviets insisted that they should be the dominant group exercising local authority as a governing body. The Petrograd Soviet was one of the largest and most active of such worker organizations, and in the spring of 1917 it was ideally situated to exercise its influence through its size and presence in the capital – an advantage that was magnified by the fact that it had managed to effectively take control of a sizeable group of soldiers in the Petrograd garrison.

Since neither group had a clear title to act by itself as a governing body, they reached an implicit agreement whereby the Provisional Government would act as the governing body for the Russian state, with the proviso that any action they took was subject to approval by the Petrograd Soviet. It was a fragile arrangement at best, one that depended on continued cooperation between political groups that represented two very different constituencies. Bourgeois liberal socialists were the dominant group in the provisional government, while the workers in the Petrograd Soviet leaned much more toward more radical leftist views. The system of "dual power" worked so long as both sides tolerated each other, and the Provisional Government managed to remove many of the more onerous restrictions placed on Russians by the Tsarist police state. But because the arrangement was based on a very shaky informal agreement, the political stability of the Russian government following the February Revolution was always uncertain. As Alexander Guchkov, the Minister of War in the Provisional Government, explained the situation:

> The Provisional Government does not possess any real power; and its directives are carried out only to the extent that it is permitted by the Soviet of Workers' and Soldiers' Deputies, which enjoys all the essential elements of real power, since the troops, the railroads, the post and telegraph are all in its hands. One can say flatly that the Provisional Government exists only so long as it is permitted by the Soviet.[32]

During the first eight months following the Tsar's abdication, there were three crises that required the formation of "coalition" governments involving significant realignments in the leadership, and there was always the threat that any controversial move on the part of the army, the Provisional Government, or the Petrograd Soviet might cause groups of supporters to once again take to the streets in protest for one side or the other. By the end of October, the question was not *whether* the Provisional Government would fall; it was a question of *when* it would fall.

Looming over all the political squabbling was the issue of what to do about the war. By March of 1917 the Austro-German armies had already overrun Galicia and were camped on the western frontier of the Russian Empire, presenting a situation that could make the economic situation even more severe if they decided to advance further east. No one was in a position to offer solutions for either of these challenges. The policy advocated by the Provisional Government immediately after the collapse of the monarchy was that Russia should resist the German invasion and continue to pursue the war in concert with its allies in the west. On March 17, Pavel Miliukov, the Minister of Foreign Affairs, assured the leaders of the Entente Powers that Russia "will fight by their side against a common enemy until the end, without cessation and without faltering."[33] Miliukov and his colleagues were hoping to attract the patriotic support of Russians who were anxious to defend the motherland by adopting a policy of "defensism" – a notion not unlike the refusal of the French infantry who insisted that the army should fight only to defend French territory.

The possibility that Russia might leave the war frightened Entente governments into sending delegations of senior diplomats to Petrograd to show their support for the defensism policy, which was preferable to Russia quitting the fighting.[34] On the same day that Miliukov sent his memo to the Entente governments the Petrograd Soviet issued a more general call for peace. "The Russian Revolution," they insisted, "will not retreat before the bayonets of conquerors, and will not allow itself to be crushed by foreign military force." However, they went on to urge people to "refuse to serve as an instrument of conquest and violence in the hands of kings, landowners, and bankers – and then by our united efforts we will stop the horrible butchery, which is disgracing humanity and is beclouding the great days of the birth of Russian freedom."[35] The Soviet's call for peace found sympathetic ears among Russians of all classes who were tired of a war that seemed to no longer have any purpose, and no end in sight. Whatever the consequences, a growing sense of frustration increased support for the position that Russia should simply pull out of the war. However, notwithstanding their opposition to the war, most Russians were not prepared to welcome the Austro-German invaders. The Petrograd Soviet grudgingly backed the efforts of the Provisional Government to defend the Russian homeland.

Vladimir Lenin and the Bolsheviks

The most vocal advocates of abandoning the war effort were those on the far left – particularly the Bolsheviks, who were led by Vladimir Lenin. In the spring of 1917 Lenin, like many of the Bolshevik leaders, had been exiled by the Tsar's police and was living in Berne, Switzerland, eagerly looking for a way to get back to Petrograd and promote a revolution. Since the Entente governments refused to allow him to travel through their countries, the only feasible route from Berne to Petrograd was to travel through enemy territory. The Germans, who were looking for ways to encourage the new regime in Russia to abandon the war, offered to provide Lenin and thirty-two of his radical colleagues with a special train that would take them from Berne through Berlin and on to the Finnish border, where they could board a train that would take them to Petrograd. Lenin accepted their offer and arrived in Petrograd on March 17. A German agent in Stockholm sent a message to Berlin saying, "Lenin's entry into Russia successful. He is working exactly as we wish."[36]

Indeed he was! Reunited with his colleagues, Lenin quickly proposed a new course of action for the Bolsheviks in the Petrograd Soviet. In a series of meetings and speeches that became known as the "April Theses," he articulated two very simple themes over and over again. The first was a call for the Bolsheviks to cease their "dual power" cooperation with the Provisional Government and instead do everything in their power to undermine the actions of the rival group, which Lenin described as nothing more than a "stinking corpse" of the Tsarist regime. He vigorously supported the slogan "All power to the Soviets!" as a rallying cry for Bolsheviks to concentrate their efforts on increasing their presence in the Petrograd Soviet, where the Bolsheviks were still a minority. The other theme that Lenin persistently put foward in his public appearances was a call for "Peace, Land, and Bread!" By "Peace," Lenin meant an immediate Russian withdrawal from the imperialist war being waged between capitalist powers in the West. He understood that ending the war was a necessary first step toward the establishment of a new Communist state.

These exhortations for revolutionary action were not enthusiastically received by the rank and file of his party. As Sheila Fitzpatrick points out, "without a Bolshevik majority in the Petrograd Soviet, Lenin's slogan of 'All power to the Soviets!' did not provide the Bolsheviks with a practical guide to action. It remained an open question whether Lenin's strategy was that of a master politician or simply that of a cranky extremist."[37] Events would show that he could be both. Lenin's revolutionary agenda may have been slightly ahead of his more conservative colleagues when he stepped off the train from Finland, but the slogans he repeated time and again touched the pulse of a rising revolutionary fervor fueled by the possibility of both reforms and the prospect of peace.

The leaders of the Provisional Government remained committed to a policy of continuing the war as an ally of the Allied Powers, which now included the United States. They also insisted that it was necessary to uphold the obligations that the Tsar's government had made to its allies over the past three years. On May 1 Pavel Miliukov sent a confidential note to the Allied governments promising that the Provisional Government would observe the obligations assumed toward the Allied Powers. When the contents of this note became public, there were strong protests from a wide spectrum of the Petrograd population who opposed continuing the conflict to support the war aims of the Allied governments, and once again the workers took to the streets to show their displeasure. Miliukov and Alexander Guchkov, the Minister of War, were forced to resign, and a coalition government was eventually formed with a noticeable shift to the left by the addition of several socialists were members of the Petrograd Soviet.

Despite the furor over Miliukov's note and the change of ministers, the coalition government remained committed to pressing the war against the Central Powers. Alexander Kerensky, the Minister of War in the new cabinet, named Aleksei Brusilov as commander of the Russian armies in Galicia and urged him to undertake a new offensive as soon as possible. Brusilov, after carefully choosing units of the army that were loyal to the Provisional Government, decided to attack the Austrian forces in the same region where he had enjoyed success the previous year. The offensive began on June 30. Unfortunately for the Russians, things did not go so well the second time around. As they had in Brusilov's earlier campaign, Austrian troops retreated in disarray following the initial artillery bombardment by the Russians. However, the Germans, who had been given warning of Brusilov's plans, rushed reserves from their forces that were able to bring the Russian attack to a standstill. Like so many efforts in this war, the "Kerensky offensive" produced horrendous casualty lists but ultimately very little tangible gain in territory. Its failure revealed just how demoralized and ineffective the Russian army had become after three years of fighting. One of Brusilov's generals reported that "in reserve, regiments declare their willingness to fight on to full victory, but then baulk at the demand to go into the trenches."[38] By the end of July, German counterattacks had pushed the Russian lines sixty miles further east. Only the inability to maintain their supply lines caused the German and Austrian troops to end their advance into Russia. One measure of how discouraged Russian soldiers had become was the number of prisoners taken or soldiers who deserted. The Russians lost more than 60,000 men taken as POWs by the Central Power troops. The Austrians suffered even greater losses through surrender or desertion in the early phases of the attack. Casualties for the Russians during the 1917 campaigns totaled just under 700,000 men, 180,000 of whom were taken prisoner.[39]

The collapse of the Russian military forces dealt a staggering blow to the credibility of the newly reorganized Provisional Government. During the week of July 16–18, which became known as "the July

Days," thousands of workers and soldiers rioted in Petrograd to protest the latest military disaster. Troops loyal to the Provisional Government were brought in from outside the capital and when order was finally restored, a new government was formed with Kerensky named as the prime minister. Despite his association with the failed offensive, as a member of both the Provisional Government and the Petrograd Soviet, Kerensky still enjoyed considerable popularity across a broad spectrum of political groups. The party that suffered the greatest setback from the disturbances of the July Days was the Bolsheviks. Answering Lenin's call for revolution, they had actively supported the demonstrations against the government and the party took much of the blame for the riots. Lenin was forced to flee to Finland and several Bolshevik leaders were arrested.[40]

In an effort to stabilize the military situation, Kerensky replaced the exhausted Brusilov with Lvar Kornilov, a conservative officer with a record as a strict disciplinarian. Kornilov did manage to restore some sense of order among troops supposedly loyal to the Provisional Government. Unfortunately, his political views were well to the right of the prime minister's centrist tendencies, and he insisted upon having complete control over the military. Kerensky soon found himself caught in a tug of war between the conservative pressures from what he termed "Bolsheviks of the Right," such as Kornilov, and the liberal demands of the "Bolsheviks of the Left," who were gaining support in the Petrograd Soviet. "I want to take a middle road," Kerensky complained, "but nobody will help me."[41] Lacking any authority to act on its own, the Provisional Government was helpless in the face of the divergent aims of the various political factions.

The Germans had remained relatively quiet throughout all this confusion, preferring to let the Russian army self-destruct rather than stirring up patriotic resistance to a foreign invader. However, early in September, German troops attacked the Baltic city of Riga, at the northern end of the Eastern Front. The success of their assault produced a new crisis in the Russian government. Fearing that the loss of Riga could trigger a German attack on Petrograd, Kornilov decided to take matters into his own hands by taking charge of the rudderless Russian ship of state. He gathered a division of troops and marched toward the capital with the apparent intention of overthrowing the Provisional Government. Kerensky, who at one point had regarded Kornilov as a political ally, was now forced to turn to the Petrograd Soviet in an effort to save his government from a military coup. The Soviet responded by gathering enough armed militia units to check Kornilov's advance and arrest the rebellious general. On October 8, another coalition government was formed with Kerensky now officially in command of the armies.[42]

The October Revolution

The Kornilov affair marked the end of any effective governance on the part of the Provisional Government. By relying on the military assistance of the Petrograd Soviet to defend his government, Kerensky had essentially transferred the balance of power to the workers. No one realized this more clearly than Vladimir Lenin, who increased his strident calls for "All power to the Soviets!" from his hiding place in Finland. By the end of October, his messages were no longer falling on deaf ears within the Bolshevik Party. It was only a matter of time before the latest coalition government would have to be reorganized, and with every passing week the strength of the Bolsheviks within the Petrograd Soviet was increasing.

Amid all this political maneuvering the economic situation in Russia continued to unravel throughout the months following the February Revolution. Our economic snapshot of the Russian economy (Figure 5.6) documented the decline of income and industrial production in 1916/17. The situation in the cities was exacerbated by shortages of fuel and food combined with a decline in manufacturing output that further eliminated jobs. The food situation was particularly frustrating because there was more than enough grain in the countryside. An indication of how severe the food shortages in the cities had become can be seen in the estimates of government grain procurements, which for August through September of 1917 averaged less than a quarter of the amount needed. These shortages were reflected by the sharp increase in wholesale and retail prices that we examined in Chapter 5.[43] The economic pressures also manifested themselves in street protests and a dramatic increase in the number of workers on strike. Blame for all these economic problems fell on the Provisional Government, which was powerless to do anything about them. Amid this chaos, Kerensky tried to fashion a new coalition that could restore some semblance of order, but he was unable to rally a sufficient bloc of supporters to form an effective government.

The Russian army was disintegrating, the Germans were advancing on the capital, and rumors were circulating that the government was preparing to abandon Petrograd and move to Moscow. Watching all this, Vladimir Lenin concluded that the time was finally ripe for the Bolsheviks to take control of the government by force. By early October, Lenin was back in Russia – though still in hiding – and he attended a meeting where the Bolshevik Central Committee approved a motion stating that an insurrection led by the Bolsheviks was "in principle" a good idea. However, a substantial fraction of the leadership remained cool to the idea of actually trying to carry out an immediate coup against the Provisional Government. One participant later recalled that "hardly any of us thought of the beginning as an armed seizure of all the institutions of government at a given hour ... We thought of the uprising as the simple seizure of power by the Petrograd Soviet."[44] Lenin had far more ambitious plans. He was convinced that a Bolshevik gamble on the use of force to overthrow the Provisional Government would succeed this time. On the evening of November 7, he wrote an open letter to the Petrograd Soviet urging his comrades to take immediate action:

> With all my might I urge comrades to realise that everything now hangs by a thread; that we are confronted by problems which are not to be solved by conferences or congresses (even congresses of Soviets), but exclusively by peoples, by the masses, by the struggle of the armed people. We must not wait! We may lose everything!
>
> ...
>
> All districts, all regiments, all forces must be mobilized at once and must immediately send their delegations to the Revolutionary Military Committee and to the Central Committee of the Bolsheviks with the insistent demand that under no circumstances should power be left in the hands of Kerensky and Co ...
>
> History will not forgive revolutionaries for procrastinating when they could be victorious today (and they certainly will be victorious today), while they risk losing much tomorrow, in fact, they risk losing everything.
>
> The government is tottering. It must be given the death blow at all costs.[45]

Lenin's call for an insurrection in November was based on his confidence that, unlike the situation in July when the Bolsheviks had lacked the resources to back up their call for action, they now had the military means and organization to successfully carry out a *coup d'état* against the Provisional Government. Plans developed for the deployment of troops commanded by members of the Petrograd Soviet to occupy key positions – chiefly bridges, telegraph offices, railway stations, and government buildings – were put in motion on November 7 and by the end of the day the Bolsheviks were in control of the capital and the government.

The Bolshevik "coup" consisted of little more than filling a vacuum left by the inability of the Provisional Government to govern. Kerensky tried to rally troops to defend his government, but given the disorganized state of the Russian army, he was able to gather only a small contingent of loyal troops to oppose the Soviet militias and a contingent of sailors from the nearby Kronstadt naval base. There was a brief skirmish of opposing troops on November 8 which ended with the withdrawal of Kerensky's forces.[46] Lenin had gambled that the time had come for the Soviets to grab power and he had won. Though they represented a distinct minority of the Russian population, the Bolsheviks had managed to grab control of the government in Petrograd.

The Treaty of Brest-Litovsk

Once in power, the Bolsheviks wasted no time addressing the problem of what to do about the war. The Germans were as eager as the Russians to end the fighting, and they agreed to a meeting in the town of Brest-Litovsk, located in eastern Poland, on December 3. The two sides quickly agreed to an armistice that effectively ended the fighting and began negotiations for a treaty that would end Russia's participation in the war a week later.

Despite the eagerness on both sides to reach a permanent agreement, the discussions did not go smoothly. The Germans, who already occupied large areas of Poland, Latvia, Lithuania, and Estonia, made it clear that they had no intention of giving those territories back to Russia. Hindenburg and Ludendorff insisted that Finland and Ukraine should also be broken away from Russia. When the Russians balked at these terms, the German armies renewed their offensive and pushed further into Russian territory. Realizing the futility of further resistance to the German military power, Lenin conceded defeat and agreed to Ludendorff's territorial demands.

A Russian delegation signed the Treaty of Brest-Litovsk on March 3, 1918.[47]

The terms of the Treaty of Brest-Litovsk are largely overlooked in accounts of the Great War because eight months after it was signed, Germany surrendered to the Allied Powers in the west, and the territorial gains that the Germans had squeezed from the Russians were eventually negated by the Treaty of Versailles. Yet at the time of its signing, the treaty between the Germans and the former Russian Empire sent shockwaves throughout the world. Map 6.2 shows the territorial rearrangements brought about by the treaty ending the war between Russia and Germany. The Russians agreed to give up all

Map 6.2 The war in the east, 1917/18

claims to the newly independent Baltic states of Estonia, Lithuania, and Latvia, along with Russian Poland and Finland. In addition, the Germans occupied an area of western Russia that included Ukraine and Crimea. By one estimate, Russia lost about 90 percent of its coal mines, 50 percent of its industry, and 30 percent of its population. Under a separate treaty negotiated on February 9, Germany was to receive 30 percent, Austria-Hungary 50 percent, and Bulgaria and Turkey 20 percent of Ukraine's grain reserves.[48] Lenin was willing to accept these terms despite considerable dissatisfaction within his own government because he needed to concentrate his efforts on the growing menace of armed opposition against the Bolshevik regime that was emerging in Russia.

For Ludendorff and the OHL the treaty was a dream come true. Kaiser Wilhelm called it one of the "greatest successes in world history." Not only did it mean that German troops could be moved from the Eastern Front to the west to launch an attack against the Allies; it also gave the Central Powers access to grain and food supplies from western Russia. There was, however, a downside to all this. The OHL soon discovered that maintaining empires can be expensive, and the former Russian territories required more than a million German and Austrian troops to patrol their new territories, and these men were not available for deployment elsewhere. One can only wonder whether the presence of those troops would have made a difference on the Western Front in the spring of 1918. What we know for sure is that the terms of the Brest-Litovsk treaty created a major tipping point in the war that was to have dramatic implications for the future of central Europe no matter who finally won the war. The terms of the treaty effectively separated a large territory of land from Russian control. Neither the Allies nor the Central Powers were inclined to return those lands to the Bolsheviks when the war finally ended. Equally important was the fact that the terms agreed to by Russia and Germany at Brest-Litovsk meant that the Russians would be excluded from the debates over the political realignment of eastern Europe created by the Paris Peace Conference after the end of the war. Britain, France, and the United States had not recognized the Bolshevik regime, and all three countries would eventually send troops to Russia to support the White Armies in an unsuccessful attempt to unseat the government Lenin and his colleagues had established.

The Sideshows

The withdrawal of Russia from the war and the occupation of large areas of Russian territory by the Germans and Austrians reduced the immediate military threat to the Central Powers from the east. However, there were three other fronts that continued to tie up large numbers of troops and this posed a significant threat to both the Habsburg and Ottoman empires. With the Russian threat out of the way, Ludendorff and the OHL would have preferred to ignore the activities in the east and focus on the Western Front. However, the risk of a collapse of the Austrians in Italy or the Ottomans in Palestine and Mesopotamia could eventually open the way for Allied forces to establish a major threat to the Central Powers from the south. There was also a threat from the Allied troops located in Macedonia. Map 6.2 identifies these three fronts and summarizes the military situation confronting the Central Powers in eastern Europe, the Balkans, and the Middle East at the end of 1917. In Italy the Austrians and the Italians continued their battles in Trentino and the Isonzo regions; British and Ottoman troops were fighting in Palestine and Mesopotamia; and in Macedonia Allied troops posed a threat from the south. Any of these "sideshows" could require attention if either side were able to make a significant breakthrough.

Caporetto: A Cosmetic Victory

The Italians and Austrians had been fighting along a narrow front that followed the Isonzo River along the border between Italy and Austria-Hungary for two and a half years with virtually no change in the front lines. In May 1917 the commander of the Italian army, General Luigi Cardona, launched the tenth battle of Isonzo. Charging into the teeth of Austrian artillery, the Italians gained a meager two miles before being thrown back with heavy losses. Cardona persisted with still another offensive in August with only slightly more favorable results; this time the Italians advanced their lines by six miles before coming to a halt. Nevertheless, the Austrians were nervous about the cost of these battles. Though they were holding their lines for the time being, it was becoming clear that their mountain battles with the Italians were inflicting losses that they could no longer afford. The modest success of the final Italian attack was enough to raise serious concerns about how long the Austrian troops could hold their present positions.

A solution to this situation might be for the Austrians to launch a strong offensive against the equally battered Italians in an effort to break the Isonzo stalemate. However, to do this, the Austrians would need German artillery support. The Austrian request for German support posed a difficult quandary for Ludendorff, who had little confidence in the Austrians' ability to carry out their proposed offensive even with the help of German artillery. The military coordination between the two allies had already become seriously strained by the poor performance of Austrian troops in Galicia, which had led to an insistence on the part of the Germans that all decisions on the Eastern Front must be approved by the OHL. As Ludendorff pondered the situation, he decided that to deny the Austrians any help at this point would further rupture the relationship between the two allies, and possibly lead to a collapse of the Austrian defense along the Isonzo front – which was the last thing Ludendorff wanted as he planned for his great offensive in the west. His solution was to offer more than just artillery support; he agreed to send the Austrians seven divisions of a newly formed German army, under the command of General Otto von Below. Von Below's army included units of "shock troops" that could employ the new tactics of infantry attack that had been developed during the Battle of Verdun. These units were trained to infiltrate behind the enemy lines rather than assaulting fortified positions. They had seen limited use at Verdun and on the Russian front, but had only recently been integrated into infantry units on a broad scale. This would provide the Germans a further test of their new tactics.

Von Below's plan was to concentrate his forces on a thirty-mile stretch of the Isonzo front just north of Trieste. The German troops attacked on October 24, 1917 and almost immediately created a huge gap in the Italian lines. The Italian army simply disintegrated. After two weeks of fighting they had retreated a hundred miles westward to the Piave River (see Map 6.3). In the course of their disorganized retreat they suffered over a quarter-million casualties and 350,000 prisoners with an equal number of men who simply deserted. "The failure to resist on the part of some units of our Second Army, which retired in cowardice without fighting or surrendered to the enemy," reported the Italian War Office in October of 1917, "allowed the Austro-German forces to break into our left wing."[49] Fortunately for the Italians, the

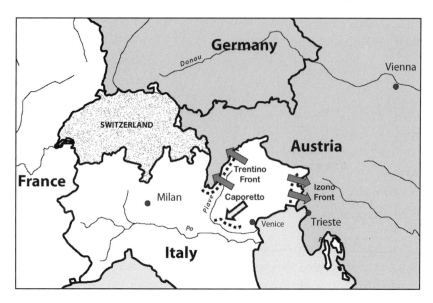

Map 6.3 The Italian front, 1917

Austro-German troops were forced to halt at the Piave River because of torrential rains, together with the usual confusion that followed an unexpected advance and an absence of equipment to deal with the problem of crossing the river.

The British and French were horrified at the possibility that Italy might drop out of the war altogether. Ferdinand Foch, the Chief of the French General Staff, and Sir William Robertson, the Chief of the British Imperial Staff, rushed to Italy to meet with the Italians and assure them that help was on the way. Eventually four French and two British divisions, along with supplies and artillery, would arrive to help stabilize the Italian line along the Piave River. For their part, the men at the OHL were content to let things rest there. Caporetto was a brilliant tactical victory that boosted morale in the Central Powers – particularly the flagging spirits of the Austrians. However, Ludendorff realized that his Italian offensive had accomplished all that could be expected, and he resisted the temptation of trying to push any further into Italy.[50]

Palestine and Mesopotamia

By the beginning of 1917, Edmund Allenby had reorganized the Egyptian Expeditionary Force into two infantry corps together with

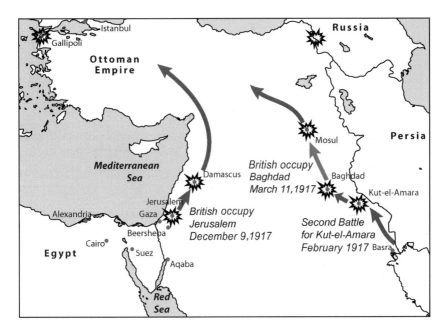

Map 6.4 Palestine and Mesopotamia, 1917

a Desert Mounted Corps which was ready to move against the Gaza–Beersheba line. Map 6.4 shows the movements of troops in Palestine and Mesopotamia. The Turks were convinced that the brunt of the British attack would be focused on Gaza. However, Allenby's plan was to concentrate his forces further west against the Turkish garrison at Beersheba, which would put his troops in a position to outflank the Turkish armies along the coast. With the clever use of some false plans that were placed in Turkish hands, Allenby was able to obtain complete surprise when his troops attacked Beersheba early on the morning of October 31. The combined attacks of infantry and cavalry broke the Turkish resistance and by the end of the day Beersheba was occupied by the British. Allenby then turned his attention to Gaza, which fell to British troops a week later, and on December 9, 1917 British troops entered Jerusalem.

The next objective for the EEF was Damascus. Allenby hoped to continue his northward advance along the coastal plain, with the Arab Revolt forces of T. E. Lawrence and Faisal moving in conjunction with his troops to the east. However, despite the recent success of the EEF. the Western Front remained at the center of the Entente war effort, and this resulted in the reassignment of two divisions of EEF troops to the European theater. Allenby had to reorganize his forces and train new recruits who were arriving from India. His plans for further action in Palestine were placed on hold until the summer of 1918. Nevertheless, the capture of Jerusalem made both Allenby and Lawrence instant heroes to a British public starved of good news after three years of disappointing news from the Western Front.

The British forces in Mesopotamia also managed to meet with some success during 1917. The surrender of 10,000 British troops at Kut-el-Amara in April of 1916 had prompted the appointment of Stanley Maude as the new commander of the Mesopotamia Expeditionary Force. Maude had been instrumental in the successful evacuation of troops from Gallipoli, and he promptly began plans for an offensive that would recapture Kut and eventually capture Baghdad. Kut fell on February 24, and Maude's troops reached Baghdad two weeks later. This sudden success was met with enthusiasm back home; Lloyd George regarded it as "a stroke which at once rehabilitated our prestige in the east and cheered our people … The name of Baghdad counted throughout the Mussulman world." The loss of Baghdad was lamented by the Germans as well. After the war Hindenburg commented that "the loss of the old city of the Caliphs was painful to us in Germany."[51] Decisions by the British War Council to withhold the troops and equipment necessary to carry on an aggressive military campaign meant that it would be another year before Allenby and his troops finally entered Damascus.

Compared with the battles that were raging on the Western Front and in Russia, the British successes in Palestine and Mesopotamia seemed to be relatively minor episodes in the Great War. Certainly, many people at the time regarded them as sideshows. Yet it is easy to overlook the fact that by allowing the French and the British to occupy major cities in the Ottoman Empire, the fate of the Ottoman Empire was sealed regardless of what else was happening in Europe. The Sykes–Picot Agreement in 1916 would eventually play a major role in the settlements in the Middle East following the end of the war.

The Macedonian Front

There was one other sideshow that largely escaped notice amid the excitement of the fighting in the Middle East. In July of 1917, Greece finally abandoned its efforts to remain neutral and entered the war on the side of Entente Powers. For the Greeks it was a difficult decision that split the country into two factions. One group, headed by Prime Minister Eleftherios Venizelos, reflected a deep antipathy among Greeks toward the Central Powers because of the recent struggles to break free from the Ottoman Empire. Venizelists wanted to ally themselves with the Western Powers and strongly opposed any arrangements that might favor the Ottoman Empire or Bulgaria. The other group was led by King Constantine I, who was sympathetic to the Central Powers because he had been educated in Germany and was married to the Kaiser's sister. Constantine anticipated a German victory, but he was not anxious to get involved in the war. He was aware that Greece would be vulnerable to a blockade by the British fleet, and, like most Greeks, he distrusted Austria and Bulgaria. So he insisted that the best course for his country was a policy of neutrality with a distinct favoritism toward Germany and the Central Powers.

Unfortunately for the king, neutrality proved to be a very difficult path to follow. The Austrian invasion of Serbia in August of 1914 had put the Greeks in a difficult position. The Serbs and Greeks had been allies in the Second Balkan War and the two sides had agreed at the end of that war that Greece would come to Serbia's aid if it were attacked by Bulgaria. However, the agreement did not say anything about an attack on Serbia by Austria. So even though most Greeks sympathized with the Serbs, Greece did not intervene in the fight between Austria and Serbia. When the Serbs succeeded in blunting the Austrian attacks at the end of 1914, the situation in the Balkans settled into a nervous game of waiting to see the outcome of the competition between the Entente and Central Powers to vigorously bid for support from Bulgaria, Greece, and Romania through the spring and summer of 1915.

Things changed dramatically in September 1915 when Bulgaria agreed to enter the war on the side of the Central Powers provided that Austria and Germany were willing to support another invasion of Serbia. The Austrians were not enthusiastic after their experience the previous summer, but Erich von Falkenhayn, the German commander–in-chief felt that a victory over Serbia would not only bring Bulgaria into the war on their side, it would also consolidate the Central Powers' position in the Balkans. On October 7, 1915, German and Bulgarian troops under the command of the German General August von Mackensen invaded Serbia and a week later Bulgaria joined the invading forces. The Serbs appealed to the Entente for help but the Western powers were in no position to supply troops in time to help the beleaguered Serbian army. The only feasible way for Entente troops to quickly reach Serbia would be to land them at the northern Greek port of Salonika, but this would violate Greece's policy of neutrality. Prime Minister Venizelos welcomed the idea of intervention by the Entente Powers, and he invited them to organize an expeditionary force and send 150,000 troops to Salonika. King Constantine vigorously opposed the proposal and made it clear that the Entente forces were not welcome in Greece. In one of the more bizarre episodes of this war, the French and the British decided to ignore the Greek king and send troops to Salonika without bothering to obtain permission from the Greek government.

The troops arrived under the command of the French General Maurice Sarrail, but they were too late to be of any use to the Serbian army, which by this time had been forced to take refuge in Albania. Consequently, Entente troops set up a large camp outside Salonika which became known as the "Bird Cage." By the middle of 1916 there were 300,000 "birds" in the "cage." In another six months, the total number of troops fighting on what was now called the Macedonian front grew to 22 divisions consisting of 600,000 men and included units from France, Britain, Italy, Serbia, and Russia.[52] Entente troops engaged German, Austrian, and Bulgarian forces in a series of inconclusive battles along a front that stretched from an area northeast of Salonika to the Aegean coast. The two sides were unable to break through one another's lines and the result was a stalemate that tied down troops to no avail for either side.

While the Macedonian front was turning into another stalemate, the same cannot be said for domestic Greek politics. Following the arrival of uninvited Entente troops in Salonika, Constantine dismissed Venizelos from office and gave orders to Greek army commanders – most of whom had remained loyal to the king – that they should not resist advances by Central Power troops into Greek territory. In May of 1916, the Bulgarian army occupied most of Thrace and parts of eastern Macedonia with little or no resistance from the Greeks. The most blatant act of surrender was the turning over of Fortress Rupert – a strategically important port in Macedonia – without a shot being fired. Constantine's policy of "Germanophile neutrality" particularly incensed a group of Greek military officers who staged a coup against the royal government in September of 1916. With the encouragement of the Entente generals in Salonika, Greek officers began to recruit volunteers to cooperate with the Entente troops fighting in northern Greece. Venizelos and his principal followers joined the mutinous officers in Salonika and in October 1916 he formed a "Provisional Government of National Defense" to rival the Athenian government. A hastily formed triumvirate consisting of Venizelos and two of the renegade officers – General Panagiotis Danglis and Admiral Pavlos Koundouriotis – was formed to organize the new government. By the end of November things were sufficiently organized that the Provisional Government declared war on the Central Powers.

There were now two Greek governments. One was a self-proclaimed Provisional Government operating out of Salonika which was cooperating with the Entente Powers; the other was the royal government in Athens which was openly cooperating with the Central Powers while insisting that Greece was neutral with respect to the war. Venizelos was clever enough not to demand the overthrow of the king, which might have touched off a bitter civil war. However, his Entente allies were not so patient. While they did not immediately recognize the Provisional Government, they backed Venizelos in his efforts to bring Greece into the Entente camp and they instituted a blockade of Greek ports. They also presented the Athens government with a list of demands that included demobilizing the Greek army and turning the Greek navy over to the Entente forces. Constantine tried to reject what amounted to a total takeover of his military authority; however, he was soon faced with the reality that the Entente Powers were prepared to use force, if necessary, to back up their demands. The king left Greece and abdicated his throne in favor of his second son, Alexander. The new king reinstated Venizelos as prime minister of a unified Greek government and on July 2, 1917 Greece formally entered the war on the side of the Entente Powers.

Greece was the last country to decide to formally enter the fighting in the First World War. It was hardly an earth-shaking or unexpected event; there were already 600,000 Entente troops fighting on the Macedonian front that had been established in 1916. Greek battle deaths in the final year and a half of the war totaled 5,000 men, about the level of deaths incurred each day on the Western Front. Yet the struggle in Greece over whether or not to enter the war had enormous repercussions for the future political structure of the country.

The split between the Venizelists and the more conservative royalists/anti-Venizelists was the beginning of the Greek "National Schism" that would dominate Greek politics for the next four decades.[53]

1917: A Year of Tipping Points

The year 1917 was a busy twelve months. Two huge tipping points had emerged that offered each side a chance to win the war. First was the entry of the United States into the war in April; next was the ceasefire signed in December by Germany and Russia that effectively took Russia out of the war. For the Allies (as they were now known) the American intervention brought a surge of confidence that the huge resources of the United States would be able to break the stalemate on the Western Front and finally force Germany to concede defeat. There was a catch to this possibility, however. To realize that advantage, the British and French had to sustain their war effort long enough for the United States to mobilize its resources. That could easily take the better part of a year – or more. For the Germans, the Russian collapse meant that for the first time since the early months of the war they could gather their forces to launch one last effort to break the stalemate on the Western Front. But time was also a key to their success; they had to gain their victory before the Americans arrived to join the fight.

As the world clock announced the arrival of 1918 all of this was still in the future. The die was cast; all that remained was to see how each side would fare in 1918.

7 THE LAST GAMBLE

Yet with such temerity and courage did [Gough] continue
to oppose and muffle the enemy's advance that, after the
first terrible fortnight was passed, the front still stood and
Ludendorff's last throw had patently failed. Amiens was saved;
so was Paris; so were the Channel ports; so was France; so
was England.

        Frederick Smith, Earl of Birkenhead (1930)[1]

Among the many changes that had taken place by the beginning of 1918 was a new cast of characters at the head of the belligerent countries. Georges Clemenceau in France and David Lloyd
George in Great Britain each took charge of his country's war effort
with a determination to pursue the war more vigorously than ever.
Erich Ludendorff and Paul von Hindenburg, the *de facto* military and
political leaders of Germany, were busily planning an offensive that
they confidently expected would win the war. In Russia the Bolshevik
government headed by Vladimir Lenin was in the process of negotiating a treaty with Germany that would take Russia out of the war. In
Vienna, Charles I, who became emperor of the Habsburg Empire upon
the death of Franz Joseph in November 1916, was desperately looking
for a way to get Austria out of the war. Woodrow Wilson, the American
who had narrowly won re-election in 1916 on a platform of keeping
America out of the war, brought a new perspective into the Allied
councils of war. He had resisted the call to arms over the *Lusitania*
sinking in 1915 and the fuss over the Zimmermann Telegraph in early

1917. But when Germany announced that it was resuming unrestricted submarine warfare, he had reluctantly brought the United States into the war in April of 1917.

Woodrow Wilson's Fourteen Points

Unlike the Europeans, whom Wilson regarded as imperial powers protecting their colonial as well as their national interests, the American president had hoped for several years that a neutral United States might prevail upon the belligerent countries to accept what he termed a "peace without victory." The role of the United States, according to Wilson, would be best served not as an ally tied to any existing treaty arrangements, but rather as a "partner" of the Entente Powers in the fight against the German Empire.[2] He remained convinced that it was important for the United States to spell out what he regarded as the necessary conditions for something akin to a peace without victory. In an address before Congress on January 8, 1918, Wilson spelled out the principles that he felt should serve as a guide to the peace that would not only end the fighting, but also provide some guidelines for a peace that would prevent future conflicts. "We entered this war," he told Congress:

> because violations of right had occurred which touched us to the quick and made the life of our own people impossible unless they were corrected and the world secure once for all against their recurrence. What we demand in this war, therefore, is nothing peculiar to ourselves. It is that the world be made fit and safe to live in; and particularly that it be made safe for every peace-loving nation which, like our own, wishes to live its own life, determine its own institutions, be assured of justice and fair dealing by the other peoples of the world as against force and selfish aggression. All the peoples of the world are in effect partners in this interest, and for our own part we see very clearly that unless justice be done to others it will not be done to us.[3]

In his speech, which is reproduced in Appendix 2, Wilson listed fourteen "points" that he regarded as essential aims of the war.

The speech went far beyond any statement of war aims espoused by the Entente or Central Powers. Wilson outlined a sweeping program of institutional arrangements for a postwar world. He began by calling for "open covenants of peace" and diplomacy that rejected the secret agreements and treaties which had characterized antebellum diplomacy; he demanded guarantees of freedom of trade and navigation everywhere; a global reduction of armaments; and a "free, open-minded, and absolutely impartial adjustment of all colonial claims."

Wilson recognized that any peace settlement must involve major changes in the political organization of central Europe and the Middle East. Germany, he said, must evacuate and return all territories that they occupied during the war. The Habsburg and Ottoman empires and their colonial territories must be reorganized into new nation-states based on ethnic and institutional similarities. Wilson was vague on the details of how these empires would be reorganized. For the Habsburg Empire he said, "peoples ... should be accorded the freest opportunity to autonomous development." For the Ottoman Empire, he thought that everyone "should be assured an undoubted security of life and an absolutely unmolested opportunity of autonomous development."

The president went to some length to point out that both the Allies and the Central Powers must come to terms with the implications of the Russian Revolution. "The treatment accorded Russia by her sister nations in the months to come," he noted, "will be the acid test of their good will, of their comprehension of her needs as distinguished from their own interests, and of their intelligent and unselfish sympathy." Wilson closed his speech with a call for the creation of a "general association of nations [that] must be formed under specific covenants for the purpose of affording mutual guarantees of political independence and territorial integrity to great and small states alike."

Looking back on the speech a century later we can see how far his ideas were ahead of his time. Neither the Allied leaders nor those of the Central Powers paid a great deal of attention to the Fourteen Points at the time of the speech and they were hardly eager to accept all of Wilson's suggestions. As it turned out, Wilson himself badly bungled the attempt to incorporate some of his principles into the postwar settlements. His failure to do so was underscored by the refusal of his own countrymen to allow the United States to join a "League of Nations" in 1920. Yet it is worthwhile to look closely at what he said at this point in our narrative because his vision of a world after the war was one of the few cogent statements of what might have been gained from this war in a more perfect world.

In the winter of 1917/18, proposals for peace never had much of a chance. The British and the French had their hands full holding off the threat of German attacks on the Western Front long enough for the American Expeditionary Force to join the fighting, while Ludendorff and the OHL were gambling that, with Russia out of the war, the German army could launch an offensive that would win the war before the Yanks arrived and make Wilson's rhetoric less relevant to the peace settlement. Having extricated themselves from the war, the Bolshevik Russians were too preoccupied with their civil war to pay very much attention to what they viewed as a capitalist war.

Once again, the leaders on all sides of the global war elected to ignore the exits on the road to war marked "Give Peace a Chance!"

The Changing Face of War

Leadership was not the only thing that had changed over the past three years. The industrial revolution that swept through Europe and North America in the nineteenth century had brought forth a new generation of weapons of war that were finally being put to use on the battlefields of western Europe. In 1914 the arsenal of twentieth-century armies and navies already included weapons such as rifles that could fire a magazine of seven to ten bullets accurately with a range of a thousand yards, machine guns that could fire hundreds of bullets in a minute, and artillery pieces that could throw huge explosive shells several miles. Navies had "capital ships" that were steam powered, reached 25 knots per hour, and mounted guns that could reach targets they could not see. These weapons had proved their worth in colonial wars, but the only significant war that had seen them used by both sides in a major conflict was the Russo-Japanese War in 1904–5. Soldiers can be drilled on how to use new weapons and tactics, but the final test of what works and what does not work is a process of "learning by doing" on the battlefield. The huge casualties suffered in trench warfare testified to the ability of artillery to destroy fixed defensive emplacements and of machine guns to mow down rows of advancing infantry in battle after battle, and the inability to break through enemy positions gave generals a strong incentive to look for new and innovative ways to overcome the power of these new weapons.

Learning by doing can be an effective way of discovering the strengths and weaknesses of new approaches, but it can also be a slow and very expensive form of education. By the end of 1917, the experience of battles had provided numerous opportunities to test new weapons and tactics that might finally break the stalemate of trench warfare. The results were sometimes promising, but none of them had worked well enough to command the full confidence needed for a large offensive campaign that would finally end the war. As commanders contemplated their options for 1918, they stepped back and considered what three and a half years of fighting offered in the way of new weapons and approaches to the war.

Artillery

Two of every three casualties in the Great War were caused by artillery shells. Generals understood that the introduction of breech-loading cannons with recoilless carriages provided armies with the ability to rain destruction down on enemy positions several miles away, or to shell advancing troops with smaller, rapid-firing field guns. They had not, however, learned how to harness this awesome power in a way that coordinated the movement of infantry and artillery barrages. Barrages that lasted hours or even days could hurl hundreds of thousands of shells on hostile positions prior to infantry attacks, but enemy soldiers soon learned that they could abandon the forward positions until the artillery stopped firing, then return to the damaged trenches and set up an effective line of defense. To counteract this problem attackers eventually tried shorter bombardments using heavier guns just prior to the attack. These attacks were intended to destroy communication centers as well as fixed fortifications. Both sides developed a practice of creating a "creeping barrage" of artillery fire that provided a protective screen 100 yards or so ahead of the advancing infantry.

Larger guns meant a longer range of fire which allowed enemy artillery positions to be placed well beyond the view of your own batteries. The problem was how to locate the position of enemy guns firing on your positions. The simplest way of doing this was the use of reconnaissance aircraft equipped with radio contact which allowed a spotter in the airplane to relay the location of enemy batteries to their own gun crews on the ground. However, verbal descriptions were not always reliable or accurate enough to pinpoint the target. A more accurate means of finding the location of enemy batteries was the development of range-finding techniques known as "sound ranging" or "flash-spotting." These techniques involved measuring the time it took for the sound from a shell fired from an enemy gun to reach your trenches. With multiple observations, the gunners could use the speed of sound and trigonometry equations to estimate the location of the gun that fired the shell. By 1916 the British had developed special microphones for picking up the sounds of enemy guns firing and were able to estimate the German gun locations within 25 yards.[4]

Tanks

Even when infantry attacks succeeded in penetrating the initial lines of defense, there was the problem of supporting the attacking troops as they moved beyond the range of accurate artillery fire. Counterattacks by enemy troops could slow the advance and limit the territory gained from the initial infantry attack. The absence of a mobile weapon that could not only help the infantry to break through the front trenches, but also provide further support to carry the attack deeper into enemy lines limited the success of frontal attacks on the Western Front. One of the best-known military innovations of the First World War was the introduction of the "tank," an armored vehicle that had the capability of plowing through barbed wire and crawling over trenches. The British took an early lead in the search for such an armored vehicle. The man credited with developing the first workable machine was Ernest Swinton, who persistently pressed his ideas for "some armoured object, petrol-driven, and caterpillar-mounted, that would squash the nests of German machine guns as boot heels do those of wasps."[5]

One of the men impressed with Swinton's ideas, and the persistence with which he presented them, was Winston Churchill, the First Lord of the Admiralty. In February 1915 Churchill created a group within the Admiralty called the Landship Committee to oversee the development of an armored vehicle that matched Swinton's proposals. The committee's existence was initially kept secret from the War Office, the Board of the Admiralty, and the Treasury – all of whom Churchill correctly believed would resist the idea until the first prototypes were completed and could demonstrate their usefulness. In July 1915, when the Landship Committee's secret operations were discovered, it was taken over by the army and renamed the "Tank Supply Committee."[6]

After several earlier prototypes had been developed and discarded, the first model Mark I tank was finished and ready for testing in January 1916. It was about 31 feet long, 8 feet high, and nearly 14 feet in beam. Fully laden with a crew of eight men it weighed 28 tons. Two models were put into production: the "male" version, which mounted two 6-pound cannons, and the "female" version, which was equipped with two sponsons mounting machine guns. The army placed an order for fifty of each type. They were put into action on the Western Front for the first time during the Battle of the Somme in the summer of 1916 with less than spectacular results. Only eleven of the forty-nine tanks engaged in the battle managed to reach the German trenches. Both Swinton and Churchill insisted that too few tanks had been rushed into action before the design had been improved to the point where they were ready for combat. With his characteristic flair, Churchill complained that "My poor 'land battleships' have been let off prematurely and on a petty scale." The Tank Supply Committee sent their personnel back to the drawing boards to correct problems of reliability and increase the tank's armor protection. By the middle of 1917 they had come up with a new and improved Mark IV tank that everyone agreed was ready for battle.

The British generals had been sufficiently impressed with the effectiveness of the few tanks that did reach the German lines at the Somme and with the improvements introduced by the Mark IV model that they were willing to give the new vehicle another test. Since early in the war the Germans had occupied a position on an elevated point known as Messines Ridge that ran parallel to the British lines near Ypres and posed a threat to any British offensive operations. Sir Herbert Plummer, commander of the British Third Army, had been working on a plan to capture the ridge since mid-1916. His idea was to employ an extensive artillery bombardment, followed by a massive detonation of more than 500 tons of explosives planted under the middle of the German position.[7] Plummer approached Douglas Haig and suggested that his plan, augmented with seventy-two of the new Mark IV tanks, could serve as a useful prelude to the larger attack that Haig was organizing to capture the Channel ports. Haig agreed to let Plummer proceed with the experiment, and the tanks proved to be an effective way of unnerving the German infantry by breaching barbed wire and reaching the enemy trenches. However, their lack of speed and mechanical problems still made them easy prey for German field artillery, and Plummer's troops did not have sufficient reserves to take advantage of the opportunity provided by the mine explosions, the heavy artillery support, and the presence of the tanks to proceed beyond the initial breakthrough in the German lines. Nevertheless, when all was said and done, the British forces were able to occupy and hold Messines Ridge and the tanks had proved their effectiveness in a major battle. When the British populace received news of this success they celebrated by ringing church bells. However, the success achieved at the Battle of Messines Ridge was soon buried amid the mud and casualties of Haig's disastrous Passchendaele campaign in the months that followed.

All this was not completely in vain. While tanks were of little or no use in the mud of Passchendaele, one of the more obvious lessons of their use in the Somme and the Messines Ridge assaults was that the appearance of such awe-inspiring behemoths caused enormous confusion among the enemy infantry units. As more tanks became available for action, the army created a "Tank Corps" of about five hundred tanks that could be assigned to support specific army units. In August 1917 General Hugh Elles from the Tank Corps and General Henry Tudor from the Artillery Corps came up with a proposal that would combine tanks, heavy artillery, and air support acting together in a surprise assault against the town of Cambrai, which served as a major supply depot for the Germans along the Siegfried–Hindenburg Line. Tudor's idea was to use the new sound technology that improved the accuracy of artillery to support his infantry attack. His original suggestion had involved only a small number of tanks to clear a path for the infantry through barbed wire, but Elles convinced him that a much larger force of tanks advancing in front of the advancing infantry and behind the artillery barrage could create a major breakthrough in the German trenches. Douglas Haig, who was anxious for any signs of success after the collapse of his Passchendaele offensive, approved the plan, apparently feeling that it was a gamble worth a try.

On November 20, more than a thousand British artillery pieces opened a concentrated barrage of fire on the surprised Germans. What began as a six-mile gap in the German lines gradually expanded to a twelve-mile breach. The artillery attack was followed by the appearance of Mark IV tanks in a massed formation moving ahead of the advancing infantry. Once again the tanks suffered heavy casualties – 179 of them were put out of action by enemy fire and 71 suffered mechanical failures. But the rest of the force managed to clear a wide path through the barbed wire and attacked the German trenches.[8] Although the German units facing the tank attack had encountered tanks in the past, the sheer number of the vehicles overwhelmed the troops in the forward trenches and forced them to withdraw. The account of one German observer was typical of the reaction of men in the trenches in defending themselves against the tanks:

> There were enemy tanks everywhere, followed by two waves of British assault troops at 200 and 300 metres distance. Nowhere did our artillery appear to be having any sort of effect. Finally the enemy realised that we had been forced into one final pocket of resistance. Tanks approached from all sides, the guns in their small turrets bringing down unbroken fire. We suffered considerable casualties and our gallant band shrank constantly as we repeatedly yielded sections of trench. Finally, faced with a hopeless situation, we gathered in the sunken road. Tanks appeared at the western edge of the ravine, which enabled them to bring their guns to bear all along it. The game was up.[9]

Historian Jack Sheldon notes that "the forward companies poured small arms fire at the infantry accompanying the tanks and against the tanks themselves, but their efforts were largely in vain. Outnumbered, overrun and overpowered they fell where they stood or were swiftly captured and sent back to the British rear in large numbers."[10]

The Battle of Cambrai provided a clear demonstration of the power and mobility that tanks could bring to the battlefields of the Western Front. Their presence provided the Allies with a weapon that could spearhead the offensives that eventually won the war in 1918. However, the battle also showed that the Mark IV tanks still had severe limitations. They were designed explicitly for use against the trench warfare that characterized the Western Front, and they were still in a very early stage of development. As John Terraine notes, "in all considerations of First World War tanks ... one has to reflect that the internal combustion engine itself was still in its infancy, that automobile output was, by modern standards, still pitifully small, and that what was now required for tank development was, in effect, an entirely new branch of technology."[11] They were slow, cumbersome behemoths that could seize a position, but they could not hold that position without infantry support, and they were extremely vulnerable to fire from German field artillery. However, the biggest problem that frustrated the British at Messines Ridge and at Cambrai was that their own artillery and infantry were unable to follow up and hold breakthroughs created by the tanks. In both battles, the Germans were able to regroup to defenses further back from the front trenches and eventually stop the British attacks from further advances. Cambrai showed that tanks could not do the job all by themselves; but these encounters also demonstrated that an attack that could make use of infantry, artillery, and tanks working together just might succeed.

Curiously, the Germans stubbornly refused to embrace the possibilities offered by the new weapon. Their attempt to design a tank was the Sturmpanzerwagen A7V, which made its way to the battlefield in early 1918 and was singularly ineffective in action. The army had ordered a hundred A7Vs to be produced, but poor performance caused them to cancel the order after the first twenty were delivered. The A7V was a 30–33 ton "moving fortress" that carried a crew of eighteen and mounted a 57 mm canon and six machine guns. It proved to be unwieldy and unable to cross trenches, and was no match for the Mark V British tanks.[12] The failure to appreciate the value of tanks on the part of the German military was one of their most serious oversights of the war. Primitive though they were, the British Mark IV and V tanks were fearsome creatures on the battlefield, and the British economy was able to produce enough of them to compensate for the high rate of attrition in battle. The British and French also employed smaller tanks, nicknamed "Whippets," that were smaller than the British Mark IV and V models, and were used as a means of mobile firepower accompanying infantry assaults.

The Germans were able to develop some reasonably effective anti-tank weapons, including a Mauser Tank-Gewehr rifle, which fired a 13 mm cartridge bullet that could disable a Mark IV tank's tread, damage the engine, or pierce the command cupola. They also found ways to employ their field artillery as anti-tank weapons. Their favorite was a 7.7 mm field artillery piece that could fire a very low trajectory shell against an advancing tank. By the middle of 1918 German gunners had become very proficient at using their artillery against advancing tanks. Jack Sheldon relates stories of German infantry at Cambrai tying three or more hand grenades together to throw at a tank, a trick that would only work if you managed to get the grenades under the tank.[13] The fact remained that without some form of support from field artillery, German infantry were almost helpless in the face of attacking tanks. A somewhat fatalistic approach to dealing with tanks was that of the Austrian General Arz von Straussenberg, who insisted that tanks posed no serious threat to his men and advised them to "simply ignore [the tanks] and concentrate on the following infantry ... who are the most dangerous opponent." Holger Herwig points out that it was fortunate that Straussenberg's advice was for soldiers fighting on the Eastern Front where there was a far more open battlefield than in the west and many fewer tanks. "Soldiers were instructed to dig fox holes and not to waste ammunition by firing on the mechanical monsters with machine guns."[14]

Airplanes

Another new weapon that the development of the internal combustion engine made possible for the first time was the airplane. In 1914 airplanes were still a novelty; however, the possibility of using them for military purposes was quickly explored. The British General Sir James Grierson, after observing the Royal Flying Corps maneuvers in 1912, commented on the promise of airplanes in future wars:

> The impression left on my mind is that their use has revolutionized the art of war. So long as hostile aircraft are hovering over one's troops all movements are liable to be seen and reported, and therefore the first step in war will be to get rid of the hostile aircraft ... Soon warfare will be impossible unless we have mastery of the air.[15]

Grierson was ahead of the curve at this point, and not everyone shared his enthusiasm for air power. In August 1914 the combined forces of Britain, France, and Germany totaled only 364 planes of all types, and their main activity was limited to observing action on the ground from above the battlefields. To be sure, this was more than a perfunctory service. It was aerial observation by British aircraft that alerted Entente commanders in September 1914 to the vulnerability of the German Fourth and Fifth armies and allowed them to organize their forces for the counterattack that stopped the Germans at the First Battle of the Marne. "This vital information-gathering," notes John Terraine, "was a striking debut for the most strikingly novel part of the Industrial Revolution's contribution to modern war."[16]

Observation and photographic reconnaissance remained an important part of the airplane's role in military operations throughout the war. As Grierson predicted, that meant control of airspace was essential. This led to the development of "fighter" aircraft that could attack or defend against enemy planes. Aerial "dogfights" over the trenches became a daily routine, and pilots with multiple "kills" became heroes who captured the imagination of people on the home front. The most famous "ace" of the war was Germany's Manfred von Richthofen. The "Red Baron" accumulated eighty kills before he was finally shot down in April of 1918 over the trenches around Amiens. As a sign of respect for a fallen foe, the Australian troops gave Richthofen a burial with full military honors. Michael Clodfelter notes that a total of just over a thousand "aces" were credited to Great Britain, France, and the United States, while Germany had 367. As a testimony to the skill involved in the war over the trenches, Michael Clodfelter estimates that about 4 percent of all fighter pilots accounted for about 50 percent of all hostile aircraft shot down.[17] While "aces" basked in the glory of individual dogfights, "formation flying" – a policy similar to the convoy system adopted by the navy to protect merchant ships – was developed to protect reconnaissance planes.[18] Reconnaissance continued to play a vital part of everyday operations, but it soon became obvious that airplanes armed with machine guns also could also act as mobile weapons capable of strafing enemy units without the need to break through enemy lines.

Putting weapons on airplanes was not a simple matter. Among the more complicated challenges was the need to develop a way to prevent the bullets from machine guns mounted on the fuselage from destroying the airplane's propeller. This led to the development of "interrupter" or "synchronization" gears that would ensure that machine guns would not fire if the bullet would hit the propeller.[19] As early as 1916 British General Hugh Trenchard, who was appointed head of the Royal Flying Corps in 1915, insisted that "An aeroplane is an offensive, not a defensive weapon," and he advocated "a policy of relentless and incessant offensive."[20] Both sides spent time and money developing and improving the design of airplanes that might temporarily give one side or the other an advantage in the contest to control the skies. The ability of Allied planes to strafe or bomb infantry positions with relative impunity introduced an added "terror" factor among enemy troops that systematically reduced their morale. A British officer described the scene of an aerial attack by more than six hundred Allied planes on Austrian troops retreating from the Italian front in October 1918:

> All along the road were broken vehicles and all the litter out of them, dead horses sometimes with limbs off or bellies ripped open, corpses of men on the road and in the fields where they had run to escape the machine guns and bombs from the planes ... I don't want to go into what I saw too much, but it was terrible.[21]

Similar scenes could be found in the desert campaigns, where Edmund Allenby found the geography of the desert was an ideal site to employ the advantages of aerial mobility to strafe and bomb enemy troops as he pushed north toward Syria.

A final note on the use of air power involves the introduction of airplanes designed to drop bombs on enemy targets behind the battle lines – including the possibility of bombing enemy towns or cities. In May of 1917 a flight of twenty-one German "Gotha" bombers crossed the English Channel to bomb the town of Folkstone. Because of the weather, only a few bombers reached the town and dropped their bombs on it, but as Martin Gilbert reports, "it was civilians who were the victims: sixteen men, thirty women and twenty-five children. When the raid was over, 95 people had been killed and 192 injured, and a new element had been introduced to warfare."[22] These attacks were only the beginning of a growing effort by both sides to use air attacks against both civilian and military objectives. Michael Clodfelter documents 435 German sorties – most of them against London – that killed or wounded more than three thousand civilians and did about £3 million in damage. German raids on Paris caused just under a thousand casualties. Air raids by the British against German cities caused about 2,500 casualties.[23] Compared with the carnage wrought by the bombing efforts of the Second World War, these casualties seem almost trivial. However, the impact of the bombings on the civilian population was due not so much to the physical destruction of lives and properties, as it was to the psychological blow of having to deal with unexpected death from the sky.

Foreign wars had always been seen as troublesome events, but the airplane brought the conflict right to your doorstep. In this sense the air raids were much more akin to the public reaction to terrorist bombings a century later than to the massive Second World War bombing raids. Even at the height of the bombings in the Great War not many people were killed or injured. But the constant threat of an attack brought forth cries of protest from frightened citizens and demands that the Royal Air Corps divert fighters to defend the skies over London. The authorities responded to the attacks by constructing an elaborate system of air defenses that included planes and anti-aircraft guns. The British air defense system in April 1918 consisted of 266 anti-aircraft guns, 353 searchlights, and 274 fighter planes. The disposition of these elements stretched from London itself to the military positions along the southern coast.[24] Lacking the sophistication of future air defenses, these attempts to "defend" against air raids were more of an effort to boost morale than to prevent the bombs from being dropped. A German report published in 1928 noted that

> The direct destructive effect of the enemy air raids did not correspond with the resources expended for this purpose. On the other hand, the indirect effect, namely, falling off of production of war industries, and also the breaking down of the moral resistance of the nation, cannot be too seriously estimated.[25]

The foundation of a major change in the paradigm for waging war had been laid. The use of air power and the development of new weapons to instill fear in enemy populations would grow dramatically over the next two decades.

Infantry Tactics

While they ignored the use of tanks, the Germans were ahead of their opponents in developing "infiltration tactics" for highly skilled units of infantry trained to exploit breakthroughs in the opposing line of trenches. The fighting on the Eastern Front in 1917 had encouraged General Oskar von Hutier to develop a complex scheme of offensive tactics that combined massive artillery bombardments with specially trained teams of *Stoßtruppen* (storm troopers) to infiltrate enemy lines and attack key points in the enemy defenses. The key to Hutier's system was the launch of sudden and unexpected attacks against the weakest points of the enemy lines. The tactics involved a short but very intensive artillery bombardment with explosive and gas shells that was intended to neutralize the enemy troops in addition to destroying fortifications.

This use of artillery barrages forced enemy soldiers to take cover or retreat before the German infantry attack. The initial shelling would be followed by a second round of artillery shells to cover the storm troopers, who would advance in dispersed groups to attack specific points of interest such as command posts, artillery positions, or supply and communication centers. Close on the heels of the storm troopers would be the arrival of special infantry groups with light machine guns and flamethrowers to attack points that had been missed or deliberately bypassed by the storm troopers on their way to other targets. Flamethrowers had been used before, although not as a normal piece of ordinance in small infantry groups. The final phase of the attack would be an assault by regular infantry units to mop up whatever enemy resistance was left. A major premise of the Hutier tactics was the use of surprise and dispersed troop movement to replace the practice of sending waves of troops going "over the top" to charge into the face of a withering enemy fire. Hutier had used the system effectively in the east, and the Germans spent the winter of 1917/18 training and developing units for the new system of attack on the Western Front in the spring.

The introduction of tanks and the development of dispersed infantry tactics brought a mobility of action that had been missing on the Western Front. However, one problem that none of the new innovations could fully resolve was the state of the battlefield that the armies were fighting on. The constant use of heavy artillery barrages left the fields filled with craters that made movement of men and equipment difficult. The reliance on heavier artillery ordinance also posed a challenge of how to move the heavy guns forward to keep up with the advancing tanks and infantry as the battle expanded. Even the most successful breakthroughs were eventually slowed by the inability to move the heavy guns over the "moonscape" battlefield. Without artillery support, the infantry was left with the option of either slowing the advance or returning to the system of massed infantry attacks that had been so futile earlier in the war.

1918: The Ludendorff Offensives

On March 3, 1918 representatives from the German and Russian governments signed the Treaty of Brest-Litovsk. This was the moment that Erich Ludendorff had been waiting for. Russia was no longer in the war. For three months, the Germans had been steadily moving men and equipment from the east to the west in preparation for one last offensive that could win this war. Thousands of artillery pieces that ranged in size from 77 mm field guns to giant 210 mm cannons had been carefully put in place along a stretch of the Siegfried–Hindenburg Line stretching from Arras to Saint-Quentin, together with seventy-six infantry divisions – more than a million men – who were ready to spring into action at a moment's notice.[26] This was, in many ways, a replay of the drama associated with the launching of the Schlieffen Plan in August of 1914 – a huge gamble calculated to win or lose the war in a single stroke.

Ludendorff had carefully considered his options. The Allied lines stretched from the British forces at Ypres to the French forces south of Verdun in the south, and Ludendorff knew that he did not have the resources to simultaneously attack both foes at once. Various members of his staff favored a concentration on either Verdun or Ypres. However, German efforts to break the enemy lines at those points had failed earlier in the war. Ludendorff decided on a series of sequential attacks that would begin with a major offensive launched against the point where the British and the Germans fought on the battlefield of the Somme in 1916. Map 7.1 shows the plan as the attacks unfolded in the spring of 1918. The objective was to create a breakthrough at the Somme which would separate the British forces from the French, and then follow with additional attacks near Ypres designed to capture the Channel ports and force the BEF out of France. The Germans would then be in a position to push the French forces south toward Paris and eventually force the French to sue for peace as they had in 1871.

The decision to attack the center of the Allied lines proved to be a very fortuitous choice. The British commander, Douglas Haig, was sure that the main German attack would come at the northern end of their lines near Ypres, and he had allocated his resources accordingly. As a result, the British sector near the Somme battlefield was held by the British Fifth Army, which was still recovering from its ordeal at Passchendaele. Their commander, Sir Hubert Gough, a former cavalryman who was not known for his organizational skills, was struggling to reorganize his troops and rebuild a section of trenches that his troops had taken over from the French. Together with Julian Byng's Third Army to the north, there were twenty-six British divisions arrayed

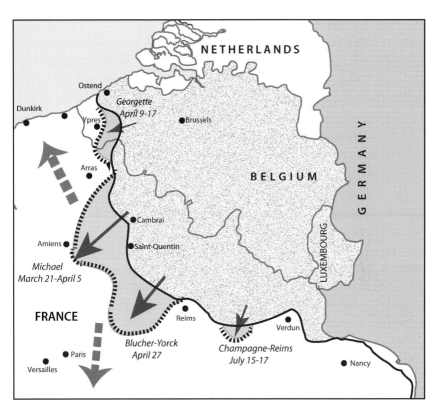

Map 7.1 The Ludendorff offensives, spring 1918

against a German force almost twice that size. Although the British were badly out-manned and out-gunned in this sector, Haig was not concerned; he remained confident that any German attack would be centered at the northern end of the British lines, not in the area of the Somme battlefield.

Haig's confidence was, as usual, terribly misplaced. Early on the morning of March 21 the trenches from Arras to Saint-Quentin erupted in a maelstrom of German artillery shells raining down on the British troops. Operation Michael, the first phase of Ludendorff's plan, was underway. In addition to holding a sizeable advantage in terms of the number of men and guns involved, the Germans had the element of surprise in their favor. The advance units of Gough's army were completely overrun by the Germans on the first day, and Byng's Third Army was forced to quickly fall back to reserve positions that opened up a huge gap in the center of the British lines. At the end of the first day the Germans had managed to push British troops back more than ten miles and occupy almost a hundred square miles of territory – an advance that equaled the total gains the British had made against the Germans in 140 days of fighting on the Somme in 1916. By early April the Germans had advanced sixty miles beyond their initial positions, and were close enough to Paris that their huge 210 mm artillery pieces could fire shells that would fall on the city.[27] Operation Michael was a huge success for the Germans. It was the first major defeat for British troops on the Western Front, and their retreat was so disorganized that at times it appeared as though the lines might completely break and open the possibility for the Germans to force the British to retreat to the Channel ports and hope for the best.

That did not happen. Byng's troops held their lines on the north edge of the breakthrough and Haig rushed every available British reserve to close the gap between the British Third and Fifth armies. The French added some troops to help stem the German tide, although their commander, Henri Philippe Pétain, was reluctant to commit more than a few divisions to assist the British because he believed – correctly, as it turns out – that the Germans were still planning an attack further south. The only other source of troops was the still untested Americans. Up to this point General John Pershing, the American commander-in-chief, had resisted all requests on the part of his allies to send individual units of American troops to fight under British or French commanders. On March 23 Lloyd George sent a telegraph to the British ambassador in Washington, DC instructing him to explain to President Wilson that "this situation is undoubtedly critical and if America delays [in providing troops] now she may be too late."[28] There had been growing frictions between Pershing and the British and French leaders over the American's refusal to allow American troops who were already in France to be pushed into action under the direction of Entente officers. At a conference in Abbeville on May 2, Pershing insisted that "the morale of the soldiers depends upon fighting under our own flag." Lloyd George later wrote to his ambassador in the United States that "It is maddening to think that though the men are there, the issue may be endangered because of the short-sightedness of one General and the failure of his government to order him to carry out their undertakings."[29] Pershing reluctantly relented and allowed five American divisions to be thrown into action.

As is so often the case in such situations, it was Hubert Gough, the commander of the Fifth Army, who took the blame for the apparent collapse of the British lines. Recognizing that he was faced with a difficult hand to play at the outset of the battle, historians have tended to be kinder to Gough than many of his contemporaries were. Gough had an army that was still in the midst of a major reorganization, yet his troops managed to rally and hang on long enough for help to arrive, and they did not allow the Germans to take Arras, which was a major British supply center. The primary force behind Gough's removal was Lloyd George, who demanded some sort of action be taken to alleviate the public outcry over the British retreat. Haig was not pleased with the removal of one of his favorite generals; he pointed out that "fewer men, extended front, and increased hostile forces were the main causes to which the retreat may be attributed." Haig also noted that, "in spite of a most difficult situation, [Gough] had never really lost his head."[30] Despite Haig's objections, Gough was replaced. A further change in the command structure of the Allied forces was the appointment on April 3 of Ferdinand Foch as the supreme commander of the French, British, and American forces. For the first time in the war, the Allied forces were under the direction of a single commander.

As Operation Michael finally ground to a halt just short of Amiens at the end of March, Ludendorff launched his second offensive, Operation Georgette, against the British lines south of Ypres. The plan had been for this attack to be coordinated with Operation Michael so that after their initial attacks the two army groups would be in a position to swing north and advance on the Channel ports. Michael had started well enough: the Germans quickly gained ten miles of territory and recaptured Messines Ridge. However, the British lines stiffened and by April 19 the German offensives had been stopped just east of Amiens and no longer posed any threat to the Channel ports. To make matters worse, the Germans had once again failed to capture Ypres.

At this point the German soldiers were beginning to lose heart. The usual problems of logistics keeping up with the troops surfaced again, and as historian Alan Palmer notes,

> [The German soldiers] were delighted at finding such fine rations abandoned by the Fifth Army in its precipitate retreat – not merely tins of corned beef, or bacon and cheese and jam, but oats for the horses – delighted, that is, until [the] more

hard-bitten veterans began to reflect that, if Britain's front-line troops had such abundance of supplies, then the U-boats could hardly have brought "England" to the verge of starvation, as German propagandists maintained.[31]

As the morale of the German troops sagged perceptibly, so did the chances of a German victory in the west. Operations Michael and Georgette had gained a large chunk of territory and inflicted enormous losses on the British army. Earlier in the war these accomplishments would have been celebrated as great victories. But there was no time to celebrate now. Neither attack had achieved its principal objectives. Arras and Ypres were still in British hands and at the end of April German losses were more severe than those incurred by the British.[32]

Ludendorff's Last Gasp

The final phase of Ludendorff's offensives, codenamed Operation Blucher-Yorck, began on April 27. Originally planned as a "diversion" from the attacks in the north, it had become a major operation that stretched along a 25-mile front north from Reims (see Map 7.1). Once again the German forces made substantial gains in their initial attacks, and by the end of May German troops had again reached the Marne. However, at this point they were forced to stop and regroup. An additional offensive launched on June 9 failed to push the advance any further.[33] In a last gasp effort to capture Reims, forty-seven German infantry divisions, with the support of more than six thousand pieces of artillery launched an attack across the Marne River. This time Foch had information warning him of the German attacks and the French were prepared. Two days before the Germans planned to begin their advance, French artillery shelled the area where the advance units of the German attack were assembling, seriously disrupting the preparations. When fourteen German divisions managed to cross the Marne just east of Reims, they were contained by counterattacks by French and American troops. Allied air power and artillery forces destroyed bridges over the Marne, seriously disrupting the German supply lines, so Ludendorff was forced to hurriedly pull the units back across the river. The Second Battle of the Marne lasted four days and effectively ended the Ludendorff offensives.

In March of 1918 morale and confidence among the German army had approached the enthusiasm of 1914. By the middle of July both the confidence and the morale of the troops had visibly sagged. Holger Herwig summarizes the situation facing Hutier at this point:

> [His] soldiers were exhausted. No petrol for trucks. No ammunition for the artillery. No reserves. Poor defensive positions. The situation is terrible. For the first time, reserves coming up to the front were met with shouts of "strike breakers" by hardened veterans. Hutier was upset that "the OHL counts only the number of divisions, not their strength and their [fighting] value." Some battalions were down from their normal strength of 900 men to just 100. British airplanes strafed the trenches with such intensity that the soldiers could neither sleep nor rest. *Operation Michael* had driven them to the limits of their moral and physical capabilities.[34]

The grand offensives had cost the Germans more than a million casualties, and more than two thousand pieces of artillery had been lost, together with huge stores of ammunition and food. Neither the men nor the supplies could be easily replaced by a German economy that was struggling from shortages caused by the tightening of the Allied blockade together with the inability of German firms to reach the production goals set by the Hindenburg economic plan.

Despite this enormous effort on the part of the Germans, the Allied lines had held. All the Germans had to show for their huge losses of manpower and equipment was a modest increase in the amount of French territory occupied by German armies. They now controlled roughly 19,500 square miles of Belgium and northern France, all of which had to be patrolled by men who were unable to take part in the attacks along the Western Front. In the final analysis, the spring offensives had failed to achieve any of their significant military objectives. Operations Michael and Georgette had not taken either Ypres or Arras, and neither Amiens nor Reims had fallen to subsequent attacks. The Channel ports, which were the ultimate objectives of the great offensives, were never seriously threatened. While Allied losses were considerable, by the end of July more than a million American troops were ready for combat, and the Germans had no way of increasing their own reserves to meet this new challenge.

Ludendorff had lost the last German gamble of the war.

100 Days: The Allies Strike Back

With the collapse of the Ludendorff offensives, the Allies were finally in a position to take control of the Western Front. They now had the men, the tactics, and the technology to wage a new form of warfare, and for the first time all the Allied armies would be under the command of one man: the French Marshal Ferdinand Foch. Foch wasted no time capitalizing on their advantage. Even before the German advance had been completely stalled at the Second Battle of the Marne, Foch was ready to take the offensive. Map 7.2 shows the Allied counterattacks that began on July 18 with a contingent of troops that included American, French, British, and Italians launching a series of counteroffensives against the German units on the Marne. Bolstered by 350 French and British tanks, the Aisne–Marne offensive erased the salient that had been created by the final German offensives of the war to threaten Paris. In three weeks of heavy fighting the front lines were shortened by twenty-eight miles.[35] The action then shifted north to the region around Amiens, where an attack on August 8 by British forces – including 600 tanks – advanced ten miles on the first day, and took 15,000 prisoners. Though the Germans managed to slow the advance of Allied troops over the course of the next few days, the success of the initial Allied attack at Amiens

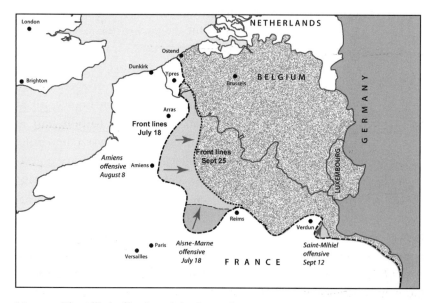

Map 7.2 The Allied offensives, July–September 1918

served notice to them that the new tactics and equipment employed by the Allied units could create a breakthrough anywhere in the German lines. When the Allies renewed their attacks in the Amiens offensive they were able to force the German army to pull back to the Siegfried–Hindenburg Line. Ludendorff called the surrender of so many troops on August 8 "the black day of the German Army in this war."

September brought more bad news for the Germans in the form of evidence that the Americans were finally ready to fight on their own. On September 12, more than 200,000 American troops attacked the Saint-Mihiel salient south of Verdun (See Map 7.2). Neither Foch nor Douglas Haig, both of whom would have preferred to continue the practice of placing the inexperienced Americans with veteran French or British units, had been particularly enthusiastic about the Saint-Mihiel operation. However, John Pershing was adamant that his army be given a chance to prove itself as an independent unit, and the Allied generals finally agreed to let the Americans get into a fight of their own. The troops still had much to learn about trench warfare, and many of them fought with weapons supplied by their French and British allies. However, in the space of four days Pershing's men cleared the German troops from the Saint-Mihiel salient. Pershing was ecstatic over the result of the battle. "An American Army," he wrote after the war, "was an accomplished fact, and the enemy had felt its power. No form of propaganda could overcome the devastating effect on the morale of the enemy of this demonstration of our ability to organize a large American force and drive it successfully through its defenses."[36] For the time being, the inexperienced "doughboys" made up for their lack of experience with unbounded enthusiasm, and Pershing was certainly correct that the Germans found the appearance of so many Americans on the battlefield – with more arriving every day – to be very demoralizing.

Foch was now convinced that the Allied forces could simply overwhelm the German troops. There was nothing subtle or complex about his approach; he organized a series of simultaneous attacks along the Allied front from Ypres to Verdun. The Belgians, who had done relatively little fighting on the front lines since the beginning of the war, fielded twelve divisions of men under the command of King Albert to attack at the north end of the Allied lines. Douglas Haig, who remained as confident as ever that one more blow would finally break the back of German resistance, would lead an attack in the area between Cambrai and Saint-Quentin. Henri Pétain, the hero of Verdun, would command the largest contingent of Allied troops in a major attack against the center of the German line. John Pershing's AEF troops would attack at the southern end of the line opposite the Argonne forest. (See Map 7.3.)[37]

Foch proved to be an excellent choice for commander-in-chief of the Allied forces. In addition to handling the logistical challenge of organizing thousands of tanks, airplanes, artillery, and transport vehicles to support more than 5 million troops, he was able to deal with the independent nature of his commanders and the concerns of politicians back at the home fronts, who had been contemplating a war that would last well into 1919. Foch was anxious to finish the job while they had the Germans reeling under the impact of Ludendorff's failed offensives, but after so many examples of offensives that had come up short of their mark, there were some voices who urged caution. Lloyd George – who still remembered both the Somme and Passchendaele disasters – had doubts about carrying out an ambitious

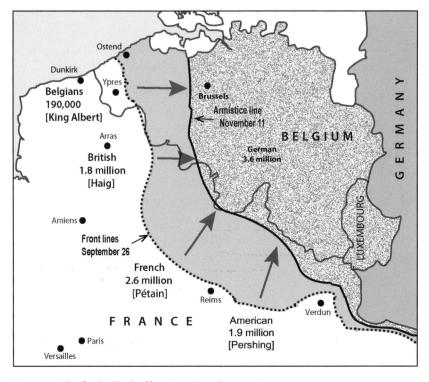

Map 7.3 The final Allied offensives, October 1918

plan without pausing to reorganize the tired Allied forces. Pershing reluctantly acceded to Foch's plan, although he personally would have preferred an attack by the AEF to the south toward Metz. Eventually, Foch succeeded in persuading all concerned to undertake his massive offensive right away.[38]

Foch's approach – "Toute le monde à la battaille" – was a slightly toned-down return to the French *élan* of 1914. Each of the four army groups was told to attack with everything at hand and maintain the pressure on the Germans until the Siegfried–Hindenburg Line had been breached. Foch was convinced that the Germans did not have the men or the equipment to turn back multiple attacks along the line, and this perception proved to be an accurate appraisal of the situation. The Allied offensives began on September 26 with the advance of 600,000 American and 240,000 French troops. The Meuse–Argonne offensive, according to Michael Clodfelter, ranks as "the bloodiest battle in which American military forces have ever been engaged in terms of casualties."[39] Over the next three days the remaining Allied armies all launched major offensives, and within a week significant portions of the Siegfried–Hindenburg Line had been overrun. After four years of stalemate, mobility had finally returned to the Western Front. As John Terraine notes, "It is a remarkable fact about this final Allied offensive that at no time were the Allies seriously held up by German action; no counter-attack threw them back from significant gain. The progress of victory was continuous."[40]

In Search of an Armistice

All this was not lost on Ludendorff and his colleagues at the OHL, who by this time were losing their confidence in the ability of the German army to hold back the Allied advance. On September 28 – the same day that Haig launched the Fourth Battle of Ypres between Cambrai and Saint-Quentin – Ludendorff met privately with Hindenburg in the older man's room at Spa. He explained that there was no longer any chance that the Germans could win the war – that the only course of action now was to seek an immediate armistice before the army collapsed. Hindenburg listened to his colleague and when the quartermaster general had finished, the old warrior silently took Ludendorff's right hand in his own and they parted "like men who have buried their dearest hopes."[41] The next day the two generals who had ruled Germany with an iron hand for the past year and a half met with the Kaiser and his advisors at the OHL headquarters at Spa.

The meeting did not go well. The generals explained that the Siegfried–Hindenburg Line had been broken and the only course of action was an immediate ceasefire. The collapse of confidence within the OHL took everyone by surprise. The confidence of the Kaiser and his cabinet had already been badly shaken by events on the battlefield. Chancellor Bethmann-Hollweg had held office since before the war began. He had been adept at maintaining a position that flip-flopped between opposing unrestricted submarine warfare and an expansion of the war and those seeking ways to reach a settlement to end the war. On July 6, 1917 Matthias Erzberger, one of the more outspoken advocates of a peace settlement, had delivered a speech in the Reichstag stating that "all our calculations as regards the submarine war are false" and that "we must do everything possible to find a way which favors the conclusion of a peace this year." Two weeks later Erzberger introduced a peace resolution which was passed by the Reichstag, 212 votes to 126, supporting "a peace of understanding and a lasting reconciliation of peoples. Any violations of territory, and political, economic, and financial persecutions are incompatible with such a peace."[42] Bethmann-Hollweg was caught between a parliamentary position that sounded like Woodrow Wilson's Fourteen Points and the commitment of the OHL to continue to pursue a "total war." He was, in the words of Hew Strachan,

> tired, committed to a policy of unrestricted submarine war in which he did not believe but which Erzberger among others had once advocated. "My position does not matter," he said when he rose to reply on 9 July. "I myself am convinced of my own limitations ... I am considered weak because I seek to end the war. A leading statesman can receive support neither from the Left nor the Right in Germany."[43]

The next day Bethmann-Hollweg resigned his position and was replaced by Georg Michaelis, who was the candidate favored by the OHL. Unable to resolve the issues between the generals and the deputies, Michaelis' tenure as Chancellor lasted only four months. In November, he was replaced by Georg Hertling.

The parade of three Chancellors in just under four months reflected the extent to which the real power in the government still rested with Ludendorff and Hindenburg at the OHL, not with either the civilian government or the Kaiser. Confronted with the OHL demand that Germany in November of 1918 accept an immediate ceasefire, Wilhelm and Hertling argued that such a step would amount to unconditional surrender. They insisted that the army should fight on long enough to allow Germany an opportunity to negotiate a ceasefire that included some assurances of what would follow a cessation of hostilities. When the generals persisted in their demand for an immediate end to the fighting, Hertling and his cabinet tendered their resignations and suggested that the Kaiser form a new government. The Kaiser now realized that he had no choice but to bow to the pressures of a rapidly worsening military situation and growing opposition to the war in the Reichstag. Wilhelm accepted the resignations of Hertling and his cabinet and appointed Prince Maximillian von Baden as Chancellor with the responsibility of forming a new cabinet with powers to negotiate terms of a ceasefire with the Allied Powers.

"Prince Max" had strongly opposed the OHL decision to resume submarine warfare in 1917, and he had been a vocal critic of Ludendorff's decision to expand the war in 1918. The Kaiser's hope was that the new prime minister's reputation as someone who had favored peace negotiations in the past would facilitate the new government's attempts to gain support in the Reichstag and with the Allied leaders. Prince Max was successful in forming a new government, but the issue of negotiating with the Allies on the terms of a ceasefire encountered some serious obstacles.

While it only takes one side to start a war, it takes an agreement that will be honored by both sides to end it. Despite the occasional efforts to give peace a chance over the previous four years, neither side had seriously considered the possibility that the military tide in the west might change so dramatically in such a short period of time as it did in the early summer of 1918. The only effort by leaders on either side of the conflict to seriously explore the basis for terms that might end the fighting had been Woodrow Wilson's speech detailing fourteen points for peace in January 1918. Though they had paid little attention to the speech while the Ludendorff offensives were underway, the OHL suddenly developed a keen interest in Wilson's approach after the German setback at the Second Battle of the Marne ended their last hope of a military victory. They now hoped that Wilson's peace platform could become a starting point for peace negotiations. For the first time in the war the OHL decided that gambling on a peaceful outcome might offer a better outcome than gambling on war.

Unfortunately, until the two sides could agree to begin talks of some sort, there would be no prospect of reaching a ceasefire. None of the Allied leaders were prepared to deal with the German military leaders, nor would they agree to meet directly with the Kaiser and his advisors. Once Prince Max had formed a new cabinet, he sent the American President a request to negotiate a ceasefire, assuring him that the reorganized German government would accept the Fourteen Points and evacuate the occupied areas of France and Belgium. At this point, Max and the Kaiser optimistically hoped that under Wilson's scheme they might be able to negotiate an agreement whereby they could retain the portion of Alsace-Lorraine that was predominately German, and keep the territories of Ukraine and Russian Poland which they had taken as part of the settlements in the Treaty of Brest-Litovsk. Some went so far as to dream that Germany could even keep its colonial holdings in Africa and the Pacific. Those hopes were quickly shattered when Wilson sent a series of notes making it clear that his vision of a peace shaped by the Fourteen Points was based on the premise that all territories that been occupied by the Central Powers – including Alsace-Lorraine – would have to be abandoned, and that the territories still occupied by Germany under the terms of the Treaty of Brest-Litovsk would become independent countries.

Wilson's hard-line attitude on the terms of a ceasefire reflected not only his deep-seated distrust of the Kaiser and his generals, but also a pessimistic view of the prospects for German democracy. He did not fully trust the "new" regime of Prince Max as a foundation of future democracy. Max, after all, was closely related to the Kaiser, and Hindenburg and Ludendorff were still in control of the OHL. Further issues were raised by Wilson's partners in the governments of the Allied coalition who had not yet agreed to all of the Fourteen Points. While they favored the idea of stopping the war, the British and French were surprised by the speed with which the German army had requested a ceasefire, and they were not at all sure how to reply. The Allied armies had yet to make any serious encroachments into German territory, and the further exchanges of notes between Wilson and the new German government raised fears that a ceasefire would simply allow the OHL to regroup its forces and resume fighting to defend the homeland. John

Pershing cautioned against rushing to approve a ceasefire, warning that "An armistice would revivify the low spirits of the German army and enable it to reorganize and resist later on."[44] In fact, such fears were not entirely without foundation. The generals at the OHL at Spa were infuriated by the tone of Wilson's responses to Prince Max's inquiries for a ceasefire, and were pondering the possibility of calling up another cohort of new recruits – about 600,000 men – to carry on the fight. On the evening of October 24, Ludendorff prepared a proclamation addressed to the troops that was cosigned by Hindenburg. Wilson's latest memo, they claimed,

> is a demand for unconditional surrender. It is thus unacceptable to us soldiers ... [It] can thus be nothing for us soldiers but a challenge to continue our resistance with all our strength. When our enemies know that no sacrifices will achieve the rupture of the German front, they will be ready for a peace which will make the future of our country safe for the great masses of our people.[45]

After some further thought, cooler heads prevailed and the announcement was withdrawn, but not before its contents had fallen into the hands of socialists in Berlin who immediately made it public. By noon the news that the OHL was prepared to continue the fight had spread all over Berlin, and there were protests in the streets. Max von Baden, who was trying to arrange a ceasefire through President Wilson, insisted that the Kaiser relieve Ludendorff of his command. The Kaiser reluctantly agreed.

Despite the bravado of the OHL proclamation, the ease with which the Allies had broken through the German lines had finally shattered what was left of Ludendorff's confidence. He had allowed his conviction that the Germans were winning the war following the Russian surrender at Brest-Litovsk to boost his confidence in the offensives undertaken in the spring of 1918, ignoring the reports from some of his generals that there were obvious flaws in the plan and that the risks of the plan if it failed would be enormous. When the offensives did fail, he was gripped by a panic that swept through Berlin as it became clear that the Germans were losing the war. On the morning of October 26, Ludendorff reluctantly offered his resignation to the Kaiser, who accepted it and told him, "You are thereby making my position very much easier. I shall endeavor, with the aid of the Socialists, to build up a new empire for myself."[46] Hindenburg also offered to resign; however, he remained a hero in the eyes of the German public, and Prince Max specifically asked the Kaiser to leave him in charge of the OHL. The Kaiser therefore refused his senior general's resignation. The next day the German government sent another message to President Wilson asking for negotiations to discuss his conditions for a ceasefire.

The Collapse of the Central Powers

While each side struggled to get their thoughts together on what would constitute acceptable terms for an armistice on the Western Front, the fighting continued. The Germans were tenuously hanging on in the west; however, their allies – Austria, Bulgaria, and the Ottoman Empire – were collapsing like a row of dominos. A glance at Map 7.4

Map 7.4 The collapse of the Central Powers, November 1918

shows the situation facing the Central Powers toward the end of 1918. The Italians, reinforced by French and British troops, were threatening to finally break through the Isonzo front in Italy and open a clear route to Vienna. On the Macedonian front a contingent of French, British, Greek, Serbian, and Italian troops under the French General Louis Franchet d'Espèrey were in position to reoccupy Serbia and move on toward Budapest and Hungary.

The first domino to fall was Bulgaria. On September 13 Allied forces under General Franchet d'Espèrey launched an offensive that finally broke the stalemate along the Macedonian front. In just over a week more than 10,000 Bulgarian and German troops were taken prisoner and the Bulgarian army was in disarray. On September 28 the Bulgarian government became the first of the Central Power to formally ask for a ceasefire. Two days later the Armistice of Salonika ended Bulgaria's participation in the war.

The next domino to fall was the Ottoman Empire. By October 1918, two British armies were preparing to advance into Turkey and occupy Istanbul. A force commanded by Edmund Allenby was ready to move north from Damascus, and a second force of British and Arab troops commanded by General Stanley Maude was prepared to advance on the Ottoman capital from Baghdad. On October 21, a Turkish tugboat flying a white flag approached the British fleet anchored near Mudros, a small town on the island of Lemnos in the north Agean Sea. On board were several Turkish diplomats and Sir Charles Townshend, the British general who had surrendered the city of Kut-el-Amara to the Ottomans in April 1916 after a prolonged siege.[47] With Townshend's help the Ottoman delegation persuaded the British authorities that the Turks wanted to negotiate an armistice. After an exchange of telegrams with the War Cabinet, Admiral Sir Somerset Gough-Calthorpe, the commander-in-chief of the British Mediteranean Fleet, was authorized to negotiate terms for a ceasefire.

Lloyd George was pleased that the negotiations on the terms of the Ottoman ceasefire would be conducted on a British warship in the north Aegean Sea. Since the Russian withdrawal from the war, the British had shouldered the burden of fighting in the Middle East, and they were anxious that the terms of any ceasefire be dictated by their interests. Given the arrangements that had been worked out with the Sykes–Picot Agreement in 1916 and various other secret agreements, Lloyd George was particularly anxious to keep Woodrow Wilson from entering the picture. The French and Italians were kept informed of progress at the talks, but the arrangements for a ceasefire to end the fighting in Mesopotamia were worked out by British negotiators. In addition to ending the fighting, terms of the ceasefire agreement dealt with the issues related to the opening of the Bosporus and the Dardanelles to Allied warships. On October 30 Admiral Calthorpe and the Ottoman Minister of Marine Affairs, Rauf Bey, signed an agreement on board the British battleship HMS *Agamemnon* that ended the Ottoman participation in the war. On November 13, General Allenby's army entered the city of Istanbul.

The final domino to fall was Austria-Hungary. Militarily the war had been a continuing disaster for the Austrians. "The price of Austria's great folly," notes Holger Herwig, "had been horrendous: of the 8 million men mobilized, 1,015,200 had died, 1,943,000 had been wounded, and 3,748,000 had been hospitalized due to illness. Additionally, 480,000 of the 1,691,000 men taken prisoner had perished over the course of the 52 months of fighting."[48] The Dual Monarchy had run out of food and it had run out of men. The victory at Caporetto had briefly boosted the morale of the Austrian forces in December of 1917; however, by early 1918 the Germans had transferred troops from the Italian front to the Western Front in preparation for the Ludendorff offensives. Reinforced by the addition of French and British troops, the Italians rallied from the disaster of Caporetto and by October 1918 they were in a position to launch a final offensive against the Austrian army. The ensuing Battle of Vittorio Veneto pushed the Austrian forces out of northern Italy and shattered what was left of the Austrian army's morale. Many of the units were grossly understaffed; soldiers no longer had uniforms; and food was in such scarce supply that troops went for days without eating.

The Habsburg Empire was rapidly disintegrating. After a week of muddled negotiations and confusion, the Austrians were willing to accept whatever terms the Allies would offer and an armistice was signed at a village nine miles east of Padua on the afternoon of November 3. Holger Herwig describes a visit by Josef Redlich, a professor and liberal politician, with the Emperor several days later:

> He found the "poor young Kaiser" stripped of all authority and power, a solitary and pathetic figure amidst the baroque splendor of the Habsburg palace built by Charles VI and Maria Theresa,

and once occupied by Napoleon I. The Army had been "split into a million atoms." Not a "trace of the power" of the old Habsburg dynasty remained, "neither in Vienna nor in Prague, neither in Budapest nor in Agram." The dichotomy between Charles' current powerlessness and the grandeur of Schonbrunn "symbolizes the deepest tragedy of earthly fame and human power." Even the brilliant rococo portraits and the dazzling uniforms of the Kaiser's military entourage exuded but a "breath of decay, the decay of a culture at once the finest but also recently grown tired."[49]

One of the oldest dynasties in Europe, which could trace its roots back to the mid-sixteeth century, had come to an abrupt end amid the chaos of the First World War.

All Quiet on the Western Front

All that remained to end the fighting was a ceasefire agreement between Germany and the Allied governments. Although Germany was suffering from the effects of the war, on paper it still had a formidable military machine that might resist an Allied invasion of its homeland. But the machine was deteriorating day by day, and the threat of civil unrest in the urban areas was growing. On November 5, the socialist deputies in the Reichstag demanded that the Kaiser abdicate, and when that did not happen they resigned *en masse*. As the Allied advance continued it became apparent that the German army could no longer affect the outcome of the war. In the hundred days since Foch ordered the counterattacks at Amiens, Allied forces had taken more than 350,000 prisoners and 6,000 guns. "This," notes Martin Gilbert, "constituted a quarter of the German Army in the field, and one half of all its guns. The warmaking power of Germany, even to defend its borders, was within a few days of collapse."[50] The Kaiser finally saw the writing on the wall. His navy was mutinying, his army could no longer defend its borders, and socialist revolutionaries were rioting in the streets of Berlin. Wilhelm hoped that he could remain in power long enough to lead his army back to Germany, but even this request was deemed unwise by his military advisors, who felt they could not guarantee his safety in light of the anti-war furor among soldiers in the army. On the morning of November 5, Kaiser Wilhelm II quietly got on a train to Holland, where he lived in exile until his death in 1941. With his abdication, control of the German government fell to Prince Max von Baden, who promptly resigned in favor of Friedrich Ebert, a socialist leader in the Reichstag. In the chaos following the end of the fighting, a group of rivals quickly challenged Ebert's leadership, touching off a political struggle that continued through 1918–19.

Animal Spirits and the Pursuit of Victory

In a poem written to commemorate the signing of the armistice on November 11, 1918, the British poet Thomas Hardy wrote:

> Calm fell. From heaven distilled a clemency;
> There was peace on earth, and silence in the sky;
> Some could, some could not, shake off misery:
> The Sinister Spirit sneered: "It had to be!"
> And again the Spirit of Pity whispered, "Why?"[51]

For those seeking "rational" answers to the questions posed by Hardy's spirits, our narrative suggests that a century after the assassination of Archduke Ferdinand, the Great War remains a tragic enigma. There was nothing inevitable about the declarations of war in the summer of 1914; indeed, historians are still searching for reasons why everyone decided to join the fight in the first place. There were periods when a negotiated settlement would certainly seem to have been the "rational" course to follow. Yet decision-makers consistently chose to carry on or even expand the war at these tipping points rather than consider other alternatives. Rational thinking was trumped by "animal spirits," which produced decisions that were based on a hope on the part of generals, kings, and prime ministers that war might somehow settle their quarrels, combined with a fear of what they might lose if they did not "do something." Leaders, in other words, displayed a strong propensity to gamble on fighting a war – even if the outcome was very risky – rather than accepting that what they viewed as a peaceful settlement might have a lower risk of failure. Once started, the war proved impossible to stop. The tendency of countries to choose war over peace was reinforced by the propensity of political leaders to leave the final decisions with regard to military strategy to generals. "What should not surprise us," notes historian Brian Bond,

is the determination (or obstinacy) with ˅
pursued the will-o'-the-wisp of victory. Nu
deemed to be lacking the will to win, or simply u
the expected results, such as Moltke, Falkenhayn, Jo
French, and Ian Hamilton, were dismissed, or "deg
the idiom of the time. The survivors, such as Foch, 1
Haig, or Allenby, were noted for their determination to s ure
victory without agonizing over the human cost.[52]

This inability on the part of political leaders to rein in the animal spirits
of their commanders was a major reason why the war continued year
after year. Time and again our narrative encountered tipping points
where, despite their concerns that the plans of their overconfident generals were too ambitious, political leaders nevertheless allowed the generals to launch new battles. Ypres (three of them), Verdun, the Somme,
Passchendaele, and the Ludendorff offensives were only the most spectacular examples of decisions made in the pursuit of victory.

We noted that the success of Bismarck's policy of "iron and
blood" during the wars to unify Germany was due in large part to
his being able to resist the temptation of allowing the animal spirits
unleashed by victories on the battlefield to override the basic goal
to be gained by fighting the war. The Iron Chancellor persuaded his
monarch that asking for territorial gains after the Prussian victory at
Königgrätz would be a serious mistake. After the war with France in
1871, Bismarck's main objective was to consolidate the position of the
German Empire in Europe, and for the next two decades he sought
to maintain a system of treaties intended to discourage wars between
major powers. However, the ascension of Wilhelm II as Kaiser in
June of 1888 dramatically changed the situation. The new Kaiser had
ambitions for the German Empire that went far beyond Bismarck's
vision of a unified Germany, and with the dismissal of Bismarck in
1890 Germany assumed a much more aggressive position in European
politics. Wilhelm was a man easily driven by animal spirits.

From there our narrative moved on to one of the most ambitious military gambles in modern history: Alfred von Schlieffen's plan
to invade France in response to a conflict between Russia and Austria
in 1914. When the Germans were stopped at the Marne, the war turned
into a bloody stalemate that was punctuated by repeated offensives
on the part of generals hoping to break through the enemy lines. The

rsistence of these unsuccessful attempts reflected an unwavering confidence that massive offensives could somehow break through the enemy lines. Experience repeatedly showed that even when breakthroughs were at least partially successful, the attackers were unable to follow up their advantage. Yet the attacks continued. For three long years this was a war of attrition. Neither side had the capability of creating a situation where a single battle would cause the enemy to agree to end the war.

Perhaps the best illustration of how powerful the pursuit of victory and the influence of animal spirits had become by the end of the war was the decision facing Erich Ludendorff and the German High Command at the end of 1917. Ludendorff was one of those people who could be influenced by animal spirits in both directions. Like the Schlieffen Plan four years earlier, Ludendorff's scheme was incredibly ambitious, and like Schlieffen's proposal it was geared to achieve a single victory that would wrap up the war. It should be noted that Ludendorff's confidence was not entirely misplaced in terms of the military situation facing the Germans. The military math shifted dramatically in Germany's favor when Russia left the war. At the beginning of 1918 Germany's composite index of military capability (%CINC) was 17.3 – the highest level since the beginning of the war. The Germans had mobilized 8 million troops, which gave them a numerical advantage over the Allies on the Western Front for the first time since 1914. The French and the British armies were both exhausted from the failed offensives they had launched in 1917, while German troops were feeling a boost from the victory against the Russians and the prospect of finally winning the war. Seen through the eyes of a military commander who had an impressive record of success throughout the war, one could perhaps understand Ludendorff's optimism.[53] His spirits were further boosted by the success of the initial attacks. Accounts at the time suggest that there was a sense of panic among the Allied forces as they retreated back to positions close to those that the Germans had held in 1914. As the German long-range guns trained their sights on Paris, the war reached the climax of its last major tipping point. "In mid-July 1918," historian Hew Strachan points out,

> the German Empire stood at its greatest ever extent. It had pushed on Paris in the west; in the east it held the Ukraine; the Baltic states were under its control; in the Caucasus, the Russian collapse had reopened the route to Baku; and in Italy

its Austrian ally had attacked on the Piave in June. For some civilians at home the army seemed poised to deliver the victory that would resolve all their domestic problems.[54]

History is full of surprises, and it is certainly possible to imagine a German victory at the Second Battle of the Marne in early 1918 that would dramatically affect the final outcome of the war.

That, of course, did not come to pass. There were too many "ifs" built into the assumptions behind the planning of the German offensives for them to have a very high likelihood of success. The biggest problem was that although the OHL had carefully thought through the issues related to the army maneuvers, Ludendorff and Hindenburg had ignored the larger pressures that four years of war had already placed on the German economy. The Hindenburg economic program had set ambitious production goals that could not be met, and paid little attention to the shortages of food for the civilian population and scarce resources needed for armament production in the preparations of their military plans. Admiral Holtzendorff's confident assertion that the U-boat blockade of the British Isles could "force England to her knees" in five months and prevent the Americans from reinforcing the beleaguered Allied armies was another case of overconfidence. By the end of 1917 the Allied navies had managed to defuse the U-boat threat with the use of convoys, and the Americans were able to ferry their troops and supplies across the Atlantic. John Pershing's reluctance to let the American troops fight under the command of French or British commanders made things a bit more dramatic for Lloyd George and Clemenceau as the Germans approached Paris in August of 1918, but as events proved, the mere presence of two million American troops made any hope of eventual German success remote at best. Nor is it clear that the Allies would have been receptive to a peace overture by the Germans even if the last great offensive had reached Paris. Britain, France, and the United States were pursuing a gamble of their own that the Americans would be able to get to France in time to save the day.

How the West Was Won

What ultimately determined the victor in this war was which side would win the "economic war" of mobilizing enough resources to keep on fighting. This was why the entry of the United States was so pivotal in determining the outcome. Compared with any of the other belligerents, the Americans had seemingly unlimited resources, and most important of all, they had a huge resource of manpower. In December 1914 Erich von Falkenhayn had predicted that, despite all the territory gained by the Central Powers in the first four months of the war, the Entente Powers still held an economic advantage that would surely increase over time. What Falkenhayn and his contemporaries on both sides of the war never imagined was the lengths to which the industrial nations could go to support a war they felt they must not lose. By the end of October 1918 when the German economy had finally run out of gas, and the German army was near collapse, Ludendorff and his compatriots at the OHL realized that there were no longer sufficient resources to fight the war. His confidence in victory was quickly replaced by a fear that military defeat would produce a socialist revolution in Germany. In a desperate attempt to stave off political chaos, the military leaders at the OHL insisted that the Kaiser and his government must seek an immediate armistice.

The last of the guns had finally been silenced on November 11, 1918, but the task of reestablishing some sort of order had barely begun.

8 THE CHAOS OF VICTORY

> The Treaty includes no provisions for the economic
> rehabilitation of Europe, nothing to make the defeated
> Central Empires into good neighbors, nothing to stabilize
> the new States of Europe, nothing to reclaim Russia; nor
> does it promote in any way a compact of economic solidarity
> amongst the Allies themselves; no arrangement was reached at
> Paris for restoring the disordered finances of France and Italy,
> or to adjust the systems of the Old World and the New.
> John Maynard Keynes (1920)[1]

On December 13, 1918, the passenger liner *George Washington*
arrived at the French port of Brest carrying Woodrow Wilson and a delegation of Americans chosen to take part in the conference to construct
a treaty that would finally end the Great War. As he stepped off the boat
to the cheers of a crowd assembled to meet him, Wilson became the first
president of the United States to visit Europe while serving in office.
Not everyone thought it was a good idea for the President to appear at
the Peace Conference in person, but Wilson was determined to attend.
"The gallant men of our armed forces on land and sea have consciously
fought for the ideals which they knew to be the ideals of their country,"
he told Congress just before he left for France. "It is now my duty to
play my full part in making good what they offered their life's blood to
obtain. I can think of no call to service which could transcend this."[2]
As he debarked from the *George Washington*, Wilson was greeted by
cheers from a welcoming crowd that included Stéphen Pichon, the

French foreign minister, who thanked him for coming to France to "give us the right kind of peace." The Americans then boarded a train for Paris, where the reception by crowds of Parisians was even more enthusiastic.

Wilson stayed in Paris long enough to meet with Premier Georges Clemenceau and discuss arrangements for the upcoming peace conference before embarking on a whirlwind tour that took him to England for a meeting with Prime Minister David Lloyd George and King George V, and brief appearances in Carlisle and Manchester. He returned briefly to Paris, then went on to Rome, where he met with Italian Prime Minister Vittorio Emanuele Orlando and King Victor Emanuel III as well as with Pope Benedict XV in Vatican City. On the way back to Paris he visited Genoa, Milan, and Turin. Everywhere he went the American president was met by crowds of friendly Europeans. By the time he arrived back in Paris on January 7 Wilson had become the man of the hour. At least for a few brief moments, his soaring rhetoric and high principles allowed people to savor the joys of victory before turning their attention back to the chaotic reality of a world that had been destroyed by the war.

The Paris Peace Conference

While the president was flitting about Europe, the diplomatic staffs of the victorious Allied Powers were organizing the greatest gathering of world leaders since the Congress of Vienna following the end of the Napoleonic wars a century earlier. The diplomats at Vienna were able to reestablish a monarchy in France, return the territories that Napoleon had occupied at various times to Prussia, Russia, and the Habsburg Empire, and lay the groundwork for a global system of political and economic arrangements that would reduce the likelihood of interstate warfare that had dominated the European continent for the two decades before 1815. The delegates arriving in Paris in January of 1919 faced a similar but far more challenging task. As British Prime Minister David Lloyd George pointed out, the diplomats meeting in Vienna in 1815 "had to settle the affairs of Europe alone. It took eleven months. But the problems at the Congress of Vienna, great as they were, sink into insignificance compared with those which we have had to attempt to settle at the Paris Conference. It is not one continent that is engaged – every continent is engaged."[3] Not only was every continent engaged; they were engaged in a fervor of revolutionary activity that challenged the *antebellum status quo* with visions of a future that no one could confidently predict amid the chaos left by the most destructive war the world had ever seen.

The first problem was how to organize a conference that included delegations from more than thirty countries and by one estimate brought 10,000 interested people to Paris.[4] It quickly became apparent to the leaders of the major powers that they needed some way of maintaining control of the Conference agenda. The solution to this problem was to agree that there would be a Supreme Council – also referred to as the Council of Ten – which would consist of the leaders from each of the four Allied Powers – Wilson, Clemenceau, Lloyd George, and Italian Prime Minister Vittorio Orlando – together with their foreign ministers and two representatives from Japan.[5] The Supreme Council became the governing body that controlled the agenda of the Conference. At Wilson's suggestion, the delegates agreed that Clemenceau be made President of the Supreme Council. The ten men met for the first time on January 18, and over the course of the next two months they would meet seventy-two times. When they were not discussing issues in sessions that were closed to the public, the four leaders listened to a parade of petitioners, expert advisors, and representatives of lesser powers who were concerned that their interests might be ignored, and examined reports from committees that had been set up to study various aspect of the peace process.

The first weeks of the Supreme Council were spent working out the many details of procedures for conducting discussions. To take an obvious and very touchy example of the challenges they faced, consider the problem of choosing which language should be used not only in their own conversations, but also in meetings and documents circulated for approval by all of the delegates. The four leaders shared three languages. Wilson and Lloyd George each spoke English, but neither knew either French or Italian. Clemenceau, who had lived in the United States for several years after the Civil War, could easily converse in English, but he preferred to speak French and he insisted that French be the only "official" language of the Conference. Orlando was not fluent in either English or French; he relied on Sidney Sonnino, his foreign minister, to translate for him. At one point, a discussion reached the point where Sonnino suggested that Italian should also be one of several languages used in the Conference, insisting that "Otherwise, it would look like Italy was being treated as an inferior by being excluded." In that case, Lloyd George retorted, they should also include Japanese. After further thought, the four men finally agreed that French and English would both be "official languages" for all Conference matters.[6]

Another touchy issue was the question of whether the proceedings of the Council should be open to the public. Wilson had made a point in his public appearances of objecting to the secret treaties and agreements that were so common in the years leading up to the war, and he was a vocal champion of "open covenants openly arrived at." He expressed a hope that the "conversations" of the Council would be carried out in an open forum. "We ought to have no formal Conferences," he argued, "but only conversations." The Europeans were aghast at the thought of opening their deliberations to the public. Clemenceau declared that it would be "a veritable suicide" to release even a daily summary of their discussions to the crowd of reporters covering the proceedings, and Lloyd George pointed out that open access to the deliberations would mean that the Conference might go on forever. After some further thought, the president finally agreed, much to the disgust of the American reporters in Paris, some of whom labeled him a "naive hypocrite."

The Supreme Council succeeded in setting up the rules of protocol for the Conference meetings. They approved appointments to fifty-eight subcommittees created to study specific problems that must be addressed by the Conference and they had lengthy "conversations" about major issues. But they did not make any perceptible progress toward reaching conclusions involving these issues. Adding to the backlog of Council business were the responsibilities of the leaders back in their own countries. In mid-February Wilson left Paris to return to Washington for a month to deal with the difficulties created by the election of a Republican Congress in the 1918 elections. Lloyd George also went home for several weeks at the end of February and into early March to deal with politics on the home front. On February 19 Clemenceau survived an assassination attempt that temporarily interrupted the proceedings of the Council.

The inability of the Supreme Council to make much progress toward shaping a peace settlement led to a growing frustration among the delegates. On March 21 the Conference attendees agreed to accept a reorganization of the Supreme Council that removed the foreign ministers and the two Japanese members.[7] The reorganized Council – now called the Council of Four – consisted of Wilson, Clemenceau, Lloyd George, and Orlando. They effectively controlled all the business before the delegates. One indication of the extent of this monopoly of power was the fact that there were only six plenary sessions held during the six months prior to the signing of treaties at the end of June.

The Council of Four

The new Council of Four met for the first time on March 24 and they continued their schedule of meeting twice a day – often on Sunday – until the end of June.[8] Streamlining the decision-making process at the top of the Conference hierarchy removed some obstacles to reaching conclusions and recommendations. However, it also meant that the Conference agenda and all the decisions reached at the Conference were governed by the confidence and fears of four men. Of course, they were not exactly alone in their deliberations. John Maynard Keynes, who accompanied the British delegation to the Versailles Peace Conference as a technical advisor to Lloyd George, had an opportunity to closely study the interactions of the Council as they struggled with the issues before them. He gradually became convinced that the three prime ministers and the president were shaping a Carthaginian Peace that Keynes felt would place undue burdens on the defeated Central Powers. Keynes resigned his position and returned to Britain to write a scathing attack on the treaty. *The Economic Consequences of the Peace* was an instant success, and it remains one of the more enduring criticisms of the problems posed by the treaty that formally ended the First World War.[9]

Keynes placed much of the blame for what he predicted would be a failed postwar economy on the inability of the four men who orchestrated the Conference to look beyond their own political agendas and address the needs of a shattered world order. Clemenceau, according to Keynes, was much too preoccupied with a need "to crush the economic life of his enemy." Lloyd George was a politician, not a diplomat, who worried about the effects of the Conference among voters back home and wanted to "do a deal and bring home something which would pass muster for a week." President Wilson was obsessed that he must "do nothing that was not just or right." Keynes' description of the deliberations of the Council provides us with a revealing glimpse into the inner workings of the governing body of the Conference. Clemenceau had a simple policy designed to "set the clock back and to undo what, since 1870, the progress of Germany had accomplished. If France could seize, even in part, what Germany was compelled to drop, the inequality of strength between the two rivals for European hegemony might be remedied for many generations." Lloyd George, by Keynes' measure, was a very clever man with an "unerring, almost medium-like sensibility to everyone immediately around him."[10] The British Prime Minister tended to act as the negotiator seeking ways to make things work. This was not an easy task. At one point Lloyd George explained to his colleagues in the House of Commons that "I am doubtful whether any body of men with a difficult task have worked under greater difficulties – stones clattering on the roof and crashing through the windows, and sometimes wild men screaming through the keyholes."[11] Keynes saved his most caustic evaluation for President Woodrow Wilson. The president was "like a nonconformist minister, perhaps a Presbyterian. His thought and his temperament were essentially theological not intellectual, with all the strength and the weakness of that manner of thought, feeling and expression." When all was said and done, Keynes concluded, Wilson "stood for stubbornness and a refusal of reconciliations."[12]

In addition to his evaluations of the eccentricities and biases of Clemenceau, Lloyd George, and Wilson, Keynes also provided an account of the way in which items of interest were discussed:

> Not infrequently Mr. Lloyd George, after delivering a speech in English, would, during the period of its interpretation into French, cross the hearthrug to the President to reinforce his case by some *ad hominem* argument in private conversation, or to sound the ground for a compromise – and this would sometimes be the signal for a general upheaval and disorder. The President's advisers would press round him, a moment later the British experts would dribble across to learn the result or see that all was well, and next the French would be there, a little suspicious lest the others were arranging something behind them, until all the room were on their feet and conversation was general in both languages. My last and most vivid impression is of such a scene.[13]

Keynes' account of the activities of the Big Four provides a useful and sometimes entertaining window into the workings of the Council of Four. However, a century of deliberations by scholars studying the postwar world suggests that his indictment of the leaders at the Paris Peace Conference as men who failed because they lacked a concern for the global problems they were addressing seems too extreme.

The inability to resolve the issues facing the Supreme Council involved much more than personalities and shortcomings of information. Keynes' theoretical framework was sound, however, the existing paradigms for understanding war, politics, or economics simply did not offer any obvious solutions for how to deal with the destruction of global institutional arrangements and the vacuum of power created by the simultaneous collapse of four major empires in Europe. The principles embedded in Wilson's Fourteen Points offered an idealistic vision of what a postwar world should look like, but they did not provide a very useful road map showing how to apply these principles to the reality of a world torn apart by war.

Adding to the difficulties of decision-making was the fact that no one expected that a war which had dragged on for almost five years would end so suddenly. The requests for ceasefire arrangements with Germany, Austria-Hungary, Bulgaria, and the Ottoman Empire that stopped the fighting were unexpected and the terms negotiated were hastily put together. While the victors were still gathering in Paris to decide what to do next, the political and economic chaos in the areas controlled by the Central Powers at the end of the war continued to escalate. Shortly after he arrived in Paris, Robert Lansing, the American Secretary of State, remarked that "all the races of Central Europe and the Balkans are actually fighting or about to fight with one another. The Great War seems to have split up into a lot of little wars."[14]

Historians have tended to focus on the activities of the Council of Four when dealing with the deliberations over the terms for the peace treaties that were signed by the combatants at the end of June 1919. At that point Wilson, Lloyd George, and Orlando went home to urge their governments to ratify the treaties they had signed with the Central Powers. However, the activities of the Conference did not end with the signing of the treaties. The decisions reached by the Council of Four covered a vast array of issues, however, the details of exactly how these terms were to be implemented were left to the large contingent of advisors, experts, and diplomats who had come to Paris to take part in the process of shaping the terms outlined by the Council of Four.

These diplomats, and their staff, stayed in Paris for another six months working on a variety of tasks, such as drawing maps for countries that were still in the process of defining their borders or writing reports and circulating memos dealing with mandates, reparations, and a host of answers for issues yet to be determined. In the decade following the Paris Peace Conference scholars tended to stress what did *not* get done during the conference, rather than the things that *did* get done. By the time the Conference closed with the inaugural session of the League of Nations in January 1920, the foundations for a new world had been laid. In the space of a few years the world of 1914 had been replaced with a new and very different world. It was not a perfect world, but at least some of the debris left by four and a half years of war had been cleared away.

Peace Treaties

The most obvious task facing the victorious Allies was to draft a series of treaties with the Central Powers that would end the war. However, before they could turn their attention to the issues of dealing with the defeated powers, the four leaders had to settle some sensitive issues between their own countries. Woodrow Wilson was particularly concerned about the various secret arrangements and treaties that had been worked out among the Allies during the war. An example of just such an arrangement was the Treaty of London, secretly signed by Britain, France, and Russia in April of 1915. As an added inducement for the Italians to join the fighting, the Entente Powers promised that if they won the war, Italy would be granted control of territory along its northern boundary and the eastern coast of the Adriatic Sea. When the issue of approving the terms of the Treaty of London was presented for discussion by the Council of Four in April 1919, Wilson strongly objected to promises made in 1915 because they did not take into consideration the question of self-determination. He particularly objected to the idea that the Italians be given control of Fiume, a city which had very few Italian residents. Orlando was sufficiently miffed by the president's objections that he left the Conference and returned to Italy. Wilson remained adamant and the Italians reluctantly abandoned their demands for gaining control of Fiume and returned to Paris after an eleven-day absence. The incident remained an unsettling reminder that the Allies were not always on the same page when it came to the details of territorial adjustments after the war.[15]

Despite their misgivings and disagreements, the four men charged with the task of overseeing the treaties had no choice but to work on drafting treaties with the new governments in Germany, the newly formed countries of Austria, Hungary, Bulgaria, and what was left of the Ottoman Empire. The treaty between Germany and the Allied countries, signed in the Palace of Mirrors at Versailles on June 28, 1919, has received the most attention from historians examining the consequences of the treaties signed in Paris. However, there were four other sets of negotiations for treaties that also had to be worked out in the suburbs of Paris:

The Treaty of Saint-Germaine-en-Laye was signed with the new state of Austria on September 10, 1919.

The Treaty of Neuilly-sur Seine was signed with Bulgaria on November 27, 1919.

The Treaty of Trianon was signed with the new state of Hungary on June 4, 1920.

The Treaty of Sèvres was signed with the Ottoman Empire on August 10, 1920.

In a dramatic break with the conventional ways of drafting international treaties, a decision was made to not allow the defeated parties to send delegates to attend the Peace Conference until drafts of the treaties had been completed. Each country would then be presented with a set of demands that must be accepted or rejected. The decision to not let the defeated states be part of the discussion over the terms of the treaties had a significant effect on the wording of the treaties. Delegations from all four of the major powers had arrived in Paris with demands that they anticipated would be negotiated with the defeated countries. With no input from delegates from the other side of the conflict, the tendency was for the Council of Four to incorporate almost all of the initial demands brought to the Conference by each of the Allied Powers into the final document in some form or another. Harold Nicolson, one of the British delegates privy to the Council debates, remarked, "Had it been known from the outset that no negotiations would ever take place with the enemy, it is certain that many of the less reasonable clauses of the Treaty would not have been inserted."[16] Common elements in all of the treaties included the question of boundaries for new nation-states, restrictions on the defeated country's military establishment, and the payment of reparations for damages suffered by Allied countries in the war.

A New Map for Europe

The collapse of governments and the movement of people during the war had obliterated the territorial boundaries that had existed in 1914 for many countries in central Europe. The terms agreed upon by Germany and Russia in the Treaty of Brest-Litovsk had left a vast area of central Europe and the Balkans occupied by German and Austrian armies (see Map 6.2). The terms of the ceasefire agreement between the Germans and the Allies in 1918 made it clear that the Germans would not be allowed to retain any of the territory they had gained as a result of the Treaty of Brest-Litovsk. There was, however, no master plan for the massive reorganization of national boundaries implied by the disappearance of three European empires. Woodrow Wilson's Fourteen Points, which the other three Allied countries had cautiously supported, provided principles of self-determination and a few broad suggestions to guide the Council of Four in their deliberations on the formation of new states in central Europe. In the absence of detailed suggestions, recognition of new governments and the establishment of new national boundaries was carried out on a very ad hoc basis. Neither Wilson nor his colleagues were familiar with the countries in central Europe, and their supporting staff proved to be of only limited help regarding the details of how the new boundary lines might be drawn.

Germany

Finding a way to create a German state that could live peacefully in a postwar Europe was the most significant hurdle to be cleared in the road to a peace settlement at the Versailles Conference. One of the stipulations of the ceasefire with Germany was the immediate evacuation of troops in Belgium and France, and any territories gained from the terms of the Treaty of Brest-Litovsk. The larger question that still needed to be decided by the Council of Four was what should be done with those territories. How could the terms of a peace settlement be used to curtail the ability of a postwar Germany to once again emerge as the most powerful economic and political force in central Europe? Even in defeat, the German economy was one of the largest and most industrialized economies among the European states.

Clemenceau pointed out that one way to limit the recovery of the German economy was to take away areas that were a crucial part of German industry. He not only demanded that the Germans should return Alsace-Lorraine to France; he also wanted to allow France to annex the Rhineland, a region of Germany which included land on both sides of the Rhine River and was one of the most industrialized areas of Europe. Wilson and Lloyd George strongly opposed such a drastic step. Both agreed that Alsace-Lorraine must be returned to France. However, the majority of people living in the Rhineland were German, not French. Transferring control of the Rhineland to France in 1919 would create a new confrontation between France and Germany similar to that posed by the German annexation of Alsace-Lorraine in 1871. Clemenceau eventually agreed to a situation where the Rhineland would become a demilitarized zone which would be occupied by French, British, and American troops for the next fifteen years. An Inter-Allied Rhineland High Commission was established to administer the region with its headquarters in Koblenz. The French were also given control of the Saar coal mines for fifteen years. Not surprisingly, the Germans strongly objected to all of these proposals.

The other territorial issue involving Germany was the question of what to do with the territories that had been occupied by German troops in eastern Europe. There was agreement that the land taken from Russia under the terms of the Treaty of Brest-Litovsk would be used to support the creation of a new state of Poland, which would also be given access to the Baltic Sea by making the city of Danzig a free city. Finally, it was decided that Germany must cede the Grand Duchy of Posen, a rich agricultural region of East Prussia, to Poland. The loss of Posen was a particularly hard blow to the Germans. Ludendorff's success in forcing Russia to sign the Treaty of Brest-Litovsk had opened up the possibility of a substantial increase in the agricultural capability of the German economy through the acquisition of new land in central Europe. Now those gains were lost amid the collapse of the German forces on the Western Front.

Map 8.1 summarizes the territorial losses to Germany as a result of the Versailles Treaty. In all, Germany lost control of more than

Map 8.1 German territorial losses, 1919

25,000 square miles of land and about six million people. The loss of agricultural land to the new Polish state meant that Germany would be more dependent than ever on imports of food after the war – a point that was not lost on those who were considering the possibility of a future conflict with Germany. As Albrecht Ritschl notes, "the thrust of Germany's imperialist drive turned away from maritime rivalry with Britain and towards territorial expansion in eastern Europe, with many of the Malthusian and Darwinist forebodings of what was to come in World War II."[17] Two other minor territorial adjustments were that the Germans had to cede the Danish-speaking area of northern Schleswig back to Denmark and give Eupen-Malmédy, a small, predominantly German-speaking region, to Belgium.

Germany also lost control of its colonial empire. Though they were late entrants in the European race for colonies in the nineteenth century, by 1914 the Germans had accumulated a significant colonial empire in Africa and some islands in the Pacific. Under the Treaty of

Versailles, responsibility for the governance of German colonies was transferred to other countries. To avoid the appearance that they were simply supporting the imperialist aims of the European colonial powers, (which, of course was exactly what they were doing,) the Council of Four set up a system of colonial "mandates" that was instituted on the principle that "the well-being and development of such peoples form a sacred trust of civilization." The new colonial masters were required to make annual reports to a Permanent Mandates Commission that was established under the auspices of the League of Nations to act as an oversight body on the governance of the former German colonies. The African colonies went primarily to the British, French, and Belgians. Japan gained control of Germany's colonial islands north of the equator, which included the Marshall Islands, the Carolines, and the Marianas. Portugal, New Zealand, and Australia also received mandates for German colonies in the Pacific.

The mandates system was far from perfect; however, it reflected a changing view of colonial empires that would emerge after the war. While it facilitated the transfer of German colonies to new colonial masters, the mandate system did little to change the existing colonial systems. The British, French, and Japanese colonial holdings all expanded during the two decades following the end of the Great War.[18]

The Habsburg Empire

By the end of the war the economic and political situation in the Habsburg Empire and the other Balkan states approached complete anarchy. In March of 1917, the Austrian Emperor Charles I, who inherited the throne after the death of Emperor Franz Joseph in 1916, had secretly approached the French government to arrange for a ceasefire with the Allies. The talks fell apart because the French insisted on including Italy in the discussion. As the economic situation in Austria-Hungary continued to deteriorate, the military situation reached a crisis when, with the help of the British, the Italians launched a major attack against the Austrian lines in October 1918. With no prospect of military support from the Germans, who were facing a crisis of their own on the Western Front, and with growing pressures on the home front to dissolve the Dual Monarchy, the Austrian army simply collapsed.

Emperor Charles resorted to some drastic measures to save his empire. On October 16, 1918, he issued a proclamation declaring that he would approve the separation of the Dual Monarchy into two states. In what became known as the "Manifesto to the Peoples," the Emperor stated that: "Austria must, in accordance with the will of its people, become a federal state, in which every nationality shall form its own national territory in its own settlement zone."[19] Far from encouraging his subjects to help him reorganize his empire, the proclamation touched off a furious scramble on the part of nationalist groups to eliminate the monarchy and establish independent national states. Desperate to save his throne, Charles issued a second proclamation on November 11 approving "the decision taken by German Austria to form a separate State" and offering to "relinquish every participation in the administration of the State, and release the members of the Austrian Government from their offices." The following day the Republic of German-Austria was proclaimed, followed by the proclamation of a Hungarian Democratic Republic on November 16, 1918. Interestingly, Charles never did say he was prepared to abdicate his throne. He regarded his proclamation as an offer to step aside while his subjects reorganized the empire so that he could resume his reign when things settled down. When that did not materialize, he moved first to Switzerland, and eventually to the Portuguese colony of Madeira, where he died in 1922 from a bout of pneumonia at the age of thirty-four.

The collapse of the Dual Monarchy and the confusion created by four years of furious fighting opened the door for additional drastic changes. Even before the war ended, political committees began lobbying for recognition as independent states. In July of 1917, a group calling themselves the "Yugoslav Committee," which had been formed in London to create a national state that would include the Slavic provinces in the south of the Austrian Empire, met with the Serbian government in exile on the island of Corfu to discuss the creation of a country that would be called the "Kingdom of Serbs, Croats, and Slovenes." The result of this meeting was the Corfu Declaration, which advocated the formation of a constitutional monarchy headed by the Serbian Prince Regent Aleksandar Karadjordjevic of Serbia. The Declaration was signed by Premier Nikola Pasic of the Serbian government in exile and by delegates of the Yugoslav Committee. At the end of October 1918, the committee formally announced the establishment of the Kingdom of Serbs, Croats, and Slovenes.

Another state to emerge from the chaos surrounding the fall of the Dual Monarchy was Czechoslovakia, which laid claim to the northern Austrian provinces of Bohemia, Moravia, and Slovakia (see

Map 8.2). The Czechoslovak National Council had been founded in Paris in 1916. The Czech leaders – Thomas Masaryk, Edvard Beneš, and Slovak Stefanik – successfully lobbied the Entente leaders for recognition of their cause, and by the summer of 1918 Italy, France, and the United States had all supported their efforts to form an independent state. On October 14, 1918, the council announced the formation of a provisional government that was quickly recognized by the rest of the Allied governments. Both the Yugoslavs and the Czechs were rewarded with an invitation to send delegations to Paris and plead their case for recognition as nations at the Paris Peace Conference.[20]

All this happened before the peacemakers had arrived in Paris to consider the question of what to do with the situation in southeastern Europe. The Allies were now faced with the need to negotiate separate treaties with the newly formed independent states of German-Austria and Hungary, and simultaneously establish borders for the new states of Czechoslovakia and Yugoslavia. Wilson's Fourteen Points had stated that "the peoples of Austria-Hungary, whose place among the nations we wish to see safeguarded and assured, should be accorded the freest opportunity to autonomous development." However, the two states created in the wake of Emperor Charles' declarations were hardly what Wilson had in mind. They appeared to be mirror images of provinces in the old Habsburg Dual Monarchy with the Emperor being replaced by slightly more representative forms of government. The Council of Four viewed these "republics" as part of the Central Powers' coalition that had brought on the war, and they worried that recognizing these states with the borders they claimed would potentially increase Germany's influence in central Europe after the war. Consequently, neither state was allowed to send delegates to the Paris Peace Conference.

On September 10, 1919, the Republic of Austria signed the Treaty of Saint Germain-en-Laye, formally ending its hostilities with the Allied powers. The Austrians lost significant territory to the new states of Czechoslovakia and Poland to the north, and to newly created Yugoslavia to the south. They also ceded a small area to Italy as a result of the Treaty of London. The Austrians were also prohibited from forming any future annexation with Germany. Map 8.2 shows the new boundaries of states formed from the Habsburg Empire and territories taken from Romania and Serbia after the war, together with the adjustments to the Bulgarian border between Greece and Turkey. The dotted areas represent areas taken from the Habsburg Empire and Romania.

Map 8.2 The new map of Austria and the Balkans

Resolving the territorial issues for the Hungarian Democratic Republic took a bit more time. The Treaty of Trianon, which was not signed until June 4, 1920, stipulated that the Hungarians must cede land to Romania, Yugoslavia, Czechoslovakia, and Poland. These territorial rearrangements left the new republics of Austria and Hungary with less than one quarter of the total population and territory of the former Habsburg Empire in 1914. The boundaries of the new states posed some challenges to the application of the principle of self-determination. The populations of both Czechoslovakia and Yugoslavia included a wide variety of ethnic groups. However, in both countries there were ethnic groups that were large enough to effectively dominate the political system. Although the constitutions of both countries provided guarantees for all ethnic minorities, the smaller ethnic groups were hard-pressed to protect their rights. In Czechoslovakia 65 percent of the population were either Czech or Slovak; in Yugoslavia 83 percent were either Serbo-Croats or Slovenes. In both countries, a significant fraction of the population were Germans who strongly objected to the rearrangement of borders.[21] Map 8.2 shows the boundaries of states formed from the Habsburg Empire.

The new states that were formed out of the Habsburg Empire had a profound effect on Bulgaria, which had entered the war as an ally of the German Empire in 1915, hoping to capitalize on the success of the German armies in eastern Europe. At the end of 1917 it looked like a rather good gamble. Bulgarian and German troops had forced Romania out of the war and the Bulgarians were promised territorial rewards by the Treaty of Bucharest in May of 1918. The collapse of the Austrian armies on the Italian front and the final breakthrough of the combined Allied forces along the Macedonian front at the end of 1918 reversed the territorial gains from the Balkan victories in the east. The Bulgarians were forced to sign a ceasefire on September 24, 1918. The Treaty of Neuilly-sur-Seine between the Allied Powers and Bulgaria closely followed the terms contained in the Treaty of Versailles. The Bulgarian gamble on war, which had looked so promising in 1917, ended in disaster. They not only had to give up the territory gained from the Treaty of Bucharest; they also lost access to the Aegean Sea by returning eastern Thrace, which they had occupied after the offensives of 1917, to the Greeks. The final irony is that Romania, which had been thoroughly defeated and forced out of the war by German and Bulgarian forces in 1916, reentered the war on the side of the Allies in 1918 and wound up being the biggest winner in the series of conflicts for land in the Balkans that began with the Balkan wars of 1912–13. By 1923 Romania had doubled its area and population (see Map 8.2).

The Polish Question

The area between Germany and Russia that had once been the Kingdom of Poland was another area with major boundary issues. At the end of the Napoleonic wars Poland had been partitioned among Prussia, Austria, and Russia. By 1914 the populations in each of these three regions had come to reflect the differing social, political, and economic conditions of their governing state. The Great War offered the Poles an opportunity to create an independent Polish state; however, for many Poles it was also a civil war. More than 3.5 million Polish soldiers fought in the war for either the Central Powers or the Entente, and the Poles themselves were deeply divided over the postwar settlement. None of the four major powers had strong interests in Poland itself; the objective of the Council of Four was to create a viable buffer state between postwar Germany and Bolshevik Russia. Woodrow Wilson argued in his Fourteen Points speech that:

> An independent Polish state should be erected which should include the territories inhabited by indisputably Polish populations, which should be assured a free and secure access to the sea, and whose political and economic independence and territorial integrity should be guaranteed by international covenant.

This was easier said than done. Identifying the "indisputably Polish populations" was a major challenge because at least one third of the Polish population was not Polish.[22] The task was made even more complicated by the fact that Bolshevik Russia had not been invited to the Peace Conference and therefore did not participate in the conversations. While the Council of Four could deal with the borderlands of western Poland that had been part of Germany and Austria, they were not in a position to unilaterally determine the eastern border between Poland and Bolshevik Russia. The Russians had a strong interest in keeping "Russian Poland" as part of Vladimir Lenin's vision of an expanding Bolshevik revolution. Lenin was prepared to use force, if necessary, to attain that goal. Though the Big Four feared the expansion of communism to the west, they realized that they were not in a position to challenge that threat in 1919. They reluctantly decided to leave the Polish question up to the Poles and the Russians. Anticipating a need to negotiate with the Bolsheviks about the eastern borders of Poland, the British Foreign Secretary Lord George Curzon had put forward a proposal that imagined a north–south line that divided Poland into two spheres. To the west of Curzon's line were the German and Austrian areas of Poland which had a large Polish population; to the east was Russian Poland which had a large population of non-Polish minorities (see Map 8.3). Curzon's line was never formally adopted as the eastern border of Poland; however, it became the basis of negotiations which the Council of Four used to construct their proposal of a Polish state that eventually was put in the Versailles Treaty.

Map 8.3 The new map of eastern Europe, 1922

The peace treaty did not end the conflict over Poland's borders. Because the Poles were not happy with the boundaries set out in the treaty, they fought a series of conflicts over the next three years, culminating with a bloody war against Bolshevik Russia which started in February 1919 and finally ended with the signing of the Treaty of Riga in March 1921.[23] Under the terms of the treaty, the final border between Poland and the Soviet state was moved about 160 miles east of the Curzon Line, a concession that gave Poland an additional 52,000 square miles of land and increased the Polish population by several million. The treaty was a compromise that was not very popular on either side.

For the Poles this added a large territory that included several sub-stantial minority populations who were not eager to be included in Poland; for the Russians it ended Vladimir Lenin's dream of forcefully imposing the Bolshevik revolution on the borderlands to the west of Russia. The Allied Powers, who were not involved in the negotiations, grudgingly accepted the outcome. Germans were infuriated by the cre-ation of what become known as the "Polish Corridor," a thin strip of land which separated East Prussia from the rest of Germany (see Map 8.2). Yet when all was said and done, the First World War ended more favorably for Poland than anyone could have imagined in 1914. The Treaty of Versailles had created a new Polish state that incorporated all three of the partitions of the Kingdom of Poland made a century earlier and gave the Poles access to the Baltic Sea. That said, this came at a horrifically high price in terms of the wars of revolution, and the ire of virtually all Poland's postwar neighbors. Subsequent events would show that Poland's struggle for stability in the postwar world had only just begun.

Russia and the Baltic States

While the Allied leaders were wrestling with the problems of how to construct boundaries for Poland and the new states from the defunct Austrian Empire, the Russian Revolution of October 1917 had expanded into the largest civil war in modern times. Vladimir Lenin had managed to extricate Russia from the European war by signing the Treaty of Brest-Litovsk, but the Bolsheviks still faced enemies from within the former Russian Empire. Over the next five years 800,000 men died in the battles to control Russia, and another 500,000 would die in the border disputes between newly formed countries in central Europe.

In his eagerness to get Russia out of the war with Germany, Lenin had agreed to cede the four Baltic states of Lithuania, Latvia, Estonia, and Finland to Germany under the terms of the Treaty of Brest-Litovsk. At the peak of German military successes on the Eastern Front, Erich Ludendorff had dreamed that these states, together with Poland, Belorussia, and Ukraine, could form the basis of an expanded German Empire in eastern Europe. Those dreams collapsed with the failure of the German offensives in the west and the armistice agreement signed with the Allies in the fall of 1918.[24]

The Treaty of Versailles officially nullified any German territorial gains from the Treaty of Brest-Litovsk and required that German troops be immediately withdrawn from those regions. This demand was complicated in the case of the Baltic states by Allied concerns that Lenin and the Bolsheviks would try to take advantage of the absence of both German and Allied troops to reclaim those states for the new Soviet state. In an effort to thwart any such actions, the Allies included a provision in the armistice that German troops stationed in Lithuania should be left there to prevent the Russians from entering the country. The German troops did not cooperate with this request. For them the war was over. They withdrew and carefully avoided the advancing Russian troops.

Amid all this confusion, the Baltic states, which were now proclaiming their independence from Bolshevik Russia, faced a major threat from Lenin, who still had thoughts of incorporating the entire Baltic region back into the Soviet state. They also had to settle disputes among themselves and with the newly created state of Poland regarding boundaries they shared. The result was a chaotic period when Bolshevik Russia, Poland, and all four of the Baltic countries had to fight to support their claim of independence and establish new national boundaries. Eventually the Bolsheviks, who were still struggling to consolidate their hold on the new government in Moscow, abandoned their efforts to keep these areas in the new Soviet state and agreed to recognize the independent status of the Baltic states. By the end of 1920 all the newly independent Baltic states had signed treaties with Bolshevik Russia establishing their statehood.[25]

There remained the question of what would happen with the southwest region of the Russian Empire, a large area which had shared borders with Russian Poland and Romania, and stretched all the way east to the Crimean Peninsula. The region had been occupied by German troops under the terms of the Treaty of Brest Litovsk in 1918 (see Map 6.2). As the German troops headed home in 1919, the province of Ukraine became a bitter battlefield for the contesting armies of the Russian Revolution, and for Ukrainian and Polish groups. Historian Liubov Zhvanko summarizes the situation as one where Ukraine "became an arena of a civil war, an armed confrontation with the Bolsheviks, White and Polish armies, and the expeditionary corps of the Entente."[26] By the end of 1922 it was clear that the Bolsheviks had finally managed to militarily subdue their opponents and the issue now was whether either Belorussia or Ukraine would gain its independence as a result of the world war.

The Soviet Union of Socialist Republics

Lenin could now turn his attention back to his goal of exporting the Soviet system of socialism to the rest of the world. His immediate strategy was to try to establish "Soviet Republics" in the states adjacent to Russia and then incorporate these states into a larger entity that would eventually become a "Union" of Soviet Socialist Republics. Although the strategy did not succeed in Poland or the Baltic states, where independence movements eventually were able to establish their own system of governments, the Bolsheviks were more successful in gaining control of the governments of the Soviet Republics of Belorussia and Ukraine. On December 29, 1922 a conference of delegations from the Russian Soviet Federative Socialist Republic and the Transcaucasian, Ukrainian, and Byelorussian Soviet Socialist Republics signed a treaty in Moscow creating the Union of Soviet Socialist Republics. Map 8.3 shows the ten independent states formed from the reorganization of territories that were once part of the German, the Austria-Hungarian, and the Russian empires.

The Ottoman Empire

Nowhere was the "chaos of victory" more evident than in the settlements which emerged from the efforts of the Paris Peace Conference to deal with the disruptions in the Middle East. The Ottoman Empire posed a very different set of challenges for the Allies than those posed by the eastern European territories. Woodrow Wilson had proposed that "the Turkish portion of the present Ottoman Empire should be assured a secure sovereignty, but the other nationalities which are now under Turkish rule should be assured an undoubted security of life and an absolutely unmolested opportunity of autonomous development." Once again, the rhetoric of Wilsonian democracy clashed with the reality of a region that was still dominated by colonial empires. The secret agreement negotiated by Mark Sykes and François Georges Picot and accepted by Russia in March of 1916 proposed a comprehensive plan to divide the Turkish holdings in the Middle East between the three powers (see Map 4.3). Though the Russians were no longer part of that arrangement, Britain and France clearly hoped that the Sykes–Picot Agreement would form the basis for a postwar settlement in the Middle East. As part of the Treaty of Brest-Litovsk the Russians had ceded their claims to Ottoman territories to the Germans; however, that agreement had been negated by the terms of the Treaty of Versailles. Although they were no longer included in the negotiations between the Allies and the Turks, the Russians still had an interest in the disposition of Ottoman territories after the war.[27] A glance at Map 8.3 suggests that the Allied efforts to use the Sykes–Picot Agreement as a blueprint for the settlement of territories in the Middle East succeeded, but the process by which these partitions were completed was a very winding road.

The ceasefire with the Ottoman Empire was negotiated by the British at the end of October 1918 without any significant consultation with the French or other Allies. Clemenceau was extremely annoyed at this omission, but Lloyd George pointed out that his country had committed more than half a million men to the campaigns in Mesopotamia, and it was only fitting that his government be in charge of the negotiations for a ceasefire.[28] The British demanded that the Ottoman Turks relinquish all claims to their territorial possessions in the Middle East and that constraints be placed on the Ottoman government in Istanbul. Anxious to keep the Americans on the sidelines, the French agreed to this arrangement, which would let Britain have colonial mandates for Transjordan and Iraq while France would take charge of mandates for Syria and Lebanon (see Map 8.4).

There were, however, significant issues that went beyond these territorial divisions on the Arabian Peninsula. Among the most perplexing was the Balfour Declaration of 1917, which called for "the establishment in Palestine of a national home for the Jewish people," an action that did not sit well with the Arab allies who had fought with British forces in Palestine. Immediately after the war the British and French set aside territory for a joint "Occupied Enemy Territory Administration" in Palestine, and in June 1922 the British obtained a mandate from the League of Nations to govern Palestine. There was an obvious problem reconciling how the British would manage to keep their commitment to make a home for the Jews in Palestine and at the same time keep the promises made to Emir Faisal that the Arabs in that region would have their independence from the Ottomans after the war. The British tried as best they could to simply ignore the contradictions in their wartime agreements. Asked about the reaction of Arabs to his

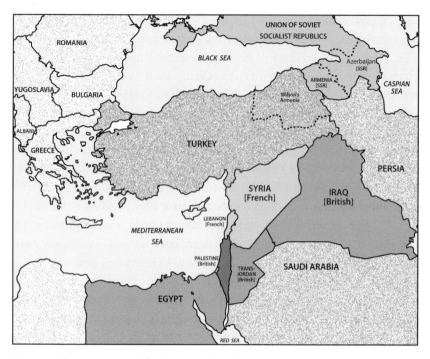

Map 8.4 The new map of the Ottoman Empire

proposal for a Palestinian mandate, Arthur Balfour replied that he hoped "they will not begrudge that small notch, for it is no more geographically, whatever it may be historically – that small notch in what are now Arab territories being given to the people who for all these hundreds of years have been separated from it."[29] There were some in the British foreign office who took a more realistic outlook on the creation of a Zionist state in the Middle East. George Curzon told Balfour that "Personally, I am so convinced that Palestine will be a ranking thorn in the flesh of whoever is charged with its mandate that I would withdraw from this responsibility while we can." The Arabs, of course, did "begrudge the small notch" and the story of Arab/Israeli conflict that arose from the creation of Palestine is one of the more lasting tragedies from the legacy of the First World War.

The Armenians

As they came up with ideas for boundaries of countries in the postwar Middle East, the peacemakers also had to wrestle with the issue

of how they could protect the rights of oppressed minoriti
many groups of ethnic minorities who suffered during t
was more oppressed than the Armenian population in the
corner of the Ottoman Empire. There had been a series
involving the systematic killing of Armenians by Turkish mil
following the second Russo-Turkish War that ended in 1878.

The rise to power of the "Young Turks" in 1908 led to increased efforts to wipe out the Armenian population. When the Ottomans entered the First World War on the side of the Central Powers the efforts to exterminate or deport the Armenian population became even more pronounced. On the night of April 24, 1915, the Turkish government ordered the arrest of more than two hundred prominent intellectuals and Armenian leaders in Istanbul. These people, according to an officer in the Ottoman War Office, were accused of being "in league with the enemy. They will launch an uprising in Istanbul, kill off the Ittihadist leaders and will succeed in opening up the straits of the Dardanelles."[30] Most of the men were subsequently murdered. That incident marked the beginning of an explicit policy of genocide carried out by the Young Turks' government against the Armenians. They made no effort to hide their murderous activity. A telegram from Ambassador Henry Morgenthau to the US State Department on July 16, 1915 warned that "deportation of and excesses against peaceful Armenians is increasing and from harrowing reports of eyewitnesses it appears that a campaign of race extermination is in progress under a pretext of reprisal against rebellion." He went on to say that "I believe nothing short of actual force which obviously [the] United States [is] not in a position to exert would adequately meet the situation."[31]

Morgenthau was not the only person to comment on these events. By the end of the war the horrors associated with the murder of so many innocent people had received attention throughout the Western world. The total number of deaths from the Armenian massacre remains open to speculation. Not all of the incidents of genocide were reported, and those that were reported often noted that the incident involved "mass killings" where the number of Armenians killed could not be accurately determined. The lowest estimate is 300,000 total deaths; Michael Reynolds cites a figure of "664,000 or about 45 percent of prewar Anatolia's 1.5 million Armenians."[32] Most observers believe the total death toll was well over a million people killed and may have been as high as 1.8 million.

When a delegation from the Armenian Revolutionary Federation arrived at the Paris Peace Conference, they asked that a region regarded as "Historical Armenia" in northeast Turkey be included in a new Democratic Republic of Armenia. They found a very sympathetic audience for their request in the Supreme Council. Woodrow Wilson was so moved by their situation that he proposed that, consistent with the argument that former Ottoman Territories be put under mandates of the League of Nations, the United States would accept responsibility for Armenia (see Map 8.4). Wilson's idea was endorsed by his colleagues on the Supreme Council, and the extended boundaries for Armenia were included in the Treaty of Sèvres. However, since the United States Senate rejected the treaty, Wilson's extended boundaries for Armenia were never implemented.[33]

So the Armenians were left to fend for themselves in their fight to resist the subsequent depredations of Turkish and Bolshevik ambitions.[34] The ink was hardly dry on the Treaty of Sèvres before the Turks attacked the Republic of Armenia and reclaimed all the land promised by Wilson. The Armenians also had to deal with the Russians. In December 1920 a Soviet party took over the Armenian Republic and signed an agreement with the Russian SFSR establishing borders between the two countries that ultimately led to the Treaty of Kars on October 13, 1921. Armenia eventually became part of the Union of Soviet Socialist Republics when that nation was formed in 1921.

The tangled story of the efforts to create an independent Armenian state underscores one of the basic problems facing the decision-makers at the Paris Peace Conference in dealing with the arrangements for land in eastern Europe and the Middle East. Though they could make decisions regarding the territorial boundaries of new states, they had no means of guaranteeing that the provisions of the treaties would in fact be enforced. The Armenian situation was one of the most obvious examples of this dilemma. Because the Allies could not back up their rhetoric with military support, the Armenians not only suffered terrible losses associated with the Armenian massacre perpetrated by the Turks, they also failed to gain the independence promised by the Paris Peace Conference. As historian John Cooper put it: "The fault lay in others, not in Woodrow Wilson; the obstacles to effective action both during and after the Great War were embedded in a political and strategic situation that worked inexorably against Armenia. That is one definition of tragedy."[35]

The Turkish Fight for Independence

The Turkish treatment of the Armenians shaped a very negative view of the leaders of the Ottoman Empire among the men on the Council of Four. The Treaty of Sèvres is generally regarded as the harshest treatment imposed upon any of the Central Power governments. The peacemakers in Paris were reluctant to establish an independent state from the remnants of the Ottoman Empire. Consequntly, the existing regime of the Sultan in Istanbul was allowed to remain nominally in charge of the area traditionally known as Anatolia, which was all that remained of the old Ottoman Empire (see Map 8.5). However, the Ottoman government's powers were drastically curtailed. Allied troops occupied Istanbul in March of 1920. They dissolved the Ottoman Parliament and appointed a "Finance Commission" comprising representatives from France, Britain, and Italy, and a Turkish representative (who acted in a consultative capacity) to exercise *de facto* control over the Ottoman budget. The Allies also took control of the war office and the mail and telegraph services. They still lacked any consistent policy with regard to the establishment of an autonomous Turkish nation. The Treaty of Sèvres had set in motion plans to partition Anatolia into regions, each of which would be under the control of one of the Allied Powers. However, diplomatic edicts issued by the Council of Four in Paris did not consider the military capabilities that would be necessary to accomplish what the peacemakers had in mind. At the time of the ceasefire with the Ottoman Empire, the only Allied

Map 8.5 The Turkish War of Independence

country with a significant military presence in the Middle East was Britain, which by the time of the armistice had committed more than a million men to its Middle Eastern war effort. However, within six months that number had fallen to just over 300,000, and demands for demobilization meant that the number of British troops in the Middle East would continue to decline.

Though they welcomed the idea of expanding their Middle Eastern empires, neither the British nor the French were interested in committing large numbers of troops to maintain peace in Anatolia on a permanent basis. Their primary concern at this point was to simply establish order in their mandates for Syria, Transjordan, and Iraq. The two countries which had the greatest interest in annexing part of Anatolia were the Armenian Democratic Republic and Greece. The Armenians hoped to gain the territory promised them by Woodrow Wilson's proposal to grant them land in northeastern Anatolia. The Greeks hoped to capitalize on the situation by expanding their boundaries east of Thrace to include a significant part of western Anatolia and the last remnants of Ottoman territory in Europe – including Istanbul. The Greek expectations were based on promises of territorial expansion made by Lloyd George to entice Greece to join the Allied forces fighting in Macedonia in 1917. The Italians also expressed a strong interest in annexing territory in western Anatolia as a result of the promises from the Entente Powers to lure them into the war in 1915 (See Map 8.5). With encouragement from the Allied command, the Greeks landed troops near Smyrna (Izmir) on the western coast of Anatolia in May of 1919. From there they advanced westward until they occupied the western third of Anatolia by the end of that year. Except for the British and French forces occupying the region around Istanbul, and some French troops in the south, there were no other significant concentrations of Allied troops in Anatolia.

While the Allies worked on trying to divide Anatolia into several distinct regions, the Turks were becoming increasingly restive and demanding their independence. Taking advantage of the absence of Allied troops in central Anatolia, they formed the Turkish National Movement and issued a decree stating that since the Sultan was a prisoner of the Allies, his decrees no longer reflected the will of the Turkish people. By February of 1920 the makings of a new Turkish state had emerged in Ankara that was strong enough to challenge the Allied control of Anatolia. Under the leadership of Mustafa Kemal "Ataturk," who had led the Ottoman forces at Gallipoli and the Dardanelles, the Turks were prepared to fight for their independence.

With encouragement and shipments of arms from Lenin and the Bolsheviks, Ataturk organized an army to push the Allies out of Turkey. The Turkish War of Independence involved more than three years of fighting between Turkish and Allied forces. Map 8.5 shows the disposition of forces in Anatolia in 1921. Ataturk had checked the encroachment on territory by the Armenians in the north and negotiated with the French for a ceasefire in the south. Turkish forces were able to stop the westward advance of the Greeks in the Battle of Sakarya and launch a vigorous counterattack that eventually recaptured the town of Smyrna in August 1921. The Greco-Turkish War cost the Greeks more casualties than they suffered in the Great War. Michael Clodfelter puts the toll for Greece at 105,000 men including 35,000 missing in action or taken prisoner. Turkish casualties were 13,000 killed and 35,000 wounded. He notes that there were also thousands of civilian deaths.[36]

The defeat of the Greek expeditionary force ended the fighting in Anatolia. All of the belligerents gathered for a conference in Lausanne, Switzerland in November 1922 to establish a new set of boundaries for the territories of the former Ottoman Empire that would replace the arrangements stipulated in the Treaty of Sèvres two years earlier. The Treaty of Lausanne, which was the result of eight months of negotiation, established an independent Turkish state and formally dissolved the Ottoman Empire. It also finalized the border arrangements for mandates and states shown in Map 8.4. Great Britain, France, Italy, Greece, and Romania all signed and eventually ratified the treaty. The Soviet Socialist Federal Republic had earlier recognized the new Turkish state with the Treaty of Moscow in March of 1921.

The task of drawing a new map of Europe and the Middle East was finally finished. It remained to be seen how long the new boundaries would last.

Gold, Guilt, and Reparations

By the end of the nineteenth century, the western European economies had fashioned a global system of multilateral trade that allowed all the countries to import and export a wide range of consumer commodities, food, and the raw materials that fueled the growth of their domestic economies. One of the institutional arrangements that facilitated this trade was the emergence of the *Gold Standard*, which established a fixed price of gold to serve as an international currency. As cliometrician Barry Eichengreen explains, "For more than a quarter of a century before World War I, the gold standard provided the framework for domestic and international monetary relations. Currencies were convertible into gold on demand and linked internationally at fixed rates of exchange. Gold shipments were the ultimate means of balance-of-payments settlement."[37]

The Gold Standard

The conventional wisdom of the time was that the gold standard depended on the presence of central banks – and in particular the Bank of England – to manage the clearing of international payments efficiently so that exchange rates did not fluctuate over time. Immediately after the war, bankers and policymakers of the period firmly believed that for the gold standard to work, in the postwar era, the Bank of England must return to a monetary policy of supporting a price of gold pegged at the level that had persisted before the war. Eichengreen takes issue with the argument that it was the policies of the central banks were the pillar of stability on which the gold standard rested before the war. The stability of the prewar gold standard, he argues,

> was instead the result of two very different factors: credibility and cooperation. Credibility is the confidence invested by the public and the government's commitment to a policy. The credibility of the gold standard derived from the priority attached by governments to the maintenance of balance of payments equilibrium ... Ultimately, however, the credibility of the prewar gold standard rested on international cooperation. When stabilizing speculation and domestic intervention proved incapable of accommodating a disturbance, the system was stabilized through cooperation among governments and central banks.[38]

The outbreak of the war in 1914 caused all the major countries to abandon the gold standard, (with the notable exception of the United States, which was still in the process of organizing the Federal Reserve System and did not yet have an operational central bank to manage the operation of a gold standard). "The argument, in a nutshell," claims Eichengreen, "is that credibility and cooperation were central to the smooth operation of the classical gold standard. The scope for both declined abruptly with the intervention of the war. The instability of the interwar gold standard reflected the loss of confidence and the constant fear of unstable markets."[39] In a world fearful of the unknown, the ties that bound the system of global payments were torn apart.

Reparation Payments

Adding to the difficulties of collapsing global financial markets immediately after the war was the imposition by the Allies of reparation payments which were levied against all the Central Powers in varying amounts. The reparation payments were a curious blend of morality and economics. The morality involved placing the blame for the war on Germany and its allies and insisting that the Central Powers were therefore morally obligated to "pay for the war." The economic challenge was to construct a reasonable estimate of the value that should be placed on that obligation.

The morality issue was settled in favor of the Allied Powers by Article 231 of the Versailles Treaty – widely known as the "War Guilt Clause" – which stated that:

> The Allied and Associated Governments affirm and Germany accepts the responsibility of Germany and her allies for causing all the loss and damage to which the Allied and Associated Governments and their nationals have been subjected as a consequence of the war imposed upon them by the aggression of Germany and her allies.[40]

Forcing the Germans to assume the blame imposed a humiliation on the enemy; asking them to pay for all the damages associated with the war was rubbing salt in the wounds. Article 232 of the treaty recognized that the resources of Germany were not adequate "to make complete reparation for all such loss and damage." In spite of this obvious reality, the treaty insisted that the Germans "will make compensation for all damage done to the civilian population of the Allied and Associated Powers and to their property during the period of the belligerency," as well as any damage from "aggression by land, by sea and from the air," and in general "all damage as defined in Annex l hereto."[41]

The Council of Four realized that they needed additional time and some assistance from their staff and colleagues to construct a detailed plan for reparations. They therefore appointed an Inter-Allied Reparation Commission that would determine "The amount of the above damage for which compensation is to be made by Germany." The commission would report its findings "to the German Government on or before May 1, 1921, as representing the extent of that Government's obligations." The next fifteen articles of the treaty explained in great detail the variety of ways that Germany could meet its obligations to the Allied governments, and the possible penalties that could be imposed if the Germans failed to meet these demands in a timely fashion. This could be in the form of monetary payments or a variety of in-kind payments such as shipments of coal, timber, chemical dyes, pharmaceuticals, livestock, agricultural machines, construction materials, and factory machinery. An estimate of damages constructed by the U.S. Army Corps of Engineers presented to the Council of Four in May of 1919 valued the damages at between 60 and 100 billion marks, with a comment that 60 billion was the most one might reasonably expect the Germans to be able to pay.[42]

On May 5, 1921, the Reparation Commission announced that it had arrived at a figure of 132 billion gold marks as the total amount due from Germany. This was a compromise figure reached by members of the commission, which at one point had flirted with the possibility that the indemnity should be set as high as 225 billion gold marks. The commission identified three classes of bonds: 12 billion gold marks of "A" bonds to cover damages in France and Belgium during the war; 38 billion gold marks of "B" bonds to cover loans between Allied countries during the war; and 82 billion gold marks of "C" bonds to serve as a contingency that could cover the possibility of additional payments if the German economy recovered.

Realizing that the Germans would be unable to pay such a huge sum immediately, the commission established a schedule of payments that required the Germans to begin payments immediately on the 50 billion gold marks of "A" and "B" bonds, with the remaining balance of 82 billion gold marks of "C" bonds deferred depending on the recovery of German economy. There was some confusion whether the "C bonds" would ever be repaid. The Germans were assured it was extremely unlikely that these bonds would ever have to be paid; however, the possibility that they might be invoked at some later date left a cloud of uncertainty over the creditworthiness of future German bonds. One interpretation of the commission's decision to include the "C" bond payments in the calculation for the total amount due is that this allowed politicians in the Allied countries to impress their constituents with the magnitude of the German reparations even though they had no intention of ever collecting the 82 million gold marks. What all of this meant in 1921 was that, after making allowance for the payments made between 1919 and 1921, the Germans still owed about 41 billion gold marks.[43]

The reparation clause and its impact have been debated at length by twentieth-century historians. A review of this literature sheds light on several questions about the impact of reparations on Germany and on the global economy.[44] The question that immediately arose in 1921 was whether the schedule announced by the commission was a figure that the Germans could reasonably be expected to pay. Initial reaction from the Germans was that it was much too high, and this view found considerable sympathy from observers in the Allied countries at the time. However, a closer look at the situation suggests that, while the figure of 132 gold marks may have been an unacceptable challenge for the Germans to meet in 1921, the 41 billion gold marks payment should not have been that daunting. Writing in 1919, Keynes suggested that the Allies should cancel all their wartime debts with each other and impose a reparations burden of 40 billion gold marks ($10 billion).[45] Many contemporary observers noted that the indemnity imposed by the victorious Prussians on France after the Franco-Prussian War was of the same order of magnitude relative to the French ability to pay in 1871. France repaid that burden in two years. Niall Ferguson insists that it cannot "credibly be maintained that the reparations total set in 1921 constituted an intolerable burden," and Albrecht Ritschl agrees, noting that "A burden this size was by no means impossible to bear."[46]

Another problem discussed at some length in the literature is whether the Germans deliberately encouraged the hyperinflation of 1919–24 in an effort to evade paying the reparations. While the intricacies of economic policy make it difficult to reach a definitive answer with regard to their motives, most observers agree that the Germans deliberately pursued a monetary and fiscal policy that fed the inflationary pressures following the war, and they were happy enough to see inflation diminish the real value of the remaining debt. "German leaders," according to Sally Marks, "clearly recognized the political implications of the reparations issue and, from beginning to end, devoted their inexhaustible energies to avoiding or reducing payments."[47] The result of all this is that the Germans eventually wound up paying only about 20 billion marks by the time the remaining debt was repudiated by Adolf Hitler in 1933. Finally, it is clear that the political implications that accompanied the imposition of reparations were more important than the economic consequences in terms of the relationships between countries in the international marketplace. Marks' summary of the situation captures the tone of a revised view of the Treaty of Versailles among many scholars looking back on the Treaty of Versailles from the twenty-first century:

> Germany saw no reason to pay and from start to finish deemed reparations a gratuitous insult. Whether it was wise to seek reparations from Germany is arguable, although the consequences of not seeking them would have been far-reaching, as the failure to obtain them proved in time to be. Certainly it was unwise to inflict the insult without rigorous enforcement. In the last analysis, however, despite the fact that reparations claims were intended to transfer real economic wealth from Germany to the battered victors and despite the financial complexity of the problem, the reparations question was a political issue; a struggle for dominance of the European continent and to maintain or reverse the military outcome of 1918.[48]

Unfortunately, this was not 1815. Metternich and his colleagues in Vienna were able to construct something resembling the *status quo antebellum* world before Napoleon. The diplomats at the Paris Peace Conference knew that they could not go back to the world of 1914, and they had little or no experience to draw upon as they tried to create new states or estimate the cost of reparations. In the space of a few weeks at the end of 1918, the imperial governments of the German, Habsburg, and Ottoman empires had all been swept away, creating a political vacuum that stretched across a vast area of Europe and the Middle East. The result was a pervasive sense of fear and uncertainty which undercut the confidence of those charged with the responsibility of establishing institutional arrangements in the world the peacemakers were trying to create. This uncertainty produced a crippling level of caution in decision-making. In the fall of 1918, Woodrow Wilson refused to negotiate with the Kaiser and his generals over the question of a ceasefire. When the Germans responded by forming a more representative government they discovered that

Wilson did not have any confidence that a more "democratic" government would work in the Germany of 1918. It soon became apparent that the president's fears about the stability of new governments being formed in Germany and eastern Europe were shared by his colleagues on the Council of Four. None of the new governments formed by the Treaty of Versailles had any experience in the formation and operation of what western Europeans thought of as a "democratic" system of government. The peacemakers were caught up in a Catch-22. They wanted democratic governments to be formed after the war, but they did not really believe that those democratic governments would work in the context of the institutional structure left by the sudden destruction of former imperial empires. Experience confirmed that their fears were well-founded. Among the new European governments formed in the wake of the First World War only one – Czechoslovakia – retained a semblance of democracy in the two decades following the Peace Conference of 1920.

An Incomplete Victory?

Our narrative of the First World War has focused on ways in which the interaction of confidence, fear, and a propensity to gamble can help explain many of the decisions made on the battlefields and in the councils on war between 1914 and the end of 1918. All the belligerents were following military and economic strategies that would protect them against *losing* the war, and they were willing to undertake considerable risks to avoid such a calamity. The promise of victory was strong enough to fashion a sense of solidarity among the high commands of both the victorious Allies and the defeated Central Powers. However, once the fighting stopped, there was no comparable strategy on either side with regard to a strategy that might produce a lasting peace. The European leaders were far more concerned with making sure that the peace would protect their interests at home than they were in promoting international cooperation. For Clemenceau, a peace settlement meant "turning the clock back to 1870" when Germany was not yet the dominant power in Europe and Alsace-Lorraine was a department in France. For Lloyd George, it meant protecting the freedom of the seas that was the lifeblood of the British Empire and finding a way to make Germany a peaceful partner rather than a threat to the rest of

Europe. For Italy, Orlando wanted to make sure that his country got the rewards promised when it joined the Entente. For Woodrow Wilson it was the creation of a League of Nations that would oversee a "peace without victory."

Was the Treaty of Versailles responsible for the failure of the peace? John Maynard Keynes' indictment of the treaty's economic and political shortcomings remains an insightful analysis of what happened over the next two decades. But we should remember that Keynes' critique was that of an economist focusing on the economic consequences that would play a major role in causing the Great Depression and the Second World War. Historians reviewing the failure of the treaty after a century of thought have suggested that the catastrophes that followed the end of the war involved more than the economics of a treaty. They emphasize that, despite its shortcomings, the treaty actually accomplished a great deal given the circumstances in 1919. In the introduction to their 1998 volume reassessing the treaty after seventy-five years the editors suggest that:

> Whatever its shortcomings, the treaty lent itself to future revision and eventually led to an era of temporary stability between 1924 and 1931. By 1932 the reparations dispute was largely resolved, the Rhineland occupation had come to an end, and Britain and the United States had signaled their readiness to enter into negotiations for a new settlement of the Polish Corridor. By contemporary standards, in short, the treaty did not prove an inflexible instrument.[49]

The Great War ended because one side could no longer carry on the fight. Once the Siegfried–Hindenburg Line was broken in the summer of 1918, the Germans realized that they could not withstand the weight of the Allied attacks that would follow. Rather than fight to the last man, they elected to ask for a ceasefire. Surprised by the suddenness of the German offer, the Allied generals and statesmen reined in their armies and hurried to put together a set of terms that would stop the fighting. Not everyone thought this was a good idea, and a case can be made that they were right. As David Stevenson points out, Germany's economy was exhausted, but its economic infrastructure was not destroyed. Amid the chaos of victory was the bitter truth that Britain, France, and Italy were as exhausted as were the Germans.

Summing up the effects of the world war on an imaginary country, Niall Ferguson presents a description of a country which

> lost 22 per cent of its national territory; incurred debts equivalent to 136 per cent of gross national product, a fifth of it owed to foreign powers; saw inflation and then unemployment rise to levels not seen for more than a century; and experienced an equally unprecedented wave of labour unrest. Imagine a country whose newly democratic political system produced a system of coalition government in which party deals behind closed doors, rather than elections, determined who governed the country.[50]

That country, notes Ferguson, was not Germany, it was Great Britain in the years immediately following the war. France and Italy were even more ravaged by the effects of the war, and the rest of Europe was totally disorganized. Once the guns were finally silenced, the European powers were hardly in a position to restrain a postwar German economic recovery as they struggled to rebuild their own economies, and they showed little interest in expending efforts to see that the terms of the treaty they had written were enforced.

The Allies won the war, but accepting a hastily constructed armistice left them with an incomplete victory. This was not so much due to a lack of will as it was a reflection of just how high the price of victory had been. Amid the chaos of victory, the peacemakers in Paris did their best to fashion a lasting peace. As Margaret MacMillan summed things up at the end of her study of the peace conference,

> If they could have done better, they certainly could have done much worse. They tried, even cynical old Clemenceau, to build a better order. They could not foresee the future and they certainly could not control it. That was up to their successors. When war came in 1939, it was a result of twenty years of decisions taken or not taken, not of arrangements made in 1919.[51]

Ferdinand Foch's prediction that the Treaty of Versailles was only a prolonged armistice turned out to be prescient indeed.

EPILOGUE: THE TRAGEDY OF A WORLD WAR

> The outbreak of war in 1914 is not an Agatha Christie drama at the end of which we will discover the culprit standing over a corpse in the conservatory with a smoking pistol. There is no smoking gun in this story; or, rather, there is one in the hands of every major character. Viewed in this light, the outbreak of war was a tragedy, not a crime.
>
> Christopher Clark[1]

It was billed as the "war to end all wars," but it was anything but that. Georges Clemenceau called it a "series of disasters ending in victory," while Woodrow Wilson hoped for a "peace without victory" and Marshall Ferdinand Foch described the treaty that ostensibly ended the war as nothing more than a "twenty-year armistice." Eric Hobsbawm summed up the view of many historians when he wrote that the war ushered in a forty-year "Age of Catastrophe" when Western civilization "stumbled from one calamity to another." Social scientists have regarded the war as an enigma through a century of study. For cliometricians Ronald Findlay and Kevin O'Rourke, the war remains "somewhat of an unexplained *diabolus ex machina*."[2]

The Great War was all of these and more: a series of enigmatic tragedies that changed the world in a way that made it impossible to return to the antebellum state of affairs. But it did not "end" wars. Christopher Clark's observation that not even Hercule Poirot could find an answer of who "started" the war points to the first of these tragedies. What should have been nothing more than a quarrel between Austria and Serbia in the Balkans became a war that involved all the major powers of Europe within a matter of a few weeks. This initial tragedy was magnified by the inability of anyone to figure out a way to end the war once it had started. As the war went on the casualties and the number of countries involved increased. The need to make sure that all those deaths were not in vain encouraged leaders to chase victory rather than search for a negotiated peace. Winning the war became an end in itself rather than a way to accomplish some prewar objective. Politicians and generals took risky gambles to attain that victory, which only magnified the cost of the war if the gambles failed.

The inability to find some means of putting an end to the fighting meant that the war did not end with a negotiated peace; it ended because the ability of one side to support their war effort had collapsed. What emerged from the Peace Conference in Paris was a two-decade "ceasefire" between Germany and the Allied countries that was written into a series of treaties which did little more than confirm the conditions spelled out in the November 1918 armistice. Four and a half years of fighting had taught people how to wage war, but they remained clueless about how to keep the peace. In 1919 "smoking guns" were still in abundance. Despite the celebrations around the globe when the ceasefire was announced, no one was happy with the outcome of the war. On the Allied side, the British and the French could finally give a sigh of relief that the German threat had been repulsed and their empires had survived – for the time being. The British returned to tending their empire and controlling the seas. The French, who still harbored an enormous fear of Germany, nervously constructed massive fortifications along the German border to fend off future invasions. The Americans refused to sign any of the peace treaties, packed up their two million troops, and went home, still convinced that it was best to stay out of European wars. The Italians were unhappy with a peace that did not reward them with the promises made in 1915 when they joined the Entente, and they eventually allied themselves with a resurgent Germany to take another gamble at empire building. The Russians, who managed to get out of the war with Germany and Austria, were left to deal with their new economic and political system amid the ruins of a lost war and a very bloody revolution. The Soviet Union was one of many enigmas to emerge from the Great War. Despite the fact that they were forced to surrender to the Allied forces in 1918, the Germans did not lose their propensity to gamble on war. They eventually managed to rebound from their defeat and prepare for an even riskier gamble – the invasion of the

Soviet Union in 1941 under the misguided direction of Adolf Hitler. In the Orient, Japan, one of the few countries to emerge relatively unscathed from the war, tried its own version of gambling on war by attacking Pearl Harbor in December of 1941. By the fall of 1939, the world was once again engaged in a world war. That is not to say that the "Second" World War was simply a continuation of the Great War of 1914–18. The Second World War was much larger, much more violent, and involved a whole new cast of characters and war objectives. The Allied victory over the Axis Powers in the summer of 1945 did at least manage to put an end to "world" wars. The surrender of Japan and Germany led to a "Cold War" that – despite some very warm moments – has managed to avoid another catastrophic world war for more than seventy years.

One of the greatest tragedies of the Great War was that after the agony of a new form of warfare that indiscriminately killed and wounded millions of soldiers and civilians and undermined the institutional framework of the global social, economic, and political systems, the First World War did not, in the end, provide a means of resolving the rivalries and jealousies of the nations that started it. "In 1914," writes historian Ruth Henig,

> countries went to war because they believed that they could achieve more through war than by diplomatic negotiation and that if they stood aside their status as great powers would be gravely affected. That was their greatest miscalculation. The balance sheet in 1918 proved how wrong they had been; by that time the status of all Europe's major powers had been greatly diminished and virtually none of the objectives of the European ruling elites had been realized.[3]

Henig's judgment reminds us that the price the world paid for the gambles on wars during the Age of Catastrophes was extraordinarily high. On the evening of August 3, 1914, as the British cabinet completed their deliberations on the declaration of war against Germany Sir Edward Grey, the British foreign secretary, turned to a colleague and said, "The lamps are going out all over Europe, and we shall not see them lit again in our lifetime."[4]

Grey's comment has become one of the iconic quotes associated with the outbreak of a war that nobody wanted, nobody understood, and nobody can forget. A century later we are still struggling to adjust to the tragic legacy of the Great War.

APPENDIX 1   THE COMPOSITE INDEX OF NATIONAL CAPABILITY SCORE

The data in Table A1.1, ranks the %CINC scores of the ten major powers with the highest %CINC score during six pivotal years between 1850 and 1935. In addition to the %CINC estimates for each country, the table presents the country ratios for three subsets of variables:

%MIL is the country's share of military personnel plus military expenditures;
%ECON is the country's share of iron production and energy use; and
%POP is the share of total plus urban population.

A glance at the %CINC rankings in Table A1.1 suggests that the estimates conform to the generally accepted view of the changing military power among states and empires in the years leading up to and through the Great War. The most obvious observation is that the ability to wage war was concentrated in a few "great powers." Great Britain and its colonial empire were clearly the most powerful military force in the world up to the midpoint of the nineteenth century with a %CINC more than twice the level of either Russia or France. The British remained atop the rankings in 1875; however, their lead diminished substantially as two new powers – the United States and the newly created German Empire – moved up. By the end of the century the Americans had moved to the top spot, with the British close behind and the Germans only slightly further behind in third place. The dominance of these three states in the %CINC rankings calls attention to a significant feature of the CINC approach to the metrics of power: the importance of *economic* and *demographic* factors in the determination of national capability to wage war. The %ECON and %POP ratios take into account the effects of the industrial revolution; by 1914 the American, British, and German %ECON variables amounted to 79 percent of the global total. The British and American cases point to another issue that we explore in our narrative. Both of these countries maintained strong navies; however, neither country maintained a standing army at anywhere near the scale of their European rivals. Consequently, their %MIL estimates are well below those of the four other powers. This meant that their *potential* for waging a major war was much higher than their ability to actually wage such a war at any point of time. This distinction becomes crucial in evaluating decisions facing leaders during crises produced by tipping points. A decision to wage war or change strategy had to take into account both the potential power and the situation at a point in time.

The changing position of the United States is particularly revealing in this regard. The Americans already had the highest %CINC score of any great power before the Great War started. As the conflict escalated, all the belligerents recognized that an American decision to enter on either side (or to remain neutral) could dramatically change the balance of power. The nagging question facing the Germans in 1917 was not how strong the Americans were; it was whether or not they could mobilize their military capability and get their military forces across the Atlantic soon enough to affect the outcome of the fighting on the Western Front. The %CINC estimates of Table A1.1 show just how important this effort was. Woodrow Wilson's administration orchestrated a war effort that mobilized and moved two million doughboys to France by the summer of 1918. When the peace treaty was finally signed in Versailles in June of 1919 the United States' %CINC had risen to 38.1, the %MIL was 40.4, and the %ECON was 57.2.

While the rapid emergence of the United States was the most dramatic example of how great the shift in the global power structure in the years immediately following the war had been, it is worth noting that the %CINC score of Weimar Germany was exceeded by only two of the victorious Allies – the United States and the British Empire. This strongly supports the idea that while the Allies had defeated the German armies, they had not eliminated the economic capability of the German economy to rearm and return to the battlefield two decades later. The First World War did not end the problems and rivalries facing the world in 1914.

Table A1.1 Composite Index of National Capabilities

1850

Country/empire	%MIL	%ECON	%POP	%CINC
British Empire	10.76	60.21	20.28	30.40
Russia	26.75	2.73	13.83	14.40
France	18.15	8.87	11.09	12.70
Habsburg Empire	14.53	2.34	8.24	8.40
United States	3.06	11.05	7.63	7.20
Prussia	4.48	5.76	4.48	4.90
German states	3.76	1.60	1.99	0.53
Ottoman Empire	2.50	0.01	9.42	4.80
Italy	1.72	0.28	1.58	1.20
Total powers	85.73	92.83	78.54	84.53
Rest of world	14.27	7.17	21.46	15.47
Total world	100.00	100.00	100.00	100.0

Note: In all tables, figures are rounded to two decimal points.

1875

Country/empire	%MIL	%ECON	%POP	%CINC
British Empire	9.82	46.54	14.29	23.55
United States	4.29	17.39	10.41	10.70
France	14.13	9.96	7.55	10.54
Germany	11.07	13.65	6.31	10.34
Russia	18.76	2.09	9.05	9.96
Habsburg Empire	6.79	3.04	4.27	4.70
Italy	4.64	0.32	4.96	3.31
Ottoman Empire	3.42	0.05	3.33	2.27
Japan	1.13	0.12	5.43	2.23
China	11.90	0.04	21.38	11.11
Total powers	85.95	93.20	86.96	88.71
Rest of world	14.05	6.80	13.04	11.29
Total world	100.00	100.00	100.00	100.00

Table A1.1 (*cont.*)

1900

Country/empire	%MIL	%ECON	%POP	%CINC
United States	6.56	36.18	19.53	18.80
British Empire	19.99	21.73	18.51	17.75
Germany	10.63	20.01	12.79	13.15
Russia	15.56	6.30	10.21	10.92
France	10.72	6.16	7.47	7.47
Habsburg Empire	4.81	3.48	4.38	4.24
Japan	3.33	0.56	4.19	2.89
Italy	4.13	0.57	3.66	2.82
Ottoman Empire	3.24	0.02	1.47	1.72
China	10.26	0.02	5.00	10.00
Total powers	89.24	95.02	87.21	89.76
Rest of world	10.76	4.98	12.79	10.24
Total world	100.00	100.00	100.00	100.00

1914

Country/empire	%MIL	%ECON	%POP	%CINC
United States	2.89	43.67	15.36	20.64
Germany	18.16	19.62	9.69	15.82
British Empire	15.10	15.75	10.53	13.79
Russia	15.16	5.83	12.25	11.08
France	13.93	4.28	4.22	7.47
Habsburg Empire	12.98	3.20	4.29	6.82
Japan	2.86	1.25	5.37	3.16
Italy	3.03	1.22	3.45	2.57
Ottoman Empire	1.77	0.03	1.24	1.01
China	3.72	0.64	18.68	7.68
Total powers	89.59	95.48	85.08	90.05
Rest of world	10.41	4.52	14.92	9.95
Total world	100.00	100.00	100.00	100.00

Table A1.1 (*cont.*)

1919

Country/empire	%MIL	%ECON	%POP	%CINC
United States	40.43	57.16	16.82	38.14
British Empire	7.66	15.19	10.44	11.10
Germany	0.71	12.83	9.52	7.69
Russia	10.67	0.77	7.52	6.32
France	11.40	2.92	4.07	6.13
Italy	8.80	0.95	3.75	4.50
Japan	2.60	2.05	5.79	3.48
Habsburg Empire	0.11	0.27	1.25	0.55
Turkey	0.62	0.02	1.11	0.58
China	6.16	0.84	18.99	8.66
Total powers	89.16	93.01	79.25	87.14
Rest of world	10.84	6.99	20.75	12.86
Total world	100.00	100.00	100.00	100.00

1920

Country/empire	%MIL	%ECON	%POP	%CINC
United States	15.66	57.88	17.31	30.28
British Empire	15.63	17.49	13.83	15.65
Russia	24.36	0.62	7.69	10.89
Germany	1.21	11.73	9.79	7.57
France	9.91	4.07	4.41	6.13
Japan	5.25	1.75	5.96	4.32
Italy	6.54	0.81	3.86	3.74
Austria	0.18	0.35	1.26	0.60
China	6.78	0.83	19.22	8.94
Total powers	85.52	95.52	83.33	88.12
Rest of world	14.48	4.48	16.67	11.88
Total world	100.00	100.00	100.00	100.00

Table A1.1 (*cont.*)

1925

Country/empire	%MIL	%ECON	%POP	%CINC
United States	8.55	51.34	16.32	25.40
Soviet Union	20.53	1.84	8.14	10.17
British Empire	9.83	13.34	11.80	11.66
Germany	2.56	12.51	9.40	8.16
France	7.48	6.69	3.88	6.02
Japan	4.52	1.89	5.50	3.97
Italy	4.22	1.40	3.71	3.11
China	15.97	0.80	17.82	11.53
Total powers	73.67	89.81	76.57	80.02
Rest of Europe	16.24	9.38	12.18	12.60
Rest of world	10.09	0.81	11.24	7.38
Total world	100.00	100.00	100.00	100.00

1930

Country/empire	%MIL	%ECON	%POP	%CINC
United States	7.21	46.07	15.15	22.81
Soviet Union	30.16	5.00	9.61	14.92
British Empire	7.10	13.25	10.86	10.40
Germany	2.14	11.99	8.05	7.39
France	7.06	7.88	3.40	6.11
Japan	4.05	2.40	5.52	3.99
Italy	4.73	1.39	3.52	3.21
China	15.04	0.78	21.94	12.59
Total powers	77.48	88.75	78.04	81.43
Rest of Europe	16.57	10.73	13.23	13.51
Rest of world	5.95	0.52	8.73	5.07
Total world	100.00	100.00	100.00	100.00

Source: The CINC figures are calculated from the Correlates of War National Capabilities Data Set, Version 4.0.

APPENDIX 2   WOODROW WILSON'S FOURTEEN POINTS

A Speech to the United States Senate, January 8, 1918

Once more, as repeatedly before, the spokesmen of the Central Empires have indicated their desire to discuss the objects of the war and the possible basis of a general peace. Parleys have been in progress at Brest-Litovsk between Russian representatives and representatives of the Central Powers to which the attention of all the belligerents has been invited for the purpose of ascertaining whether it may be possible to extend these parleys into a general conference with regard to terms of peace and settlement.

The Russian representatives presented not only a perfectly definite statement of the principles upon which they would be willing to conclude peace but also an equally definite program of the concrete application of those principles. The representatives of the Central Powers, on their part, presented an outline of settlement which, if much less definite, seemed susceptible of liberal interpretation until their specific program of practical terms was added. That program proposed no concessions at all either to the sovereignty of Russia or to the preferences of the populations with whose fortunes it dealt, but meant, in a word, that the Central Empires were to keep every foot of territory their armed forces had occupied – every province, every city, every point of vantage – as a permanent addition to their territories and their power.

It is a reasonable conjecture that the general principles of settlement which they at first suggested originated with the more liberal statesmen of Germany and Austria, the men who have begun to feel the force of their own people's thought and purpose, while the concrete terms of actual settlement came from the military leaders who have no thought but to keep what they have got. The negotiations have been broken off. The Russian representatives were sincere and in earnest. They cannot entertain such proposals of conquest and domination.

The whole incident is full of significances. It is also full of perplexity. With whom are the Russian representatives dealing? For whom are the representatives of the Central Empires speaking? Are they speaking for the majorities of their respective parliaments or for the minority parties, that military and imperialistic minority which has so far dominated their whole policy and controlled the affairs of Turkey and of the Balkan states which have felt obliged to become their associates in this war?

The Russian representatives have insisted, very justly, very wisely, and in the true spirit of modern democracy, that the conferences they have been holding with the Teutonic and Turkish statesmen should be held within open, not closed, doors, and all the world has been audience, as was desired. To whom have we been listening, then? To those who speak the spirit and intention of the resolutions of the German Reichstag of the 9th of July last, the spirit and intention of the Liberal leaders and parties of Germany, or to those who resist and defy that spirit and intention and insist upon conquest and subjugation? Or are we listening, in fact, to both, unreconciled and in open and hopeless contradiction? These are very serious and pregnant questions. Upon the answer to them depends the peace of the world.

But, whatever the results of the parleys at Brest-Litovsk, whatever the confusions of counsel and of purpose in the utterances of the spokesmen of the Central Empires, they have again attempted to acquaint the world with their objects in the war and have again challenged their adversaries to say what their objects are and what sort of settlement they would deem just and satisfactory. There is no good reason why that challenge should not be responded to, and responded to with the utmost candor. We did not wait for it. Not once, but again and again, we have laid our whole thought and purpose before the world, not in general terms only, but each time with sufficient definition to make it clear what sort of definite terms of settlement must necessarily spring out of them. Within the last week Mr. Lloyd George has spoken with admirable candor and in admirable spirit for the people and Government of Great Britain.

There is no confusion of counsel among the adversaries of the Central Powers, no uncertainty of principle, no vagueness of detail. The only secrecy of counsel, the only lack of fearless frankness, the only failure to make definite statement of the objects of the war, lies with Germany and her allies. The issues of life and death hang upon these definitions. No statesman who has the least conception of his responsibility ought for a moment to permit himself to continue this tragical and appalling outpouring of blood and treasure unless he is sure beyond a peradventure that the objects of the vital sacrifice are part and parcel of the very life of Society and that the people for whom he speaks think them right and imperative as he does.

There is, moreover, a voice calling for these definitions of principle and of purpose which is, it seems to me, more thrilling and more compelling than any of the many moving voices with which the troubled air of the world is filled. It is the voice of the Russian people. They are prostrate and all but hopeless, it would seem, before the grim power of Germany, which has hitherto known no relenting and no pity. Their power, apparently, is shattered. And yet their soul is not subservient. They will not yield either in principle or in action. Their conception of what is right, of what is humane and honorable for them to accept, has been stated with a frankness, a largeness of view, a generosity of spirit, and a universal human sympathy which must challenge the admiration of every friend of mankind; and they have refused to compound their ideals or desert others that they themselves may be safe.

They call to us to say what it is that we desire, in what, if in anything, our purpose and our spirit differ from theirs; and I believe that the people of the United States would wish me to respond, with utter simplicity and frankness. Whether their present leaders believe it or not, it is our heartfelt desire and hope that some way may be opened whereby we may be privileged to assist the people of Russia to attain their utmost hope of liberty and ordered peace.

It will be our wish and purpose that the processes of peace, when they are begun, shall be absolutely open and that they shall involve and permit henceforth no secret understandings of any kind. The day of conquest and aggrandizement is gone by; so is also the day of secret covenants entered into in the interest of particular governments and likely at some unlooked-for moment to upset the peace of the world. It is this happy fact, now clear to the view of every public man whose thoughts do not still linger in an age that is dead and gone, which makes it possible for every nation whose purposes are consistent with justice and the peace of the world to avow now or at any other time the objects it has in view.

We entered this war because violations of right had occurred which touched us to the quick and made the life of our own people impossible unless they were corrected and the world secure once for all against their recurrence. What we demand in this war, therefore, is nothing peculiar to ourselves. It is that the world be made fit and safe to live in; and particularly that it be made safe for every peace-loving nation which, like our own, wishes to live its own life, determine its own institutions, be assured of justice and fair dealing by the other peoples of the world as against force and selfish aggression. All the peoples of the world are in effect partners in this interest, and for our own part we see very clearly that unless justice be done to others it will not be done to us. The program of the world's peace, therefore, is our program; and that program, the only possible program, as we see it, is this:

I. Open covenants of peace, openly arrived at, after which there shall be no private international understandings of any kind but diplomacy shall proceed always frankly and in the public view.

II. Absolute freedom of navigation upon the seas, outside territorial waters, alike in peace and in war, except as the seas may be closed in whole or in part by international action for the enforcement of international covenants.

III. The removal, so far as possible, of all economic barriers and the establishment of an equality of trade conditions among all the nations consenting to the peace and associating themselves for its maintenance.

IV. Adequate guarantees given and taken that national armaments will be reduced to the lowest point consistent with domestic safety.

V. A free, open-minded, and absolutely impartial adjustment of all colonial claims, based upon a strict observance of the principle that in determining all such questions of sovereignty the interests of the populations concerned must have equal weight with the equitable claims of the government whose title is to be determined.

VI.   The evacuation of all Russian territory and such a settlement of all questions affecting Russia as will secure the best and freest cooperation of the other nations of the world in obtaining for her an unhampered and unembarrassed opportunity for the independent determination of her own political development and national policy and assure her of a sincere welcome into the society of free nations under institutions of her own choosing; and, more than a welcome, assistance also of every kind that she may need and may herself desire. The treatment accorded Russia by her sister nations in the months to come will be the acid test of their good will, of their comprehension of her needs as distinguished from their own interests, and of their intelligent and unselfish sympathy.

VII. Belgium, the whole world will agree, must be evacuated and restored, without any attempt to limit the sovereignty which she enjoys in common with all other free nations. No other single act will serve as this will serve to restore confidence among the nations in the laws which they have themselves set and determined for the government of their relations with one another. Without this healing act the whole structure and validity of international law is forever impaired.

VIII. All French territory should be freed and the invaded portions restored, and the wrong done to France by Prussia in 1871 in the matter of Alsace-Lorraine, which has unsettled the peace of the world for nearly fifty years, should be righted, in order that peace may once more be made secure in the interest of all.

IX.   A readjustment of the frontiers of Italy should be effected along clearly recognizable lines of nationality.

X.   The peoples of Austria-Hungary, whose place among the nations we wish to see safeguarded and assured, should be accorded the freest opportunity to autonomous development.

XI.   Rumania, Serbia, and Montenegro should be evacuated; occupied territories restored; Serbia accorded free and secure access to the sea; and the relations of the several Balkan states to one another determined by friendly counsel along historically established lines of allegiance and nationality; and international guarantees of the political and economic independence and territorial integrity of the several Balkan states should be entered into.

XII. The Turkish portion of the present Ottoman Empire should be assured a secure sovereignty, but the other nationalities which are now under Turkish rule should be assured an undoubted security of life and an absolutely unmolested opportunity of autonomous development, and the Dardanelles should be permanently opened as a free passage to the ships and commerce of all nations under international guarantees.

XIII. An independent Polish state should be erected which should include the territories inhabited by indisputably Polish populations, which should be assured a free and secure access to the sea, and whose political and economic independence and territorial integrity should be guaranteed by international covenant.

XIV. A general association of nations must be formed under specific covenants for the purpose of affording mutual guarantees of political independence and territorial integrity to great and small states alike.

In regard to these essential rectifications of wrong and assertions of right we feel ourselves to be intimate partners of all the governments and peoples associated together against the Imperialists. We cannot be separated in interest or divided in purpose. We stand together until the end. For such arrangements and covenants we are willing to fight and to continue to fight until they are achieved; but only because we wish the right to prevail and desire a just and stable peace such as can be secured only by removing the chief provocations to war, which this program does remove. We have no jealousy of German greatness, and there is nothing in this program that impairs it. We grudge her no achievement or distinction of learning or of pacific enterprise such as have made her record very bright and very enviable. We do not wish to injure her or to block in any way her legitimate influence or power. We do not wish to fight her either with arms or with hostile arrangements of trade if she is willing to associate herself with us and the other peace-loving nations of the world in covenants of justice and law and fair dealing. We wish her only to accept a place of equality among the peoples of the world, – the new world in which we now live, – instead of a place of mastery.

Neither do we presume to suggest to her any alteration or modification of her institutions. But it is necessary, we must frankly say, and necessary as a preliminary to any intelligent dealings with her on our part, that we should know whom her spokesmen speak for when they speak to us, whether for the Reichstag majority or for the military party and the men whose creed is imperial domination.

We have spoken now, surely, in terms too concrete to admit of any further doubt or question. An evident principle runs through the whole program I have outlined. It is the principle of justice to all peoples and nationalities, and their right to live on equal terms of liberty and safety with one another, whether they be strong or weak.

Unless this principle be made its foundation no part of the structure of international justice can stand. The people of the United States could act upon no other principle; and to the vindication of this principle they are ready to devote their lives, their honor, and everything they possess. The moral climax of this the culminating and final war for human liberty has come, and they are ready to put their own strength, their own highest purpose, their own integrity and devotion to the test.

ACKNOWLEDGMENTS

I have many people to thank for the assistance given me in the writing of this book. My greatest intellectual debts are to Douglass North, who introduced me to cliometrics as a graduate student at the University of Washington in the early 1960s and remained a role model for the next four decades; and to Richard Sutch, who teamed with me to teach a graduate course at the University of California, Berkeley in the spring of 1967 and became my partner in an intellectual partnership that has lasted fifty years.

The historical narrative presented in this book rests upon the research of many scholars who have studied war and economics in the modern era, and I have made every effort to give them the credit they are due in the comments and footnotes of each chapter. I also benefited from the comments and assistance of colleagues and friends who read all or part of the manuscript and commented on presentations of my work. Michael Bonner and Lindsay Johnson edited and improved multiple drafts of chapters as they evolved. Among the many people who offered help and encouragement by reading all or part of the manuscript are Paul d'Anieri, Claude Diebolt, Jonathan Eacott, Barry Eichengreen, Paul Gatrell, Michael Haupert, Phillip Hoffman, Peter Lindert, Anne McCants, Peter McCord, Doug McCulloh, Joel Mokyr, Phillip Mongin, and Kevin O'Rourke.

Writing a manuscript is only the first step in producing a book, and I owe particular thanks to Michael Watson's editorial expertise at Cambridge University Press, and his assistant Lisa Carter, who pushed me through the various stages of preparing the manuscript for review and publication. Carol Fellingham Webb and Céline Durassier offered numerous corrections and improvements by copyediting the final drafts of the manuscript.

I owe a huge debt to my wife, Connie, who has always been my greatest supporter, and to my grandson, Jared McKenzie, who pitched in to finish the final draft and index for the manuscript.

Finally, the book would not have been possible without the assistance of the medical team at the Riverside Medical Clinic. In the fall of 2014 I was diagnosed with multiple myeloma cancer. My primary care doctor, Andrew Corr, my oncologist, Vaishali Saste, and a large group of doctors, medics, and assistants helped me wage a war against cancer that provided the strength and the will to finish this manuscript.

To all of these people – and many more – all I can say is THANKS!

NOTES

Prologue

1 Ronald Findlay and Kevin H. O'Rourke, *Power and Plenty: Trade, War, and the World Economy in the Second Millennium* (Princeton University Press, 2007), xxi.
2 Findlay and O'Rourke obviously gave some thought to adding it to their list; however, they stopped short of doing so because "World War I still appears as somewhat of a *diabolus ex machina* in our account. [T]here are only so many cans of worms that one can open in the course of writing a book, and this is one can that we have decided to leave closed." Ibid., xxv.
3 Cliometrics is an approach to economic history that involves the application of economic theory and quantitative analysis to "predict" the past with ever greater precision. It was initially hailed as the "New Economic History," a field of study that evolved in economics departments during the late 1950s. The term "cliometrics" originated with the formation of the Cliometric Society in 1960 at Purdue University. In 1993 Robert Fogel and Douglass North – my thesis advisor at the University of Washington – were awarded the Nobel Prize in economics for their work in establishing the field of cliometrics.
4 Donald Kagan, *On the Origins of War and the Preservation of Peace* (New York: Doubleday, 1995).

1 Confidence, Fear, and a Propensity to Gamble

1 Carl von Clausewitz, *On War*, trans. Michael Howard and Peter Paret, indexed edn (Princeton University Press, 1984), 85.
2 Eric Hobsbawm, *The Age of Extremes: A History of the World, 1914–1990* (New York: Pantheon, 1994), 6.
3 John Maynard Keynes, *The Economic Consequences of the Peace* (New York: Penguin Books, 1988), 12.
4 Quoted in Lewis D. Eigen and Jonathan Paul Siegel, *The Macmillan Dictionary of Political Quotations* (Toronto: Macmillan, 1993), 689.
5 Phillip Hoffman, *Why Did Europe Conquer the World?* (New York: Princeton University Press, 2015), 1.

6 Ibid., 15–16.

7 See the discussion in ibid., 37–54.

8 The term "European" in our analysis of Figure 1.1 and Table 1.1 includes the United States, and for the period before 1920, data for Great Britain includes the resources of the British Commonwealth countries of Canada, Australia, New Zealand, and South Africa.

9 Other wars in this group include the Carlist Rebellion in Spain during the 1830s and the Balkan wars between Romania, Greece, Bulgaria, and Serbia that shaped the boundaries of countries following the withdrawal of the Ottoman Empire, and eventually produced the spark that started the First World War.

10 Trevor Royle, *Crimea: The Great Crimean War, 1854–1856* (New York: Palgrave MacMillan, 2000), 514; Michael Clodfelter, *Warfare and Armed Conflicts: A Statistical Reference to Casualty and Other Figures, 1500–2000*, 2nd edn (Jefferson, NC: McFarland & Company, 2002), 201.

11 The estimate of 618,000 is actually a conservative estimate of the number of deaths in the Civil War. J. David Hacker has constructed estimates of deaths in employing a survival technic that uses census data showing that more than 750,000 men died as a result of the war. The most widely accepted estimate is 624,000. See J. David Hacker, "A Census Based Count of the Civil War Dead," *Civil War History* 57, no. 4 (2011).

12 Gary Gallagher, *The Confederate War: How Popular Will, Nationalism, and Military Strategy Could Not Stave Off Defeat* (Boston: Harvard University Press, 1997), 168–9.

13 An excellent account of the Confederate political economy and their war effort is Michael Bonner, *Confederate Political Economy: Creating and Managing a Southern Capitalist Nation* (Baton Rouge: Louisiana State University Press, 2016). For the Union mobilization and management of the war, see Mark Wilson, *The Business of Civil War: Military Mobilization and the State, 1861–1865* (Baltimore: The Johns Hopkins University Press, 2006).

14 For an analysis of the American Civil War as a precursor of modern warfare and the First World War, see John Terraine, *White Heat: The New Warfare, 1914–1918* (London: Sidgewick & Jackson, 1982), 11–17.

15 On the evolution of Sherman's notion of "destructive" war, see John F. Marszalek, *Sherman: A Soldier's Passion for Order* (New York: Free Press, 1993). On the demoralizing effects of Union successes on the Confederate population, see Gallagher, *The Confederate War* and Drew Gilpin Faust, "Alters of Sacrifice: Confederate Women and the Narratives of War," *Journal of American History* 76 (March 1990). One of the less-celebrated aspects of both these campaigns was the effect the Union invasions had on the slave population. By the time Sherman reached Savannah, there were more than forty thousand escaped slaves following his army. See Joseph T. Glatthaar, *The March to the Sea and Beyond: Sherman's Troops in the Savannah and Carolinas Campaigns* (New York University Press, 1985).

16 Grant's "Overland Campaign" in the summer of 1864 began with the Battle of the Wilderness on May 5, 1864 and was followed by encounters at Spotsylvania Courthouse, the North Anna River, and Cold Harbor.

17 For more on the "economics" of the American Civil War, see Roger L. Ransom, "The Civil War in American Economic History," in *Oxford Handbook of American Economic History*, ed. Louis Cain (Oxford University Press, 2018).

18 Clodfelter, *Warfare and Armed Conflicts*, 479. There are mountains of statistics relating to casualties in the two world wars. Because they rely on many different

sources and definitions to construct the estimates, it is extremely difficult to compare figures across regions and time periods. To keep the definitions of statistics consistent throughout this study, I have relied on two sources for most of the battle statistics: the data sets of the Correlates of War Project and Michael Clodfelter's comprehensive study of casualty figures from 1500 to the present.

19 Ibid., 582. An excellent summary of the difficulties of estimating the human toll of the Second World War is Niall Ferguson, *The War of the World: Twentieth Century Conflict and the Descent of the West* (New York: Penguin, 2006), 647–54.

20 Clodfelter, *Warfare and Armed Conflicts*, 581.

21 To name just a few examples of this tendency, see Peter Temin, *Lessons from the Great Depression* (Cambridge, MA: The MIT Press, 1989); Barry Eichengreen, *Hall of Mirrors: The Great Depression, the Great Recession and the Uses – and Misuses – of History* (Oxford University Press, 2015); Adam Tooze, *The Deluge: The Great War, America, and the Remaking of the Global Order, 1916–1931* (New York: Viking Penguin, 2014); Findlay and O'Rourke, *Power and Plenty*; Charles Feinstein, Peter Temin, and Gianni Toniolo, *The World Economy between the World Wars* (Oxford University Press, 2008); Richard Overy, *The Inter-War Crisis, 1919–1939*, 2nd rev. edn (Harlow: Pearson, 2010).

22 John Stoessinger, *Why Nations Go to War*, 8th edn (New York: Beford/St. Martin's, 2001), 1–2.

23 John Maynard Keynes, *The General Theory of Employment, Interest, and Money* (New York: Harcourt Brace and World, 1936), ii.

24 Ibid., 129.

25 George A. Akerlof and Robert J. Shiller, *Animal Spirits: How Human Psychology Drives the Economy, and Why It Matters for Global Capitalism* (Princeton University Press, 2009). Akerlof and Shiller identify five animal spirits that they claim influence economic behavior: Confidence; Fairness; Corruption and Bad Faith; Stories; and what economists call the "Money Illusion."

26 Ibid., 13.

27 Clausewitz, *On War*. For more on Clausewitz's influence on military thinking, see Peter Paret, "Clausewitz," in *Makers of Modern Strategy: From Machiavelli to the Nuclear Age*, ed. Peter Paret (Princeton University Press, 1986).

28 Dominic D. P. Johnson, *Overconfidence and War: The Havoc and Glory of Positive Ilusions* (Cambridge, MA: Harvard University Press, 2004), 34.

29 Daniel Kahneman and Amos Tversky, "Prospect Theory: An Analysis of Decision under Risk," *Econometrica* 47, no. 2 (1979).

30 Ibid., 263.

31 Jack S. Levy, "Loss Aversion, Framing Effects, and International Conflicts: Perspectives from Prospect Theory." In *Handbook of War II*, edited by Manus I. Mildarsky, 193–221 (Ann Arbor, MI: University of Michigan Press, 2000).

32 There is a considerable literature on the application of prospect theory to decisions on war. An excellent summary of the theory's implications for war is provided by Levy, "Loss Aversion, Framing Effects." For more on the evolution of the model behind prospect theory, see Daniel Kahneman, *Thinking, Fast and Slow* (New York: Farrar, Strauss, and Giroux, 2011); Richard Thaler, *Misbehaving: The Making of Behavioral Economics*, Kindle edn (New York: W. W. Norton, 2015).

33 Kahneman, *Thinking, Fast and Slow*, 342.

34 Jack S. Levy and William Thompson, *The Causes of War*, Kindle edn (Chichester, West Sussex: John Wiley/Blackwell, 2010), Loc. 2363.

35 Rober J. Shiller, *Irrational Exuberance* (Princeton University Press, 2000), 150.
36 Stephen Van Evera, *Causes of War: Power and the Roots of Conflict* (Ithaca: Cornell Universty Press, 1999), 14.
37 John A. Vasquez, *The War Puzzle* (Cambridge University Press, 1993), 154.
38 Thomas S. Kuhn, *The Structure of Scientific Revolutions* (University of Chicago Press, 1962).
39 Kuhn argues that researchers saw no reason to question accepted paradigms because "they shared two essential characteristics. Their achievement was sufficiently unprecedented to attract an enduring group of adherents away from competing modes of scientific activity. Simultaneously, it was sufficiently open-ended to leave all sorts of problems for the redefined group of practitioners to resolve." To Kuhn, this open-endedness is not a shortcoming of the paradigm; it is only encouragement for further research to improve – not destroy – the paradigm.
40 Kuhn, *Structure of Scientific Revolutions*, 76.
41 John Kenneth Galbraith coined the phrase in his book *The Affluent Society* (Boston: Houghton Mifflin, 1958), insisting that there should be a "name for the ideas that are esteemed at any time for their acceptability, and it should be a term that emphasizes ... predictability." For more on his application of the term, see William Breit and Roger L. Ransom, *The Academic Scribblers*, 3rd edn (Princeton University Press, 1998), 166–9.
42 Keynes, *The General Theory of Employment, Interest, and Money*, 328.
43 Two obvious examples of military path dependency were the resistance to the development of the tank by the Allies and the introduction of new infantry by the Germans in 1918. Both of these innovations involved substantial retraining of troops. See the discussion in Chapter 7 on the changing face of war.
44 Hobsbawm, *The Age of Extremes*, 7.
45 For more information, see Correlates of War Project, "Project History," http://correlatesofwar.org/COWhistory.htm.
46 Singer and Small established a definition of war and presented a body of statistical data on warfare that became the foundation for a vast body of research on wars in the modern era. See J. David Singer and Melvin Small, *The Wages of War, 1816–1965: A Statistical Handbook* (New York: John Wiley and Sons, 1972). They subsequently published a second volume that carried the research forward to 1980. For a bibliography of publications relating to the project and its users, see Correlates of War Project, "Correlates of War Bibliography," www.correlatesofwar.org.
47 Correlates of War Project, *National Material Capabilities Data Documentation*, Version 4.0 edn (2010), 3, 6.
48 Ibid., 3.
49 The formulas are:
Country Ratio = Country Production / Global Production
Where the global production of each variable is the total of all the countries reporting that variable in a given year
CINC score = Sum of Country Ratios / six
%CINC score = CINC Score x 100
Note that the %CINC index has the convenient property that the sum of all the country CINC scores will add to 100.
50 For a more detailed discussion of the variable descriptions and the construction of the CINC score, see Correlates of War Project, *National Material Capabilities Data Documentation*, Version 4.0. For more on the COW data sets on wars, see

the codebooks for each of the three types of wars on the COW website, www
.correlatesofwar.org/data-sets.

2 Otto von Bismarck and the Changing Paradigm of War

1 Theodore Hamerow, ed. *Reflections and Reminiscences of Otto Von Bismarck*
(New York: Harper Torchbooks, 1968).

2 Joachim Remak, *The Origins of World War I*, 2nd edn (New York: Harcourt Brace,
1995), 5.

3 For a discussion of the formation of the German Federation, see Dennis Showalter,
The Wars of German Unification, Kindle edn (London: Bloomsbury, 2015),
chapter 1.

4 Cited in Hamerow, *Reflections and Reminiscences of Otto Von Bismarck*, 192.

5 For more on the dispute with Denmark, see Erich Eyck, *Bismarck and the German
Empire* (New York: W. W. Norton, 1950; repr. 1968), 77–107.

6 The initial members of the Zollverein were: Prussia, Hesse-Darmstadt, Hesse-
Kassel, Bavaria, Wurttemberg, Saxony, Thuringia, Baden, Nassau, and the city of
Frankfurt.

7 The role of the Zollverein in unifying Germany has not received the attention it
deserves in the literature. Two recent works that emphasize its significance in the eco-
nomic unification of Germany are: Carol Shuie and Wolfgang Keller, "Endogenous
Formation of Free Trade Agreements: Evidence from the Zollverein's Impact on
Market Integration," *Journal of Economic History* 74 (December 2014) and Florian
Ploeckl, "The Zollverein and the Formation of a Customs Union," *University of
Oxford Discussion Papers in Economic and Soical History* 84 (August 2010).

8 Cited in G. Craig, *The Politics of the Prussian Army* (Oxford University Press,
1955), 110.

9 The most important German states joining the war on the Austrian side included
Baden, Bavaria, Hanover, Saxony, and Wurttemberg. The only large state to side
with Prussia was Mecklenburg.

10 "In terms of numbers involved and casualties incurred," writes Michael Clodfelter,
"it was the greatest battle fought in the 90-year period between Waterloo in 1815
and the Liao-yang in 1904, surpassing in numbers even the battle of Gettysburg in
the American Civil War." Clodfelter, *Warfare and Armed Conflicts*, 206. For more
on the Seven Weeks War, see Geoffrey Wawro, *The Austro-Prussian War: Austria's
War with Prussia and Italy in 1866* (Cambridge University Press, 1997),
chapters 9–10; Showalter, *Wars of German Unification*, chapter 5; Brian Bond,
The Pursuit of Victory: From Napoleon to Saddam Hussein (Oxford University
Press, 1996), 61–7.

11 Wawro, *The Austro-Prussian War*, 295–6.

12 For more on Bismarck's machinations on the Ems Telegram and the decision to provoke a war with France, see Showalter, *Wars of German Unification*, Loc. 6048–64.

13 The negotiations were complicated by the disturbances of the Paris Commune
which continued from the middle of March to the end of June 1871. For a summary of the negotiations and settlement, see Michael Howard, *The Franco-Prussian
War: The German Invasion of France, 1870–71*, Kindle edn (London: Routlege,
2008), chapter 8.

14 Showalter, *Wars of German Unification*, Loc. 80.

15 For more on the problems associated with the League of the Three Emperors, see Eyck, *Bismarck and the German Empire*, 188–94; A. J. P. Taylor, *The Struggle for Mastery in Europe, 1848–1918* (Oxford University Press, 1980).

16 In addition to seven European states, representatives from four Balkan states – Greece, Serbia, Romania, and Montenegro – also attended the conference, but they were not members of the Congress.

17 Eyck, *Bismarck and the German Empire*, 250.

18 J. David Singer, "The Etiology of Interstate War: A Natural History Approach," in *What Do We Know About War?*, ed. John A. Vasquez (Lanham, MD: Rowman and Littlefield, 2000), 19.

19 Bond, *Pursuit of Victory*, 49.

20 David G. Herrmann, *The Arming of Europe and the Making of the First World War* (Princeton University Press, 1996), 3.

21 The figures for military personnel are from the Correlates of War data set. "Military Personnel" is defined as troops under the command of the national government, intended for use against foreign adversaries, and held ready for combat.

22 The demography of Europe had changed dramatically with the advent of the industrial revolution. William McNeill is one of many historians who feel that the "experiences in coping with population growth go far to explain the attitudes and behavior of the European powers on the eve of World War I" (*The Pursuit of Power: Technology, Armed Force, and Society since AD 1000* (University of Chicago Press, 1982), 311.

23 J. A. S. Grenville, *A History of the World in the Twentieth Century* (New York: Belknap Press, 1994), 255.

24 Stolypin was a dominant figure in Russian politics during the first decade of the twentieth century. In addition to the reorganization and financing of the Russian military, he proposed sweeping land reforms to increase the productivity of Russian agriculture. Unfortunately, he was unwilling to accept any form of compromise with those who sought to undermine the monarchy, and he was brutal in his suppression of the 1905–6 protesters. This not only crippled efforts to bring about any real reforms, it led to his assassination in November 1911. See the account in Grenville, *A History of the World in the Twentieth Century* and Martin A. Gilbert, *A History of the Twentieth Century, vol. i: 1900–1933* (New York: William Morrow, 1997).

25 Cited in John Keegan, *The Price of Admiralty: The Evolution of Naval Warfare* (New York: Viking Press, 1988), 100.

26 For more on Tirpitz's "risk theory" and the naval arms race it started, see Keegan, *The Price of Admiralty*; Niall Ferguson, *The Pity of War: Explaining World War I* (New York: Basic Books, 1999), 82–7; Robert K. Massie, *Dreadnought: Britain, Germany, and the Coming of the Great War* (New York: Random House, 1991).

27 The article was coauthored by a journalist, W. T. Snead, and titled "The Truth about the Navy."

28 An excellent summary of the building of the *Dreadnought* from its conception in a committee hand-picked by Jackie Fisher through its trial voyage around the world is in Massie, *Dreadnought*, chapter 26. For more on the development of capital ships in the years leading up to and during the war, see Terraine, *White Heat*, chapter 3.

29 Quoted in McNeill, *Pursuit of Power*, 277.

30 Stevenson provides data on the naval construction budgets of Britain and Germany (in millions of pounds):

Year	Britain	Germany
1907	10.6	6.6
1909	11.2	11.5
1911	18.9	13.1
1913	17.1	11.4

David Stevenson, *Armaments and the Coming of War: Europe, 1904–1914* (Oxford: Clarendon Press 1996), 8.

31 Ibid., 9.

32 See the %CINC measures in Table A1.1 of Appendix 1.

33 The quote is from Grey's postwar memoirs published in 1926; see Ferguson, *The Pity of War*, 82.

34 Comment made during the Congress of Berlin in 1878, as quoted in Andrei Navrozov, "European Diary," *Chronicles* 32 (2008).

3 Schlieffen's Gamble

1 A statement attributed to General Alfred von Schlieffen regarding his plan for the disposition of German troops invading Belgium, in Robert Foley, ed., *Alfred Von Schlieffen's Military Writings* (London: Frank Cass, 2003).

2 There is an extensive literature dealing with the emergence of a "treaty system" leading up to the First World War. See, for example, Paul Kennedy, *The Rise and Fall of the Great Powers: Economic Change and Military Conflict from 1500 to 2000* (New York: Vintage Books, 1987), chapter 5; Remak, *The Origins of World War I*; Kagan, *On the Origins of War and the Preservation of Peace*, chapter 2; Christopher Clark, *The Sleepwalkers: How Europe Went to War in 1914* (New York: HarperCollins, 2012), chapters 3–6; Margaret MacMillan, *The War that Ended Peace: The Road to 1914*, Kindle edn (New York: Random House, 2013),

3 Herrmann, *Arming of Europe*, 15–16. Also see Terraine, *White Heat*, chapter 4.

4 Herrmann, *Arming of Europe*, 228.

5 Robert Foley, ed., *Alfred von Schlieffen's Military Writings*.

6 See the comments in ibid.

7 Ibid., 179.

8 Terence Zuber, *Inventing the Schlieffen Plan: German War Planning, 1871–1914* (Oxford University Press, 2002). For a very different view of the impact of Schlieffen's planning, see Gerhard Ritter, *The Schlieffen Plan: Critique of a Myth* (New York: Frederick Praeger, 1958); Annika Mombauer, "Of War Plans and War Guilt: The Debate Surrounding the Schlieffen Plan," *Journal of Strategic Studies* 28, no. 5 (2005).

9 Richard Hamilton and Holger Herwig, *Decisions for War, 1914–1917* (Cambridge University Press, 2004), 82.

10 Mombauer, "War Plans and War Guilt," 879.

11 Stephen Van Evera, "The Cult of the Offensive and the Origins of the First World War," in *Military Strategy and the Origins of the First World War*, ed. Steven E. Miller, Sean Lynn-Jones, and Stephen Van Evera (Princeton University Press, 1991). In addition to the analysis of Van Evera, the discussion of Plan XVII in the text draws on Samuel R. Williamson, "Joffre Reshapes French Strategy,

1911–1913," in *The War Plans of the Great Powers, 1880–1914*, ed. Paul Kennedy (Boston: Allen and Unwin, 1985); Roger Chickering and Stig Forster, eds., *Great War, Total War: Combat and Mobilization on the Western Front, 1914–1918* (Cambridge University Press, 1999).

12 Williamson, "French Strategy," 150.

13 A final endorsement was offered by the President of France, Clement Fallières, who insisted that "the offense alone is suited to the temperament of French soldiers." The quotes are from Van Evera, "Cult of the Offensive, 61–62.

14 Stevenson, *Armaments and the Coming of War*, 306–7.

15 For more on the shortcomings of Joffre's estimates, see the comments by Williamson, "French Strategy," 134.

16 Ferguson, *The Pity of War*, 45.

17 Kennedy, *Rise and Fall of the Great Powers*, 233. Kennedy provides an excellent summary of the changing military and economic positions for each of the great powers between 1885 and 1914.

18 Cited in Ferguson, *The Pity of War*, 80.

19 Annika Mombauer, *The Origins of the First World War: Controversies and Consensus* (London: Pearson, 2002), 17.

20 The full text of the telegram is online at www.firstworldwar.com/source/blankcheque.htm

21 Between July 29 and August 1, the two rulers exchanged ten telegrams: seven were sent by the Kaiser; three by the Tsar. The telegrams are reproduced at www.firstworldwar.com.

22 Tsar to Kaiser, July 29, 1914, 1 a.m., www.firstworldwar.com.

23 Kaiser to Tsar, July 29, 1914, 1:45 a.m., www.firstworldwar.com.

24 Kaiser to Tsar, July 29, 1914, 6:30 p.m., www.firstworldwar.com.

25 Tsar to Kaiser, July 30, 1914, 1:20 a.m., www.firstworldwar.com.

26 Kaiser to Tsar, July 31, 1914, www.firstworldwar.com.

27 Tsar to Kaiser, July 31, 1914, www.firstworldwar.com/source/Willy-Nicky,htm.

28 The message stated that "It is essential for the self-defence of Germany that German troops be allowed to enter Belgium. Should Belgium oppose the German troops, and in particular should it throw difficulties in the way of their march by a resistance of the fortresses on the Meuse, or by destroying railways, roads, tunnels, or other similar works, Germany will, to her regret, be compelled to consider Belgium as an enemy." Cited online at firstworldwar.com/source/belgium_germanrequest.htm.

29 It is interesting to note that the Austrians were preoccupied fighting the Serbs, and did not formally declare war against Russia until August 6, two days after the Germans invaded Belgium.

30 Gilbert, *A History of the Twentieth Century*, 332. There is an enormous literature dealing with the "decision for war" in July and August of 1914. In addition to Gilbert's account, the description in the text draws heavily on Ruth Henig, *The Origins of the First World War* (New York: Routledge, 1993); Barbara Tuchman, *The Guns of August* (New York: Macmillan, 1962); Correlli Barnett, *The Swordbearers: Supreme Command in the First World War* (London: Cassell, 1963); Ferguson, *The Pity of War*.

31 Cited in Barnett, *The Swordbearers*, 83–4.

32 Williamson, "French Strategy," 212. For a description of the battles of the Frontier and the Marne, also see John Keegan, *The First World War* (New York: Alfred A. Knopf, 1998), chapter 4.

33 Clodfelter, *Warfare and Armed Conflicts*, 455.
34 Keegan, *The First World War*, 145–7.
35 Ibid., 146.
36 Norman Stone, *The Eastern Front, 1914–1917* (London: Penguin, 1998), 19.
37 Ibid., 122.
38 For a more detailed account of the "Austrian Emergency" and the German offensive, see ibid., chapter 6. Peter Gatrell provides an assessment of the impact of the loss of territory on the Russians. Peter Gatrell, *Russia's First World War: A Social and Economic History* (Harlow, UK: Pearson Education, 2005), 19–21.
39 The figures for casualties are from Clodfelter, *Warfare and Armed Conflicts*, 439, 459. The totals by country are: France – 995,000; Britain – 97,000; Russia – 1.75 million; Austria-Hungary – 1.3 million; and Germany – 952,000. These casualties equaled 22.3 percent of the estimated 32.7 million casualties reported by Clodfelter and others for the entire period of the war.
40 See Clodfelter, *Warfare and Armed Conflict*, 439–42.
41 Gerd Hardach, *The First World War, 1914–1918* (Berkeley: University of California Press, 1977), 88, 57. For a description of the shell shortage in Russia in 1915, see Stone, *The Eastern Front*, chapter 7.
42 Falkenhayn's memo is reported by Marc Frey, "Bullying the Neutrals: The Case of the Netherlands," in Chickering and Forster, eds., *Great War, Total War*, 118.
43 For an intriguing counterfactual analysis of a German victory in the First World War, see Niall Ferguson, "The Kaiser's European Union," in *Virtual History: Alternatives and Counterfactuals*, ed. Niall Ferguson (London: Macmillan, 1997), 228–80

4 A War of Attrition

1 "In Flanders Fields," was written by a Canadian medical officer, Lieutenant Colonel John McCrae, as a eulogy for one of his comrades killed at the Second Battle of Ypres in May 1915. The poem was published by *Punch* magazine in December 1915 and is one of the best-known British "war poems" of the First World War. Poppies became the symbol of remembrance for veterans in Britain, France, and the United States. The version quoted above is taken from Gilbert, *A History of the Twentieth Century*, 389–90.
2 Martin Gilbert *The First World War: A Complete History* (New York: Henry Holt, 1994), 117. While there is some controversy over the extent of fraternization between soldiers in the German and Entente armies, there are enough reports of instances where exchanges of pleasantries did take place to suggest that it was widespread. For an example of the sort of activities, see the description of the Christmas truce by Bruce Bairnsfather, reproduced in Gilbert, *A History of the Twentieth Century*, 349.
3 Gilbert, *The First World War*, 117.
4 Hew Strachan, ed., *The First World War: A New Illustrated History* (New York: Simon and Schuster, 2003), 148.
5 Japan, Italy, Portugal, and Romania joined the Entente Powers; the Ottoman Turks and Bulgaria joined the Central Powers.
6 Quoted in David Fromkin, *A Peace to End All Peace: The Fall of the Ottoman Empire and the Creation of the Modern Middle East* (New York: Henry Holt, 1989), 75. Fromkin offers a detailed analysis of the complex intrigues that led

to the entry of the Turks into the war; also see Ulrich Trumpener, *Turkey's War* (Oxford University Press, 1998).

7 Winston Churchill later claimed that de Robeck's refusal to renew the naval attack on the Dardanelles the following day was a lost opportunity because the Turks had expended most of their ammunition and would not have been able to resist a second attack. Though it became part of the lore that has surrounded the Gallipoli campaign, Churchill's claim has not been upheld by historians examining the battle, most of whom now agree with de Robeck's assessment that the combination of Turkish batteries and mines would probably have produced another day of disaster for the Entente fleet. See the comments by Eric Brose, *A History of the Great War: World War One and the International Crisis of the Early Twentieth Century* (Oxford University Press, 2010), 164; Edward Erickson, *Gallipoli and the Middle East, 1914–1918: From the Dardanelles to Mesopotamia* (London: Amber Books, 2008), chapter 1.

8 One of the best accounts of the Gallipoli campaign is Alan Morehead, *Gallipoli* (New York: Harper Row, 1956). For a more recent view, see Erickson, *Gallipoli and the Middle East*; Lawrence Sondhaus, *The Great War at Sea: A Naval History of the First World War*, Kindle edn (Cambridge University Press, 2014), chapter 6. The casualty figures cited in the text are from Clodfelter, *Warfare and Armed Conflicts*, 465.

9 Fromkin, *A Peace to End All Peace*, 215.

10 See Fromkin, *A Peace to End All Peace*, 218–21; Erickson, *Gallipoli and the Middle East*, 161–74.

11 The comments were included in the *Arab Bulletin* issued on May 31, 1917. See Fromkin, *A Peace to End All Peace*, 223.

12 For more on the creation of the Arab Bureau, see Fromkin, *A Peace to End All Peace*, 168–87.

13 For a more detailed discussion of the deliberations in Italy over the question of neutrality or war in 1914, see David Jordan, *The Balkans, Italy and Africa, 1914–1918: From Sarajevo to the Piave and Lake Tanganyika* (London: Amber Books, 2008), 101–14.

14 Clodfelter, *Warfare and Armed Conflicts*, 466.

15 The battle casualties are from ibid., 467–8.

16 Cited in Herman deJong, "Between the Devil and the Deep Blue Sea: The Dutch Economy in World War I," in *The Economics of World War I*, ed. Stephen Broadberry and Mark Harrison (Cambridge University Press, 2005), 139.

17 For data on Dutch exports and imports to Germany, see Frey, "Bullying the Neutrals," 233–7; deJong, "The Dutch Economy in World War I," 138–44.

18 See Clodfelter, *Warfare and Armed Conflicts*, 442–3.

19 Ibid., 443.

20 For an excellent summary of the agreements reached at the conference at Chantilly, see Robin Prior and Trevor Wilson, *The Somme*, Kindle edn (New Haven: Yale University Press, 2005), chapter 1.

21 Quoted in Alistair Horne, *The Price of Glory: Verdun 1916* (New York: Penguin, 1993; first published 1962), 36. For an exposition of Falkenhayn's strategic thinking in planning the Verdun offensive, see Holger Afferbach, "Planning Total War? Falkenhayn and the Battle of Verdun," in Chickering and Forster, eds., *Great War, Total War*.

22 The troop rotation was popular among the troops; however, Joffre chaffed at the constant requests for fresh troops that Pétain demanded. Michael Clodfelter reports

that "out of 96 French divisions on the Western Front, 66 passed through the fires of Verdun at one time or another." *Warfare and Armed Conflicts*, 444.

23 The trains carried food and supplies for the horses; the *Sacré Voie* was able to accommodate 1,200 truckloads a day bringing troops, ammunition, and food. See Elizabeth Greenhalgh, *The French Army and the First World War*, Kindle edn (Cambridge University Press, 2014), 146–8; Paul Jankowski, *Verdun: The Longest Battle of the Great War* (Oxford University Press, 2013), 71–3.

24 Getting reliable estimates of enemy losses at the time was a difficult task. The German military intelligence people consistently exaggerated French losses far beyond their actual level. This overstatement of losses contributed to Falkenhayn's confidence that he should persist in his battle of attrition. "Our own losses," he reported to the foreign office in March, "are in the view of the General Staff, only a third of the French." (Afferbach, "Planning for Total War?," 126). In fact, they were about equal to the French losses.

25 Clodfelter, *Warfare and Armed Conflicts*, 445. He goes on to point out that the killing at Verdun did not end with the French capture of Fort Douaumont. Over the entire course of the war casualties were as high as 400,000 men killed and another 800,000 wounded. For a discussion of the casualties at Verdun, see the "Appendix on Sources" in Jankowski, *Verdun*.

26 John Keegan, *The Face of Battle* (New York: The Viking Press, 1976), 226–7. There is a considerable literature on the Battle of the Somme; Keegan's account is still one of the very best sources on the tactics and outcome of the battle. For a more detailed account of the battle, see Prior and Wilson, *The Somme*; Holger Herwig, *The First World War: Germany and Austria-Hungary, 1914–1918* (Oxford University Press, 1997), 195–204.

27 Haig's reaction is quoted in Prior and Wilson, *The Somme*, Loc. 0061-6003.

28 See, for example, the comments in Keegan, *First World War*, 286–9; Peter Hart, *The Somme: The Darkest Hours on the Western Front*, Kindle edn (New York: Pegasus Books, 2012), chapter 14.

29 Prior and Wilson, *The Somme*, Loc. 6072.

30 Clodfelter, *Warfare and Armed Conflicts*, 446.

31 Horne, *The Price of Glory: Verdun 1916*, 324.

32 Attending the meeting were three army commanders: Generals Aleksei Kuropatin (Northern Front), Aleksei Evert (Northwestern Front), and Aleksei Brusilov (South Western Front), together with General Mikhail Alekseyev (Chief of the General Staff), General Dimitri Shuhvaev (Minister for War), Grand Duke Sergei Mikhailovich (Inspector General of the Artillery), and Admiral A. I. Rusin (Chief of Naval Staff). Tsar Nicholas II acted as chair of the meeting, though he was not an active participant in the discussion.

33 Timothy C. Dowling, *The Brusilov Offensive*, Kindle edn (Bloomington: Indiana University Press, 2008), Loc. 222. See also Stone, *The Eastern Front*, 234–41.

34 Gatrell, *Russia's First World War*, 21.

35 Clodfelter, *Warfare and Armed Conflicts*, 458.

36 Stone, *The Eastern Front*, 265.

37 Herwig, *The First World War*, 222.

38 For more information on the Romanian campaign, see ibid., 217–22; Hamilton and Herwig, *Decisions for War*, chapter 9; Stone, *The Eastern Front*, 265–81.

39 Because of its limited level of military preparedness in 1914–16, it was easy to underestimate the military capability of the United States to wage war. The COW

composite indicator of national capability measure shows that the United States in 1913 had a %CINC score of 20.6, which was significantly higher than any other country that would get involved in the conflict.

40 Wilson received 277 electoral votes to 254 for Charles Evans Hughes. He carried 30 states, largely in the southeast and west, while Hughes carried 18 states in the northeast and Midwest.

41 Woodrow Wilson, "Speech to the United States Senate, January 22, 1917," www .firstworldwar.com.

42 Ibid.

43 Ibid. See Tooze, *The Deluge*, 35–6.

44 Gilbert, *The First World War*, 299–300.

5 Economies at War

1 Tuchman, *The Guns of August*, 335.

2 Avner Offer, *The First World War: An Agrarian Interpretation* (Oxford University Press, 1989), 1.

3 Findlay and O'Rourke, *Power and Plenty*, 435.

4 Note that the price indices are plotted in Figure 5.1 using a semi-log scale, which means that the upward slope of the line reflects the annual rate of inflation presented in Table 5.3.

5 Hardach, *The First World War*, 152–3.

6 For a discussion of the effects of bond sales and the problem of inflation in the United States during and after the war, see Richard Sutch, "Financing the Great War: A Class Tax for the Wealthy, Liberty Bonds for All," in Berkeley Economic History Laboratory Working Papers Series (Berkeley: University of California, 2015).

7 The figures are from Brian R. Mitchell, *European Historical Statistics, 1750–1993*, 4th edn (New York: Stockton Press, 1998), Table E-1.

8 The figures are from the Correlates of War "National Materials Capability" data set, version 4.0.

9 Ritschl, "The Pity of Peace: Germany's Economy at War, 1914–1918 and Beyond," in Broadberry and Harrison, *The Economics of World War I*, Table 2.3, 46.

10 Ibid., Table 2.9, 53.

11 Ibid., 45–7.

12 Offer, *The First World War*, 24. Among the most significant reductions in food were the wheat imports from Russia.

13 In addition to the lengthy discussion of diets and food shortages in Offer, *The First World War*, see Broadberry and Harrison, *The Economics of World War I*, 18–22; Hardach, *The First World War*, 108–23.

14 Jay Winter and Antoine Prost, *The Great War in History: Debates and Controversies, 1914 to the Present*, Kindle edn (Cambridge University Press, 2005), 124.

15 Max-Stephan Schulze, "Austria-Hungary's Economy in World War I," in Broadberry and Harrison, *The Economics of World War I*, 107.

16 Pierre-Cyrille Hautcoeur, "Was the Great War a Watershed? The Economics of World War I in France," in Broadberry and Harrison, *The Economics of World War I*, 172.

17 Hardach, *The First World War*, 87–8.

18 The trade figures are from Hautcoeur, "Economics of World War I in France," Table 6.7, 182. On the arrangements that made this financing possible, see 190–1.

19 Hardach, *The First World War*, 131–2.

20 The British value of imports from Germany before the war was considerably more than the value of exports, because Germany was the major supplier of sugar beet to the British economy. The loss of German sugar beet imports had a significant effect on the supply of sugar throughout the war, in a country famous for its "sweet tooth."

21 The data on the external accounts in this paragraph comes from the discussion of the British external accounts in Broadberry and Harrison, *Economics of World War I*, 220–2. Unfortunately for British investors, the largest debtor was Russia (£568 million), which defaulted on the debt after the war; the other large debtors were France and Italy.

22 Hardach, *The First World War*, 124.

23 Between 1900 and 1913 production of wheat, sugar beet, and barley all doubled, and output of oats and potatoes expanded by more than 50 percent. Mitchell, *European Historical Statistics, 1750–1993*, 300–1

24 The economic indices portrayed in Figure 5.6 for the Russian economy are far less reliable that those for the more developed economies of Germany, France, and Britain. We do not have estimates of gross domestic product, and as Peter Gatrell notes, there has been only one serious attempt at estimating aggregate national income in Russia during the war. Figure 5.6 presents Gatrell's index of his best estimate of national income. Gatrell, *Russia's First World War*.

25 Gatrell, "Poor Russia, Poor Show: Mobilizing a Backward Economy," in Broadberry and Harrison, *The Economics of World War I*, 244–5, Table 8.5.

26 Hardach, *The First World War*, 134.

27 Gatrell, "Poor Russia, Poor Show," 250–1, Table 8.11.

28 Hardach, *The First World War*, 134.

29 McNeill, *Pursuit of Power*, 329.

30 Gatrell, "Poor Russia, Poor Show," 239.

31 See, for example, Tooze, *The Deluge*, chapter 9; Hugh Rockoff, "Until It's Over, Over There: The US Economy in World War I," in Broadberry and Harrison, *The Economics of World War I*.

32 Rockoff, "The US Economy in World War I," 331. Hugh Rockoff goes on to point out that the eventual entry into the war in 1917 "unleashed a torrent of federal spending."

33 Tooze, *The Deluge*, 39.

34 McNeill, *Pursuit of Power*, 345. McNeill's discussion of the interaction between state and private sectors in each of the major powers provides an excellent summary of the move toward a command or "corporatist" economy. See 317–45. For surveys of wartime economic organization in each of the belligerent countries, see the essays in Broadberry and Harrison, *Economics of World War I*; Hardach, *The First World War*, chapters 4–7. Additional detail for Russia can be found in Gatrell, *Russia's First World War*, chapter 5.

35 For an excellent summary of these blockades, see Lance E. Davis and Stanley L. Engerman, *Naval Blockades in Peace and War* (Cambridge University Press, 2006), chapters 1–4.

36 Ibid., 209–10.

37 The British lost fourteen ships, including three battle cruisers, three armored cruisers, and eight destroyers. The German High Seas Fleet lost eleven ships,

including one pre-dreadnought battleship, one battle cruiser, four light cruisers, and five destroyers. See Clodfelter, *Warfare and Armed Conflicts*, 274.

38 Keegan, *The Price of Admiralty*, 131.

39 Clodfelter, *Warfare and Armed Conflicts*, 472. See Hardach, *The First World War*, 35–40; Holger Herwig, "Total Rhetoric, Limited War: Germany's U-boat Campaign, 1917–1918," in Chickering and Forster, eds., *Great War, Total War*, 191–9; Davis and Engerman, *Naval Blockades*, 160–75.

40 Quoted in Herwig, "Total Rhetoric, Limited War," 191.

41 Davis and Engerman, *Naval Blockades*, Table 5.12.

42 Document on file at *The World War I Document Archives*; http://wwi.lib.byu.edu.

43 Hardach, *The First World War*, 39–41.

44 For a discussion of how the estimates behind the decision to resume unrestricted U-boat activity were reached, see Davis and Engerman, *Naval Blockades*, 163–76; Herwig, "Total Rhetoric, Limited War," 192–9.

45 Hardach, *The First World War*, 43.

46 See Hardach, *The First World War*, chapter 3; Avner Offer, "The Blockade of Germany and the Strategy of Starvation, 1914–1918: An Agency Perspective," in Chickering and Forster, eds., *Great War, Total War*; Davis and Engerman, *Naval Blockades*, 206–22.

47 David and Engerman, *Naval Blockades*, 230.

48 See Ritschl, "The Pity of Peace," 65.

49 Gerald Feldman, *Army Industry and Labor in Germany, 1914–1918* (Princeton University Press, 1966), 153.

50 Ibid. Feldman's book provides the most extensive study of the Hindenburg Program. See also Herwig, *The First World War*, 259–66.

51 Feldman, *Army Industry and Labor*, 301.

52 McNeill, *Pursuit of Power*, 340.

6 War and Revolution

1 Excerpt from the "Report on Peace" submitted to the Second All-Russia Congress of Soviets of Workers' and Soldiers' Deputies on November 8, 1917. The full text of the report is available at www.firstworldwar.com/source/decreeonpeace.htm.

2 Cited in Herwig, *The First World War*, 251. For a discussion of the strategic options facing each side at the beginning of 1917, see Jack Sheldon, *The German Army in the Spring Offensives 1917: Arras, Aisne and Champagne*, Kindle edn (Barnsley: Pen and Sword Books, 2015).

3 Prince Maximillian was a controversial figure who had served briefly as a staff officer in the German army at the beginning of the war, but resigned his position because of ill health and disagreements stemming from his role in the military. By 1917 "Prince Max" had become an outspoken critic of the policies introduced by Hindenburg and Ludendorff's OHL, particularly their support for resumption of unrestricted submarine warfare early in 1917. The quote is cited by Alistair Horne, *The Price of Glory: Verdun 1916*, 331.

4 Most of the southern end of the Russian frontier was manned by Austrian and Bulgarian troops. However, all units on the Eastern Front were commanded by German officers, and the military plans of activities in the east were directly controlled by Hindenburg, Ludendorff, and the OHL.

5 Cited in Dirk Steffen, "The Holtzendorff Memorandum of 22 December 1916 and Germany's Declaration of Unrestricted U-boat Warfare," *Journal of Military History* 68 (January 2004).

6 Cited in ibid.

7 A translation of Holtzendordff's memo is reproduced along with some comments on the Pless meeting in ibid. For additional descriptions of the meeting at Pless and the decision to resume unrestricted submarine warfare, see Barbara Tuchman, *The Zimmermann Telegram: America Enters the War, 1917–1918* (New York: Random House, 2014; first published 1958), 125–9; Herwig, *The First World War*, 312–25; Sondhaus, *The Great War at Sea*, Loc. 5248–86.

8 Sondhaus, *The Great War at Sea*, Loc. 5271.

9 For more on the shortcomings of Holtzendorff's calculations and quantitative evidence of what actually happened, see the comments in Davis and Engerman, *Naval Blockades*, 173–9.

10 A copy of the full text of the telegram is in Tuchman, *The Zimmermann Telegram*, 133.

11 A major problem for the British and American governments was how they could release the contents of a top-secret message to the rest of the world without revealing that they were able to read and decipher coded German messages. Barbara Tuchman provides a detailed account of the efforts to provide a false lead that would prevent the Germans from concluding that Room 40 – an operation that only a few of the top officials in either the United States or Britain were aware existed – had the ability to decipher German codes. Tuchman turns all this into a spy thriller in the best spirit of John LeCarré's' sleuth, George Smiley. See Tuchman, *The Zimmermann Telegram*, 141–64.

12 The Hearst *World* went even further with a series of lesser headlines covering most of the front page that ended with an assurance that the "public will be amazed if all evidence of the plot is made public." See Tuchman, *The Zimmermann Telegram*, 159–61.

13 Tooze, *The Deluge*, 65–6.

14 The contents of the notes were revealed in Wilson's address to Congress on February 3, 1917; see www.firstworldwar.com/ source/uboat_wilson.htm.

15 For a detailed look at the planning and execution of the Nivelle offensives, see Greenhalgh, *The French Army*, chapter 5; David Murphy, *Breaking Point of the French Army: The Nivelle Offensives of 1917* (Barnsley: Pen and Sword Books, 2015).

16 Elizabeth Greenhalgh notes that "Although Pétain and Poincaré both used it at the time for lack of any better, the term 'mutiny' is too strong for the incidents of collective indiscipline that occurred between May and June 1917, following Nivelle's failed offensive. The various incidents were so disparate in type, extent and duration that it has proved hard to define what constituted the 1917 'mutiny.'" She estimates that the official records reported 170 incidents, while estimates by other historians who have studied the records range as high as 250 incidents. Greenhalgh suggests that "a good half of all French divisions at the time" were reporting some form of discipline problems, noting that "the numbers involved may have been between 25,000 and 30,000" and could have been much more. See Greenhalgh, *The French Army*. Martin Gilbert also provides an account of the mutinies in the context of larger collective opposition to the war: *The First World War*, chapter 17.

17 Michael Clodfelter reports the arrest of 23,385 "ringleaders," of whom 55 were executed: *Warfare and Armed Conflicts*, 447. Elizabeth Greenhalgh puts the number of executions at "around 25." One reason for the lower estimates of executions is that many sentences of death were quietly commuted and the men eventually assigned to colonial posts. Nivelle himself was relegated to a command in North Africa for the remainder of the war. Greenhalgh, *The French Army*, chapter 6.

18 French casualties for the two months of the Nivelle offensive totaled 81,000 or just over 40,000 per month, For the other twelve months of activity from January 1, 1916 to the end of February 1918, monthly losses averaged 10,000 men.

19 Brose, *A History of the Great War*, 259–60.

20 Cited in Robin Prior and Trevor Wilson, *Passchendaele: The Untold Story* (New Haven: Yale University Press, 1996), 39.

21 Cited in ibid., 194.

22 Cited in ibid., 39.

23 There are many accounts of the tug of war within the War Cabinet between the prime minister and the commanding general as well as the battle that followed. Prior and Wilson provide a very complete description that is equally critical of both sides of the decision to proceed with the Ypres attack. See *Passchendaele: The Untold Story*.

24 The statistics are from Clodfelter, *Warfare and Armed Conflicts*, 447.

25 Ibid., 448.

26 For more on the problems of food distribution in Russia, see Gatrell, *Russia's First World War*, 154; James D. White, *The Russian Revolution: A Short History* (New York: Edward Arnold, 1994), 101–4.

27 Gilbert, *A History of the Twentieth Century*, 440. The discussion of the Russian Revolution in the text draws heavily on the chronology of events presented in Gilbert's *History of the Twentieth* and *The First World War*; Sheila Fitzpatrick, *The Russian Revolution*, 3rd edn (Oxford University Press, 2008), chapter 2; White, *The Russian Revolution*, chapter 4; Gatrell, *Russia's First World War*, chapter 9. Establishing a timeline for events is complicated by the fact that in 1917 Russia was still on the Julian calendar, which was thirteen days behind the Gregorian calendar that had been adopted by most countries by that time. Consequently, what the Bolsheviks refer to as the "February Revolution" took place in March, and what they call the "October Revolution" was in November according to the Gregorian calendar. The Bolsheviks adopted the Gregorian calendar in 1918. Unless otherwise noted, the text follows the example of Gilbert, Fitzpatrick, and Gatrell (along with many others) in using the Gregorian dates for the events described.

28 Gilbert reports that 655 soldiers, 587 demonstrators, and 73 policemen were killed between March 11 and 13. Gilbert, *A History of the Twentieth Century*, 442.

29 Gilbert, *A History of the Twentieth Century*, 440.

30 Cited in Fitzpatrick, *The Russian Revolution*, 46.

31 Steve Smith claims that "some 700 soviets sprang up in March and April, embracing around 200,000 deputies by summer. By October there were 1,429 soviets, of which 455 were soviets of peasants' deputies. Peasant soviets, however, did not really get off the ground until the end of 1917." Steve Smith, *The Russian Revolution: A Very Short Introduction*, Kindle edn (Oxford University Press, 2002). An excellent outline of the establishment of the Petrograd Soviet is in White, *The Russian Revolution*, 71–3.

32 Cited in Fitzpatrick, *The Russian Revolution*, 47.

33 Gilbert, *A History of the Twentieth Century*, 424.

34 See the discussion in White, *The Russian Revolution*, 94–7.

35 Petrograd Soviet, "Call to the Peoples of the World," March 27, 1917. It is reproduced on the Digital History Reader Website: www.dhr.history.vt.edu.

36 Gilbert, *A History of the Twentieth Century*, 448. More than a few Russians thought that Lenin was actually working for the Germans as a spy. His vehement opposition to the war after travelling through Germany made him particularly vulnerable to this charge, and the accusations persisted throughout the October Revolution. See the discussion in Alexander Rabinowitch, *The Bolsheviks Come to Power* (Bloomington: University of Indiana Press, 1976), 14–19.

37 Fitzpatrick, *The Russian Revolution*, 51.

38 Cited in Keegan, *First World War*, 338.

39 See Clodfelter, *Warfare and Armed Conflicts*, 458–9.

40 On the July Days demonstrations and the Bolshevik involvement, see Rabinowitch, *The Bolsheviks Come to Power*, chapters 1–2; Fitzpatrick, *The Russian Revolution*, 57–61; White, *The Russian Revolution*, 107–12.

41 Fitzpatrick, *The Russian Revolution*, 59.

42 There are many accounts of the capture of Riga and the abortive coup by Lvar Kornilov. The sequence of events described in the text draws upon Peter Hart, *The Great War: A Combat History of World War I*, Kindle edn (Oxford University Press, 2013), 295–308; White, *The Russian Revolution*, chapter 7; Rabinowitch, *The Bolsheviks Come to Power*, chapters 6–8.

43 The data presented in this section draws on Gatrell, *Russia's First World War*, 206–14, and "Poor Russia, Poor Show," 269–71.

44 Cited in Fitzpatrick, *The Russian Revolution*, 62. Also see Rabinowitch, *The Bolsheviks Come to Power*.

45 The letter is reproduced in V. I. Lenin, *Collected Works*, vol. XXVI (Moscow: Progress, 1972), 234–5.

46 For more on Kerensky's effort to rescue his government, see Rabinowitch, *The Bolsheviks Come to Power*, 139–43.

47 For an assessment of the treaty from the perspective of the Germans in early 1918, see Herwig, *The First World War*, 382–7; Bond, *Pursuit of Victory*, 117–18. On the details of the negotiations, see White, *The Russian Revolution*, 177–82.

48 The estimates are cited in Herwig, *The First World War*, 384.

49 Quoted in Jordan, *The Balkans, Italy and Africa*, 182.

50 For more on the Battle of Caporetto, see Herwig, *The First World War*, 336–45; Alan Palmer, *Victory 1918* (New York: Atlantic Monthly Press, 1998), chapter 9; Jordan, *The Balkans, Italy and Africa*, chapter 6.

51 Cited in Palmer, *Victory 1918*, 76.

52 Clodfelter, *Warfare and Armed Conflicts*, 468–9.

53 For more on the Greek decision to go to war and its aftermath, see Jordan, *The Balkans*, chapter 2

7 The Last Gamble

1 Frederick E. Smith, *Turning Points in History* (London: Hutchinson, 1930). Lord Birkenhead's comment refers to the performance of General Sir Hubert Gough in the spring of 1918.

2   Though it agreed to join the Entente Powers in their fight against Germany, the United States never declared war against either Austria-Hungary or the Ottoman Empire.

3   Wilson, "Speech to the United States Senate, January 8, 1918."

4   For more on the role of innovation and change in the British artillery over the course of the war, see the comments in the *Long, Long Trail* website: www.longlongtrail.co.uk/how-the-british-artillery-developed-and-became-a-war-winning-factor-in-1914-1918/.

5   Swinton's description of his proposed vehicle is from A. J. Smithers, *Cambrai: The First Great Tank Battle, 1917*, Kindle edn (London: Leo Cooper, 1992), Loc. 897.

6   Because the project was secret they needed a code name for the strange-looking machines they were producing. The idea of calling the vehicle a "tank" emerged because the initial prototypes looked like giant tanks of water on tractor treads. For more on the "stories" behind the development of British tanks, see Smithers, *Cambrai: The First Great Tank Battle*, chapter 3; Terraine, *White Heat*, 238–46.

7   The explosives were placed in nineteen tunnels, the longest of which was 2,000 feet, and some of which were as deep as 100 feet under the center of the German trenches. All but two of the mines exploded, creating a crater that was 430 feet in diameter. The explosion could be heard in Lille, fifteen miles away, and was felt as a mild earthquake throughout southern England. See the comments in Gilbert, *The First World War*, 336–7.

8   There is some discrepancy among historians on the number of tanks used in the attack. Clodfelter sets the number at three tank brigades totaling 475 tanks in his account of the battle (*Warfare and Armed Conflicts*, 448). John Keegan places the number at "over 300" (*First World War*, 369) and Martin Gilbert claims 324 tanks "took part in the attack" (*The First World War*). All the estimates suggest that this was by far the largest mass of tanks to take part in an assault up to this point in the war.

9   Jack Sheldon, *The German Army at Cambrai*, Kindle edn (Barnsley: Pen and Sword Books, 2009), Loc. 1388–93.

10 Ibid., Loc. 1257–9.

11 Terraine, *White Heat*, 238.

12 On April 24, 1918 a Mark V destroyed an A7V in the first battlefield action between enemy tanks. See David Bocquelet, "Sturmpanzerwagen A7V," www.tanks-encyclopedia.com/ww1/germany/sturmpanzerwagen_A7V.

13 Sheldon, *German Army at Cambrai*, chapter 3.

14 Herwig, *The First World War*, 435.

15 Cited in Terraine, *White Heat*, 31.

16 Ibid., 103.

17 Clodfelter, *Warfare and Armed Conflicts*, 428.

18 The British rules stated that each reconnaissance plane in a mission had to be accompanied by three fighters, and the mission was to be aborted if any planes were shot down. See Terraine, *White Heat*, 198–9.

19 For more on the problem of propellers and machine guns on airplanes, see https://en.wikipedia.org/wiki/Synchronization_gear.

20 Cited in Terraine, *White Heat*, 200. Terraine points out that one of the disadvantages of the British policy that insisted on taking the fight to the enemy is that the dogfights tended to be over the German lines. This meant that when a British plane was shot down, the pilot was lost for further action even if he survived the crash.

21 Cited in Gilbert, *The First World War*, 486.

22 Gilbert, *The First World War*, 335.

23 Clodfelter, *Warfare and Armed Conflicts*, 478. The Germans also used Zeppelins as weapons of aerial attack.

24 For more on the air war in 1917–18, see Terraine, *White Heat*, 264–75.

25 Cited in ibid., 275.

26 Michael Clodfelter lists the German guns in the initial attack as 3,965 field guns of 7.7–100 mm, together with 2,435 heavy guns of 150 mm and 75 superheavy guns of 210 mm or more. An additional 3,532 mortars supported the advancing troops. In five hours, more than a million shells fell on the British trenches. The attack was also supported by 750 aircraft. Over the course of the next two weeks the Germans fired more than 2 million gas shells. *Warfare and Armed Conflicts*, 451.

27 There were nine huge cannons that had a range of seventy-five miles and hurled a shell weighing about 275 pounds. During the course of the spring offensives the Germans fired 367 shells that hit Paris, killing or injuring more than eight hundred people. Clodfelter, *Warfare and Armed Conflicts*, 450.

28 Gilbert, *The First World War*, 408.

29 Ibid.

30 Cited in Lyn Macdonald, *To the Last Man: Spring 1918* (New York: Penguin, 1999), 340. Macdonald provides a detailed account of the British withdrawal based on interviews with and the dairies of participants.

31 Palmer, *Victory 1918*, 170–1.

32 British losses were 177,339 including 25,000 killed or wounded and included 72,000 prisoners. They also lost 1,100 guns, 200 tanks, and 400 aircraft. German casualties totaled 350,000 men with 68,000 deaths. This made March and April of 1918 the deadliest two months of casualties for Germany on the Western Front during the entire war. Clodfelter, *Warfare and Armed Conflicts*, 450.

33 The initial attack of Operation Blucher-Yorck consisted of seventeen German divisions with thirteen divisions held in reserve and 3,700 artillery guns firing a barrage of 2 million shells in less than three hours. Across from the German lines was a force of nine French and three British divisions.

34 Herwig, *The First World War*, 419.

35 The Aisne–Marne offensive is also known as the Battle of Soissons. The breakdown of units by country was twenty-three French, eight American, four British, and two Italian divisions. Clodfelter, *Warfare and Armed Conflicts*, 52–4.

36 Quoted in Nick Lloyd, *Hundred Days: The Campaign that Ended World War I* (New York: Basic Books, 2014), 131. Lloyd provides an interesting account of the Saint-Mihiel battle, arguing that the outcome justified Pershing's demands for an independent command for the Americans. Also see John Mosier, *Myth of the Great War: A New Military History of World War I* (New York: HarperCollins, 2001), 306–26; Gilbert, *The First World War*, 457–60; Palmer, *Victory 1918*, 207–11.

37 The figures for troops shown in Map 7.3 are estimates of the total number of troops available for action on the Western Front in the respective areas as reported in Michael Neiberg, *The Military Atlas of World War I* (New York: Chartwell Books, 2014), 95. For a summary of the armies actually involved in the various battles, see Terraine, *White Heat*, 300–18; Clodfelter, *Warfare and Armed Conflicts*, 452–5.

38 Metz was a major rail terminus supplying the German front in France and Belgium. On the continuing problems between Foch and Pershing involving the deployment of an independent American army, see Lloyd, *Hundred Days*, 133–40.

39 Clodfelter, *Warfare and Armed Conflicts*, 453. By the end of the battle 1.3 million doughboys had seen action. Numerous writers have attributed the high rate of American casualties to Perishing's advocacy of open assaults, not unlike those used by the European armies earlier in the war.

40 Terraine, *White Heat*, 302.

41 A description of this meeting is in D. J. Goodspeed, *Ludendorff: Soldier, Dictator, Revolutionary* (London: Rupert Hart-Davis, 1966), 211.

42 Erzberger's comments are cited by Strachan, *The First World War*, 265. The Reichstag resolution is available online at http://firstworldwar.com/source/reichstagpeaceresolution.htm.

43 Ibid., 265.

44 Cited in Gilbert, *The First World War*, 486.

45 Cited in Goodspeed, *Ludenorff*, 215. The details of the negotiations between the Allied and German governments to reach an armistice have been covered at some length in many accounts of the ending of the war. Among the most useful for our narrative are the blow-by-blow accounts of Herwig, *The First World War*, chapter 9; Gilbert, *The First World War*, chapter 26; Tooze, *The Deluge*, chapter 11; David Stevenson, *With Our Backs to the Wall: Victory and Defeat in 1918* (Cambridge, MA: Harvard University Press, 2013), chapter 8; together with more general summaries by Lloyd, *Hundred Days*, chapters 15–16; Keegan, *First World War*, 414–27; Palmer, *Victory 1918*, chapter 18.

46 Goodspeed, *Ludenorff*, 217. Goodspeed's description is based on Ludendorff's verbatim account of the interview with the Kaiser, which "although almost certainly true in the main, is unreliable in detail."

47 At this point in the war, Townshend was highly regarded by the British for his brave resistance to the Turkish forces that eventually captured Kut. The Turks offered him his freedom if he would assist them in opening negotiations with the British. He later came under strong criticism in Britain for accepting comfortable treatment while his troops were badly mistreated during their imprisonment.

48 Herwig, *The First World War*, 439.

49 Ibid. In addition to Herwig's account of the Austrian surrender, see Palmer, *Victory 1918*, 267–73.

50 Gilbert, *The First World War*, 499.

51 Cited in Gilbert, *The First World War*, 504.

52 Bind, *Pursuit of Victory*, 105.

53 The combined %CINC score for France and Britain was 23.1. The military personnel of the two sides was roughly equal, though most observers agree that the element of preparation and surprise gave the Germans an initial advantage in taking the offensive.

54 Strachan, *The First World War*, 290–1.

8 The Chaos of Victory

1 Keynes, *The Economic Consequences of the Peace*.

2 Woodrow Wilson, State of the Union Speech, December 2, 1918.

3 Cited in Klaus Richter, "Baltic States and Finland," in *1914–18 Online Encyclopedia of the First World War*, ed. Ute Daniel et al. (Berlin: Freie Universität Berlin, 2017), 1.

4 Erik Goldstein, *The First World War Peace Settlements, 1919–1925* (New York: Longmans, 2002), 9. Goldstein notes that the American delegation alone brought 1,300 people to Paris. Margaret MacMillan puts the size of the British delegation at "well over 400 officials, special advisors, clerks and typists, it occupied five hotels near the Arc de Triomphe." Margaret MacMillan, *Paris 1919: Six Months that Changed the World* (New York: Random House, 2001), 46. By contrast, the British delegation to the 1815 Vienna Conference was fourteen people, headed by Lord Castlereagh.

5 The foreign ministers were Robert Lansing (United States), Arthur Balfour (Great Britain), Stephon Pichon (France), and Sidney Sonnino (Italy).

6 The exchange is reported by Margaret MacMillan, who added that "The Japanese delegates, who had trouble following the debates whether they were in French or English remained silent" (MacMillan, *Paris 1919*, 56). John Maynard Keynes observed that since Orlando "knew only French and the Prime Minister and President only English . . . it is of historical importance that Orlando and the President had no direct means of communication." (*The Economic Consequences of the Peace*, 31).

7 The Japanese were not entirely happy at being pushed off the Council of Ten. However, the language issue and the fact that the only major issue they had strong feelings about was the disposition of German colonial territories in the Pacific persuaded Baron Makino Nobaki that he did need to sit in on the deliberations dealing with European and Middle Eastern issues. The Japanese representative and the other foreign ministers formed a group that dealt with issues passed on to them by the Council of Four.

8 There are many accounts of the challenges in organizing the Conference. Among the most useful sources for the discussion above are MacMillan, *Paris 1919*, chapters 1 and 2; Ruth Henig, *Versailles and After, 1919–1933*, 2nd edn (New York: Routledge, 1995); Alan Sharp, "The Big Four: Peacemaking in Paris in 1919," *History Review*, 68 (2009); Goldstein, *First World War Peace Settlements*, chapter 1.

9 *The Economic Consequences of the Peace* eventually sold more than 100,000 copies and was translated into eleven languages – including German.

10 The quotes are from Keynes, *The Economic Consequences of the Peace*, 226–8.

11 Quoted in Erik Goldstein, "Great Britain: The Home Front," in *The Treaty of Versailles: A Reassessment after 75 Years*, ed. Manfred Boemeke, Gerald Feldman, and Elisabeth Glaser (Cambridge University Press, 1998), 164.

12 Keynes, *The Economic Consequences of the Peace*, 226.

13 Ibid., 31.

14 Cited in Richter, "Baltic States and Finland," 4.

15 For more on the Fiume incident, see Sharp, "The Big Four," 6; MacMillan, *Paris 1919*, chapter 22.

16 Richter, "Baltic States and Finland," 6.

17 Ritschl, "The Pity of Peace," 73.

18 For a summary of the impact of the war on colonialism, see James Kitchen, "Colonial Empires after the War/Decolonization," in Daniel et al., eds., *1914–18 Online Encyclopedia of the First World War*.

19 Ibid. The complete text of the proclamation is available on www.firstworldwar .com.

20 On the emergence of Czechoslovakia and Yugoslavia, see Katrin Boeckh, "Crumbling of Empires and Emerging States: Czechoslovakia and Yugoslavia as

(Multi)National Countries," in Daniel et al., eds.,*1914–18 Online Encyclopedia of the First World War*; Ignac Romsics, *The Dismantling of Historic Hungary: The Peace Treaty of Trianon, 1920*, trans. Mario Fenyo (Wayne, NJ: Center for Hungarian Studies and Publications, 2002). Margaret MacMillan provides a look behind the scenes for each country in *Paris 1919*.

21 See Boeckh, "Crumbling Empires," 8.

22 The demographic statistics for Poland in the period 1918 through 1921 are incomplete at best because of the problems created by border changes and the confusion created by the war. The COW population estimates give a figure of 21.8 million Poles for 1918, growing to a total of 27.9 million after the end of the Polish–Soviet War in 1922, an increase of 30 percent in four years. Estimates of the minority population are also subject to possible error. According to the first census, taken in 1921, national minorities in Poland accounted for 30.8 percent. However, this is surely a lower bound estimate because it left out major areas of Poland. Josef Marcus cites estimates that could push the figure near 40 percent. *Social and Political History of the Jews in Poland, 1919–1939* (Berlin and Boston: De Gruyter Mouton, 2011; first published 1983).

23 The Polish "border wars" included conflicts with Ukraine over eastern Galicia (November 1, 1918–July 2, 1919), a series of uprisings in Germany (December 1918 to October 1920), and a war with Bolshevik Russia that according to the COW estimates cost 40,000 Polish and 60,000 Russian battle deaths.

24 See the discussion of Ludendorff's plans for eastern expansion in Chapter 7; see also Richter, "Baltic States and Finland," 10–17.

25 Klaus Richter notes that each of the four Baltic states took a very different path to what he calls "Constitutionalized Statehood." The peace treaties negotiated with Russia that fixed their boundaries and gave then *de jure* recognition were the Treaty of Tartu with Estonia (February 2, 1920); the Treaty of Moscow with Lithuania (July 12, 1920); the Treaty of Riga with Latvia (August 11, 1920); and the Treaty of Tartu with Finland (October 14, 1920). See Richter, "Baltic States and Finland," 17.

26 Liubov Zhvanko, "Ukraine," in Daniel et al., *1914–18*; for more on the Ukrainian situation, see Peter Gatrell, "War, Population Displacement and State Formation in the Russian Borderlands, 1914–1924," in Homelands: War, Population and Statehood in Eastern Europe and Russia, 1918–1924, ed. Nick Baron and Peter Gatrell (London: Anthem Press, 2004).

27 See the discussion in Fromkin, *A Peace to End All Peace*, 465–92.

28 After the war Clemenceau grumbled that if Britain had sent these troops to the Western Front the Allies could have won the war sooner. His comment is a measure of the extent to which the French regarded anything other than the Western Front as a "sideshow." See MacMillan, *Paris 1919*, 374–5.

29 Cited in ibid., 421–4.

30 For a more detailed summary of the decision by the Young Turks to escalate the extermination of Armenians, see Vahakn N. Dadrian, *The History of the Armenian Genocide: Ethnic Conflict from the Balkans to Anatolia to the Caucasus* (Oxford: Berghahn Books, 1995), 202.

31 This telegram, along with another elaborating the situation, is reproduced in Wikipedia. See https://en.wikipedia.org/wiki/Armenian_Genocide. For additional reactions by American and German observers to the reports of genocide in Armenia, see Fromkin, *A Peace to End All Peace*, 13.

32 See Michael Reynolds, *Shattering Empires: The Clash and Collapse of the Ottoman and Russian Empires, 1908–1918*, Kindle edn (Cambridge University Press, 2011), 154.

33 For a more detailed analysis of Wilson's view of the Armenian massacre and his recommendation to have the United States accept a mandate for a larger Armenia, see John M. Cooper, "A Friend in Power? Woodrow Wilson and Armenia," and Lloyd E. Ambrosius, "Wilsonian Diplomacy and Armenia: The Limits of Power and Ideology," both in *America and the Armenian Genocide of 1915*, ed. Jay Winter (Cambridge University Press, 2003).

34 For more on the emergence of the Armenian SSR, see Christopher J. Walker, *Armenia: The Survival of a Nation* (London: Palgrave Macmillan, 1990).

35 Cooper, "A Friend in Power?," 112.

36 Clodfelter, *Warfare and Armed Conflicts*, 388.

37 Barry J. Eichengreen, *Golden Fetters: The Gold Standard and the Great Depression, 1919–1939* (Oxford University Press, 1992), 3.

38 Ibid., 7. Eichengreen provides a much more complete analysis of the operation of the gold standard in the specie flow mechanism of gold and the money supply that produced a stabilizing equilibrium in the world economy of the late nineteenth and early twentieth century. See the introduction and chapters 3–4 for a discussion of the impact of the war.

39 Ibid., 12. For more on the collapse of confidence, see Findlay and O'Rourke, *Power and Plenty*, chapter 8; Feinstein et al., *World Economy*, chapter 2; Nikolaus Wolf, "Europe's Great Depression: Coordination Failure after the First World War," in *The Great Depression of the 1930s*, ed. Nicholas Crafts and Peter Fearon (Oxford University Press, 2013). Charles P. Kindleberger, *The World in Depression, 1929–1939*, revised and enlarged edn (New York: Penguin Books, 1986), chapters 1–3, discusses the role of central banks as "lenders of last resort." All these books look at the disruption of the Great War and the difficulties of 1919–21 as major disruptions that contributed to the global financial crisis of 1929 and the Great Depression.

40 Articles 231 through 247 dealing with reparations in the Treaty of Versailles are available at: www.firstworldwar.com/source/versailles/231-247.htm.

41 Annex 1 defined nine categories of damages during the war to persons and property as a result of German actions during the war. At the insistence of Lloyd George, the definition of damages to persons included the costs of pensions and payments to families of soldiers who were wounded or killed during the war. See www.firstworldwar.com/source/versailles/231–247.htm.

42 On the debates over the size of the reparations within the Council of Four, see the comments in Sally Marks, "Smoke and Mirrors: In Smoke-Filled Rooms and the Galerie des Glaces," in Boemeke et al., eds., *The Treaty of Versailles: A Reassessment after 75 Years*, 343–5.

43 Ferguson, *The Pity of War*, 414.

44 For a detailed summary of the literature dealing with the reparation payments, see the entry at Wikipedia: https://en.wikipedia.org/wiki/World_War_I_reparations.

45 Keynes, *The Economic Consequences of the Peace*, 147.

46 Ferguson, *The Pity of War*, 414; Ritschl, "Reparations, Deficits and Debt Default: The Great Depression in Germany," in *The Great Depression of the 1930s*, ed. Nicholas Crafts and Peter Fearon (Oxford University Press, 2013), 114.

47 Sally Marks, "Mistakes and Myths: The Allies, Germany, and the Versailles Treaty, 1918–1921," *Journal of Modern History* 85, no. 3 (2013): 655.

48 Ibid., 654–5.
49 Boemeke et al., eds., *The Treaty of Versailles: A Reassessment after 75 Years*, 3.
50 Ferguson, *Pity of War*, 395.
51 MacMillan, *Paris 1919*, 493–4.

Epilogue: The Tragedy of a World War

1 Clark, *The Sleepwalkers*, 561.
2 Findlay and O'Rourke, *Power and Plenty*, xxv. Note the negative connotation in this statement which would translate as an "Act of the Devil."
3 Henig, *The Origins of the First World War*, 54.
4 In his memoirs published in 1925 Grey did not recall making the famous remark. An account of the comment was published in 1927 by John Spender, a journalist who recalled that "We were standing together at the window looking out into the sunset across St. James Park and the appearance of the first lights along the Mall suggested the thought." John A. Spender, *Life, Journalism and Politics* (New York: Frederick A. Stokes Comany, 1927), 14–45.

BIBLIOGRAPHY

Afferbach, Holger. "Planning Total War? Falkenhayn and the Battle of Verdun." In *Great War, Total War: Combat and Mobilization on the Western Front, 1914–1918*, edited by Roger Chickering and Stig Forster, 113–52. Cambridge University Press, 2000.

Akcam, Taner. *A Shameful Act: The Armenian Genocide and the Question of Turkish Responsibility*. New York: Metropolitan Publishers, 2007.

Akerlof, George A., and Robert J. Shiller. *Animal Spirits: How Human Psychology Drives the Economy, and Why It Matters for Global Capitalism*. Princeton University Press, 2009.

Ambrosius, Lloyd E. "Wilsonian Diplomacy and Armenia: The Limits of Power and Ideology." In *America and the Armenian Genocide of 1915*, edited by Jay Winter, 113–46. Cambridge University Press, 2003.

Badsey, Stephen. *The Franco-Prussian War, 1870–71*. New York: Osprey Publishing, 2003.

Balakian, Peter. *The Burning Tigris: The Armenian Genocide and America's Response*. New York: HarperCollins, 2005.

Barnett, Correlli. *The Swordbearers: Supreme Command in the First World War*. London: Cassell, 1963.

Blum, Matthias, Jari Eloranta, and Pavel Osinsky. "Organization of War Economies." In *1914–18 Online Encyclopedia of the First World War*, edited by Ute Daniel, Peter Gatrell, Oliver Janz, Heather Jones, Jennifer Keene, Alan Kramer, and Bill Nasson. Berlin: Freie Universität Berlin, 2017, www.1914-1918-online.net/.

Bocquelet, David. "Sturmpanzerwagen A7v." www.tanks-encyclopedia.com/ ww1/ germany/sturmpanzerwagen_A7V.

Boeckh, Katrin. "Crumbling of Empires and Emerging States: Czechoslovakia and Yugoslavia as (Multi)national Countries." In *1914–18 Online Encyclopedia of the First World War*, edited by Ute Daniel, Peter Gatrell, Oliver Janz, Heather Jones, Jennifer Keene, Alan Kramer, and Bill Nasson. Berlin: Freie Universität Berlin, 2017, www.1914-1918-online.net/.

Boemeke, Manfred, Gerald Feldman, and Elisabeth Glaser, eds. *The Treaty of Versailles: A Reassessment after 75 Years*. Cambridge University Press, 1998.

Bond, Brian. *The Pursuit of Victory: From Napoleon to Saddam Hussein*. Oxford University Press, 1996.

Bonker, Dirk. "Naval Race between Germany and Great Britian, 1898–1921." In *1914–18 Online Encyclopedia of the First World War*, edited by Ute Daniel, Peter Gatrell, Oliver Janz, Heather Jones, Jennifer Keene, Alan Kramer, and Bill Nasson. Berlin: Freie Universität Berlin, 2017, www.1914-1918-online.net/.

Bonner, Michael. *Confederate Political Economy: Creating and Managing a Southern Capitalist Nation*. Baton Rouge: Louisiana State University Press, 2016.

Breit, William, and Roger L. Ransom. *The Academic Scribblers*. Third edn. Princeton University Press, 1998.

Broadberry, Stephen, and Mark Harrison, eds. *The Economics of World War I*. Cambridge University Press, 2005.

Broadberry, Stephen, and Peter Howlett. "The United Kingdom During World War I: Business as Usual?" In *The Economics of World War I*, edited by Stephen Broadberry and Mark Harrison, 206–34. Cambridge University Press, 2005.

Brose, Eric. "Arms Race Prior to 1914, Armaments Policy." In *1914–18 Online Encyclopedia of the First World War*, edited by Ute Daniel, Peter Gatrell, Oliver Janz, Heather Jones, Jennifer Keene, Alan Kramer, and Bill Nasson. Berlin: Freie Universität Berlin, 2017, www.1914-1918-online.net/.

A History of the Great War: World War One and the International Crisis of the Early Twentieth Century. Oxford University Press, 2010.

Brudek, Pawel. "Revolutions (East Central Europe)." In *1914–18 Online Encyclopedia of the First World War*, edited by Ute Daniel, Peter Gatrell, Oliver Janz, Heather Jones, Jennifer Keene, Alan Kramer, and Bill Nasson. Berlin: Freie Universität Berlin, 2017, www.1914-1918-online.net/.

Catton, Charles, ed. *The History of World War I*. London: Amber Books, 2008.

Chickering, Roger, and Stig Forster, eds. *Great War, Total War: Combat and Mobilization on the Western Front, 1914–1918*. Cambridge University Press, 1999.

Clark, Christopher. *The Sleepwalkers: How Europe Went to War in 1914*. New York: HarperCollins, 2012.

Clausewitz, Carl von. *On War*. Translated by Michael Howard and Peter Paret. Indexed edn. Princeton University Press, 1984.

Clodfelter, Michael. *Warfare and Armed Conflicts: A Statistical Reference to Casualty and Other Figures, 1500–2000.* Second edn. Jefferson, NC: McFarland, 2002.

Cooper, John M. "A Friend in Power? Woodrow Wilson and Armenia." In *America and the Armenian Genocide of 1915*, edited by Jay Winter, 103–13. Cambridge University Press, 2003.

Correlates of War Project. "Correlates of War Bibliography." www.correlatesof war.org/.

  National Material Capabilities Data Documentation. Version 4.0 edn. 2010.

  "Project History." http://correlatesofwar.org/COWhistory.htm.

Crafts, Nicholas, and Peter Fearon, eds. *The Great Depression of the 1930s: Lessons for Today.* Oxford University Press, 2013.

Craig, G. *The Politics of the Prussian Army.* Oxford University Press, 1955.

Dadrian, Vahakn N. *The History of the Armenian Genocide: Ethnic Conflict from the Balkans to Anatolia to the Caucasus.* Oxford: Berghahn Books, 1995.

Davis, Lance E., and Stanley L. Engerman. *Naval Blockades in Peace and War.* Cambridge University Press, 2006.

deJong, Herman. "Between the Devil and the Deep Blue Sea: The Dutch Economy in World War I." In *The Economics of World War I*, edited by Stephen Broadberry and Mark Harrison, 137–69. Cambridge University Press, 2005.

Dockrill, Michael, and John Fisher, eds. *The Paris Peace Conference: Peace without Victory?* London: Palgrave, 2001.

Dowling, Timothy C. *The Brusilov Offensive.* Kindle edn. Bloomington: Indiana University Press, 2008.

Eichengreen, Barry. *Golden Fetters: The Gold Standard and the Great Depression, 1919–1939.* Oxford University Press, 1992.

  Hall of Mirrors: The Great Depression, the Great Recession and the Uses – and Misuses – of History. Oxford University Press, 2015.

Eigen, Lewis D., and Jonathan Paul Siegel. *The Macmillan Dictionary of Political Quotations.* Toronto: Macmillan, 1993.

Erickson, Edward. *Gallipoli and the Middle East, 1914–1918: From the Dardanelles to Mesopotamia.* London: Amber Books, 2008.

Ermacora, Matteo. "Civilian Morale." In *1914–18 Online Encyclopedia of the First World War*, edited by Ute Daniel, Peter Gatrell, Oliver Janz, Heather Jones, Jennifer Keene, Alan Kramer, and Bill Nasson. Berlin: Freie Universität Berlin, 2017, www.1914-1918-online.net/.

Eyck, Erich. *Bismarck and the German Empire.* New York: W. W. Norton, 1968; first published 1950.

Faust, Drew Gilpin. "Alters of Sacrifice: Confederate Women and the Narratives of War." *Journal of American History* 76 (March 1990).

Feinstein, Charles, Peter Temin, and Gianni Toniolo. *The World Economy between the World Wars*. Oxford University Press, 2008.

Feldman, Gerald. *Army Industry and Labor in Germany, 1914–1918*. Princeton University Press, 1966.

The Great Disorder: Politics, Economics, and Society in the German Inflation, 1914–1924. Oxford University Press, 1997.

Ferguson, Niall. *The Pity of War: Explaining World War I*. New York: Basic Books, 1999.

The War of the World: Twentieth Century Conflict and the Descent of the West. New York: Penguin, 2006.

Ferguson, Niall, ed. *Virtual History: Alternatives and Counterfactuals*. London: Macmillan, 1997,

Findlay, Ronald, and Kevin H. O'Rourke. *Power and Plenty: Trade, War, and the World Economy in the Second Millennium*. Princeton University Press, 2007.

Fink, Carole. "The Minority Question at the Paris Peace Conference: The Polish Minority Treaty, June 18, 1919." In *The Treaty of Versailles: A Reassessment after 75 Years*, edited by Manfred Boemeke, Gerald Feldman, and Elisabeth Glaser, 249–74. New York: St. Martins Press, 1998.

Fitzpatrick, Sheila. *The Russian Revolution*. 3rd edn. Oxford University Press, 2008.

Foley, Robert, ed. *Alfred von Schlieffen's Military Writings*. London: Frank Cass, 2003.

French, David. "'Had We Known How Bad Things Were in Germany, We Might Have Got Stiffer Terms': Great Britain and the German Armistice." In *The Treaty of Versailles: A Reassessment after 75 Years*, edited by Manfred Boemeke, Gerald Feldman, and Elisabeth Glaser, 69–86. Cambridge University Press, 1998.

Frey, Marc. "Bullying the Neutrals: The Case of the Netherlands." In *Great War, Total War: Combat and Mobilization on the Western Front, 1914–1918*, edited by Roger Chickering and Stig Forster, 247–64. Cambridge University Press, 2000.

Friedman, Milton, and Anna J. Schwartz. *Monetary Trends in the United States and the United Kingdom: Their Relation to Income, Prices, and Interest Rates, 1867–1975*. University of Chicago Press, 1982.

Fromkin, David. *A Peace to End All Peace: The Fall of the Ottoman Empire and the Creation of the Modern Middle East*. New York: Henry Holt, 1989.

Fulwider, Chad. "Revolutions." In *1914–18 Online Encyclopedia of the First World War*, edited by Ute Daniel, Peter Gatrell, Oliver Janz, Heather Jones, Jennifer Keene, Alan Kramer, and Bill Nasson. Berlin: Freie Universität Berlin, 2017, www.1914-1918-online.net/.

Galbraith, John Kenneth. *The Great Crash, 1929*. New York: Houghton Mifflin 1954.

Gallagher, Gary. *The Confederate War: How Popular Will, Nationalism, and Military Strategy Could Not Stave Off Defeat*. Boston: Harvard University Press, 1997.

Gatrell, Peter. "Poor Russia, Poor Show: Mobilizing a Backward Economy." In *The Economics of World War I*, edited by Stephen Broadberry and Mark Harrison, 235–75. Cambridge University Press, 2005.

——. *Russia's First World War: A Social and Economic History*. Harlow: Pearson, 2005.

——. "War, Population Displacement and State Formation in the Russian Borderlands, 1914–1924." In *Homelands: War, Population and Statehood in Eastern Europe and Russia, 1918–1924*, edited by Nick Baron and Peter Gatrell, 10–34. London: Anthem Press, 2004.

Gilbert, Martin A. *The First World War: A Complete History*. New York: Henry Holt, 1994.

——. *A History of the Twentieth Century, vol. 1: 1900–1933*. New York: William Morrow, 1997.

Glatthaar, Joseph T. *The March to the Sea and Beyond: Sherman's Troops in the Savannah and Carolinas Campaigns*. New York University Press, 1985.

Goldstein, Erik. "The Eastern Question: The Last Phase." In *The Paris Peace Conference: Peace without Victory?*, edited by Michael Dockrill and John Fisher, 141–56. London: Palgrave, 2001.

——. *The First World War Peace Settlements, 1919–1925*. New York: Longmans, 2002.

——. "Great Britain: The Home Front." In *The Treaty of Versailles: A Reassessment after 75 Years*, edited by Manfred Boemeke, Gerald Feldman, and Elisabeth Glaser, 147–66. Cambridge University Press, 1998.

Goodspeed, D. J. *Ludendorff: Soldier, Dictator, Revolutionary*. London: Rupert Hart-Davis, 1966.

Greenhalgh, Elizabeth. *The French Army and the First World War*. Kindle edn. Cambridge University Press, 2014.

Grenville, J. A. S. *A History of the World in the Twentieth Century*. New York: Belknap Press, 1994.

Hacker, J. David. "A Census Based Count the Civil War Dead." *Civil War History* 57, no. 4 (2011).

Hamerow, Theodore, ed. *Reflections and Reminiscences of Otto von Bismarck*. New York: Harper Torchbooks, 1968.

Hamilton, Richard, and Holger Herwig. *Decisions for War, 1914–1917*. Cambridge University Press, 2004.

Hardach, Gerd. *The First World War, 1914–1918*. Berkeley: University of California Press, 1977.

——. "War Finance and Monetary Consequences: The German Case Revisited." In *1914–18 Online Encyclopedia of the First World War*, edited by Ute Daniel,

Peter Gatrell, Oliver Janz, Heather Jones, Jennifer Keene, Alan Kramer, and Bill Nasson. Berlin: Freie Universität Berlin, 2017, www.1914-1918-online.net/.

Hart, Peter. *The Great War: A Combat History of World War I*. Kindle edn. Oxford University Press, 2013.

The Somme: The Darkest Hours on the Western Front. Kindle edn. New York: Pegasus Books, 2012.

Hautcoeur, Pierre-Cyrille. "Was the Great War a Watershed? The Economics of World War I in France." In *The Economics of World War I*, edited by Stephen Broadberry and Mark Harrison, 169–205. Cambridge University Press, 2005.

Henig, Ruth. *The Origins of the First World War*. New York: Routledge, 1993.

Versailles and After, 1919–1933, 2nd edn. New York: Routledge, 1995.

Herrmann, David G. *The Arming of Europe and the Making of the First World War*. Princeton University Press, 1996.

Herwig, Holger. *The First World War: Germany and Austria-Hungary, 1914–1918*. Oxford University Press, 1997.

"Total Rhetoric, Limited War: Germany's U-boat Campaign, 1917–1918." In *Great War, Total War: Combat and Mobilization on the Western Front, 1914–1918*, edited by Roger Chickering and Stig Forster, 189–206. Cambridge University Press, 2000.

Hobsbawm, Eric. *The Age of Extremes: A History of the World, 1914–1990*. New York: Pantheon, 1994.

Hoffman, Phillip. *Why Did Europe Conquer the World?* Princeton University Press, 2015.

Holquist, Peter. *Making War, Forging Revolution: Russia's Continuum of Crisis, 1914–1921*. New York: Harvard University Press, 2002.

Horne, Alistair. *Hubris: The Tragedy of War in the Twentieth Century*. Kindle edn. New York: HarperCollins, 2015.

The Price of Glory: Verdun 1916. New York: Penguin, 1993; first published 1962.

Howard, Michael. *The Franco-Prussian War: The German Invasion of France, 1870–71*. Kindle edn. London: Routledge, 2008; first published 1961.

Innerhofer, Ian. "Post-War Societies (South East Europe)." In *1914–18 Online Encyclopedia of the First World War*, edited by Ute Daniel, Peter Gatrell, Oliver Janz, Heather Jones, Jennifer Keene, Alan Kramer, and Bill Nasson. Berlin: Freie Universität Berlin, 2017, www.1914-1918-online.net/.

Jack, Albert. *Pop Goes the Weasel: The Secret Meanings of Nursery Rhymes*. London: Allen Lane, 2008.

Jankowski, Paul. *Verdun: The Longest Battle of the Great War*. Oxford University Press, 2013.

Jeffery, Keith. *1916: A Global History*. Kindle edn. New York: Bloomsbury, 2016.

Johnson, Dominic D. P. *Overconfidence and War: The Havoc and Glory of Positive Illusions*. Cambridge, MA: Harvard University Press, 2004.

Jordan, David. *The Balkans, Italy and Africa, 1914–1918: From Sarajevo to the Piave and Lake Tanganyika*. London: Amber Books, 2008.

Jukes, Geoffrey. *The Russo-Japanese War, 1904–1905*. Oxford: Osprey Publishing, 2002.

Kagan, Donald. *On the Origins of War and the Preservation of Peace*. New York: Doubleday, 1995.

Kahneman, Daniel. *Thinking, Fast and Slow*. New York: Farrar, Strauss, and Giroux, 2011.

Kahneman, Daniel, and Amos Tversky. "Prospect Theory: An Analysis of Decision under Risk." *Econometrica* 47, no. 2 (1979): 263–91.

Keegan, John. *The Face of Battle*. New York: Viking Press, 1976.

The First World War. New York: Alfred A. Knopf, 1998.

The Price of Admiralty: The Evolution of Naval Warfare. New York: Viking Press, 1988.

Keiger, John. "Poincaré, Clemenceau, and the Quest for Total Victory." In *Great War, Total War: Combat and Mobilization on the Western Front, 1914–1918*, edited by Roger Chickering and Stig Forster, 247–64. Cambridge University Press, 2000.

Kennedy, Paul. *The Rise and Fall of the Great Powers: Economic Change and Military Conflict from 1500 to 2000*. New York: Vintage Books, 1987.

Kennedy, Paul, ed. *The War Plans of the Great Powers, 1880–1914*. Boston: Allen and Unwin, 1985.

Keynes, John Maynard. *The Economic Consequences of the Peace*. New York: Penguin, 1988; first published 1920.

The General Theory of Employment, Interest, and Money. New York: Harcourt Brace and World, 1936.

Kindleberger, Charles P. *The World in Depression, 1929–1939*, revised and enlarged edn. New York: Penguin Books, 1986.

Kindleberger, Charles, and Robert Aliber. *Manias, Panics and Crashes: A History of Financial Crises*. 5th edn. Hoboken, NJ: John Wiley & Sons, 2005.

Kitchen, James. "Colonial Empires after the War/Decolonization." In *1914–18 Online Encyclopedia of the First World War*, edited by Ute Daniel, Peter Gatrell, Oliver Janz, Heather Jones, Jennifer Keene, Alan Kramer, and Bill Nasson. Berlin: Freie Universität Berlin, 2017, www.1914-1918-online.net/.

Knock, Thomas. "Wilsonian Concepts and International Realities at the End of the War." In *The Treaty of Versailles: A Reassessment after 75 Years*, edited by Manfred Boemeke, Gerald Feldman, and Elisabeth Glaser, 111–29. New York: St. Martins Press, 1998.

Kuhn, Thomas S. *The Structure of Scientific Revolutions*. University of Chicago Press, 1962.

Lehnstaed, Stephan. "Occupation during and after the War (East Central Europe)." In *1914–18 Online Encyclopedia of the First World War*, edited by Ute Daniel, Peter Gatrell, Oliver Janz, Heather Jones, Jennifer Keene, Alan Kramer, and Bill Nasson. Berlin: Freie Universität Berlin, 2017, www.1914-1918-online.net/.

Lenin, V. I. *Collected Works*. Moscow: Progress, 1972.

Lesaffer, Randall, and Mieke van der Linden. "Peace Treaties after World War I." *Max Planck Encyclopedia of Public International Law* (2013), http://opil.ouplaw.com.

Levy, Jack S. "Loss Aversion, Framing Effects, and International Conflicts: Perspectives from Prospect Theory." In *Handbook of War II*, edited by Manus I. Mildarsky, 193–221. Ann Arbor, MI: University of Michigan Press, 2000.

Levy, Jack S., and William Thompson. *The Causes of War*. Kindle edn. Chichester, West Sussex: John Wiley/Blackwell, 2010.

Lloyd, Nick. *Hundred Days: The Campaign that Ended World War I*. New York: Basic Books, 2014.

Macdonald, Lyn. *To The Last Man: Spring 1918*. New York: Penguin, 1999.

MacMillan, Margaret. "Lessons from History? The Paris Peace Conference of 1919." O. D. Skelton Lectures, 2013.

Paris 1919: Six Months that Changed the World. New York: Random House, 2001.

The War That Ended Peace: The Road to 1914. Kindle edn. New York: Random House, 2013.

McNeill, William Hardy. *The Pursuit of Power: Technology, Armed Force, and Society Since AD 1000*. University of Chicago Press, 1982.

Mantoux, Paul. *The Deliberations of the Council of Four (March 24–June 28, 1919)*. Translated by Arthur Link and Manfred Boemeke. 2 vols. Princeton University Press, 1992.

Marcus, Josef. *Social and Political History of the Jews in Poland, 1919–1939*. Berlin: De Gruyter Mouton, 2011; first published 1983.

Markevich, Andrei, and Mark Harrison. "Great War, Civil War, and Recovery: Russia's National Income, 1913 to 1928." *Journal of Economic History* 71, no. 1 (2011): 672–703.

Marks, Sally. "Mistakes and Myths: The Allies, Germany, and the Versailles Treaty, 1918–1921." *Journal of Modern History* 85, no. 3 (2013): 632–59.

"Smoke and Mirrors: In Smoke-Filled Rooms and the Galerie des Glaces." In *The Treaty of Versailles: A Reassessment after 75 Years*, edited by Manfred Boemeke, Gerald Feldman, and Elisabeth Glaser, 337–70. Cambridge University Press, 1998.

Marszalek, John F. *Sherman: A Soldier's Passion for Order*. New York: Free Press, 1993.

Martel, Gordon. *The Month that Changed the World: July 1914*. Oxford University Press 2014.

Massie, Robert K. *Dreadnought: Britain, Germany, and the Coming of the Great War*. New York: Random House, 1991.

Mawdsley, Evan. "International Responses to the Russian Civil War (Russian Empire)." In *1914–18 Online Encyclopedia of the First World War*, edited by Ute Daniel, Peter Gatrell, Oliver Janz, Heather Jones, Jennifer Keene, Alan Kramer, and Bill Nasson. Berlin: Freie Universität Berlin, 2014, www.1914-1918-online.net/.

Mazza, Roberto. "Occupation during and after the War (Middle East)." In *1914–18 Online Encyclopedia of the First World War*, edited by Ute Daniel, Peter Gatrell, Oliver Janz, Heather Jones, Jennifer Keene, Alan Kramer, and Bill Nasson. Berlin: Freie Universität Berlin, 2017, www.1914-1918-online.net/.

Miller, Michael B. "Sea Transport and Supply." In *1914–18 Online Encyclopedia of the First World War*, edited by Ute Daniel, Peter Gatrell, Oliver Janz, Heather Jones, Jennifer Keene, Alan Kramer, and Bill Nasson. Berlin: Freie Universität Berlin, 2017, www.1914-1918-online.net/.

Minkov, Stefan. "The Treaty of Neuilly-sur-Seine." In *1914–18 Online Encyclopedia of the First World War*, edited by Ute Daniel, Peter Gatrell, Oliver Janz, Heather Jones, Jennifer Keene, Alan Kramer, and Bill Nasson. Berlin: Freie Universität Berlin, 2017, www.1914-1918-online.net/.

Minsky, Hyman. "The Financial Instability Hypothesis: Capitalist Processes and the Behavior of the Economy." In *Financial Crises: Theory, History, and Policy*, edited by Charles Kindleberger, 13–47. Cambridge University Press, 1982.

Mitchell, Brian R. *European Historical Statistics, 1750–1993*. 4th edn. New York: Stockton Press, 1998.

Mombauer, Annika. *The Origins of the First World War: Controversies and Consensus*. London: Pearson, 2002.

"Of War Plans and War Guilt: The Debate Surrounding the Schlieffen Plan." *Journal of Strategic Studies* 28, no. 5 (2005): 857–85.

Mongin, Philippe. "A Game-Theoretic Analysis of the Waterloo Campaign and Some Comments on the Analytic Narrative Project." *Cliometrica*, forthcoming.

Morehead, Alan. *Gallipoli*. New York: Harper Row, 1956.

Mosier, John. *Myth of the Great War: A New Military History of World War I*. New York: HarperCollins, 2001.

Murphy, David. *Breaking Point of the French Army: The Nivelle Offensives of 1917*. Barnsley: Pen and Sword Books, 2015.

Navrozov, Andrei. "European Diary." *Chronicles* 32 (2008).

Neiberg, Michael. *The Military Atlas of World War I*. New York: Chartwell Books, 2014.

Offer, Avner. "The Blockade of Germany and the Strategy of Starvation, 1914–1918: An Agency Perspective." In *Great War, Total War: Combat and*

Mobilization on the Western Front, 1914–1918, edited by Roger Chickering and Stig Forster, 169–88.Cambridge University Press, 2000.

The First World War: An Agrarian Interpretation. Oxford University Press, 1989.

Overy, Richard. *The Inter-War Crisis, 1919–1939.* 2nd rev. edn. Harlow: Pearson, 2010.

Palmer, Alan. *Victory 1918.* New York: Atlantic Monthly Press, 1998.

Paret, Peter. "Clausewitz." In *Makers of Modern Strategy: From Machiavelli to the Nuclear Age*, edited by Peter Paret, 186–216. Princeton University Press, 1986.

Ploeckl, Florian. "The Zollverein and the Formation of a Customs Union." *University of Oxford Discussion Papers in Economic and Social History* 84 (August 2010).

Prior, Robin, and Trevor Wilson. *Passchendaele: The Untold Story.* New Haven: Yale University Press, 1996.

The Somme. Kindle edn. New Haven: Yale University Press, 2005.

Prusin, Alexander. *The Lands Between: Conflict in the East European Borderlands, 1870–1992.* Oxford University Press, 2010.

Rabinowitch, Alexander. *The Bolsheviks Come to Power.* Bloomington: University of Indiana Press, 1976.

Ransom, Roger L. "The Civil War in American Economic History." In *Oxford Handbook of American Economic History*, edited by Louis Cain. Oxford University Press, 2018.

"Confidence, Fear, and a Propensity to Gamble: The Puzzle of War and Economics in an Age of Catastrophe 1914–45." *Social Science History* 40 (2016).

Remak, Joachim. *The Origins of World War I.* 2nd edn. New York: Harcourt Brace, 1995.

Reynolds, Michael. *Shattering Empires: The Clash and Collapse of the Ottoman and Russian Empires, 1908–1918.* Kindle edn. Cambridge University Press, 2011.

Richter, Klaus. "Baltic States and Finland." In *1914–18 Online Encyclopedia of the First World War*, edited by Ute Daniel, Peter Gatrell, Oliver Janz, Heather Jones, Jennifer Keene, Alan Kramer, and Bill Nasson. Berlin: Freie Universität Berlin, 2017, www.1914-1918-online.net/.

Ristović, Milan. "Occupation during and after the War (South East Europe)." In *1914–18 Online Encyclopedia of the First World War*, edited by Ute Daniel, Peter Gatrell, Oliver Janz, Heather Jones, Jennifer Keene, Alan Kramer, and Bill Nasson. Berlin: Freie Universität Berlin, 2014, www.1914-1918-online.net/.

Ritschl, Albrecht. "The Pity of Peace: Germany's Economy at War, 1914–1918 and Beyond." In *The Economics of World War I*, edited by Stephen Broadberry and Mark Harrison, 71–6. Cambridge University Press, 2005.

"Reparations, Deficits and Debt Default: The Great Depression in Germany." In *The Great Depression of the 1930s*, edited by Nicholas Crafts and Peter Fearon. Oxford University Press, 2013.

Ritter, Gerhard. *The Schlieffen Plan: Critique of a Myth*. New York: Frederick Praeger, 1958.

Rockoff, Hugh. "Until It's Over, Over There: The US Economy in World War I." In *The Economics of World War I*, edited by Stephen Broadberry and Mark Harrison. Cambridge University Press, 2005.

Romsics, Ignac. *The Dismantling of Historic Hungary: The Peace Treaty of Trianon, 1920*. Translated by Mario Fenyo. Wayne, NJ: Center for Hungarian Studies and Publications, 2002.

Rowe, Steven E. "Labor." In *1914–18 Online Encyclopedia of the First World War*, edited by Ute Daniel, Peter Gatrell, Oliver Janz, Heather Jones, Jennifer Keene, Alan Kramer, and Bill Nasson. Berlin: Freie Universität Berlin, 2017, www.1914-1918-online.net/.

Royle, Trevor. *Crimea: The Great Crimean War, 1854–1856*. New York: Palgrave Macmillan, 2000.

Sarkees, Meredith Reid, and Frank Wayman. *Resort to War: 1816–2007*. New York: CQ Press, 2010.

Schneer, Jonathon. *The Balfour Declaration: The Origins of the Arab–Israel Conflict*. Kindle edn. New York: Random House, 2012.

Schröder, Joachim, and Alexander Watson. "Occupation during and after the War (Germany)." In *1914–18 Online Encyclopedia of the First World War*, edited by Ute Daniel, Peter Gatrell, Oliver Janz, Heather Jones, Jennifer Keene, Alan Kramer, and Bill Nasson. Berlin: Freie Universität Berlin, 2016, www.1914-1918-online.net/.

Schuker, Stephen. "The Rhineland Question: West European Security at the Paris Peace Conference of 1919." In *The Treaty of Versailles: A Reassessment after 75 Years*, edited by Manfred Boemeke, Gerald Feldman, and Elisabeth Glaser, 275–313. New York: St. Martins Press, 1998.

Schulze, Max-Stephan. "Austria-Hungary's Economy in World War I." In *The Economics of World War I*, edited by Stephen Broadberry and Mark Harrison, 77–111. Cambridge University Press, 2005.

Sharp, Alan. "The Big Four: Peacemaking in Paris in 1919." *History Review*, 68 (2009).

"A Comment." In *The Treaty of Versailles: A Reassessment after 75 Years*, edited by Manfred Boemeke, Gerald Feldman, and Elisabeth Glaser, 131–44. New York: St. Martins Press, 1998.

Sharp, Allen. "The Paris Peace Conference and its Consequences." In *1914–18 Online Encyclopedia of the First World War*, edited by Ute Daniel, Peter Gatrell, Oliver Janz, Heather Jones, Jennifer Keene, Alan Kramer, and Bill Nasson. Berlin: Freie Universität Berlin, 2017, www.1914-1918-online.net/.

Sheldon, Jack. *The German Army at Cambrai*. Kindle edn. Barnsley: Pen and Sword Books, 2009.

The German Army in the Spring Offensives 1917: Arras, Aisne and Champagne. Kindle edn. Barnsley: Pen and Sword Books, 2015.

Shiller, Robert. "Rational and Irrational Bubbles." In *Diverse Views on Asset Bubbles*, edited by William C Hunter, George G Kaufman, and Michael Pomerleano, 35–40. Cambridge, MA: The MIT Press, 2003.

Shiller, Robert J. *Irrational Exuberance*. Princeton University Press, 2000.

Showalter, Dennis. "Mass Warfare and the Impact of Technology." In *Great War, Total War: Combat and Mobilization on the Western Front, 1914–1918*, edited by Roger Chickering and Stig Forster, 73–92. Cambridge University Press, 2000.

The Wars of German Unification. Kindle edn. London: Bloomsbury, 2015.

Shuie, Carol, and Wolfgang Keller. "Endogenous Formation of Free Trade Agreements: Evidence from the Zollverein's Impact on Market Integration." *Journal of Economic History* 74 (December 2014): 1–54.

Singer, J. David. "The Etiology of Interstate War: A Natural History Approach." In *What Do We Know about War?*, edited by John A. Vasquez, 3–21. Lanham, MD: Rowman and Littlefield, 2000.

Singer, J. David, and Melvin Small. *The Wages of War, 1816–1965: A Statistical Handbook*. New York: John Wiley and Sons, 1972.

Smith, Frederick E. *Turning Points in History*. London: Hutchinson, 1930.

Smith, Leonard. "Post War Treaties (Ottoman Empire/Middle East)." In *1914–18 Online Encyclopedia of the First World War*, edited by Ute Daniel, Peter Gatrell, Oliver Janz, Heather Jones, Jennifer Keene, Alan Kramer, and Bill Nasson. Berlin: Freie Universität Berlin, 2017, www.1914-1918-online.net/.

Smith, Steve. *The Russian Revolution: A Very Short Introduction*. Kindle edn. Oxford University Press, 2002.

Smithers, A. J. *Cambrai: The First Great Tank Battle, 1917*. Kindle edn. London: Leo Cooper, 1992.

Sondhaus, Lawrence. "Civilian and Military Power." In *1914–18 Online Encyclopedia of the First World War*, edited by Ute Daniel, Peter Gatrell, Oliver Janz, Heather Jones, Jennifer Keene, Alan Kramer, and Bill Nasson. Berlin: Freie Universität Berlin, 2017, www.1914-1918-online.net/.

The Great War at Sea: A Naval History of the First World War. Kindle edn. Cambridge University Press, 2014.

Spender, John A. *Life, Journalism and Politics*. New York: Frederick A. Stokes Company, 1927.

Steeples, Douglas. "The Depression of 1893." http://eh.net/encyclopedia/the-depression-of-1893.

Steffen, Dirk. "The Holtzendorff Memorandum of 22 December 1916 and Germany's Declaration of Unrestricted U-boat Warfare." *Journal of Military History* 68 (January 2004): 215–24.

Steiner, Zara. "The Treaty of Versailles Revisited." In *The Paris Peace Conference: Peace without Victory?*, edited by Michael Dockrill and John Fisher, 14–34. London: Palgrave, 2001.

Stevenson, David. *Armaments and the Coming of War: Europe, 1904–1914*. Oxford: Clarendon Press 1996.

"French Srategy on the Western Front." In *Great War, Total War: Combat and Mobilization on the Western Front, 1914–1918*, edited by Roger Chickering and Stig Forster, 297–345. Cambridge University Press, 2000.

"War Aims and Peace Negotiations." In *World War I: A History*, edited by Hew Strachan, 204–15. Oxford University Press, 1998.

With Our Backs to the Wall: Victory and Defeat in 1918. Cambridge, MA: Harvard University Press, 2013.

Stoessinger, John. *Why Nations Go to War*. 8th edn. New York: Beford/St. Martin's, 2001.

Stone, Norman. *The Eastern Front, 1914–1917*. London: Penguin, 1998; first published 1975.

Strachan, Hew, ed. *The First World War: A New Illustrated History*. New York: Simon and Schuster, 2003.

Sumpf, Alexandre. "Russian Civil War." In *1914–18 Online Encyclopedia of the First World War*, edited by Ute Daniel, Peter Gatrell, Oliver Janz, Heather Jones, Jennifer Keene, Alan Kramer, and Bill Nasson. Berlin: Freie Universität Berlin, 2014, www.1914-1918-online.net/.

Sutch, Richard. "Financing the Great War: A Class Tax for the Wealthy, Liberty Bonds for All." Berkeley Economic History Laboratory Working Papers Series. Berkeley: University of California, 2015.

Sutch, Richard, and Susan Carter, eds. *Historical Statistics of the United States, Earliest Times to the Present: Millennial Edition*. 5 vols. Cambridge University Press, 2006.

Szlanta, Piotr. "Poland." In *1914–18 Online Encyclopedia of the First World War*, edited by Ute Daniel, Peter Gatrell, Oliver Janz, Heather Jones, Jennifer Keene, Alan Kramer, and Bill Nasson. Berlin: Freie Universität Berlin, 2015, www.1914-1918-online.net/.

Taylor, A. J. P. *The Struggle for Mastery in Europe, 1848–1918*. Oxford University Press, 1980.

Temin, Peter. *Lessons from the Great Depression*. Cambridge, MA: The MIT Press, 1989.

Terraine, John. *White Heat: The New Warfare, 1914–1918*. London: Sidgewick and Jackson, 1982.

Thaler, Richard. *Misbehaving: The Making of Behavioral Economics*. Kindle edn. New York: W. W. Norton, 2015.

Thompson, James. "Labour Movements, Trade Unions and Strikes." In *1914–18 Online Encyclopedia of the First World War*, edited by Ute Daniel, Peter

Gatrell, Oliver Janz, Heather Jones, Jennifer Keene, Alan Kramer, and Bill Nasson. Berlin: Freie Universität Berlin, 2017, www.1914-1918-online.net/.

Tooze, Adam. *The Deluge: The Great War, America, and the Remaking of the Global Order, 1916–1931*. New York: Viking Penguin, 2014.

Trgovcenic, Ljubinja. "Yugoslavia." In *1914–18 Online Encyclopedia of the First World War*, edited by Ute Daniel, Peter Gatrell, Oliver Janz, Heather Jones, Jennifer Keene, Alan Kramer, and Bill Nasson. Berlin: Freie Universität Berlin, 2017, www.1914-1918-online.net/.

Trumpener, Ulrich. *Turkey's War*. Oxford University Press, 1998.

Tuchman, Barbara. *The Guns of August*. New York: Macmillan, 1962.

The Zimmermann Telegram: America Enters the War, 1917–1918. New York: Random House, 2014; first published 1958.

Van Evera, Stephen. *Causes of War: Power and the Roots of Conflict*. Ithaca: Cornell University Press, 1999.

"The Cult of the Offensive and the Origins of the First World War." In *Military Strategy and the Origins of the First World War*, edited by Steven E. Miller, Sean Lynn-Jones, and Stephen Van Evera, 59–108. Princeton University Press, 1991.

Vasquez, John A. *The War Puzzle*. Cambridge University Press, 1993.

Vlossak, Elizabeth. "Alsace Lorraine." In *1914–18 Online Encyclopedia of the First World War*, edited by Ute Daniel, Peter Gatrell, Oliver Janz, Heather Jones, Jennifer Keene, Alan Kramer, and Bill Nasson. Berlin: Freie Universität Berlin, 1917, www.1914-1918-online.net/.

Walker, Christopher J. *Armenia: The Survival of a Nation*. London: Palgrave Macmillan, 1990.

Wandycz, Piotr. "The Polish Question." In *The Treaty of Versailles: A Reassessment after 75 Years*, edited by Manfred Boemeke, Gerald Feldman, and Elisabeth Glaser, 35. New York: St. Martins Press, 1998.

Wawro, Geoffrey. *The Austro-Prussian War: Austria's War with Prussia and Italy in 1866*. Cambridge University Press, 1997.

The Franco-Prussian War: The German Conquest of France in 1870–71. Kindle edn. Cambridge University Press, 2003.

A Mad Catastrophe: The Outbreak of World War I and the Collapse of the Hapsburg Empire. Kindle edn. New York: Basic Books, 2014.

White, James D. *The Russian Revolution: A Short History*. New York: Edward Arnold, 1994.

Williamson, Samuel R. "Joffre Reshapes French Strategy, 1911–1913." In *The War Plans of the Great Powers, 1880–1914*, edited by Paul Kennedy, 119–32. Boston: Allen and Unwin, 1985.

"On The Way to War." In *1914–18 Online Encyclopedia of the First World War*, edited by Ute Daniel, Peter Gatrell, Oliver Janz, Heather Jones, Jennifer Keene, Alan Kramer, and Bill Nasson. Berlin: Freie Universität Berlin, 2014, www.1914-1918-online.net/.

Wilson, Mark. *The Business of Civil War: Military Mobilization and the State, 1861–1865*. Baltimore: The Johns Hopkins University Press, 2006.

Wilson, Woodrow. "Speech to the United States Senate, January 8, 1918." www .firstworldwar.com 1918.

"Speech to the United States Senate, January 22, 1917." www.firstworldwar .com.

Winter, Jay, and Antoine Prost. *The Great War in History: Debates and Controversies, 1914 to the Present*. Kindle edn. Cambridge University Press, 2005.

Wolf, Nikolaus. "Europe's Great Depression: Coordination Failure after the First World War," in *The Great Depression of the 1930s*, edited by Nicholas Crafts and Peter Fearon. Oxford University Press, 2013.

Yavuz, M. Hakan, and Peter Sluglett, eds. *War and Diplomacy: The Russo-Turkish War of 1877–1878 and the Treaty of Berlin*. Utah Series in Middle East Studies. Salt Lake City: University of Utah Press, 2011.

Zhvanko, Liubuv. "Ukraine." In *1914–18 Online Encyclopedia of the First World War*, edited by Ute Daniel, Peter Gatrell, Oliver Janz, Heather Jones, Jennifer Keene, Alan Kramer, and Bill Nasson. Berlin: Freie Universität Berlin, 2014, www.1914-1918-online.net/.

Zuber, Terence. *Inventing the Schlieffen Plan: German War Planning, 1871–1914*. Oxford University Press, 2002.

INDEX